Conditionality and Coercion

OXFORD STUDIES IN DEMOCRATIZATION

Series editor
Laurence Whitehead

Oxford Studies in Democratization is a series for scholars and students of comparative politics and related disciplines. Volumes concentrate on the comparative study of the democratization process that accompanied the decline and termination of the Cold War. The geographical focus of the series is primarily Latin America, the Caribbean, Southern and Eastern Europe, and relevant experiences in Africa and Asia.

Conditionality and Coercion

Electoral Clientelism in Eastern Europe

ISABELA MARES AND LAUREN E. YOUNG

OXFORD
UNIVERSITY PRESS

OXFORD
UNIVERSITY PRESS

Great Clarendon Street, Oxford, OX2 6DP,
United Kingdom

Oxford University Press is a department of the University of Oxford.
It furthers the University's objective of excellence in research, scholarship,
and education by publishing worldwide. Oxford is a registered trade mark of
Oxford University Press in the UK and in certain other countries

First Edition published in 2019

Impression: 3

Published in the United States of America by Oxford University Press
198 Madison Avenue, New York, NY 10016, United States of America

British Library Cataloguing in Publication Data
Data available

Library of Congress Control Number: 2019946758

ISBN 978-0-19-883277-5 (hbk.)
ISBN 978-0-19-883278-2 (pbk.)

Printed and bound by
CPI Group (UK) Ltd, Croydon, CR0 4YY

Acknowledgments

In the course of researching and writing this book, we have incurred many professional and institutional debts. It is our great pleasure to acknowledge these.

In Hungary, we are grateful to colleagues at the Central European University for helping us launch the study. We are grateful to Lili Török for extraordinary research assistance. Doro Bohle, Bela Greskovits, Gergö Medve-Bàlint, and Krisztóf Szombati advised and helped us during the early stages of research. Roland Ferkovics, Daniel Kovarek, Norbert Monti, Szilvia Nagy, Marton Szarvas, and András Vigvári provided extraordinary research assistance.

In Romania, we are very grateful to colleagues at the National University of Political Studies and Public Administration for their support in carrying out the study. Dr. Aurelian Muntean assisted with the locality selection, elaboration of a respondent sampling strategy, and formulation of survey questions and the logistics of the fieldwork implementation. We are also grateful to George Matu for his help in sampling and locality selection and for organizing the surveys. Elena Barcaru, Corina Cosmescu, David Diaconu, Cosmina Dobrota, Ana Paraschiv, Elena Radu, and Anca Yastremskyi provided research assistance. Finally, we are grateful to Lacrima Iuga for conducting a large part of the qualitative interviews and for helping us understand the qualitative findings.

We have presented parts of the research for this book at a number of seminars and workshops and are grateful to seminar participants for their feedback. We are grateful to seminar participants in NYU Abu Dhabi, University College London, Harvard, Virginia, University of Wisconsin Madison, Cornell, Princeton, Brigham Young University, Central European University, Yale, Syracuse, Chicago, Duke, Berkeley, Rochester, and ITAM (Mexico City). For comments, we would like to thank Pablo Beramendi, Rikhil Bhavnani, John Carey, Thad Dunning, Federico Estevez, Margarita Estevez-Abe, Scott Gehlbach, Dimitar Guergiev, Wade Jacoby, Jan Kubik, Lucas Leeman, Noam Lupu, Ed Malesky, Melanie Manion, Carol Mershon, Bing Powell, Jessica Preece, Gretchen Ritter, Vidal Romero, Todd Sechser, David Siegel, Alberto Simpser, David Waldner, and Yuhua Wang. We want to thank especially David Rueda and Sherill Stroschein for sending us detailed written comments on different chapters.

We held a final book conference discussing the book manuscript at CDDRL Stanford in August 2018. We are grateful to Francis Fukuyama and Larry Diamond for hosting this conference and to Josephine Andrews, Carles Boix,

Alberto Diaz-Cayeros, Miriam Golden, Jessica Gottlieb, Herbert Kitschelt, and Jason Wittenberg for extremely insightful comments and suggestions.

We are grateful to Dominic Byatt, our editor at Oxford University Press, for his enthusiasm for the manuscript and to Céline Louasli for her help in the production of the book.

Contents

List of Figures

List of Tables

List of Abbreviations

ALDE	Alianța Liberalilor și Democraților	Alliance of Liberals and Democrats	Romania
FDSN	Frontul Democrat al Salvării Naționale	Front of Democratic National Salvation	Romania
Fidesz	Fiatal Demokraták Szövetsége	Alliance of Young Democrats	Hungary
FSN	Frontul Salvării Naționale	Front of National Salvation	Romania
MSZP	Magyar Szocialista Párt	Hungarian Socialist Party	Hungary
PCR	Partidul Comunist Român	Communist Party of Romania	Romania
PD	Partidul Democrat	Democratic Party	Romania
PMP	Partidul Miscarea Populară	Popular Movement	Romania
PNL	Partidul Național Liberal	National Liberal Party	Romania
PRM	Partidul România Mare	Greater Romanian Party	Romania
PSD	Partidul Social Democrat	Social Democratic Party	Romania
PSDR	Partidul Democratiei Sociale din Romania	Party of Social Democracy in Romania	Romania
PUNR	Partidul Unității Națiunii Române	Party of Romanian National Unity	Romania
SZDSZ	Szabad Demokraták Szövetsége	Alliance of Free Democrats	Hungary
USL	Uniunea Social Liberală	Social Liberal Union	Romania
USR	Uniunea Salvați România	Save Romania Union	Romania

1

Introduction

NM. is a small Hungarian locality with less than ten thousand inhabitants located in close vicinity to the border with Slovakia. It is accessible only via a narrow road that meanders through endless kilometers of tobacco fields. As with many similar localities throughout Eastern Europe, NM.'s economic outlook bears the imprint of two decades of economic reforms. During the communist period, most of the town's residents were employed in the local agricultural cooperative and in enterprises located in small neighboring urban localities. Many of the industrial enterprises in neighboring localities closed down during the first years of the post-communist transition, once subsidies from the central government that had sustained their economic activity were no longer available. After the local agricultural cooperative closed down, agricultural activities shifted to subsistence farming. A local farm, owned by the mayor, provides seasonal employment to a small number of people.

As the local economy has been doubly hit by the forces of deindustrialization and de-agrarianization, citizens in NM. have no local employment opportunities. Their only option to access a steady income-stream is the workfare program, a relatively new initiative in the policy landscape of Hungary's welfare state. While the Socialist government of Gordon Bajnai pioneered the introduction of this policy, the final adoption of the workfare policy occurred in Hungary only in 2010, during Viktor Orbán's first administration (Szöke 2014: 3). Beginning in 2010, social assistance benefits were conditioned on participation in the workfare program and local governments were tasked with the organization of this program, a responsibility for which localities were initially ill-prepared (Szöke 2014; Csoba 2010). In NM., the policy provides a monthly income that ranges from fifty to seventy thousand Hungarian Forint, or between two and three hundred US dollars. In exchange for these benefits, workfare employees must perform public work in the interest of the community. Projects in this locality include repairing the drainage system and the local road and repainting the school. The town's mayor of the locality and other local administration employees, called brigade leaders, monitor the workfare employees as they undertake these tasks.

The presence of the workfare program—its use and its economic and social consequences for the community—gives rise to political tensions within the locality. The most important source of this tension is the limited number of positions: the program provides too few employment opportunities to meet the needs of the town's many unemployed. Everyday interactions in this community involve frequent conflicts between participants in the workfare program and people who missed the opportunity to qualify for access to social policy benefits, because of their age or access to part-time employment elsewhere. In addition to these economic grievances, the ethnic polarization in the locality between Hungarians and Roma further contributes to the politicization of the workfare program. Due to the strong correlation between Roma ethnicity and extreme poverty, the frontlines of the ethnic and economic friction overlap. Many respondents we encountered in this locality consider that ethnic Roma abuse the workfare program by failing to perform the required work. The theme of the "work-shy Roma" that was used by Jobbik, Hungary's right-wing party during the 2010 electoral campaign, resonates extremely well with many voters in localities like this one (Szombati 2016). During Hungary's 2010 parliamentary election, about one-third of the voters in the locality voted for the candidate running for the far-right Jobbik party.

The mayor of NM. skillfully exploits his prerogative to control access to the workfare program and seeks to extract electoral advantages from this position. He cultivates an image of repressive paternalism that seeks to convey not only strength, but also capriciousness in allocating the right to participate in the workfare program. The mayor raises the administrative hurdles to access the program, humiliating applicants for no reason. Violating the administrative provisions of the workfare legislation, the mayor also employs workfare employees on a farm he owns. Such cumulation of economic and political power gives the mayor quasi-feudal control over the economic opportunities of many low-income citizens in this community. As local or parliamentary elections approach, employees in the workfare program become a reserve army of voters whom the mayor can mobilize to achieve a particular electoral goal. One electoral strategy that this mayor uses towards employees in the workfare program involves the threat that current beneficiaries will lose access to the program and hence, to an important stream of future income, if they fail to support his preferred candidate. To increase the credibility of the threat of loss of workfare benefits, outspoken critics have actually been dismissed from the workfare program. The mayor combines such threats with systematic efforts to pierce voting secrecy and ascertain the political intentions of voters at the time ballots are cast. In this locality, the primary method used by the mayor to verify the political loyalties of workfare employees is brigade leaders.

In neighboring Romania, a similar anti-poverty policy provides mayors with tools for the coercive mobilization of voters during elections. The Romanian anti-poverty legislation adopted in 2001 gave mayors full control over the distribution of anti-poverty benefits within the locality. In exploiting their position as gate-keepers to a long-term stream of policy benefits, mayors condition participation in the program on political support. One commonly used coercive strategy is that of blackmail. Throughout the mandate, workfare employees are allowed to draw workfare benefits without fulfilling all of the obligations defined by the law. Then, when elections come up, mayors exploit the enhanced vulnerability of low-income voters and extort their votes in exchange for the right to continue participating in the program.

BF., another locality in central Hungary, shares many economic and demographic conditions with NM. For many low-income voters in both localities, political rights represent only a hollow promise. In BF., the mayor seeks to control the electoral choices of many low-income voters by deploying moneylenders as intermediaries that mobilize such voters on the day of elections. Control over the long-term debt carried by vulnerable voters in this locality gives moneylenders an important lever they can use to influence voters' electoral choices. The threat that is often invoked by these moneylenders is that failure to support the lender's preferred candidate may result in worsening of a debtor's credit, or, in worse cases, the repossession of land and household items.

In this book we examine electoral strategies by which mayors or brokers operating on their behalf use threats to worsen ongoing economic exchanges or cut off access to critical state benefits as coercive electoral strategies. These coercive strategies coexist with positive inducements. Mayors attempt to influence voters' electoral decisions using offers of preferential access to policies or administrative decisions under their control. Most administrative decisions controlled by mayors can be transformed into political favors, including offers of certificates, land rights, policy benefits, and so on. Offers of favors involve the creation of expectations of political reciprocity. As a mayor of Q., a locality in Southern Romania, comments on this strategy, such electoral appeals are premised on the personalization of the delivery of routine policy benefits. During parliamentary or presidential elections, leaders of regional party organizations lean on mayors to deliver a certain number of votes for their respective parties. To deliver these blocks of votes, mayors activate the ties of reciprocity they have established through the provisions of favors.

In addition to exploiting the resources of the state, candidates compete by offering small goods or monetary inducements. Candidates distribute a variety of such goods to incentivize voters to support them, including buckets of flour, bottles of oil, corn, sausages, packets of meat, or money. These gifts can be either targeted to specific voters, or distributed to broad swathes of voters immediately prior to the election.

The above examples raise a number of theoretical questions about the use of different clientelistic strategies by candidates. Given that candidates can choose from a broad menu of clientelistic strategies, how do they structure the mix of positive and negative inducements? What explains the choice between clientelistic strategies that politicize the resources of the state or that use private resources? How do political conditions in a locality, such as its fragmentation or competitiveness, affect the choice of different clientelistic strategies? Do ethnic or economic divisions condition the choice between negative and positive inducements and, if so, how?

The second set of questions concerns voters' evaluation of different non-programmatic strategies. How do voters evaluate candidates who use electoral coercion, such as welfare threats, compared to candidates that use positive electoral inducements, such as favors? Do voters punish the use of positive and negative non-programmatic strategies with equal intensity? Do voters have different tolerance thresholds for different types of illicit electoral strategies? If so, what explains the variation in such thresholds?

Electoral practices premised on the use of coercion or offers of contingent favors also provide us with an opportunity to examine a set of broader questions about the achievements and shortcomings of democratic elections in Eastern Europe. How successful are the electoral rules and nominal commitment to ballot secrecy in protecting voters' electoral autonomy? What are the most significant strategies deployed by candidates competing in these elections to undermine voters' autonomy and unduly influence their electoral choices? How extensive is the use of clientelistic strategies like the ones discussed above and how do they affect the ability of elections to reflect voters' electoral will successfully?

The study of these questions allows us to evaluate both the achievements but also the limitations of the democratic transformations in post-communist countries, such as Hungary and Romania. The literature examining democratic transitions in Eastern Europe is vast and includes scholarship examining democratic consolidation, political parties, and voting behavior. In existing studies examining the quality of democracy in Eastern Europe, the tone and broad assessments have changed dramatically over time. The initial tone of the literature was triumphalist and excessively optimistic and shared the anticipation that Eastern European countries would slowly but inevitably converge on the democratic electoral experience that is common in Western European countries (Przeworski 1991; Offe 1994; Elster et al. 1998; Ekiert and Hansom 2003). In recent years, this optimistic mood has been replaced by a concern about the democratic backsliding witnessed by some of the success stories of the early democratization (Fish 2001; Rupnik and Zielonka 2016). Yet while it is common to express normative concerns about the gap between democratic ideals and everyday political practices, so far, few studies have marshaled systematic evidence about the magnitude and variation in this gap. The magnitude of infringements on voters' democratic freedoms at times of elections has not been yet systematically documented in the literature.

Our study draws on novel quantitative and qualitative evidence to address questions about democratic quality and democratic accountability in Eastern Europe. Current studies of post-communist transitions have relied on elite-level interviews with party leaders and country experts and close readings of primary documents such as party positions to derive general inferences about democratic quality. What is missing from existing scholarship is the detailed and nuanced examination of everyday electoral practices in the post-communist region. Such a description of electoral practices might include, among other things, precise descriptions of the actors who mediate between candidates and voters, and of the strategies by which these intermediaries to appeal to voters. This type of evidence is crucial in characterizing the gap between democratic ideals and the electoral experience of voters.

Using a wealth of ethnographic and survey-based evidence, our study brings to light a rich array of actors and strategies that are otherwise absent from studies of partisan politics and election outcomes. The recurrent figures in our account include mayors, employees of the local administration, rural employers, and money lenders. We seek to characterize the variety of strategies used by such actors in the long interval between elections and on election days. In addition to documenting the wide heterogeneity in such non-programmatic strategies, our study proposes and tests an explanation for this variation. We draw from the existing literature to contend that two broad factors might account for the mix of non-programmatic strategies. The first set of factors is the political conditions in each locality, which influence the types of endowments that candidates can mobilize for clientelistic exchanges with voters. The second set of factors involves the size of coalitions with opposing positions on the existing distribution of social policy. We argue that these demographic variables affect the electoral costliness of using clientelism because different forms of clientelism may carry policy signals that resonate with certain groups of voters. As a result, politicians can lessen the electoral costs of clientelism by using a form that aligns with voters' social policy preferences. Ultimately, we find that the second set of factors that shapes the electoral costs of the clientelism for candidates explains a much larger proportion of the variation in which forms of clientelism are used.

1.1 The Argument in Brief

Our study of everyday electoral practices examines the range of non-programmatic electoral strategies deployed by candidates to influence voters' choices. We draw on Hicken's (2011) definition of electoral clientelism as chains of dyadic relations between politicians, clients, and voters. Such relationships involve contingent exchanges premised on informal understandings that voters will provide electoral support in exchange for some agreed-upon behavior by the principal (Hicken 2011). Our definition of clientelistic exchanges excludes promises of benefits that do not hinge on how an individual or a small group of individuals personally votes. It also excludes fraud, which involves circumventing rather than influencing voters' choices, although in some discussions we will touch on substitutions between clientelism and fraud.

Current studies examining electoral clientelism in Latin America, Africa, or South Asia have primarily examined exchanges where candidates mobilize voters using small monetary inducements, such as gifts, offers of food, or money. The typical brokers involved in such vote-buying transactions are hired on spot markets. On many occasions, such brokers are incentivized to work on behalf of the candidate through monetary inducements that are only a bit larger than those offered to voters. In contrast to these studies, we suggest that the menu of clientelistic strategies that can be deployed by candidates is broader and that it may include either policy resources financed by tax revenues or economic resources. Similarly, candidates can rely on a wide variety of brokers that are integrated in different positions within the party organization. Such intermediaries may include employees of local municipalities, and economic brokers, such as employers, or moneylenders, or tenant farmers. The goal of our study is to examine the factors accounting for the heterogeneity in non-programmatic strategies and its consequences for electoral behavior.

Consider first the variation in the type of resources that can be deployed to incentivize voters. Candidates can appeal to voters using either public or private resources. Public resources include both policies and regulations that can be used to influence voters' electoral decisions. By contrast, private resources can originate with the candidate himself, a political party, or private actors who operate as brokers. We posit that the choice among different clientelistic strategies that involve different resources is affected by the relative availability of public versus private resources. A variety of political factors increases the candidates' ability to access and politicize those public resources in clientelistic exchanges with voters. They include length of incumbency, copartisanship with the national incumbent party, and the presence of a mayor-aligned majority in the local city council. By contrast, in localities where such conditions are absent, candidates are more likely to use clientelistic strategies that politicize private resources.

Clientelistic strategies vary not only in the type of resources that are used to incentivize voters, but also in the ways such resources are deployed by brokers. A broad distinction can be made between positive and negative inducements. The former include offers of goods or favors, or privileged access to policies; the latter threats, harassment, or coercion. We contend that the use of favors and coercion are not informationally neutral strategies. Both strategies present candidates with the opportunity to send voters additional information about their policy positions or personal attributes. To return to the example used at the beginning of this chapter, the use of clientelistic strategies based on coercion allows the mayor of NM. to send voters signals about his policy position on the workfare program, an issue that is extremely divisive in the community. The harshness and brutality in his interaction with the beneficiaries of the workfare program and his systematic violation and infringement of their dignity allow this mayor to signal his opposition to the workfare program and thereby appeal to voters that oppose the current allocation of workfare benefits – ironically also while gaining some coerced votes from workfare recipients.

Candidates consider these signaling opportunities when calibrating their choices between the coercion and favors. We submit that the distribution of voters' preferences in a particular locality affects the importance candidates attach to the policy signals that can be conveyed by different clientelistic strategies. Coercive strategies are more valuable to candidates and brokers in localities where a large part of the population resents the current allocation of social policy benefits. The use of coercive strategies allows candidates to signal their opposition to the workfare program and appeal electorally to voters who oppose the current allocation of welfare benefits. By contrast, the use of non-programmatic strategies premised on favors allows candidates to send signals of paternalism and benevolence, or personal generosity. These efforts attempt to activate voters' norms of reciprocity, which imply that supporting their patron at the polls is the right thing to do and is also required to get continuous access to the benefits. At the same time, distributing favors may enable candidates to signal concerns about the personal circumstances and livelihood of low-income voters. We contend that such policy signals are particularly valuable to candidates competing in localities where demand for social policy benefits is high, but where distributional conflict over the allocation of social policy benefits is low.

Our study thus suggests that the use of clientelistic strategies creates opportunities for candidates to send voters signals about both their personal competence and their policy positions. Existing studies of electoral clientelism draw a strong distinction between programmatic and clientelistic strategies (Kitschelt 2000). In contrast to these studies, we suggest that the distinction between programmatic and clientelistic politics is, in fact, less pronounced. The use of different forms of clientelism allows candidates to send a range of policy signals to voters who are not even directly targeted by clientelistic inducements. Using evidence drawn from a variety of surveys, we show that voters' responses to different non-programmatic strategies are mediated by their social policy preferences: voters with different views about the desirability of redistribution draw different inferences about the policy positions and characteristics of candidates who use favors rather than coercion.

Our book provides some insights about the factors accounting for the persistence of clientelistic strategies in democratic elections. First, we highlight the fact that the multidimensionality of strategies creates opportunities for candidates to substitute between different forms of electoral clientelism. Political campaigns that seek to reduce or eliminate clientelism by increasing the legal penalties for the use of one particular clientelistic strategy may backfire, as they will create opportunities for candidates to switch to clientelistic strategies that are less visible and where they will be treated more leniently. As such, efforts to close off particular channels for clientelistic influence may result not in an overall reduction in the level of clientelism, but only in the reallocation of candidates' resources and effort towards different strategies.

Secondly, our signaling theory suggests that clientelism offers opportunities for candidates to obfuscate severe infringements of democratic practices. By using of clientelistic strategies to signal policy competence or personal attributes, candidates lessen the electoral costs of a behavior that most voters find normatively undesirable. Such signals weaken voters' ability to sanction clientelistic policies and may contribute to the election of "bad" politicians. At the same time, candidates' ability to rely on clientelistic policies to signal programmatic policy positions explain the persistence of clientelism in the region and the difficulties encountered by efforts to reform this phenomenon.

1.2 Relationship to Existing Studies

The study of clientelistic practices now occupies a central position in political science (Kitschelt and Wilkinson 2007; Stokes et al. 2013; Weitz-Shapiro 2014; Diaz-Cayeros et al. 2016). Clientelistic practices have been documented in both established and developing democracies, in countries as diverse as Argentina, Austria, Benin, Costa Rica, Kenya and Uganda. Recent studies of electoral clientelism have attempted to understand the non-programmatic appeals and the identity of voters targeted by different non-programmatic strategies.

In an important recent contribution to the study of clientelism, Susan Stokes and her collaborators have highlighted the important role played by brokers or intermediaries that mediate in the relationship between candidates and voters (Stokes et al. 2013). They demonstrate that brokers may have divergent interests from candidates and examine the electoral consequences of this divergence in preference for the type of voters who are targeted using clientelistic strategies.

Our book shares the premise of this study and other more recent approaches that emphasize the importance of brokers or political intermediaries for understanding clientelistic exchanges (Stokes et al. 2013; Holland and Palmer-Rubin, 2015). We complement existing studies by documenting the existence of a wide heterogeneity among brokers who mediate between candidates and voters. We also demonstrate that brokers control a variety of resources that can be used to influence the electoral choices of voters. Documenting such heterogeneity is important not only for analytical and descriptive purposes, but also because it allows us to consider possible interventions that may be devised to reduce the overall incidence of electoral clientelism altogether. We contend that current interventions designed to limit clientelistic practices have often missed important opportunities because they have focused solely on only one type of political exchange—vote buying—and have excluded other non-programmatic strategies.

Secondly, our study contributes to the literature on electoral clientelism by documenting the use of electoral coercion in contemporary elections and the variety of forms that coercion may take. With very few exceptions, existing studies probing clientelistic exchanges have only examined strategies premised on positive inducements, such as offers of money, goods, or policy benefits conditional on political support, while ignoring or neglecting the coercive dimension of clientelism (Stokes et al. 2013; Weitz-Shapiro 2014). Our study documents the existence of a wide range of coercive strategies. We also unpack the political considerations that make candidates willing to rely more strongly on coercive strategies as opposed to clientelistic strategies premised on positive inducements.

Our study investigates not only the political and economic conditions that are conducive to different types of clientelistic strategies, but also the variation in how voters assess candidates who make use of different non-programmatic strategies. Much of the existing research on clientelism regards clientelistic and programmatic strategies as mutually exclusive. Our study demonstrates that different forms of clientelism carry different informational signals about candidates' policy positions and personal characteristics. We find that when politicians use forms of clientelism that are more aligned with a particular voter's policy preferences, that voter tends to use a candidate less harshly for using clientelism. For example, when a voter who thinks that the current social policy programs care benefitting the 'undeserving poor' sees a candidate use a positive form of clientelism, they infer that the candidate's policy positions and personal characteristics are not in line with their own. However, when the same voter sees a candidate who uses a coercive form of clientelism—for example a candidate who demands and threatens workfare recipients—that voter uses the candidate less harshly. These informational signals ultimately affect the cost of clientelism in the eyes of a broader group of voters in a community. Our signaling theory of clientelism suggests that the distinction between clientelistic and programmatic policies is much weaker than currently assumed.

Beginning with the earliest studies on clientelism, scholars have highlighted the importance of poverty as a facilitating condition for electoral clientelism. Banfield and Wilson's study of political machines argued that "almost without exceptions, the lower the average income and the fewer the average years of schooling in a ward, the more dependable the ward's allegiance to the machine" (Banfield and Wilson 1965: 118). Likewise, Judith Chubb's study of clientelism in Italy argues that "political machines thrive upon poverty and social fragmentation. The machine, through its ties to national power can perpetuate the conditions of dependency and underdevelopment in which it is rooted and which impede the mobilization of mass support along alternative lines" (Chubb 1982: 251). In recent years, numerous contributions have documented the existence of such linkages between poverty and clientelism in a variety of contexts and have tested for a variety of mechanisms that may account for this relationship (Stokes 2005; Blaydes 2006; Stokes et al. 2013: ch. 6).

A common theme in the recent literature investigating the relationship between poverty and clientelism is the homogeneity of many low-income voters.

Invariably, the existing scholarship on clientelism presents low-income voters as an undifferentiated group or, to borrow the well-known metaphor Marx used in *The Eighteenth Brumaire*, as a "sack of potatoes" (Marx 1963 [1852]: ch. 7). In contrast to these studies, we argue that environments that experience high levels of poverty are sites of intense distributional conflicts among low-income voters. Throughout the book, we will refer to such distributional conflicts among low-income voters as "poor-versus-poor" conflicts. Social policy programs are one important source of such conflicts pitting low-income voters against each other. Such policies may engender a conflict between low-income voters who meet the eligibility threshold for benefits and low-income voters who cannot quality for these programs. People who cannot meet the eligibility threshold for a particular policy are likely to resent social policy beneficiaries and rationalize this hostility with perceptions that welfare beneficiaries are morally bankrupt and thus undeserving of social support. If high levels of poverty are correlated with membership in a different ethnic group, then economic and inter-ethnic conflicts overlap and reinforce each other. While "rich-versus-poor" conflicts have been a central theme in the political economy literature for decades, to our knowledge no study examines the consequences of distributional conflicts among low-income voters for incidence of different forms of electoral malfeasance.

In contrast to existing studies of clientelism that treat the poor as an undifferentiated mass of voters, our study examines the consequences of this distributional conflict between low-income voters for the use of clientelistic strategies. We argue that in communities where this distributional conflict among low-income voters is salient, the use of clientelistic strategies premised on coercion becomes more attractive for candidates. In using coercive strategies, brokers may extort the vote of workfare recipients, while signaling a punitive position on workfare to voters who are dissatisfied with the current allocation of workfare benefits. By contrast, in localities where such distributional conflict is absent, candidates may find clientelistic strategies premised on positive electoral inducements as a more attractive electoral strategy. In such localities, extending promises of workfare benefits or other social benefits to voters is likely to meet with lower levels of political opposition from voters do not meet the eligibility threshold for such benefits. Taken together, these considerations suggest that environments characterized by high levels of poverty can be conducive to multiple types of clientelistic strategies and that the choice of favors versus coercion depends on the salience and intensity of the distributional cleavage among low-income voters.

While contributing to the broader literature on clientelism, our study also seeks to advance the study of electoral politics in Eastern Europe. Previous studies of clientelism and patronage in Eastern Europe have focused on the first decade of the post-communist transition and have noticed the abundance of resources that could be politicized by parties for electoral purposes during the process of privatization, when the vast majority of state resources were "up for grabs" and "for sale" (Grzymała-Busse 2006; O'Dwyer 2006). As Anna Grzymała-Busse characterizes the context of the transition, "After the fall of communism, barely constituted democratic political parties simultaneously had to establish electoral rules, constituency relationships and functioning markets and democracies" (Grzymała-Busse 2006: 21). The decade we study differs in important ways from the first years of the post-communist transition. The first difference concerns the levels and amount of political resources that could be controlled by party leaders for political patronage and clientelism. In contrast to the first decade of the post-communist period, when the entire apparatus of the state was "up for sale," in recent years, party leaders have controlled significantly fewer resources that can be exploited for clientelistic purposes. Thus, while the economic environment of the first decade of the post-communist period was characterized by the abundance of resources that could be politicized, the current environment is one of resource scarcity. Secondly, the economic environment in which clientelistic strategies unfold differs significantly across these two periods. Poverty, unemployment, and labor market exclusion have been a much more pressing concern in recent years than in the first decade after the collapse of communism. As we will show, this changing economic environment characterized by higher levels of unemployment represents a fertile political terrain for the use of multiple forms of clientelistic strategies. In particular, the intensification of political conflict over the allocation of social policy benefits has made the use of coercive forms of clientelism a highly attractive electoral strategy in recent decades.

Our study also revisits several prominent hypotheses about the determinants of variation in the use of clientelistic strategies in the region developed by scholars of Eastern European party systems (Kitschelt 2002, 2003). The first of these hypotheses attributes differences in clientelistic strategies to pre-transitional factors, such as the mixes of coercion and accommodation exhibited by communist regimes (Crawford 1996; Ágh 1998). In a well-known formulation of this hypotheses, Herbert Kitschelt refers to these families of explanations as the "excessively deep explanations" of post-communist regime diversity (2003: 66). A second explanation of variation in non-programmatic strategies traces the diversity to the relative strength of parties with ties to the pre-communist period. According to this account, communist successor parties were more likely to make use of clientelistic strategies than parties that emerged during the transition period. The higher appetite of communist successor parties' propensity to use clientelistic strategies can be attributed not only to the parties' organizational legacies, but also to their leaders' ability to seize state resources during the immediate political transition (Kitschelt 1992).

Our findings provide very little support for either of these hypotheses. First, pre-communist legacies remain a less salient predictor of variation in clientelistic strategies during current decades as compared to the first years of the post-communist transition. While some cross-national differences in the levels of clientelistic strategies between Hungary and Romania exist, such differences are relatively small. Moreover, as our study will demonstrate, the salient variation in the use of electoral clientelism is the variation among different types of clientelistic strategies—those that involve positive or negative inducements and in those that rely on different types of brokers—and not the cross-national variation in regime legacies. Secondly, our results find also little support for the hypothesis that communist successor parties hold a political monopoly over the use of clientelism. In Hungary, the implosion of the Socialist Party after 2010 reduced dramatically its ability to engage in clientelistic strategies during recent elections. Here, we document the use of electoral clientelism in a political environment dominated by a party that emerged during the post-communist transition (Fidesz) and which faced electoral challenge from a newly formed party on the right (Jobbik). In Romania, the communist successor party appeared to retain an initial monopoly over the use of electoral clientelism during the first decade of the post-communist transition. However, as recent scholars of Romanian party development have argued, parties on the political right have successfully imitated this electoral strategy and have "learned" to exploit resources of the state for clientelistic purposes (Gherghina 2013; Giugăl 2015). At the time of our study, we find only very small differences in the use of clientelistic strategies among the successor of the post-communist party, on the one hand, and parties on the right, on the other hand.

Rather than explaining variation among clientelistic strategies either through specific cross-national differences or through factors that are specific to particular political parties, we trace this variation to specific locality-level conditions. As we will show, local factors include both differences in political endowments, which affect candidates' access to different types of political resources, and differences in the salience of distributional conflict, which originate in different demographic and labor market characteristics. Thus, to understand clientelistic practices in contemporary elections in Eastern Europe, we must unravel how such locality-level conditions create distinct electoral incentives for candidates to use different electoral strategies.

1.3 Empirical Strategy

In examining how clientelism functions, our study seeks to capture what historians of democratization call "the quotidian experience of electoral politics" or "electoral democracy with a human face" (Anderson 2000: 14). Methodologically, we attempt to bring together methodological tools that have been developed by two types of approaches to the study of illicit electoral practices. The first set of methods are found in the tool-kit of anthropologists and historians, the second comprises survey methods designed to capture illicit activities or to capture citizens' evaluations of such activities. We will briefly preview here the methodological choices we made, but present a richer account of them in Chapter 3.

The first component of our empirical strategy draws on such in-depth research consisting of over four hundred interviews with politicians, brokers, and voters in rural and urban communities in Hungary and Romania carried out over a period of eighteen months. This qualitative research combines participation in the daily activities of the respective communities, including the observation of public events (such as elections or rallies) and everyday interactions between mayors, officials of the welfare administration, and voters. We recorded, transcribed, and analyzed all these interviews and also relied on a complementary method of data analysis that involved field notes drafted by skilled and trained field researchers.

The overwhelming majority of our interviews were semi-structured. They occurred in the houses and backyards of the respondents, in city halls, in fields, in mines and other enterprises, in schools or churches. In each of the interviews, we followed a common structure that began with more neutral topics—such as the state or the locality, the economic conditions and opportunities—before breaching sensitive political topics including electoral irregularities. This allowed us to develop trust with our respondents over the course of long sessions and some-times over the course of multiple sessions. While these techniques were successful on many occasions, on others we could only note that respondents chose to resist our questions, to close down, or to carefully filter the information they were willing to provide. The interpretation of this rich interview-based data also posed unique challenges. We followed the strategy adequately described by Allina-Pisano as reading "against the grain" (2008: 25). This involved an effort to remain alert to statements that our respondents believed we wanted to hear and to "listen to comments that emerged in the interstices of the conversation" (Allina-Pisano 2008: 25). We also carefully avoid reporting evidence that could not be corroborated by multiple sources.

In addition to ethnographic research, our empirical strategy makes use of unobtrusive survey techniques such as list experiments that allow us to measure the incidence of a variety of electoral irregularities. These unobtrusive survey techniques allow respondents to report clientelistic strategies without incriminat-ing themselves or admitting to stigmatized behavior. We fielded the surveys in the aftermath of the 2014 parliamentary election in Hungary and in the aftermath of the 2014 presidential election in Romania. Our analysis of these surveys allows us to characterize the most salient correlates of the variation in the incidence of clientelistic strategies across different localities and across different voters.

A third component of our empirical strategy are survey-based experiments. In these surveys, we use a variety of realistic vignettes to obtain fine-grained meas-ures of how voters interpret forms of electoral clientelism and the informational signals about candidate qualities and platforms that are embedded in different non-programmatic strategies. The vignettes also give us a high degree of precision over the exact form of clientelism, allowing us to isolate how specific differences in the way that clientelism is structured might affect voters' reactions.

Existing studies of electoral clientelism have successfully used either survey-based methods or ethnographic research to shed light on such practices. To our knowledge, no study has combined the two research strategies to the extent that we do in this book. Both research strategies share a common analytical goal, which involves searching for political micromechanisms. Each method provides researchers with different analytical tools to identify such micromechanisms. As such, leveraging multiple methods within the same study represents an important methodological strength. In combination, the methods allow us to measure carefully a variety of unobtrusive and hidden practices but also to describe and characterize the beliefs and expectations of the actors involved in such exchanges: voters, brokers, and candidates.

1.4 Looking Ahead

Chapter 2 presents the theoretical framework of our analysis. We clarify definitional and conceptual issues related to the study of electoral clientelism and propose a classification of non-programmatic strategies that differentiates among the resources that are used to finance clientelistic exchanges, and among the ways that those incentives can be structured, particularly whether they are offered as negative threats or positive inducements. Next, we develop our theory which begins by conceptualizing how voters who are directly and indirectly exposed to different forms of clientelism perceive and react to it. Drawing on normative theories, we conjecture that voters are likely to punish coercive strategies more severely than strategies premised on positive inducements. While candidates incur political audience costs from using various non-programmatic strategies, they may attempt to reduce the severity of this constraint by sending voters signals about their personal attributes, their relation position vis-à-vis their competitor, and their policy position. This chapter develops theoretical expectations about the positive informational signals that may result from the use of different non-programmatic strategies for voters with certain policy preferences or characteristics.

Chapter 2 also conceptualizes how these considerations about the electoral costs of different forms of clientelism and resource constraints shape the choices that politicians make about the level and form of clientelism that they use. We argue that the potential effectiveness of different clientelistic strategies is affected by voters' normative reactions and their likelihood of complying with the clientelistic exchanges. On the other hand, we conjecture that politicians' abilities to employ different forms of clientelism are shaped by access to resources, including, most importantly, control of local flows of social policy through the local city hall.

Chapter 3 provides background on the most significant political parties and the most notable dimensions of programmatic competition in the countries included in our study. We also examine the most significant policies that provide opportunities for exploitation of state resources for electoral purposes. This chapter also presents our research design and explains how the three different methodologies we deploy in combination allow us to test the various elements of our empirical strategy.

In Chapter 4, we examine the use of non-programmatic strategies where political brokers deploy state resources—privileged access to policy resources or administrative favors—to incentivize the electoral choices of voters. Drawing on ethnographic research, we document the strategies by which these brokers (mayors or employees in the local administration) seek to establish norms of political reciprocity amongst voters and to activate these norms during elections. We also discuss the strategies used by brokers to ensure that voters comply with their political promises and vote for the correct candidate. Using list experiments, we document the use of these strategies during recent elections and examine the variation across localities in the use of such strategies. Finally, we examine the informational opportunities and constraints associated with the use of this non-programmatic strategy. Using survey-based experiments, we show that the use of clientelistic strategies premised on favors creates opportunities for candidates to signal pro-poor concerns. Consequently, we find that favors are common in localities with large groups of homogeneous voters who depend on or desire state resources, but that in areas where there is conflict over those resources, favors are less prevalent.

Chapter 5 examines the use of non-programmatic strategies based on welfare coercion. Drawing on ethnographic research, we document the use of different coercive practices used by candidates in both countries. "Blackmail" involves the initial toleration of some irregularities (such as non-payment of taxes), which are then exploited at elections. "Welfare coercion," by contrast, involves threats to cut off access to long-term benefits from the state. This chapter argues that the use of coercion is a politically attractive strategy in places where eligibility for welfare benefits is particularly politicized. In such localities, the use of coercion allows mayors to maximize electoral support from beneficiaries of social policies, while at the same time signaling a "tough on welfare" position to opponents of the social policy programs. Using list experiments, we document the use of coercive strategies and show that the incidence of such strategies is higher in localities where a larger share of the voters cannot meet the eligibility criteria for social policy benefits.

Chapter 6 turns to the analysis of another clientelistic coercive strategy, where brokers exploit long-term economic exchanges with voters to induce them to support a particular candidate. In urban settings, candidates rely on employers as brokers. This chapter documents the use of coercive strategies where employers may threaten to reduce employees' wages or lay them off if they support the incorrect candidate. In rural settings, we document candidates' reliance on moneylenders as brokers. The incidence of such strategies varies across localities and is determined by economic conditions that affect the costs of economic coercion incurred by such brokers.

In Chapter 7, we examine the use of vote buying or offers of small goods in exchange for political support. The chapter documents important differences between vote buying, on the one hand, and non-programmatic strategies that politicize state resources, on the other hand. These strategies differ with respect to the types of brokers used in these exchanges, the goods offered to voters, and the identity of the voters targeted by these strategies. We document the use of both cash and in-kind forms of vote buying, such as offers of meals. While we find that voters view candidates who use in-kind forms of clientelism less negatively than those who offer cash handouts, we find little evidence that either type of vote buying leaves voters with important impressions of what candidates will do once in office. There is also little evidence that vote buying is strategically allocated across localities.

Chapter 8 discusses the implications of its findings for ongoing debates about the persistence of electoral clientelism in current democracies. First, we show that our account of electoral clientelism presents new tools to characterize the endogenous emergence of political parties in countries with weakly institutionalized party organizations. We show that the incentives for internal integration of brokers are a function of the different non-programmatic strategies.

The chapter also discusses the implications of our findings for discussions of the adoption of electoral reforms that aim to reduce the incidence of electoral clientelism. Our study identifies two reasons why such reforms may lead only to modest reductions in the incidence of electoral clientelism. First, candidates may continue to use clientelistic practices to send signals to voters about their personal attributes or policy position, which is likely to reduce the determination of voters to sanction such strategies and may even lead to the re-election of candidates who engage in non-programmatic exchanges. Secondly, electoral reforms may be less successful in closing down opportunities for substitution among different clientelistic strategies. The imposition of higher punishments for particular electoral strategies may create opportunities for candidates to strategically switch to non-programmatic strategies that are punished less severely. The analysis of electoral clientelism advanced in this book provides policymakers with a better analytic framework to consider possible opportunities for substitution among various clientelistic practices and equip policymakers with better tools to approach reforms.

We conclude on a rather pessimistic note. Given that clientelistic strategies provide ample opportunities for electoral differentiation among candidates and candidates seem able to effectively 'spin' clientelism to avoid punishment even from their supporters, candidates will have few incentives to abandon such strategies. Practices of welfare favors, welfare coercion, vote buying, and intimidation are likely to continue to remain an enduring feature of the political landscape of these countries.

2

Disaggregating Clientelism

Resource Constraints and Informational Signals

In elections around the world, candidates seek to influence voters' decisions using not only past performance or general promises, but also individualized promises and threats. Such practices are as old as mass politics. They have been documented in European countries such as Britain, France, or Germany during the immediate decades following the introduction of mass suffrage. Such practices of undue influence are also a common occurrence in electoral campaigns in recently democratized countries in Africa, Latin America, Asia or Eastern Europe. Political scientists have studied such electoral strategies using the term electoral clientelism (Kitschelt and Wilkinson 2007).

In this chapter, we lay out a conceptual framework for understanding variation in electoral clientelism, and the forces that shape why one form is used over another. We make the case for the need to disaggregate among different types of non-programmatic strategies, and we propose a classification that disaggregates electoral clientelism along two dimensions. The first dimension considers variation in the resources used to incentivize the choices of voters or brokers. Here we distinguish between clientelistic strategies that deploy state resources, and strategies that deploy private resources, financed by candidates, parties, or other private actors. The second dimension captures how candidates and brokers structure voters' incentives. We differentiate between clientelistic strategies based on promises of positive inducements and strategies premised on coercive threats.

We argue that these two dimensions—whether clientelism is financed by state or private resources, and whether it is structured as a positive or negative incentive—are important for several reasons. First, there are important differences in how strongly these different forms of clientelism violate important ethical principles. Coercive strategies are particularly offensive because they take away voters' choices to opt out of clientelism. Clientelism involving state resources also violates basic principles of equal access to state resources. Second, coercive and state-based forms of clientelism may have a stronger effect on voters' behavior than the archetypical one-off vote-buying transactions. For all of these reasons, it is important to understand not only the overall level of clientelism, but also where it is likely to take its more powerful and morally odious forms.

Incorporating this classification, the chapter then formulates a set of hypotheses about the factors explaining the choice of different forms of non-programmatic strategies. We draw on existing theory to propose two families of explanations for how much clientelism should occur, and what form it should take. One family of explanations focuses on the availability and attractiveness of the resources used to finance clientelistic transactions. We will refer to these theories as "resource-based explanations." These explanations focus on the supply side of clientelism to argue that the existence and manipulability of political resources shapes candidates' choices of whether to use state versus private funding in the personally targeted incentives that they offer to voters. These explanations suggest that politicians prefer to use state resources such as social policy benefits or procedural favors to incentivize voters rather than their own campaign resources when possible. However, their ability to do so varies systematically across localities and according to local political conditions.

The second type of explanation focuses on the demand for clientelism, or more specifically, on how voters perceive and punish or reward candidates who use clientelism. We call this family of theories "informational explanations." This emerging view emphasizes that voters who are offered material incentives in clientelistic transactions, or who hear about these transactions secondhand, may also update their beliefs about the characteristics of the clientelistic candidate. In other words, clientelism may carry important informational signals. In small communities where information about clientelism quickly becomes common knowledge, these informational signals can affect how costly it is for politicians to use clientelism. At one extreme, voters might judge candidates who use clientelism so harshly that it is no longer attractive to the candidate. At the other extreme, clientelism might send positive signals about candidates to some voters. As a result, politicians and brokers must take into account the extent to which voters are willing to punish or reward candidates who use different clientelistic strategies. The way that voters judge candidates may also depend on whether they offer material incentives that are positive or negative, and state-based versus privately funded. Thus, this view implies that the distribution of voters' preferences in a particular locality should affect the informational advantages or costs that candidates derive from a particular clientelistic strategy.

We contend that local social conditions, particularly the level of distributional conflict over social policy benefits among poor voters, play an important role in shaping whether local electorates punish or reward particular clientelistic practices. Distributional conflicts pit low-income voters who can access social policy benefits against those who fall below the eligibility threshold for such benefits due to their demographic and labor market characteristics. These conflicts often center on whether different groups of poor voters are deserving of generous state support. The ways that candidates and their brokers manage local resources and treat different groups of poor voters are a strong signal of candidates' policy positions in this distributional conflict. We predict that the use of programmatic strategies premised on positive inducements, particularly those involving state resources, signals a pro-poor concern and a desire to maintain or expand the current distribution of social policy benefits. By contrast, the use of coercive clientelistic strategies that threaten to impose harsh and abusive sanctions, particularly on recipients of social policy benefits, signals that the candidates are willing to treat current social policy beneficiaries more harshly, and perhaps reallocate resources to more "deserving" citizens.

These informational signals could merely lower the cost of using clientelism, or they could actually make it more likely that certain voters will support clientelistic candidates. Either way, to the extent that these informational signals are strong they should inform the relative attractiveness of different clientelistic strategies. We argue that candidates' choices between clientelistic strategies based on positive inducements and those based on coercion thus depends on the relative size of the different constituencies in the locality. The use of coercion is an attractive electoral strategy in localities where the size of the political constituency supporting social policy retrenchment is large. By contrast, in places where size of the electoral constituency favoring an expansion of the existing social policy benefits is large, candidates should choose non-programmatic strategies premised on positive inducements. Candidates should be even more likely to use coercive forms of clientelism when both groups are large, which should create the conditions for social conflict over state resources.

Our explanation of electoral clientelism departs from the existing literature by demonstrating that clientelistic strategies create opportunities for candidates to also convey signals about their policy positions and personal characteristics even to voters who are not directly engaged in clientelistic exchanges. These signals, and the existence of distributional conflicts between groups of poor voters, help explain why voters sometimes fail to harshly judge candidates who use even morally reprehensible coercive forms of clientelism. In the final section of the chapter, we discuss the observable implications of this account of clientelism at both the individual and locality levels. At the individual level, we lay out predictions for how demographic characteristics translate into social policy preferences that then shape how voters update their beliefs about candidates who use various forms of clientelism. At the locality level, we discuss what this informational demand side and the resource-based supply-side argument imply about where different forms of clientelism should be used. While resource-based theories focus on variables measuring local political control over social policy resources, informational theories lead us to make predictions around the size of different demographic groups.

2.1 Disaggregating Electoral Clientelism

We begin by clarifying our definition of clientelism. Clientelistic exchanges are electoral strategies where politicians rely on intermediaries to incentivize voters to support a particular candidate. We draw on Hicken's (2011) definition of clientelism as chains of dyadic relationships between politicians, brokers, and voters. Behavior in clientelistic relationships involves a political quid pro quo: in exchange for some agreed behavior by political intermediaries, voters agree to a particular electoral behavior. Our definition of clientelism exclusively considers exchanges between candidates, political intermediaries (or brokers), and voters. We exclude political exchanges at higher levels of aggregation that do not target voters directly such as allocations by federal or regional governments to local governments.[1] While political criteria may be present in the allocation of such benefits, the distribution of these grants does not require a voter to reciprocate at the ballot box.[2]

In the next subsection, we disaggregate forms of clientelism along two dimensions: first, whether voters are offered positive or negative inducements, and second, whether they involve state or private resources. While many criteria could be used to disaggregate clientelism, we believe that these two dimensions are both inherently and instrumentally justifiable. First, distinguishing between promises, or voluntary exchanges, and coercive threats is important because coercion violates voters' autonomy. By taking away a voter's option to opt out of a clientelistic exchange, coercive threats are normatively worse than voluntary (although still harmful) positive forms of clientelism. Second, clientelism powered with public revenues is arguably more harmful than that based on private resources. State-based forms of clientelism not only pervert electoral processes, but also distort public spending and erode trust in the state. Finally, as we will argue in the remainder of the chapter, the resource-based and informational theories of clientelism imply that the forms of clientelism differentiated along these dimensions should be used in different localities.

2.1.1 Offers and threats

While coercion was a central component of early studies of electoral clientelism, it has fallen out of focus in recent years. We conceptualize positive inducements or proposals as a category that involves offers of money, goods, or favors. This includes the most prominent form of clientelism in the literature: vote buying. Negative inducements include the threat of economic or physical sanctions for an individual's voting behavior. Such negative inducements include threats to cut voters off from benefits on which they depend, removing them from their land or residences, or violence, including assault and death.[3]

Early research on electoral clientelism considered coercion to be an important component of clientelistic exchanges. Scott (1972a: 99–100), for instance, considers coercive strategies such as threats of punishment or withdrawal of benefits as central to the conceptualization of clientelism. Other scholars of clientelism consider that coercion is used in combination with other types of incentives (Powell 1970: 412; Lemarchand 1972; Lemarchand 1981: 17–19; Özbudun 1981; Chubb 1982: 80). More recently, while some scholars have differentiated between positive and negative inducements, most consider both offers and threats as part of the same strategy and have tended to limit the definition of coercion to only include the use of physical force. A number of scholars have examined the trade-off between clientelism, violence, and programmatic politics both theoretically (Robinson and Torvik 2009; Collier and Vicente 2012) and empirically (Fujiwara and Wantchekon 2013). Yet the dominant definition of clientelism still centers on offers of goods or services that are contingent on voters' actions but that voters enter into freely. We challenge this definition based both on theoretical distinctions between positive and negative inducements, and on empirical evidence that voters perceive some of the incentives that politicians offer them during elections as threats.

Voter expectations or beliefs matter for distinguishing between positive and negative strategies. If a voter does not expect to receive a sack of grain in the week before an election, and then she does receive it in exchange for a promise to vote for a specific party, the grain serves as a positive inducement. However, if she expects to receive it or feels entitled to it, then an effort to use the grain to incentivize her vote would take the form of a negative inducement, a threat to withhold the grain if she votes for the principal's non-preferred party. Although this difference is subjective and thus cannot be measured without micro-level measures of voters' beliefs and expectations, it may impact behavior. There is significant evidence that individuals think about gains and losses in very different ways. Being in the domain of gains (positive inducements) rather than losses (negative inducements) has implications for how individuals think about risk and how much utility they derive from different states (Kahneman and Tversky 1979). For the vast majority of individuals, a negative sanction has a much larger impact on an individual's utility than a gain of the same size.

In general, the literature on clientelism has elided the distinction between positive and negative electoral strategies. With regard to access to entitlements or assets such as welfare transfers, jobs, or land, a deeper understanding of voters' expectations or reference points could explain why these are such effective patronage tools. Threatening to take away a job that a voter expects to keep for years should be a much more powerful inducement than offering to give him the same job. Yet to date, jobs and welfare have typically been conceptualized as positive inducements that voters can take or leave.

Another important difference between positive and negative strategies involves whether the incentive worsens a voter's baseline condition, that is, his condition if he rejects the broker's offer. When a broker presents a vote-buying proposal—"If you vote for me, you get X, and if you don't, you get nothing"—a voter can either accept it or turn it down. Turning down the offer does not affect the voter's status quo. Coercion, however, can be used to push a voter into accepting a deal to which he otherwise would not consent (Wertheimer 1987). For example, threatening voters with a reduction of their social policy benefits if they do not support a particular candidate can be conceptualized as reducing the attractiveness of the status quo, or outside options, of those voters. If they do as the broker says, they get to remain in their status quo state. If they do not, they are much worse off than before. Strategies premised on coercion therefore have more severe normative implications than offers of positive inducements do because they violate a principle of autonomy.

Positive inducements and coercion vary in the autonomy exercised or retained by the voter targeted by the transaction.[4] Voters who are offered positive inducements have the freedom to opt in and out of vote-buying exchanges, unlike those who face a threat. Referring to this lack of autonomy, James Scott (1972a: 98) called voters who are "coerced by the landlord or their employer" as "locked-in electorates." This type of voter is "connected to the larger political system through his agent-patron whose *control over his political will* was a function of his control over his means of subsistence" (Scott 1972a: 98, emphasis added). Similarly, Carl Landé discusses the relationship between coerced voters and their patrons, noting that it is "made clear to such voters that he remains perpetually a debtor" despite their "continuous display of deference and obedience" (Landé 1977: xxvii). Although in much of the recent literature on clientelism it is taken as an assumption that all clientelistic transactions are voluntary, we seek explicitly to examine variation in the level of autonomy of clients that the case study literature has identified.

2.1.2 State and private resources

A second distinction among non-programmatic strategies concerns the type of resources that brokers present as incentives. Specifically, we distinguish between forms of clientelism that are powered by the resources of the state and those powered by private resources. Previous studies have referred to clientelistic strategies that exploit state resources as "patrimonial" or "neopatrimonial" strategies (Bratton and van de Walle 1997; Giraudy 2007; Hale 2014). We take a broad view of the type of state resources that can be used for clientelistic mobilization and consider offers of employment, privileged access to policy benefits, and promises of administrative favors as state resources that can be used as clientelistic incentives.

Early studies of clientelism considered offers of employment in the public sector as the quintessential clientelistic strategy. The importance of such promises of public sector employment in exchange for votes in the overall mix of non-programmatic strategies is likely to have been overstated. The total number of public sector jobs that can be offered in exchange for support is likely to be small, especially in recent decades, when the size of the public sector has decreased significantly. This strategy is also likely to be very costly compared to other policy alternatives because other state resources are likely to be more cost-effective and more abundant than jobs. Such resources include policy benefits and promises of licenses and other administrative advantages. State resources can be used both as positive inducements but also coercively, as threats to induce a particular behavior or as punishment for failure to comply with a political request.

In the case of policy coercion, brokers seek to influence the choices of voters by threatening to withhold public resources that represent important sources of income to voters. We will refer to strategies of policy coercion as those strategies where the negative incentive used to influence the voter's choice is a particular resource or a right that is defined by the state. Examples of coercion involve the threat to rescind a property right that gives a voter the right to use land if the voter does not support a candidate. Alternatively, brokers may threaten voters to remove long-term access to a policy benefit unless the voter supports a certain candidate. In many cases in the region we study, the right or benefit used to threaten voters is access to welfare.

2.2 A Typology of Clientelistic Strategies

Table 2.1 summarizes the preceding discussion and maps out the four distinct types of clientelism that we examine in this book. The two columns in this table differentiate forms of clientelism based on the resources that are used to finance it. We distinguish clientelism that involves the authority and resources of the state from clientelism financed by private revenues or powers. Second, we differentiate clientelism based on the ways that political intermediaries structure the incentives that they offer to voters. Here we distinguish between strategies structured as threats and those premised on promises.

Our classification departs from current research on clientelism in two ways. First, we emphasize the multidimensional character of clientelism. While the earliest research on electoral clientelism—as exemplified by Schmidt et al.'s 1977

Table 2.1 A typology of clientelistic strategies

		Are state resources used to finance the clientelistic incentive?	
		No	Yes
Is the clientelistic incentive the threat of a negative sanction?	No	Vote buying	Policy favors
	Yes	Economic coercion	Policy coercion

volume *Friends, Followers and Factions*—considered a broad range of non-programmatic strategies, most recent contributions have considerably narrowed the scope of the empirical analysis, equating clientelism with vote buying. By broadening our view of clientelism beyond a single type of non-programmatic exchange, we paint a more complete picture of its prevalence and drivers, and can study the trade-offs between different strategies.

Our study also departs from existing research on electoral clientelism by considering the importance of coercion in the bundle of non-programmatic strategies. Earlier studies of electoral politics in young democracies recognized the importance of electoral coercion. Discussing different forms of electoral corruption in the Philippines, Wurfel (1991 [1988], 770–2) notes that vote buying emerged as a non-programmatic strategy only after coercion by employers declined in importance. In an analysis of clientelistic strategies in England, Scott also commented on the transition from coercion to positive inducements. As he noted, "No longer being able to threaten voters physically or to stuff ballot boxes on a scale sufficient to win, candidates and parties were obliged to proffer material rewards as a means of persuasion" (Scott 1972a: 94). By contrast, the most recent literature on clientelism has avoided the study of electoral coercion altogether. One important goal of our study is to illustrate the continuous presence of coercion in the menu of non-programmatic strategies and to characterize the trade-offs encountered by candidates as they consider positive inducements rather than coercion.

Although our typology is not defined by broker types, we recognize the importance of the political intermediaries or brokers who mediate the relationship between candidates and voters. Such brokers use their control over a good that is valuable to voters to influence voter behavior. The most well-known brokers are affiliated to particular parties, and have taken a variety of names in different contexts, including *intepretes* or "go-between" in ancient Rome (Davis 1910: 13), *cabo eleitoral* in Brazil during the 1930s, *capituleros* in Peru, *gestor* or *padrino politico* in Mexico, *caudillo barrial* or *punteros* in Argentina (Auyero 1999: 302), and *capibastone* in Southern Italy (Gambetta 1996: 307). However, many clientelistic exchanges are brokered by agents who also fill other functions, including the heads of civic associations (Holland and Palmer-Rubin 2015), civil servants (Oliveros 2016), and employers (Mares 2015). While these groups may not be known primarily for their roles as political brokers, in many cases they do serve as highly influential conduits for personalized election-time inducements.

Our typology is not driven by variation in brokers, although the variation between state and non-state resources does sometimes track broker types. For instance, brokers who are not affiliated with the state are unlikely to be able to use state resources to incentivize voters. However, many brokers are able to engage in both positive and negative forms of clientelism. In our cases in Eastern Europe, for example, mayors can use state resources to both make promises and threats. The dimensions that define our typology thus cut across broker types even if they are not completely independent from them.

The typology we propose is focused on economic incentives and excludes violence. In theory, violence can be used as a form of coercive clientelism when politicians and brokers tell voters that they will be face physical sanctions if they do not vote in a certain way. We suspect that our theory could be extended to include physical threats as a third form of incentives in addition to positive and negative material inducements. For reasons that will become clear in Section 2.3.2 when we discuss the supply and demand factors that explain variation in the form of clientelism, we think that violence is qualitatively different from economic threats. However, because threats of violence are not a common strategy in the cases we cover in this book, we leave a full discussion of substitutions between economic and physical electoral incentives to future work. In the following sections we discuss the definitions and intellectual history of the four types of clientelism we consider.

2.2.1 Policy favors

Policy favors are state resources that are offered to voters in clientelistic transactions. A wide variety of resources financed by general tax revenues can be used for policy favors, including public sector jobs (Chubb 1982), public services (Fox 1994), unemployment benefits (Giraudy 2007), and food assistance (Weitz-Shapiro 2014). For example, in Mexico under the Institutional Revolutionary Party (PRI) government, Fox notes the importance of a variety of programs that distribute "sewage and potable water, health, education, food distribution, electrification, street paving, housing and soft loans for low-income producers" (Fox 1994: 167). In Venezuela under Hugo Chávez, the Misiones program, which includes educational campaigns, food and housing subsidies, and the construction of housing and clinics, was a primary source of funding for political mobilization (Penfold-Becerra 2007: 65; Diaz-Cayeros et al. 2016: 35; Stokes et al. 2013).

The modalities of policy favors have changed over time with trends in public sector management and social policy. Zolberg noted in the 1960s that politicians competing in countries with expanding public sectors made so many promises of government jobs that it created an "inflationary process of demand formation" (Zolberg 1968: 149). As neoliberal reforms were put into place globally in the 1980s and 1990s, the availability of jobs to reward supporters became more rare. By contrast, as many clientelistic countries have expanded their social policy, the use of offers of access to public policies in exchange for such electoral support has increased. Public policies that have been used for clientelistic exchanges include housing, unemployment assistance, family benefits, and poverty relief.

Scholars of clientelism in many developing countries have also documented the use of state resources to incentivize both brokers and voters. Studies of Indian politics have argued that rural programs based on agricultural loans may be the primary factor accounting for the Congress Party's hold in rural areas (Weiner 1967: 464; Scott 1972a). Wilkinson, for instance, estimates that around 10 percent of the budget for rural development programs was used as political patronage (Wilkinson 2007: 124–5). In Africa, van de Walle argues that Constituency Development Funds were an important source of clientelistic practices in Ghana, Kenya, Malawi, Tanzania, Uganda, and Zambia (van de Walle 2014: 239). Others have documented the use of agricultural inputs such as land, fertilizer, and seeds as rewards for political support (Beck 2008: 75; Zamchiya 2011).

In addition to employment and access to policy, local bureaucrats can also politicize the provision of administrative regulations they control, and condition access to administrative decisions—such as certificates or titles—on political support. As Chandra writes,

> The state also dominates the everyday business of existence, especially in rural India, and especially for the poor. Citizens require a minimum set of goods to attest to their existence and then to survive—birth certificates, death certificates, caste certificates, land titles, appointment letters, ration cards, hospital beds, loans, drinking water, electricity, sanitation, and so on—and procuring each of these requires contact with the state, which in turn can be influenced by politicians. The standard promise of the candidate at the constituency level, therefore, is 'Vote for me and I will get your work done'.   (Chandra 2014: 161)

For policy favors, state employees are the most important brokers. Early studies of party machines in US cities like Chicago and Philadelphia estimated that most party brokers were public servants (Kurtzman 1935; Gosnell 1968 [1937]: 54). The use of state employees as brokers has also been observed in a variety of contemporary contexts. In a study of three Argentinean municipalities, Oliveros (2013) documents the use of a variety of state employees as brokers. Public teachers in particular appear as important brokers in a number of cases including Mexico (Larreguy et al. 2017), Colombia (Eaton and Chambers-Ju 2014), and Indonesia (Aspinall, 2014 553).

2.2.2 Vote buying

The second non-programmatic strategy we examine is vote buying. Much like the provision of policy favors, vote buying is a strategy premised on positive inducements, but in our definition of vote buying the goods used to incentivize voting behavior are not financed out of general tax revenues. Descriptively, the goods offered as part of vote-buying exchanges are quite heterogeneous. Consider some historical examples of vote-buying strategies. In nineteenth-century US elections, party agents offered voters goods such as boots or shoes, pants, bushels of corn, or plugs of tobacco (Bensel 2004: 59). In Third Republic France, men could trade their votes for bread, cigarettes, or clothes (Journal Officiel de la République Française, Débats Chambre des Députés, 23 January 1898; 7 July 1898). Party operatives campaigning in Chicago during the period of the Great Depression distributed not only food but also more durable goods such as clothes (Gosnell 1968 [1937]: 72).

Studies of vote buying in contemporary elections have also documented wide heterogeneity in the goods offered in these exchanges. A study of Argentinian brokers found that they distributed "medicine, a metal sheet for the rook, pairs of sneakers for their sons and daughters, a *choripan* (meat sausage sandwich) on the day of the rally" (Auyero 1999: 301). One broker in Paraguay described vote-buying exchanges as follows: "the operative does his work, buying the conscience of the voter with money, with alcohol, buying his id card, a little medicine, sugar, bread, tea and in this way he goes buying and winning adherents" (Finan and Schechter 2012: 867).

Many vote-buying exchanges include offers of money. A study of Nigerian elections found that 68 percent of the respondents who were offered positive inducements were offered money. The amounts offered were small, averaging around four dollars (Bratton 2013: 126). A study of electoral practices in Ghana also notes that during these campaigns, "one of 'the boys' (runners and body-guards) continue to feed the candidate with small notes for handouts from a small envelope" (Lindberg 2003: 129).

Brokers used in vote-buying exchanges often differ from those used to offer state policy resources. In many cases, vote-buying brokers come from the same low-income background as the voters they target (e.g. see Aspinall 2014: 58 on Indonesia). Networks of brokers used in vote-buying exchanges are established on an ad hoc basis. Brokers are "free hand operatives" (Bensel 2004: 63) who are recruited into "highly fluid organizations" (Aspinall 2014: 58) in spot transactions and paid small amounts of money that are often only slightly higher than the amounts that they subsequently use to incentivize voters (Aspinall 2014; Finan and Schechter 2012: 867). Networks of vote-buying brokers are also often bloated, with one study of clientelistic mobilization in Taiwan documenting a ratio of one broker to twenty voters (Wang and Kurzmann 2007: 234).

2.2.3 Policy coercion

Both vote buying and favors are non-programmatic strategies premised on posi-tive inducements. In the case of coercive strategies, brokers seek to influence the choices of voters by threatening to withhold resources that voters perceive as a critical part of their livelihoods. We define policy coercion as the threat to withhold publicly financed resources on which voters depend. Examples of policy coercion include the threat to rescind a property right or the removal of access to a policy benefit the voter receives or anticipates. In this way, electoral coercion is not a freely entered into exchange but rather "the political subordination of clients" (Karl 1995: 73; see also Fox 1994).

Reports of policy coercion are extremely common in clientelistic political systems. Official French publications document cases of local officials threatening welfare beneficiaries with the loss of assistance from their communes if they did not vote for a specific candidate (Journal Officiel de la République Francaise, Débats Chambre des Députés, 30 June 1902). There is also evidence that such threats are carried out in contemporary elections: in the case of Brazil, for example, Nichter (2014) documents that people who voted against a mayoral candidate were subsequently excluded from public temporary employment.

Land is another common resource that bureaucratic brokers can threaten to withhold from voters. Coercive strategies occur when the politician or broker threatens voters by exploiting imperfections in the definition of land property rights. Scholars of electoral politics in Mexico have documented how PRI mayors have selectively used ambiguity regarding legal access to land to influence voters' choices (Diaz-Cayeros et al. 2016). Scholars of African politics have also analyzed the conditionality of land rights on political support. For example, Boone and Kriger have documented the decisions of Laurent Gbagbo in Côte d'Ivoire to remove the land rights of known opponents of his political regime (Boone and Kriger 2012).

2.2.4 Economic coercion

The final strategy we consider is economic coercion, or threats to cut voters off from resources that are not financed by the state. In one of the earliest conceptualizations of economic coercion, Scott and Kerkvliet (1977: 449) describe it as the ability of economic elites to "extract compliance from the clients in return for not seizing his land, for not jailing him and so on." The ability of such brokers to coerce stems from their market power. Scott and Kerkvliet define the brokers involved in economic coercion as "most often in a position to supply goods unilaterally which the potential client and his family need for their survival and well-being" (442). It is this position as a "monopolist or at least an oligopolist for critical needs" that puts the broker "in an ideal position to demand compliance" (442).

Landowners and employers were the dominant brokers encountered in a variety of settings at the time of the early democratizations. Studies of economic coercion in nineteenth-century Europe documented a large number of coercive strategies used by landlords to influence electoral choices of voters. These included threats of dismissals, termination of leases, or eviction (Mares 2015: 87–8; Kühne 1994). Consider Lavinia Anderson's discussion of post-electoral reprisals used by landlords in East Prussia:

> Against voters who ignored their wishes, the agents of the Hohenlohes employed all the usual means by which a landlord could make life hard for his dependents. They withdrew the small offices (such as the supervision of the town clock) that enabled a man to earn a tiny income. They terminated gleaning and grazing privileges. They called in outstanding debts, raised taxes and canceled tenancies. They evicted.   (Anderson 2000: 165)

Bensel describes how powerful the threat of economic losses was in the case of the United States: "A landowner or factory owner could use his power over employees or tenants to influence their voting decisions. For intimidation to be effective, it was not necessary that this threat be explicit. When a man was sufficiently sensitive to the prospect of unemployment, all was required was a public announcement by an employer of a party preference" (Bensel 2004: 77). Similarly, employers and landowners have played an important role in contemporary elections in Chile (Bauer 1995; Baland and Robinson 2008). Recent studies have documented such practices of economic intimidation in Russia and Ukraine and even in democratic settings such as the United States.

Actors in the informal or criminal economies have also been implicated in economic coercion. Throughout much of Latin America and Spain, political brokers known as *caciques* have used a range of economic activities to threaten voters. Friedrich (1968: 247) defines *caciques* as "strong and autocratic leaders in local and regional politics, using an informal, personalistic and arbitrary rule." In Mexico, *caciques* are involved in a variety of economic activities including trafficking in lots or permits for land, informal lending, and exploitation of local mineral rights (Cornelius 1977: 339). In a study of electoral clientelistic in urban Mexican communities, Cornelius documents the unprecedented economic and political influence exerted by these brokers within their respective communities. In three-quarters of the settlements where Cornelius conducted his research, "caciques were involved in a variety of illicit activities. Such activities included trafficking in lots or permits to occupy land within the settlement, fraudulent collection of money for personal use, [and] commercial exploitation of local mineral resources" (Cornelius 1977: 339). At election time, *caciques* mobilized these economic resources to provide support for a particular candidate and used a combination of coercive strategies and sanctions on opponent or resistant voters. *Caciques* rewarded political support by granting access to loans and by allowing squatters to occupy some of the land they controlled.

Illicit businesses including illegal moneylenders and organized crime gangs are a final common broker of economic coercion. Gosnell, for example, documents the involvement of "underworld personnel" providing services to candidates in Chicago in the 1930s. In describing their influence, Gosnell noted that "when word is passed down from gangster chiefs, all proprietors of gambling houses and speak-easies, all burglars, pick-pockets, pimps, prostitutes, fences and their like are whipped into line. In themselves, they constitute a large block of votes and they frequently augment their value to the machine by corrupt election practices. Chain voters, colonized voters, and crooked election boards are recruited from the ranks of organized crime" (Gossnell 1968 [1937]: 42). Similarly, the mafia has been implicated in threatening voters in Italian elections (Arlacchi 1983; Gambetta 1993), and scholars of Thai politics have documented the importance of local godfathers (*chao pho*) involved in illegal smuggling, mining, and harvesting timber, mobilizing voters through blackmail or threats (Charntornvong 2000: 53–73).

2.3 Explaining the Mix of Clientelism

In the remainder of the chapter, we develop an explanation for the variation across localities in the use of clientelistic strategies. Prior to developing our explanation, we outline two important theoretical perspectives developed to explain the use of clientelism. The first highlights the importance of material resources held by different candidates. The second emphasizes the informational consequences of different clientelistic strategies in terms of how clientelistic candidates are viewed by voters. Our proposed explanation for the variation in the use of clientelistic strategies integrates insights developed by both approaches to explain why clientelism takes different forms in different localities. We argue that the use of different clientelistic strategies could be affected both by differential opportunities to politicize resources and by differential costs in terms of the loss of support of voters who judge clientelistic candidates.

2.3.1 Why do candidates use clientelism? Resource-based and informational explanations

Why do candidates use clientelistic strategies and what factors enhance or diminish opportunities for their use? Existing studies provide two different answers to this question. The first set of studies considers that the use of clientelistic strategies can be explained by examining the political resources that candidates can access. The second set of studies suggests the main factor shaping the costs and benefits of clientelism to candidates is the propensity of voters to punish such electoral corruption, and conditions that might make such punishment less likely, or even lead voters to reward candidates for using clientelism.

Resource-based explanations for clientelism have pointed to differences in access to the types of resources that can be politicized as the main predictor of the use of clientelism and patronage. In one of the first systematic examinations of patronage, Martin Shefter (1994) proposes the distinction between "insider" and "outsider" parties and documents that the use of political patronage was higher among parties that were in power or formed the government coalition. Other studies of clientelism confirm this general observation by noting that the use of clientelistic strategies is higher among parties that have benefitted from long-term incumbency, such as the PRI in Mexico, the Christian Democratic Party in Italy, and the Liberal Democratic Party in Japan (Scheiner 2006; Magaloni 2006).

Other studies point to the importance of economic resources in explaining clientelistic strategies. Studies of political development in Europe following the adoption of mass suffrage have pointed to the ample incidence of economic coercion used by employers. The incidence of such coercion varies across localities and is significantly higher in districts where employers control opportunities for employment and output, or in other words, localities with high levels of economic concentration (Mares 2015). Baland and Robinson (2008) document that the incidence of economic electoral intimidation is greater in regions with high levels of economic inequality. We refer to this type of argument as "resource-based" or "supply side" because it is focused on constraints on factors that increase or constrain access to the resources that candidates use to supply clientelism.

In contrast to these explanations, other studies consider that an important motivation accounting for the use of clientelism is the propensity of different types of voters to reward or punish candidates for using clientelism. The studies that fall under this line of research, which we weave into a consolidated theoretical framework, show first that clientelism sends informational signals about candidates to voters. These signals might be positive: offering gifts to voters may signal that a candidate is generous, well-resourced, and likely to help the groups that are targeted with gifts. They may also be negative if voters judge that clientelistic candidates are more likely to be corrupt and ineffectual once in office.

One early formulation of this signaling logic goes back to an early study of the vote-buying practices in Senegal by Bill Foltz (1977). In his study, Foltz discusses offers of gifts—what he refers to as patterned gift-giving—and suggests that it reflects the intention of candidates to signal personal attributes, such as generosity:

> The size of a person's clientship is likely to be proportional to his generosity and his ability to further his client's fortune. However—and the distinction is of great importance—a patron does not buy his clients' support and recognition. Rather, his generosity, particularly to members of lower casts, shows that he is an individual worthy of popular acclaim. Thus, public gift-giving is a patterned process, designed to ennoble the giver and reflect his 'concern for honor' not an underhanded and reprehensible attempt to buy support or status.   (Foltz 1977)

Other studies point to the use of vote-buying strategies as signals of a candidate's wealth. Using qualitative evidence from Benin and Nigeria, van de Walle suggests that candidates distribute goods and money to signal their wealth and capability to win elections (van de Walle 2007: 64; see also Kitschelt and Wilkinson 2007: 64). Candidates who use vote buying seek both to signal generosity and that they will not steal from the citizenry (Banégas 1998; Schatzberg 2001: 82; van de Walle 2005: 64). In a study of clientelism in Ghana, Lindberg considers that "the use of cash handouts is not simply a buying of votes ... it is an institutionalized behavior signifying willingness to take care of your people" (Lindberg 2003). More recent work using survey experiments on electoral handouts has similarly argued that parties that provide handouts are perceived as having more positive qualities (Conroy-Krutz 2013; Kramon 2016).[5]

On the other hand, others have documented that voters often have strong normative stances against clientelism and other forms of electoral corruption. Survey experiments in India and Central America have shown that the average voter judges harshly citizens who participate in clientelistic transactions, and candidates who have received bribes or engaged in violent crime (Banerjee et al 2014; Gonzalez-Ocantos et al. 2014). Weitz-Shapiro (2014) argues that clientelism signals to voters that candidates will govern poorly, and that candidates therefore consider the electoral costs of alienating voters, particularly those in the middle classes, when deciding whether and how to use clientelism.

There is also evidence that the electoral costs and benefits of clientelism's informational signals vary greatly across different types of voters. Kramon (2016) finds in Kenya that the positive effects of electoral handouts are concentrated among poor voters. In Latin America, Gonzalez-Ocantos et al. (2014) find that respondents with more education are more likely to condemn citizens who sell their votes. Finally, Weitz-Shapiro (2014) argues that in Argentina clientelism is permitted by the poor, but punished by the middle class. As a result, she argues that the attractiveness of clientelism as an electoral strategy decreases as the size of the middle class in the electorate grows.

We distinguish between a strong and weak form of arguments about the informational signals of clientelism. The strong form of this argument asserts that clientelism actually has a positive effect on how candidates are viewed by voters. Kramon (2016) is a good example of this strong informational argument. In his words, "electoral handouts help politicians establish credibility by conveying information" about their competence, trustworthiness, and electoral viability (455). This strong version of the informational argument implies that the material incentives provided by clientelism are secondary, or non-existent, to the positive effects of these informational signals with some or all voters. The weaker form of the informational argument, exemplified by Weitz-Shapiro's (2014) book, asserts that clientelism usually leads voters to update negatively about candidates' personal qualities or propensities to deliver policy benefits once in office.

However, voters with certain characteristics such as low education or high poverty may be willing to forgive candidates for clientelism. This version of the argument implies that, from the perspective of the candidate, these negative informational effects are balanced against the positive material incentives that clientelism sets for voters.

While both resource-based and informational explanations provide important insights accounting for the use of clientelism, few studies have attempted to integrate insights generated by both approaches. The goal of our study is to provide a unified framework that examines the relative importance of political resources and informational considerations in explaining variation in the use of different non-programmatic strategies across localities. As we will argue in the following section, the variation across localities in the use of different clientelistic strategies can be explained by considering the availability of existing resources and the propensity of voters to either reward or punish candidates who engage in different forms of clientelism.

2.3.2 Variation in the incidence of different forms of clientelism across localities

When and under what conditions do candidates use different forms of clientelism? We contend that the political incentives to use different clientelistic strategies vary in significant ways across localities. This variation is largely affected by a combination of two types of factors. One set of factors can be understood more broadly as "supply-side conditions" and results from differences in institutional and partisan conditions across different localities that enable candidates and brokers to politicize local public policy. Another set of factors can be understood as "demand-side conditions" and refers to variation in voters' propensities to judge and punish candidates who use clientelism.

To anticipate our discussion, we argue that past theory gives us reasons to believe that both supply-side and demand-side conditions should influence variation among clientelistic strategies. On the one hand, supply-side conditions should affect the relative availability of resources that can be politicized by the candidate for electoral purposes. As such, supply-side conditions should especially affect the choice between clientelistic strategies that use resources of the state relative to strategies that rely on private resources. On the other hand, demand-side conditions should affect whether candidates choose to structure clientelistic incentives as positive offers or negative threats. Specifically, we predict that the presence of social conflict over the distribution of social policy resources should enable politicians to use coercive forms of clientelism without facing harsh punishments by other voters. We argue that social conflict arises in localities that have large populations of poor voters who are benefitting from valuable social

Table 2.2 Conditions favoring the use of different clientelistic strategies

		Supply-side factors: Access to state resources	
		Low	High
Demand-side factors: Conflict over social policy	Low	Vote buying	Policy favors
	High	Economic coercion	Policy coercion

policy, and large groups of voters who are poor but ineligible for the same benefits. Table 2.2 summarizes our main predictions about locality-level variation in the incidence of clientelism and intends to guide the reader for the remainder of this section.

A candidate who considers using clientelistic strategies to incentivize voters faces a first choice regarding the type of resources that can be used during his interaction with voters. Should voters be incentivized with policy resources financed by general tax revenues, or should they be incentivized using private resources instead? One candidate competing in Third Republic France addressed the trade-off between clientelistic strategies that involve state resources and private resources by noting that "in using resources of the state one does not pay from one's own money. Rather, the state is the one who pays" (Journal Officiel de la République Française, Débats Chambre des Députés, 30 June 1902). Similarly, a party operative of the Republican Party machine in Philadelphia suggested that "the Philadelphia organization does not do this with money. They perform their political work by service" using state bureaucrats (Kurtzman 1935).

The relative availability of state resources should condition the answer to this question. In localities where candidates can access state resources with relative ease, we conjecture that candidates will choose to utilize such resources to structure the relationship to voters. By contrast, candidates will turn to clientelistic strategies that use private resources in localities where political resources of the state are only difficult to politicize. These conjectures revert the expectations about the importance of vote-buying exchanges in the menu of non-programmatic strategies one encounters in the current literature. While much of the existing studies considers clientelistic exchanges premised on vote buying as the "default" strategy used by candidates, we predict that vote buying emerges only as a "second-best" strategy that is deployed when the political resources of the state are unavailable.

The availability of state resources to be captured for clientelistic mobilization should be affected by a variety of political conditions in a locality. In our empirical analysis in the remaining part of the book, we will consider the consequences of three such variables that are relevant in the Eastern European cases in our study. The first variable is the length of incumbency. Longer incumbency is likely to enhance access to a larger pool of state employees who can be mobilized as brokers. Such employees of the local administration, in turn, can mobilize a host of different policies and programs to incentivize voters.

A second political variable that may enhance the ability of a candidate to access policy resources of the state is co-partisanship with the national incumbent. A resource asymmetry between incumbent and non-incumbent parties is likely to be present in any political system: incumbent parties control more resources that allow them to incentivize and recruit electoral brokers as compared to parties that do not enjoy this presence in office. Co-incumbency with the national political party not only affects the resources available to a candidate, but also the willingness of brokers to supply effort into targeting and enforcing clientelistic transactions.

A third political variable that may affect the ability of a candidate to access state resources for electoral exchanges is the political fragmentation in the locality. In localities where government is unified such that mayors are coupled with a city council with a similar partisanship, candidates are more likely to benefit from greater room to maneuver to politicize state resources for electoral purposes. In these cases, the "horizontal accountability" of mayors to the city council is low. This is not the case of localities with a politically divided administration. In such cases, city council and mayors are likely to heavily scrutinize their respective political activities. These "checks and balances" are likely to limit the ability of mayors to politicize resources of the state. These considerations imply that access to political resources of the state is likely to be higher in localities with unified government.

To sum up, we predict that incumbency, co-partisanship with the national incumbent, and political fragmentation of the city council increase the likelihood of clientelistic strategies that deploy state resources. We regard access to state resources as factors *enabling* the use of these clientelistic strategies, rather than necessitating their use. In other words, we see factors such as united local government or unification of the city council as increasing the likelihood of the use of particular clientelistic strategies, but not as having a deterministic influence on their use.

Our predictions about the use of clientelistic strategies that deploy private resources follow from the above discussion. More specifically, we expect to find either no relationship between the variables measuring local political control and the incidence of clientelistic strategies that use private resources, or a negative relationship between local political control and private forms of clientelism if public and private forms of clientelism are substitutes. In localities where neither incumbents nor challengers can access the political services of state employees, candidates will have to turn to private resources to organize clientelistic exchanges. In the case of vote buying, candidates will establish networks of brokers hired on spot markets who seek to mobilize voters using in-kind gifts or monetary inducements. Alternatively, candidates can incentivize private actors—such as employers or moneylenders—who control significant economic resources to act as their brokers, often in longer-term relationships.

2.3.3 Informational costs and benefits

The previous section has drawn on resource-based explanations for clientelism and considered how the absence of local political control affects the ability to use policy resources in clientelistic exchanges. We now turn to informational explanations. We conjecture that political conflicts over the allocation of social policy benefits shape the opportunities and costs for candidates to use clientelism to signal their positions in such conflicts. The relative magnitude of the constituencies in conflicts over the distribution of social policy benefits create different incentives for candidates to choose between clientelistic strategies that use favors as compared to strategies that use coercion. Ultimately, we contend that it is the presence of such social conflict that enables candidates to get away with—or even be rewarded for—the use of clientelism.

Poor communities are often sites of intense distributional conflict. Tensions and hostilities among poor voters often originate in disagreements about the distribution over economic and policy resources that are in scarce supply. Examples of resources that may amplify such poor against poor conflict are access to land, access to a particular social policy, or employment opportunities.

Anti-poverty programs represent an important source of a political conflict among low-income voters. Such conflict pits actual and potential recipients of social policy benefits against persons who fall outside of the eligibility threshold for the particular program or cannot qualify for benefits. In other words, the eligibility criteria for social policy benefits often create a cleavage within the class of low-income voters. We will refer to the constituencies that fall on each side of the threshold defining eligibility for a particular social policy as the coalition favoring social policy expansion, versus the coalition for policy retrenchment. On one side of this conflict, we find low-income voters who either draw on the social policy at the moment or expect to gain access to the program at some future time. These low-income voters who can qualify for social policy benefits under existing policy rules are likely to favor the social policy status quo or its expansion. On the other side of the conflict, we find low-income voters who barely miss the eligibility criteria to receive social policy benefits, due to a combination of demographic or labor market characteristics. Such a constituency may include the elderly (who are usually not eligible for poverty benefits), and the working poor. We refer to this constituency as the retrenchment coalition. The term retrenchment is, inevitably, a shorthand for the complex social policy views of such voters. Because these voters are also low-income, many of them do not necessarily want social policy to be cut back. Instead, they should prefer social policy to be reallocated so that they, the "deserving poor," are eligible. Resenting their inability to access desirable social policy benefits, such voters are more likely to favor a change in the eligibility criteria for benefits and a reallocation of social policy benefits rather than the wholesale elimination of the anti-poverty program.

The existence of this distributional conflict between a constituency of low-income voters who welcome the current distribution of social policy benefits and a constituency of voters who are resentful of the current social policy beneficiaries creates opportunities for candidates to use different clientelistic strategies to signal their position on this divisive issue. The use of clientelistic strategies premised on positive inducements allows candidates to signal support for the low-income voters who depend on the current allocation of benefits. The expansion of social policy benefits targeted on these groups—even if such benefits are granted in exchange for political support at the ballot box—in contexts where the main anti-poverty programs are supported by a sizable group of voters represents a signal that the candidate supports the policy status quo.

On the other hand, the candidate can choose to exploit the eligibility conditions for the social program coercively by threatening to reduce or eliminate the benefits of social policy beneficiaries depending on their political choices. The candidate may combine these coercive electoral strategies with other forms of harassment of recipients of poverty benefits that disregard the dignity and rights of many low-income voters. The use of such coercive strategies carries a fundamentally different signal than the use of strategies that are based on positive inducements. The use of coercive electoral strategies signals the opposition of the candidate to the current allocation of social policy benefits in the community and, indirectly, a support for policy retrenchment. In choosing coercive strategies, the candidate explicitly sides with opponents to the current allocation of social policy benefits.

Policy positions are just one of the factors that voters consider when evaluating candidates. They also consider general qualities, including personal characteristics, the propensity for corruption, and management capabilities, as well as how competitive the candidate is in the election. When voters view clientelism as a form of electoral corruption, they should also negatively update their beliefs about candidates' general qualities. This is especially true for general qualities that are more closely related to clientelism, like how corrupt the candidate will be once in office. However, to the extent that candidates are using forms of clientelism that are aligned with voters' positions on the key issue of social policy benefits, we expect that they should be more forgiving or even view candidates who use clientelism more positively.

As discussed earlier in this chapter, we suggest that there is both a strong and weak version of the informational argument. In the strong version of the argument, clientelism actually provides electoral benefits to candidates who use it with aligned groups of voters. For example, if the strong informational story were correct, then positive forms of clientelism would make voters who support the current distribution of social policy benefits believe that those candidates are more aligned with their policy positions and have more positive general qualities than candidates who do not use clientelism. In the weak version of the informational argument, voters never update their views positively about candidates who use clientelism, but they update less negatively about candidates who use clientelism that is in line with their social policy preferences. For example, the reputational cost of coercive clientelism would be less negative with voters who prefer that social policy benefits are retrenched and reallocated than with those who want it to be expanded.

Both the strong and weak versions of this informational theory imply that the electoral costs and benefits of different forms of clientelism are affected by the relative size of constituencies favoring policy expansion versus retrenchment at the local level. In localities where the electoral constituency favoring expansion is large, candidates will find the use of clientelistic strategies based on positive inducements attractive. In this case, the candidate uses the clientelistic strategy to indirectly appeal to voters favoring the current allocation of policy benefits. By contrast, in localities where the electoral constituency favoring a reallocation of social policy benefits is large, candidates will favor clientelistic strategies premised on coercion. In using coercive strategies, such as threats to cut access to social policy benefits or to lay off workers who make the incorrect electoral choices, candidates and brokers operating on their behalf pursue two different objectives. On the one hand, candidates seek to capture the vote of these dependent voters and induce such voters to trade the vote in exchange for maintaining a future stream of income. On the other hand, such coercive strategies are a credible signal that the candidate shares the retrenchment coalition's view that current beneficiaries are unworthy of state support. Such voters may therefore interpret coercive strategies as signals of the resoluteness of the candidate to reallocate social policy benefits to more deserving beneficiaries, and that they are willing to mete out punishments to those unworthy of support.

Clientelistic strategies that use the policy resources of the state—such as welfare favors or welfare coercion—provide the most direct ways for candidates to signal their positions on issues that are distributionally divisive. Such signaling opportunities are weaker in the case of clientelistic strategies that make use of private resources, such as economic coercion or vote buying. Nevertheless, the decision of a candidate to ally himself with economic brokers such as moneylenders who in turn coerce low-income voters using their private resources is still likely to signal disregard for the rights of the poorest voters—current social policy beneficiaries—in the community. By contrast, a clientelistic strategy based on positive inducements is likely to signal concern for these groups of poor voters who are the main current beneficiaries of social policy.

To a political strategist, it may seem puzzling that retrenchment voters would interpret coercive forms of clientelism as a signal that candidates support reallocating social policy benefits to their group. In theory, sophisticated voters should see that candidates who gain the coerced votes of social policy beneficiaries have little interest in retrenching the program. Yet in practice, we find this logic sets a high bar for the political calculations of the average voter. Instead of such a strategic calculation, our theory argues that voters buy into the symbolic politics of abusing and threatening a demographic that is disliked and envied. While this strategy may lose its credibility if the program is not actually retrenched, we suspect that it will take several electoral cycles to become truly ineffectual.

To summarize, our explanation of the variation across localities in the use of different clientelistic strategies brings together two different views of the constraints and benefits of clientelism from the perspective of candidates. On the supply side, we consider that local political control should enable access to policy resources for use in clientelistic transactions. On the demand side, we argue that the propensity of voters to punish or reward candidates for using different forms of clientelism shapes the electoral costs of electoral corruption. We argue that positive and negative forms of clientelism carry different signals of a candidate's position on the distribution of local social policy. Positive forms of clientelism like policy favors and vote buying signal that a candidate supports the existing distribution of social policy, while negative forms like policy and private coercion signal that the candidate views current social policy beneficiaries as undeserving and is relatively likely to retrench existing programs and reallocate state support to different groups of low-income voters.

2.3.4 Clientelism and vote-choice: a new micro-level perspective on clientelism

We conclude this chapter by considering some implications of our theoretical approach for understanding voters' political responses to different clientelistic practices. How do voters evaluate candidates that make use of different clientelistic strategies? What are the most salient factors that account for differences across voters in the way they evaluate different non-programmatic strategies? What are the consequences of voters' evaluations of different clientelistic strategies for the persistence of electoral clientelism?

Our study provides new micro-foundations for understanding citizens' responses to different non-programmatic strategies. First, our approach suggests that the share of the electorate affected by clientelistic strategies is broader than the voters who are directly targeted by such strategies. Clientelistic strategies influence two distinct electoral constituencies. The first such constituency are the voters who are directly targeted by clientelistic strategies. At the same time, candidates use clientelistic strategies to appeal to a broader group of voters in the constituency who are not targeted by clientelistic strategies directly, but who learn about different clientelistic strategies indirectly, from persons who have been targeted by these candidates or from competitors of these candidates. Such voters who are indirectly exposed to clientelistic practices are likely to use this information to update their position about the candidate. This implies that to understand the consequences of clientelism for vote choice, we need to disaggregate carefully how such material and informational effects differ across various groups of voters and across different clientelistic strategies.

Clientelistic strategies convey two types of information about a candidate. First, clientelistic strategies convey information about the personal competencies and characteristics of a candidate. As discussed above, previous studies on clientelism have noted that voters derive information about a candidate's wealth, generosity, or electoral viability by observing offers of money or gifts. At the same time, clientelistic strategies convey information about the policy positions of candidates. The choice between coercive strategies and strategies premised on positive inducements carries information about the position of a candidate on questions of policy that are distributionally divisive in the locality. Clientelistic strategies differ in the mix of information about competence and policy position they convey. Unsurprisingly, clientelistic strategies that use policy resources of the state should convey more information about the policy positions of a candidate as compared to non-programmatic strategies that use private resources.

To understand the variation in responses to clientelistic strategies, we begin with a discussion of the results of previous studies that have analyzed voters' responses to offers of vote buying. These findings can be considered as a limit case in a more general theory that allows clientelistic strategies to contain both signals about the competence of a candidate but also information about the policy positions of a candidate. We will discuss this more general explanation next.

How do voters evaluate the competence of candidates that offer money or gifts to voters? As discussed above, scholars of vote-buying exchanges have noted that such clientelistic strategies are used as a signal of the electoral viability of a candidate. In a recent study of vote buying in Kenya, Kramon (2016: 463) argues that such clientelistic offers allow candidates to strengthen their claims of being a "high quality candidate." He defines "high quality" or competence of a candidate as an aggregate of three attributes, comprising expertise, trustworthiness, and electoral viability. As Kramon explains, "the distribution of handouts allows candidates to improve voters' perceptions along each of these dimensions, thus helping them establish credibility with respect to the future provision of resources" (464).

Previous studies have found that the level of income is the most significant source of heterogeneity among voters in their responses to non-programmatic strategies. The finding that low-income voters are less willing to punish politicians that engage in clientelistic exchanges is a relatively robust finding reported in contexts as diverse as Argentina, Brazil, and Kenya, (Weitz-Shapiro 2012; Winters and Weitz-Shapiro 2013; Kramon 2016). Existing studies propose a variety of possible explanations for the relationship linking poverty and a lower tolerance for vote buying, but often lack a convincing strategy that adjudicates among the mechanisms postulated by these explanations. Poor voters, these studies argue, are less willing to punish politicians who engage in clientelism because they have a higher marginal utility for the goods offered as part of these exchanges or because the poor, due to "the pressures of meeting basic needs, are less likely to have the time or inclination to care about the quality of governance" (Winters and Weitz-Shapiro 2013: 426; see also Kurer 2001). Kramon argues that low income voters are more likely to respond favorably to offers of money and goods and elections, because "such electoral handouts demonstrate that candidates understand the needs of their predominantly poor constituents and that they are aware of their responsibility to allocate resources to them" (Kramon 2016: 466). Finally, other studies seek to explain this relationship by invoking the lower tolerance threshold for clientelism of middle-income voters. Weitz-Shapiro (2012: 571) argues that middle income voters are more likely to punish politicians that engage in vote-buying exchanges because they are more likely to view clientelism as an indicator of the low quality of a politician and of their inability to deliver the desirable levels of public goods.

In contrast to these studies, we argue that clientelistic strategies also include information about a candidate's policy position. The use of anti-poverty programs, unemployment benefits, or conditional cash transfer programs as positive inducements creates some opportunities for candidates to mask clientelistic exchanges as pro-poor concerns. Voters may process information about the distribution of anti-poverty benefits as indicative of politicians' concern for low-income voters. On the other hand, candidates may use coercive strategies to signal their commitment to austerity, social policy retrenchment or cutbacks in the social policy entitlements of particular groups. The use of strategies that blatantly and unabashedly disregard the economic and political rights of welfare beneficiaries is a signal of opposition to existing social programs. In using welfare coercion, a candidate may signal an "anti-welfare" position that is closer to that held by political parties on the right.

Let us consider now how voters evaluate these non-programmatic strategies. Our central conjecture is that voters' evaluations of different clientelistic strategies are mediated by their social policy preferences. We take a broad understanding of social policy preferences to include both preferences towards responsibilities of the government to provide resources to low-income voters, to redistribute income between rich and poor voters, and preferences about which type of poor voters are truly deserving of assistance. Voters' social policy preferences therefore affect the lens through which voters interpret and judge clientelistic strategies.

Consider first voters' responses to clientelistic strategies premised on positive inducements. If voters are supportive of redistribution of resources to the poor through transfers or taxes, they may be less willing to punish politicians who use clientelistic strategies based on positive inducements. We conjecture that voters supportive of an expansive role of the state should be less willing to sanction or punish clientelistic social policies based on positive inducements as compared to retrenchment voters. By contrast, voters opposed to social policy transfers are likely to view such clientelistic strategies less favorably as compared to voters who are supportive of a broad redistributive role of the government.

Similarly, voters' responses to clientelistic strategies that use coercion are likely to vary depending on voters' preferences for social policy redistribution. As we have argued above, the use of strategies that blatantly disregard the economic and political rights of welfare beneficiaries may signal the opposition of the candidate to the *current* allocation of benefits. In using clientelistic strategies such as welfare coercion, a candidate may signal an "anti-welfare" position that is close to the position held by political parties on the right. As a result, we expect that the opposition to redistribution will be an important factor that mediates voters' responses to this non-programmatic strategy. Voters who hold the belief that the "current allocation of social policy benefits is excessive" or that "recipients of social policy benefits are lazy" will be more likely to positively evaluate such coercive strategies. By contrast, we expect that voters supportive of redistribution will negatively evaluate candidates who use coercive strategies.

Table 2.3 summarizes the main components of our argument about the informational signals of different forms of clientelism. In the left column are

Table 2.3 Consequences of clientelistic strategies for voting behavior

		Are state resources involved?	
		No	Yes
Is the inducement coercive?	No	**Vote buying** • Signal strength: Weak • Policy signal: Current social policy expansion • Personal signal: Generosity • Target audience: Roma, unemployed	**Policy favors** • Signal strength: Strong • Policy signal: Current social policy expansion • Personal signal: Generosity • Target audience: Roma, unemployed
	YES	**Economic coercion** • Signal strength: Weak • Policy signal: Current social policy retrenchment • Personal signal: Authority • Target audience: Employed, retired	**Policy coercion** • Signal strength: Strong • Policy signal: Current social policy retrenchment • Personal signal: Authority • Target audience: Employed, retired

clientelistic strategies based on private resources, namely vote buying and economic coercion, while on the right are policy favors and policy coercion, both based on public funds. The first bullet point under each strategy summarizes our prediction that private forms of clientelism should send weaker informational signals than clientelism financed out of public coffers, particularly when it comes to signals of policy positions. The top and bottom rows differentiate between positive and negative inducements, respectively. The next two bullet points summarize our predictions that positive forms of clientelism signal that the candidate is committed to a policy platform of expanding the current social policy and is personally generous, while negative forms of clientelism signal that the candidate will retrench social policy and act as a strong authority. The final bullet point summarizes the social groups that are likely to view candidates who use these strategies favorably. In the case of positive forms of clientelism, groups that prefer expansion of the current social policy (in our case, the unemployed and Roma populations) should view candidates who use positive inducements more positively, while in the case of negative inducements, groups who have been excluded from the current social policy distribution (the working poor and retirees) should view candidates who use coercive forms of clientelism more positively.

2.4 Relationship to Previous Studies

In this book we depart from existing explanations of electoral clientelism in several important ways. First, our explanation posits a different mechanism by which clientelism affects voting behavior compared to previous studies. Existing studies have drawn a very strong distinction between the material incentives offered in clientelistic exchanges and the ideological appeals to voters. Diaz-Cayeros et al. (2016) assume that voters do not have ideological positions such that their partisanship is purely a function of the history of benefits that they receive. Stokes (2005) and Stokes et al. (2013) define voters' ideological positions as fixed along a one-dimensional left–right scale. Parties' positions are also fixed and are known by voters. In this framework, when a party offers a material benefit to a voter, it has no impact on the voter's own ideological position, or on the voter's perception of the party's position on issues that she cares about. At the other extreme, Kramon (2016) argues that vote buying is actually not intended to provide a material incentive for voters, but is purely an informational signal about the candidate's credibility.

Our theoretical framework allows voters to have true policy preferences, and relaxes the assumption that they are not updating their views of candidates based on their experiences with clientelism during the election and pre-election periods.

We follow the assumption made by Stokes and her co-authors that voters in countries with clientelistic exchanges have policy preferences that make them favor one party over another, regardless of the material incentives they've received in the past. However, we contend that voters do not have complete information about parties' positions. As a result, clientelistic exchanges that voters experience first- or second-hand lead them to update their beliefs about how well each party's programmatic position aligns with their political preferences. In this way, we depart from Stokes by considering the perceived difference between voters' preferences and parties' positions as endogenous to clientelistic transactions. Similarly, we depart from the study by Diaz-Cayeros et al. (2016), by allowing the effect of material incentives offered by candidates to voters to be either positive or negative.

Finally, we depart from existing research by identifying a new dimension of voter heterogeneity that conditions how voters judge candidates who use various forms of clientelism. Existing studies have identified demographic characteristics such as high poverty and low education as factors that make voters treat vote buying permissively, or even positively (Gonzalez-Ocantos et al. 2014; Weitz-Shapiro 2014; Kramon 2016). We contend that voters' social policy preferences may be driving the existing effects on income by moderating voters' evaluation of clientelistic strategies. Central to our argument is the idea that voters' willingness to reward or support particular clientelistic strategies is shaped by their demand for enhanced or reduced spending on different social policy programs. Voters who disagree about the appropriate scope of social policy also disagree about the evaluation of candidates that use different types of clientelistic strategies. As a result of this differential evaluation of candidates that use different clientelistic strategies, the use of clientelism may further contribute to the polarization of the electorate.

Our research thus echoes work emphasizing the role of envy and relative deprivation in policy preferences. Social conflict emerges not as a function of absolute levels of poverty, but poverty relative to other local social groups and beliefs about how deserving they are of state support. In this our work builds on a behavioral literature showing that individuals are willing to engage in costly punishment for behavior that they perceive as unfair (Fehr and Gachter 2000; Henrich et al. 2006), and reduce others' material payoff merely to increase their own relative payoff (Fehr et al. 2008). It also builds on a growing body of evidence from the Unites States showing that individuals just above the threshold to qualify for a social program may oppose that program because it decreases their status relative to those who are just barely eligible (Kuziemko et al. 2014). Our informational theory suggests that in localities where large groups of voters are ineligible for valuable social policy benefits, social conflict may drive these ineligible voters to put up with harshly coercive forms of electoral corruption that are likely to leave all voters worse off.

2.5 Conclusion

This chapter has formulated the conceptual groundwork for the empirical analysis we will present in subsequent chapters. We have argued that electoral clientelism is a multidimensional concept, encompassing a heterogeneity of different strategies and practices that can be explained by different political logics.

We began by mapping out the broad variation among clientelistic strategies and proposed to classify these strategies along two distinct dimensions. The first dimension considers the source of the resources or powers that are used to influence the electoral choices of voters. Here we distinguish between clientelistic strategies that use state resources and those that involve resources that are financed by political parties or private actors. The most important resources of the state that can be leveraged by candidates for clientelistic exchanges are public employment, policies, or administrative favors. State resources can be used both to incentivize brokers and to influence the electoral choice of voters. The second dimension that we consider is whether the incentive that voters face is a positive offer or a negative threat. These dimensions are important because clientelism that is coercive or based on state resources is likely to have larger negative welfare effects, and is normatively more objectionable. In addition, existing theory suggests that forms of clientelism differentiated along these dimensions are likely to be driven by different local conditions.

Second, we develop a number of propositions that explain the variation across localities in the use of these four non-programmatic strategies. Existing theory suggests that this variation can be explained by the distribution of different political resources that can be deployed by candidates, and by the presence of political conflict over the allocation of access to social policies within the localities. We predicted that clientelistic strategies premised on positive inducements should be more attractive to candidates in localities with low levels of contestation over the allocation of social policy benefits. In localities where distribution of social policy benefits is not politicized, candidates should use clientelistic strategies to incentivize directly targeted voters, and to send the broader pool of voters signals of their redistributive intentions and pro-poor concerns. In such localities, candidates should rely on policy favors or on vote buying, depending on the availability of public resources that can be politicized at elections. By contrast, we have conjectured that candidates find clientelistic strategies that involve coercion attractive in localities where the distribution of policy benefits is contested and where a large group of the electorate resents the current allocation of benefits. In such localities, candidates should use coercive strategies to signal their disdain for current social policy beneficiaries, opposition to the current allocation of benefits, and support for retrenchment and the reconfiguration of benefits. Thus, the existence of distributional conflict over the allocation of social policy benefits explains the choice of coercive over positive forms of clientelism.

In the final section of the chapter, we developed a number of theoretical expectations about voters' evaluations of candidates that engage in different non-programmatic strategies. While clientelistic strategies are normatively undesirable, they create opportunities for candidates to obfuscate their nondemocratic intentions and send signals about their personal attributes or policy positions. We argue that individual support for redistribution conditions voters' evaluations of different non-programmatic strategies. Voters opposed to redistribution are likely to forgive or reward candidates that engage in coercive electoral strategies and punish candidates that engage in social policy expansion. By contrast, voters that support a more expansive role of the state in providing for social spending are more likely to forgive or reward candidates that use clientelistic social policies premised on favors and punish the use of coercive strategies. Given that clientelistic strategies are conditional on the policy preferences of voters, the use of these strategies contributes to a further polarization in the electorate.

Notes

1. We note, however, that monitoring does not necessarily need to occur at the individual level for an individual exchange to be upheld. As long as a broker has some signal of whether or not a voter makes good on his electoral promise, individual inducements can be used (Rueda 2017).
2. Stokes et al. (2013) and Golden and Min (2013) review and summarize recent studies that have analyzed such political exchanges.
3. While the threat of violence technically falls under our definition of negative sanctions, we do not consider it here because it is not prevalent in the cases under study. In addition, the conditions that would make the resources and informational signals more conducive to physical sanctions would most likely differ from those that are conducive to economic sanctions. To give one basic example, while control of the local welfare administration should facilitate the use of negative economic sanctions, control of the police force or courts might play a more important role in facilitating physical sanctions.
4. In our study, we disaggregate coercive strategies based on the type of resources used by the broker. In an unpublished manuscript, Kitschelt differentiates between two different types of coercive strategies, which he calls act-coerciveness and situative coerciveness. Act coerciveness encompasses relationships when the client is entrapped and includes patron–client exchanges that involve goods such as policy benefits or procurement contracts. In the case of the second type of coercive strategy, situative coerciveness, our ability to classify a transaction as coercive depends on a variety of other contextual factors. These include the availability of alternative suppliers of the good, the relative scarcity of the good, and so on. Kitschelt would classify most coercive strategies analyzed in this book as examples of situative coerciveness rather than act coerciveness. We are grateful to Herbert Kitschelt for clarifying this point.

5. Conroy-Krutz hypothesizes that electoral handouts should increase the attractiveness of a candidate to the average Ugandan voter, but actually finds that in a survey question where respondents were asked to choose between two similar candidates, one of whom unconditionally distributed bags of sugar at his rally, almost two-thirds of respondents did not support the distributing candidate (2013: 364).

3

Context and Research Design

In this chapter, we discuss both the political context in which we carried out our research, and the research design that we developed to test the implications of our theory. First, we introduce the most significant partisan actors and characterize the temporal changes in the party system in Hungary and Romania. We also discuss the most significant non-clientelistic strategies pursued by different parties to win office. In the second part of the chapter, we discuss the empirical strategy that we designed to test how electoral clientelism functions at the individual and locality levels. In particular, we describe steps that we took to solve key empirical challenges, including pairing qualitative and quantitative data and using experimental survey methodologies that reduce the role of social desirability bias.

During the post-communist period, political parties in Hungary and Romania used a combination of three distinct strategies to compete for office. The first strategy involved ideological positioning and differentiation from other political parties. We discuss the choices made by different parties about their positioning in the ideological space and discuss how parties altered their electoral appeals to improve their opportunities for electoral survival in the years before the elections under study in this book. We also document instances of the realignment of the entire partisan landscape that resulted from the different strategies pursued by different parties to reposition themselves in the policy space.

The second strategy pursued by the parties involved investment in the creation and development of formal organizations. We find variation across parties in their efforts to develop viable party organizations and in the type of formal party organizations they established. Such variation can be attributed to the institutional legacies inherited from the post-communist period, to their relationships to social movements, and to their political leadership.

The third strategy was premised on the use of patronage and clientelistic mobilization. Patronage refers to the exploitation of state resources to reward loyal party members, while clientelism refers to strategies directed at voters (Stokes et al. 2013: 7). Parties began to exploit the resources of the state for clientelistic mobilization beginning in the mid-1990s. Recognizing the importance of clientelism for their electoral survival, parties used their positions in office to enact a number of policy changes that enabled such electoral practices, particularly by local administrators. Some of these policy changes involved efforts to incentivize different administrative actors located throughout the territory to act as electoral brokers that could mobilize electoral support at elections. Parties pursued a variety of strategies to incentivize these brokers: directing fiscal resources towards municipalities with cooperative mayors, using administrative decrees to encourage partisan switches by mayors, and so on. These strategies created broad networks of electoral brokers that complemented the existing formal party organizations.

The importance of patronage and clientelism has been noted by numerous studies of post-communist party systems (Kitschelt 1995; Grzymała-Busse 2002; O'Dwyer 2006; Kopecký 2006; Kopecký et al. 2012). However, the informal and illicit nature of these exchanges has posed large challenges for the empirical study of these phenomena. In the final section of the chapter, we discuss the different strategies that assess clientelistic practices and comment on their relative advantages and disadvantages.

In the following section, we present our empirical approach, which draws on a variety of methods to assess non-programmatic strategies. First, we attempt to document the existence of clientelistic strategies using surveys that include non-obtrusive techniques that allow us to measure the incidence of these illicit practices. We complement these survey-based analyses with qualitative analyses that allow us to document the micro-level strategies pursued by different candidates and brokers and the responses of voters that are targeted by these non-programmatic strategies. Finally, we assess voters' responses to non-programmatic strategies using list experiments that present voters with information about different candidates who use various forms of clientelistic strategies. In combination, these different methods are particularly well-suited to test the theoretical propositions formulated in Chapter 2.

3.1 Partisan Competition in Hungary and Romania during the Post-Communist Period

In both Hungary and Romania, the successors to the former communist parties remained key players in subsequent elections. These successor parties underwent dramatically different trajectories during the first decades of the post-communist period. In Romania, the main successor of the Romanian Communist Party (PCR) is the Social Democratic Party (Partidul Social Democrat or PSD). The party adopted the current name (Social Democratic Party) only in 2000. The party was known as the Front of National Salvation between 1989 and 1992, the Front of Democratic National Salvation or FDSN between 1992 and 1993, and the Party of Social Democracy in Romania (PDSR) between 1993 and 2000. The Front of National Salvation was established during the 1989 Romanian revolution. At the time, former communist party members marginalized student protesters and declared themselves the "Supreme Leaders of the Revolution" and the "steering committee of the nation" (Murer 2002). The Social Democratic Party dominated electoral politics in Romania during the post-communist period, winning six out of seven elections held between 1990 and 2016. The average level of electoral support enjoyed by the PSD across these elections stood at 30 percent. PSD has formed coalition governments with a variety of parties on the political right, including the Conservative Party and the National Liberal Party. The continuity and strength of the former communist party is particularly remarkable in a political context characterized by high levels of electoral volatility (Gherghina 2014).

Throughout the post-communist transition, PSD was relatively unsuccessful in projecting an image of an ideologically modernized party that embraced market-oriented reforms and in jettisoning their connection to the communist past. At a time when the Hungarian Socialists presided over the adoption of shock therapy, the Romanian Social Democrats took a very cautious approach to the adoption of market-oriented reforms. The party platform rejected the "temptations of aggressive liberalism, which proliferated phenomena specific to wild capitalism, such as fraudulent privatization, speculative practices and the plundering of public wealth" (PDSR 2000). While in government, the party exercised extreme caution in privatizing state-owned enterprises and in liberalizing prices. Such caution reflected both ideological considerations and the party elites' pragmatic desire of party elites to control and micromanage the process of privatization in order to reap personal gains from the process. Throughout the first decade of the post-communist transition, the Socialists controlled with an iron hand all appointments to the institutions privatizing state assets and the Audit Court; they also carefully managed the prices and distribution of assets formerly held by the state.

Socialists also competed by appealing to nationalism. The Socialist Party platform called for "returns to Romanian values" (PDSR 2000). On repeated occasions, Ion Iliescu, the leader of the party and Romania's president for a decade, referred to market-oriented reforms as "an effort of Western countries to take advantage of Romania's difficult economic situation" (Oprea 2006: 230) and to attack Romania's sovereignty by "destroy[ing]" its economic base (Ban 2014: 146). In the mid-1990s, the Socialist party (which at the time was called the Democratic National Salvation Front) formed a coalition government with two extreme nationalist parties, the Party of Romanian National Unity (PUNR) and the Greater Romania Party (PRM).

The investment in a strong party organization remains an important factor that contributed to the remarkable electoral success of the PSD. Studies of the organization of the party during the mid-1990s consider that the organizational density of the PSD was similar to that of other successor parties in the region (Ishiyama 1999). Socialists pursued an intensive set of strategies to recruit new members and enlarge the number of local organizations. These strategies were successful, transforming the Social Democratic Party into one of the largest parties in the region. Between 1992 and 1996, the membership of the party increased dramatically, from 60,000 to 309,000 members (Gherghina 2014). By 2008, PSD had about 385,000 members or over 2 percent of the electorate. At the same time, the Socialists developed a highly centralized organization, which limited their vulnerability to factional politics and internal party conflicts.

In addition to strategies of ideological positioning and organizational reconstruction, the Social Democratic Party also invested in and perfected clientelistic strategies. In an early study of post-communist party systems, Herbert Kitschelt (1995) conjectured that communist successor parties display a particular affinity for clientelistic strategies. The strategies pursued by the Romanian PSD confirm this theoretical expectation. The PSD used its access to governmental positions during the 1990s to direct significant policy resources toward local mayors which enabled such mayors to consolidate their electoral strength. In addition, assets gained from the privatization of state enterprises were used as source of party patronage.

In Hungary, the communist successor party was the Hungarian Socialist Party (Magyar Szocialista Párt or MSZP), which was established in October 1989 (Racz 1993). Following their electoral loss during the first post-communist election, Socialists attempted to modify the party's ideological position and to soften the image of a post-communist successor party (Racz 1993). The electoral program of the party was "Janus-faced", signaling a commitment to "modernization" and "Europeanization" while also maintaining a rhetoric that appealed to low-income Hungarians, the "man-of-the-street" (Bozóki 2002: 90). The party also attempted to develop an image of technocratic expertise, by emphasizing their readiness to provide "A Secure Future" for Hungary, while at the same time appealing to the nostalgia for the government of experts during Hungary's last years of communism (Tóka 1996: 108; Bozóki 2002: 101). Grzymała-Busse discusses the strategy of moderation of the MSZP, "in an atmosphere increasingly dominated by the nationalist-religious outbursts from the ruling Hungarian Democratic Forum (MDF), the MSZP made non-ideological, pragmatic appeals centering around efficient management" (Grzymała- Busse 2002: 218). Public opinion polls conducted during the mid-1990s demonstrated the effectiveness of this strategy. A large majority of voters felt that MSZP politicians were likely to be "competent managers" and that the party could maintain political stability in Hungary (Grzymała-Busse 2002: 218 based on Tóka 1996). Finally, the Socialist Party also pursued a number of strategies that allowed it to extend its appeal beyond its natural electoral base of wage earners and salaried employees and appeal to middle-class voters (Enyedi 2005).

The political modernization of the Socialist Party paid off electorally and laid the groundwork for its electoral victory during the 1994 election (Racz 2000). In 1994, the Socialist Party gained 51 percent of the parliamentary mandates and formed a coalition government with the Alliance of Free Democrats (SZDSZ), Hungary's Liberal Party. Once in power, the party adopted a severe program of economic austerity in 1995, known also as the "Bokros package." This "shock therapy," which took effect in 1995, included a reduction in governmental spending, a devaluation of the currency, and a very restrictive monetary policy. While the adoption of these policies contributed to a reduction in inflation and preempted a major macro-economic crisis, they also contributed to a dramatic decline in the incomes and wages of the vast majority of Hungarians. The adoption of these neoliberal reforms allowed the party to distance itself from its communist past and position itself as a "modern" Social Democratic Party that embraces a market economy.

In organizational terms, the MSZP invested in its party apparatus to retain its electoral competitiveness. Although the MSZP had inherited the organizational legacy of the former communist party, its leaders decided early on during Hungary's post-communist transition that holding on to these assets created more liabilities than advantages. As a result, the MSZP decided to restitute to the state the assets inherited from the former communist party (Waller 1995). At a time when many parties on the right maintained a presence in the media only, but not in the countryside, the socialists made extensive efforts to invest in their party organization (Ágh 2000; Magyar 2016: 45). Most importantly, Socialists attempted to develop local party branches and to maintain a secure organizational network throughout the country (Morlang 2003: 70). Socialists used these branches both to recruit, but also to train new members (Tavits 2013: 88). The party also remained relatively successful in maintaining remarkably high levels of internal unity in a period when controversial economic reforms drove a significant wedge between its members.

At the same time, the MSZP was relatively unsuccessful in recruiting new members. Remarkably, the total number of party members remained constant for the period between 1994 and 2006 (Gherghina 2014: 109). The number of MSZP party members stood at 36,000 or 0.45 percent of the electorate. MSZP party members were generally aging persons who "were strongly attached to the earlier organs of the regime, or the remaining structure of the vast care systems (public administration, healthcare, education)," which allowed the party to retain a "nostalgic, bureaucratic and apparatchik nature" (Magyar 2016: 45). While the MSZP membership levels remained comparable to those of other political parties in Hungary, the membership of the Hungarian Socialists (normalized by the size of the electorate) lagged significantly behind the membership achieved by Romanian Socialists or other political parties in the region. As with other Hungarian political parties, the low MSZP membership rates made it somewhat difficult for the party to fill its list of candidates or to generate interest in local-level politics (Van Biezen 2003; Enyedi and Tóka 2007: 149; Gherghina 2014: 108).

Finally, like other parties in post-communist Eastern Europe, MSZP made use of patronage and clientelistic strategies (Meyer-Sahling 2008: 41). Among scholars of post-communist party systems, a lively controversy exists about the importance of patronage strategies in Hungary during the post-communist period. While the early literature coded Hungary as a country that displayed low levels of patronage (Grzymała-Busse 2006; O'Dwyer 2006), recent studies have pushed back vigorously against this characterization, arguing that the use of patronage in Hungary was comparable in its levels to that in Bulgaria and the Czech Republic (Meyer-Sahling 2008; Meyer-Sahling and Jáger 2012). These studies conclude that both political parties exploited the porousness of all levels of the Hungarian bureaucracy as sources of patronage appointments. The MSZP possessed a larger available pool of loyal party members with previous administrative expertise who could be appointed to various offices of the Hungarian state and who could generate additional electoral returns to the party by exploiting such resources. As such, scholars consider that MSZP had a resource advantage in the use of patronage over parties on the right (Meyer-Sahling 2008: 41).

In both Romania and Hungary, the partisan landscape on the political right was extremely fragmented at the beginning of the post-communist transition. Over time, a process of concentration took place. One of the most successful right-wing parties was the Romanian National Liberal Party (Partidul Național Liberal or PNL), established in January 1990. From its inception, the party claimed the ideological legacy of the interwar National Liberal Party which was one of the dominant parties on the Romanian political scene prior to the communist takeover. During Romania's first post-communist election, characterized by ample irregularities and intimidation, the Liberals obtained only 10 percent of the vote. During the subsequent parliamentary election, held in 1992, parties opposing the Communist Party formed an informal alliance called the Democratic Convention, which won around 40 percent of the votes cast. Between 1994 and 2008, the Liberals participated in several governmental coalitions.

The National Liberal Party competed on a platform that combined an anti-communist message with support for market-oriented reforms. The party advocated for the adoption of the standard package of neoliberal economic reforms, which included privatization of state-owned enterprises, the reduction of public employment, and the creation of a fiscal environment supportive of a business sector. Such an electoral platform was appealing to middle-class voters, but found less support among employees of state enterprises, who feared its consequences for their incomes and employment. The PNL came to government for the first time in the fall of 1996 as part of a larger alliance of right-wing parties and adopted a shock-therapy economic package that involved ample structural reforms, the dramatic reduction of subsidies to failing enterprises, and significant measures of fiscal austerity (Ban 2016: 160; Gabor 2010). The *Economist* characterized this set of reforms being one of the most radical reforms adopted by former communist countries (Economist Intelligence Unit 1997).

With respect to the development of a party organization, PNL pursued a different strategy from the Social Democratic Party. The National Liberal Party developed and encouraged a highly decentralized party organization. The party maintains a variety of county-level, regional, and local organizations and they play a significant role in selecting candidates (Gherghina 2014: 91). This organizational fragmentation has been a double-edged sword. On the one hand, it has given PNL the ability to adapt to mergers rapidly; on the other, in recent decades it has contributed to higher factionalism and to numerous splits in the party (Gherghina 2014: 92).

The third largest player in Romania's party system is the Democratic Party (Partidul Democrat or PD). The party originated as a dissenting faction of the Front of National Salvation (FSN) early on during the post-communist transition. By 1994, the party had adopted its new name. The Democratic Party underwent a dramatic repositioning in the ideological space. In its early days, the party attempted to offer voters a left-wing alternative to the former communist party. As such, the party took an intermediate economic position between the Socialist Party and other parties on the right by supporting privatization and market-oriented reforms but opposing restitution of property seized during the communist period. During the first years of its existence, the Democratic Party was a member of the European Federation of Left Parties and of the Socialist International. Gradually, though, the Democratic Party perceived an electoral strategy that required a differentiation from the Socialist Party as too difficult and too risky. As a result, the Democratic Party shifted ideologically to the right and began to advocate for more far-reaching economic reforms, a reduction in taxation, and of the adoption of a flat tax.

The Democratic Party achieved its most significant electoral breakthrough in 1996, when the party's candidate, Traian Băsescu, won election to Romania's presidency. Băsescu skillfully used the dissatisfaction with the economic and political corruption to narrowly defeat the PSD candidate. Between 2008 and 2012, the Democratic Party governed Romania, initially as part of a coalition with the National Liberal Party and later as a minority government. These governments accentuated the speed of economic reforms and adopted a number of austerity measures that significantly reduced both employment and the wages of many public sector employees.

During the first decade of its existence, the Democratic Party had very little success in developing its party organization. The party hemorrhaged members when it split from the FDSN. The decline in membership stabilized after the PD won the presidency and other elected offices (Gherghina 2014). By 2008, the party had around 150,000 members, which represented a 15 percent increase over its 1996 membership (Soare 2007). While the PD's membership lagged behind the Social Democratic Party, it is important to point out that, in comparative terms, the organizational density of all major Romanian parties was higher than that of Hungarian parties. In 2004, the ratio between party members and voters was 0.82 for PDL, 0.81 for PNL, and 2.09 for PSD. By contrast, in 2006 the ratio of party members to eligible voters in Hungary was 0.49 for Fidesz and 0.45 for MSZP (Gherghina 2014: 109–13).

Both the PNL and the PD used their participation in government to appropriate fiscal resources and consolidate their party organizations through the use of patronage (Giuğal 2015). In the Romanian political context, the Socialist Party had pioneered these clientelistic strategies beginning in the mid-1990s. Parties on the right (such as the PNL and PD) entered this game later and had to play catch-up with the Socialists. Existing studies on the use of patronage by Romania's parties on the right point out that eventually they successfully adapted to the use of this strategy (Giuğal 2015). The presidents of regional county organizations for both the PNL and PD mimicked the strategies of the Socialists "local barons" and rewarded mayors who brought in higher vote shares for the party in parliamentary or presidential elections with higher fiscal transfers. Similar to the Socialists, both the PNL and PD used fiscal inducements to attract migrant mayors from other political parties. This strategy of patronage allowed parties on the right to gain an increasing share of Romania's rural vote and to hold on to this rural electorate election after election (Giuğal 2015).

The political development of Fidesz (Fiatal Demokraták Szövetsége or the Alliance of Young Democrats) is one of the most remarkable stories in Hungary's post-communist transition. Fidesz was founded as an underground student movement in 1988. During Hungary's first two post-communist elections, Fidesz competed on the basis of a libertarian program, offering voters liberal and radical alternatives (Bozóki 1989 cited in Enyedi 2005). The party's electoral performance during these first two elections was unimpressive. Fidesz received around 9 percent of the votes in 1990 during Hungary's first post-communist election and 7 percent in 1994.

Following its electoral defeat in 1994, Fidesz repositioned itself ideologically in an effort to coordinate the right-wing opposition. It did so by adding the word "national" to the party name and by embracing a rhetoric that emphasized the demands of Hungarian Churches. This included support for higher levels of governmental subsidies to Churches, support for policies that enhanced the family, and so on. On the rural–urban dimension, an important cleavage line in Hungarian politics, Fidesz positioned itself as a party aligned with the interests of rural and small urban localities against large urban centers, such as Budapest. In an effort to coordinate electoral opposition to the Socialist Party, Fidesz emphasized its resolute opposition to future electoral alliances with the Socialists (Enyedi 2005). This conservative ideological turn was not entirely painless, and contributed to a split in party membership. Several of the founders of the party left Fidesz and joined other liberal parties, such as the SZDSZ.

In addition to its ideological reorientation, Fidesz also invested in the development of its party organization. During the first years of its existence, Fidesz had not invested in a functional party organization. This choice could be attributed to the party's origin as a student movement and to the fact that the initial Fidesz organizations "were formed under the wings of SZDSZ" (Magyar 2016: 46). As Tavits comments on this decision to forego the development of a party organization,

Fidesz considered "organizational linkages to be superfluous in a modern democracy and believ[ed] that elections can be won without a strong membership base, a network of branches or efficient management" (Tavits 2013: 93; cf. Bozóki 1992 and Toole 2003).

Following its narrow electoral loss in 2002, Fidesz changed its organizational strategy and began to invest more aggressively in the development of party organizations. One observer of this political transformation commented on the change: "the party publicly acknowledged that the weak organizational networks and the purely parliament- and media-centered strategy were obstacles in the way of stabilizing the party as a major player. The leadership realized that the party needed a Hinterland, a network of organizations, media forums and elite groups that could bring social legitimacy, expertise and various other resources" (Enyedi 2005). To enhance their organizational density, Fidesz leaders began to co-opt right-wing societal organizations, including military veterans, clergy members, and veterans of the 1956 Hungarian uprising (Csizmadia 1999). Fidesz offered leaders of these societal organizations positions and promotions within the party. At the same time, Fidesz promoted the development of subsidiary societal organizations, such as the Smallholder Civic Society and the Hungarian Christian Democratic Society. In 2002 alone, 10,000 such Citizens' Circles (Polgári Körök) were established in Hungary. While these Citizens' Circles were not integrated directly into the party, they could be mobilized effectively when needed.

Fidesz leaders regarded the development of this network of Civic Circles as a stepping-stone to the further development of political party branches. As such, the party leadership encouraged members of local party networks to maintain constant activity, even outside of the regular election cycle (Enyedi 2006). Enyedi and Linek discuss Fidesz's intensive efforts toward organizational development, noting that "the central office measured all potential outputs of local organizations, such as the number of new members, number of organized events, local turnout at elections and referendums, the number of signatures collected and so on" (Enyedi and Linek 2008: 464). Commenting on the importance of the Civic Circles for the party, Magyar noted that they "preempted the threat that the hierarchical discipline of the party could be eroded by a mass overflow," while allowing the formation of a "shared identity among its followers" (Magyar 2016: 47).

The 2010 parliamentary election marked a dramatic turning point in Hungary's political development. At that time, the system of political parties established during the early communist period collapsed. The Socialist Party could not recover from the scandal caused by Ferenc Gyurcsány's infamous "Oszöd Speech," a secretly taped speech in which the MSZP prime minister reported to parliament that his party had made no significant progress during its tenure and had lied to the electorate. In the 2010 parliamentary election, MSZP was able to win only 21 percent of the votes. Jobbik, a new political party on the right, made its successful entry into the Hungarian parliament, winning 16 percent of the vote. The remarkable winner of the election was Fidesz, which won 53 percent of the vote. This trend continued during the 2014 election. At that time, the Socialists won 25 percent of the vote, while Jobbik continued its upward trend to win 20 percent of the vote. Fidesz became Hungary's largest political party, taking advantage of a boost given by the electoral formula allocating parliamentary seats to votes, and winning a full two-thirds of those seats. This supermajority gave Fidesz the necessary number of votes to embark on far-reaching constitutional changes.

Fidesz's dramatic ascent during the most recent elections can be attributed to the skillful crafting of an appeal based on a "stolen transition from communism," which resonated with Hungarian voters (Krekó and Mayer 2015: 183). The party attacked the "colonialism" of Brussels, the irresponsibility and greed of banks, and the corruption of Hungary's political elite. It proposed to restore economic growth using a combination of tax decreases and decreases in spending to "irresponsible citizens," a code word for Hungary's ethnic Roma minority.

In addition to the rise of Fidesz, a second significant development in Hungary's most recent elections is the rise of Jobbik, which became Hungary's second largest political party. Jobbik or the Movement for a Better Hungary was founded as a right-wing student organization in 1999 and became a political party in 2003. In its founding manifesto, the new party defined itself as a "national-Christian force with the mission to lead Hungary to the road of 'freedom and self-determination'" (Szombati 2016). Jobbik's remarkable electoral success can be attributed to two distinct factors. The new party capitalized on Hungarians' overall dissatisfaction with their elected politicians and staged a number of anti-corruption protests. Jobbik also skillfully exploited localized conflicts between ethnic Hungarian and Roma voters and propelled the question of the "imminent Gypsy threat" into Hungarian public discourse (Szombati 2016).

Beginning in 2010, Fidesz used its parliamentary majority to implement far-reaching policy and institutional changes that captured Hungary's democratic institutions. Fidesz reduced the powers of the Constitutional Court and the size of the parliament and radically transformed Hungary's judicial system. By weakening the institutional system of checks and balances, Fidesz marginalized opponents and appointed loyal partisan supporters to all major state institutions. Observers commented on these practices that hollowed out existing institutions by noting that "the main political weapon of the party was the legal instrumentalism of the state machinery, since the two-thirds majority was, in fact, a constitution-making majority." Thereby all anti-democratic actions of the second Orbàn government were strictly made legal (Enyedi 2014; Scheppele 2014).

We have surveyed the evolution of party competition during the post-communist period and documented the most significant changes in the ideological positioning of the main parties, which have, in turn, contributed to the realignment of the party system. In both countries, the political parties have taken various approaches to develop their organizations, investing in different types of party structures and structuring their relationships to social movements in diverse ways. While such organizational development strategies have been key to the electoral success of the different parties, it is important not to overstate their influence (Tavits 2013). The implosion of the Hungarian Socialist Party in recent elections illustrates that even a strong organization cannot ensure survival when parties consistently fail to deliver expected policy benefits. The comparison between Hungary and Romania also reveals that political parties in Romania invested in stronger organizations than Hungarian political parties did (Gherghina 2014).

Both patronage and clientelism have played an important role in the toolkits of different political parties throughout the period. The resources available for use in clientelistic transactions underwent a change throughout the period. In the first years of the post-communist period, the process of privatization of state-owned assets generated immense opportunities for patronage. Grzymała-Busse noted the opportunities available to parties at the time: "the privatization of state enterprises and party holdings meant an unprecedented availability of state resources for 'carrying off' by state representatives for their own use. Enormous state holdings were now to be restructured, privatized and sold off and the profits ploughed back into the reconstruction of the state" (Grzymała-Busse 2006). Candidates and parties took advantage of these privatization opportunities and expropriated immense financial rents, which they then transformed into economic and political power. Similarly, all parties appointed loyalists to all levels of the bureaucracy and used such appointments to generate electoral advantages (Meyer-Sahling 2008; Roper 2008).

As the opportunities created by the process of privatization to sustain clientelistic exchanges dried up, parties searched for other resources that could be exploited for clientelistic mobilization. To this end, parties in both countries modified existing social policy legislation to create opportunities for its use in electoral exchanges with voters. Two significant policy changes established the preconditions for the electoral use of social policy benefits. The first of these policy changes increased mayoral discretion over the allocation of welfare benefits, transforming mayors into the main gatekeepers of the social policy programs. The second change introduced more stringent eligibility criteria for the receipt of anti-poverty programs, by transforming them into workfare programs. This policy change further enhanced opportunities for clientelistic manipulation by increasing the frequency of contact between officials of the social policy administrators and low-income voters, and by increasing state officials' ability to condition access to these programs.

3.2 Research Design and Methodology

Scholars examining party development in Eastern Europe have acknowledged the importance of clientelistic strategies for political parties (Grzymała-Busse 2002, 2006; Kopecký 2006; Tavits 2013; Magyar 2016). Despite the importance of this phenomenon, research examining such clientelistic practices in the region is scarce. We are not the first to note the dearth of scholarship on electoral clientelism in Eastern Europe. Several recent studies of political practices in Eastern Europe have noted the paucity of studies on the informal processes by which parties mobilize voters (Rupnik and Zielonka 2013; Ágh 2016). Both Ágh and Rupnik and Zielonka have noted that the large gap between formal electoral rules and electoral practices in Eastern Europe has not yet been sufficiently examined; they point out that while "informal practices may be equally important in shaping and in some cases eroding democracy, we know little about them" (Rupnik and Zielonka 2013: 3).

The scarcity of systematic research on electoral clientelism can largely be attributed to high, if not insurmountable, problems of empirical measurement. Commenting on these difficulties, Wilson's early study of political patronage noted that "so much secrecy is maintained in city politics that no exact data on patronage may ever be obtained in cities of any size" (Wilson 1961: 372). Geddes goes even further, arguing that the study of patronage or clientelism is impossible due to the severity of measurement issues: "there is no way to measure amounts of patronage" (Geddes 1994: 105).

To operate in this research environment, characterized by little existing empirical evidence and severe measurement problems, we developed a research methodology with two key characteristics. First, we adopted a mixed methods approach that combines intensive qualitative case studies and the extensive collection of quantitative data at the individual and locality level. This multi-methods approach enabled us to generate, rigorously test, and richly illustrate novel hypotheses about how clientelism affects voters and where politicians deploy it. Second, we employed a variety of methods to measure individuals' attitudes towards and participation in illicit, socially undesirable phenomena. In this section we discuss each of these design choices in turn.

Our mixed-methods approach produced an abundance of data that allows us to home in on and analyze variation in clientelism. We created qualitative profiles of fifty-one localities: eighteen in Hungary and thirty-three in Romania. The locality profiles were based on between two and twenty-three individual interviewees per locality as well as extensive observation of everyday social and political practices. The latter included interactions between officials of the local welfare administration and social policy beneficiaries, interactions between mayors and citizens requesting administrative permissions or other licenses, economic interactions between workfare employees and their employers and supervisors of the social policy administration, political rallies and other campaign events, and so on. In recording such events, we relied on the extensive use of field notes, a standard research strategy in anthropology (Emerson et al. 2011).

In order to measure the sensitive phenomenon of clientelism, we used a combination of traditional research methods and novel survey methods, including list experiments, and conjoint and survey-based experiments. One of the ways that we tried to reduce measurement error in the qualitative interviews was to conduct the qualitative component in collaboration with teams of local researchers. In the initial stages of their study, these researchers relied on referrals from non-governmental organizations (NGOs), journalists, or other local connections to secure an entry-point in the respective communities. After this initial entry, these members of our research team embedded themselves in these communities by conducting repeated interviews over an extended period of time. They also returned to several of these communities on multiple occasions, to either observe political developments over repeated elections or to clarify questions about local political dynamics that remained unclear. In the quantitative interviews, we used experimental techniques including conjoint experiments and list experiments to preserve plausible deniability and reduce social desirability bias.

3.2.1 Integrating insights from three methodologies

Over the past twenty years, there have been increasing calls for researchers to combine multiple research methods, particularly with research designs that marry quantitative and qualitative data and analysis (Tarrow 1995; Lieberman 2005; Humphreys and Jacobs 2015). We employ a mixed-methods approach for two primary reasons. First, each method serves a different function. We use the qualitative case studies primarily to generate hypotheses and observe subtle, ongoing dynamics that are difficult to measure in a survey. The two quantitative survey methods that we chose then test our theory at different levels of analysis: large-N, representative surveys measure exposure to different forms of clientelism at the locality level, and survey experiments based on vignette and conjoint designs test the individual-level implications of our theory. Second, the mixed-methods approach enables us to increase our confidence in our measurements of clientelism, as each method is susceptible to a different form of measurement error. We discuss this second advantage of our methodology in more depth in Section 3.2.2, which details the multiple steps that we took to accurately measure this sensitive phenomenon.

3.2.1.1 Locality case studies
The first method we employ in our research design uses in-depth semi-structured interviews and observation to develop qualitative case studies of different

localities. Ethnographic research is an extremely valuable research strategy and is currently experiencing a return in political science, both as a stand-alone method and in combination with other methods, such as surveys or experimental research (Cramer 2016). This method allows us to unpack the beliefs of voters subjected to different clientelistic strategies and to document in an open-ended way both clientelistic strategies, including how they are implemented by brokers and then interpreted by voters. At the same time, ethnographic research allows us to document what other scholars have called "informal electoral practices" (Anderson 2000; Rupnik and Zielonka 2013; Ágh 2016). Calling for the study of such informal strategies, Rupnik and Zielonka note that "cultural anthropologists are probably more suited than political scientists to study such phenomena" (2013: 14).

The main purpose of the case studies is to generate a thick description of how clientelism operates in this context and to enrich our hypotheses about the factors that influence where and how it occurs. Because there has been little empirical research on clientelism in Eastern Europe, one of our first steps involved understanding basic questions about whether it was occurring at all, and, if so, who was brokering clientelistic transactions, what incentives were being offered, how voters were monitored, and so on. We needed some insight into these questions in order to design a survey instrument, define independent variables or interest, and set a sampling protocol to collect quantitative data. In a second stage, we used the insights generated by our qualitative research to generate further hypotheses about how the incidence of different clientelistic strategies varied across localities. We carried out the case studies at the locality level between 2014 and 2016 using local researchers whom we trained in general research practices as well as a specific protocol for selecting and interviewing respondents in each locality.

Given the sensitivity of the interviews, we took a number of steps to protect respondents from potential breaches of confidentiality. First, although all members of our research team were experienced interviewers, we provided a half-day of training on human subjects' protection before they were allowed to go into the field. This session included training on principles of ethical research and elements of informed consent. Second, although we relied on referrals to recruit respondents, the researchers were trained not to reveal the names of past respondents (including during the referral process). Finally, the researchers kept the audio files of the interviews for as little time as possible on their recording devices in order to minimize the risk of confidentiality breaches.

Because the goal of our locality case studies was to identify the dynamics of clientelism where it existed, for our sampling we purposively selected localities where we thought we could collect rich, illustrative data. This led us to identify two primary criteria. First, some localities were selected based on accessibility to members of our research team. In some cases, our researchers had pre-existing contacts in certain localities through past research or connections to local NGOs and, on a few occasions, personal ties. Such connections facilitated community entry and respondent recruitment. Other localities were chosen at a later stage based either on their demographic characteristics or on the levels of clientelism that we had documented in our surveys that measured the incidence of different forms of clientelism. In the latter case, we selected localities based on socio-economic characteristics that were expected to contribute to variation in the incidence of clientelistic practices, such as the share of Roma voters, or unemployed voters.

Within each locality, our research team followed a semi-structured protocol for recruiting and interviewing respondents. We gave the researchers a list of types of respondents to target that included welfare recipients, opponents and supporters of the mayor, local administrators of social assistance programs, and potential elect-oral brokers. We also trained them to record field notes and to write a final locality report. These locality reports included summaries of the main findings, an assessment of the strategies used to win elections in the locality, and, if clientelism was used, an assessment of the actors that were involved, of the targeted voters, and of the strategies used to monitor voting behavior. Researchers were also given a semi-structured interview guideline that provided sample questions in our main areas of inquiry including the locality's economic conditions, debt, ethnic relations, mayor's strategies, the use of social assistance benefits, and electoral campaigns. The researchers built on the sample questions, reacting to what the respondents said and adding additional questions based on what they learned in prior interviews.

On average, in the fifty localities where our team completed the case studies, each analysis was based on ten interviews, with a maximum of twenty-three interviews in one Romanian locality. In total, our team conducted over 400 individual interviews, the majority of which were recorded and transcribed. Appendix A4 lists the topics and questions discussed during these semi-structured interviews, while Appendices A1–A3 list all of the anonymized interviews that were conducted as part of the study.

We analyze this qualitative data by using it to describe how clientelism occurs in the localities in the study. We do not try to draw inferences about causal processes, or analyze variation across cases to determine where clientelism occurs, using our qualitative data. Thus, the qualitative details presented in the following chapters should be taken as illustrative, but not representative, examples of how clientelism actually occurs in this set of cases.

Analyzing such interview data on sensitive phenomena also posed additional challenges involving the assessment of the truthfulness and accuracy of individ-uals' accounts. Although respondents were repeatedly informed that both the individual and locality-level information of these interviews would be anonym-ized, we were concerned that some people would make false accusations in hopes of bringing about retribution on political or personal enemies. We took several steps to minimize this risk. First, in analyzing the data we make note of reasons for bias such as political opposition, and include these in the field notes when applicable. Second, because we conducted multiple interviews per locality, we can identify inconsistencies between respondents' accounts. In particular, we sought to corroborate respondents' accounts in multiple interviews. We also discounted evidence from interviews that deviated from others in the locality. Finally, and, perhaps, most obviously, we put more credence in first-hand evidence than that based on second-hand accounts.

Another choice that we had to make in the development of our qualitative methodology was how to balance research transparency with the protection of human subjects. During the course of our fieldwork between 2015 and 2018, political science experienced an active debate over the conditions under which qualitative evidence should be made publicly available. In contexts where the research subjects are highly vulnerable populations and topics involve highly sensitive information, qualitative researchers experience a sharp trade-off between considerations about the protection of human subjects and the objective of research transparency. These considerations about the need to protect our research subjects limited our ability to post the full transcripts of our interviews, even after we anonymized the names of localities and our respondents. Because the case studies contain details of stories and personal characteristics that could be identifying to a reader with local knowledge and ill intent, we did not feel confident that we could post the full interview transcripts, while upholding the promise of confidentiality made to the participants in our study.

Ultimately, the qualitative evidence that we present in the following chapters should be interpreted as illustrative accounts of an illicit and largely undocumented phenomenon. This qualitative evidence not only painted a picture of illicit clientelistic practices, but also informed the development of our hypotheses at the locality and individual level, and of several subsequent surveys we have conducted in both countries.

3.2.1.2 Representative surveys to measure locality-level dynamics

The second significant component of our methodology is the use of large-N surveys to measure the incidence of four different forms of clientelism across a range of localities. This component of the research is designed to test our predictions about the type of locality-level conditions that enable clientelism, including the types of resources that facilitate its use and the social conditions that reduce citizens' propensities to punish clientelism. To do so, we surveyed 1,880 respondents in one hundred localities in Hungary and 1,497 people across eighty localities in Romania shortly after the parliamentary and presidential elections in 2014, respectively. We measure the incidence of clientelism by embedding list experiments (described in more detail in Section 3.2.2.2), in the survey. We merged this original data with comprehensive, locality-level data on economic, political, and social conditions from the countries' censuses and electoral agencies. This combination of original and official data enables us to combine the benefits of sophisticated techniques for measuring socially undesirable behavior with the comprehensive coverage of official data.

Our sampling strategy for these surveys was designed both to focus on a subset of localities where we expected clientelism to be present, and to ensure variation on the locality-level independent variables that we expected to affect its incidence. Given that one of the goals motivating our study is to investigate the correlates of cross-sectional variation in the use of different clientelistic strategies, we chose to implement the survey in a large number of localities where we expected the incidence of such irregularities to be relatively high. We first selected first-level administrative units in each country (three counties in Hungary and two provinces (judeţ) in Romania) where we expected clientelism to be prevalent. Given the strong expectation from the existing literature and previous research that it is easier to violate ballot secrecy in localities with small populations, we restricted our sample to localities with less than 10,000 inhabitants. We then stratified the list of localities based on the level of unemployment, the proportion of workers employed in agriculture, the proportion of residents who identified as Roma, and whether the mayor at the time of the survey was a co-partisan of the executive. From these sixteen strata, we selected one hundred localities in Hungary and eighty-six in Romania.[1] For the selection of respondents within each municipality in Hungary we used a random walk methodology to select the household, and the nearest-birthday method to select the respondent within a household. For the selection of respondents within each municipality in Romania, we used quota-based sampling using demographic information from the recent census to define the gender, age, and ethnicity quotas. We could not implement a random-walk methodology in Romania, due to the adverse climactic conditions because the survey was carried out during a very cold and rainy month.

In Hungary, we fielded the main survey measuring the incidence of clientelism in the aftermath of the parliamentary election held in May/June 2014. In Romania, we followed up with a similar survey that we fielded in the aftermath of the presidential election held in December 2014. In Hungary, the survey was implemented by a respected survey firm with twenty-five years of experience in public opinion polling. In Romania, it was implemented by an academic collaborator at the National School of Political Science and Public Administration (SNSPA). In both cases we conducted a series of pilots, each with 100–150 respondents, both with the survey teams who implemented the full survey and with separate survey teams. These pilots primarily served to fine-tune the list experiments (and are explained in more detail in Section 3.2.2.2), but they also enabled us to pretest the other questions in the survey.

After the survey data was collected, it was merged at the locality level with data from the most recent census and most recent elections. The census, last administered in 2014 in Hungary and 2011 in Romania, includes information on the population, on what proportion of the population that identifies as Roma and on employment statuses, and poverty rates by locality. The electoral management bodies in both countries also provide information on the past elections and we used it to code the political characteristics of each locality, including the partisanship and incumbency of the mayor at the time of the elections under study, the mayor's last margin of victory, and the composition of the city council.

After building these two country-level datasets with data on both individual and locality characteristics, we analyze the data using a multilevel mixed-effects model. Multi-level models are an efficient way to analyze data that combines variables of interest at both the group and individual unit level. In our case, we have variables at both the individual and locality level and model random intercepts. We analyze the results of the list experiments by interacting these individual and locality characteristics with an indicator that the respondent was assigned to the treatment version of the list. This specification enables us to estimate the difference between respondents assigned to the treatment list and the control list, our estimate of the incidence of the sensitive item, for respondents with different characteristics.

3.2.1.3 Survey experiments to test signaling value of clientelism

The third component in our mixed-methods research design is the use of survey experiments to test our hypotheses about the effects of different forms of clientelism at the individual level. These experiments are designed to obtain causal estimates of the effects of hypothetical scenarios describing political campaign tactics on voters' perceptions of those candidates.

Hypothetical scenarios are well suited for our research for several reasons. First, they enable us estimate the effect of fine-grained differences between clientelistic strategies. Because we are primarily interested in how voters view clientelistic promises differently from threats, this control is very important, as it enabled us to isolate this information. Importantly, this design enabled us to hold constant the value of the inducements being offered or withheld in the scenarios, which would have been difficult to control for in an observational design because positive inducements, in practice, are often one-off, low-value goods like meals, cash, or small favors. By contrast, many negative economic inducements are carried out with valuable entitlements like welfare or employment.

Second, because we can randomly assign hypothetical scenarios, they enable us to estimate the causal effect of these strategies on voters' perceptions of candidates. This is critically important because politicians presumably target certain clientelistic strategies on voters and localities where they believe they are most likely to be effective. If this systematic targeting is at all related to the way that voters perceive these strategies, then observational tests of the effects of clientelism on voter perceptions will be biased by this variation across voters. Using randomized scenarios enables us to break down this link between voter characteristics and the strategies that those voters are exposed to, and thus identify how different groups of voters would perceive candidates if they were exposed to each clientelistic strategy, or to no clientelism at all.

While we contend that hypothetical scenarios in survey experiments are the best methodology for testing our set of individual hypotheses, they are not without drawbacks. First, hypothetical scenarios are useful only if they accurately match the real-life situations that they represent. We carried out our survey experiments after conducting qualitative case studies and quantitative surveys measuring the same forms of clientelism that we examine in the hypothetical scenarios in over two hundred similar localities. This extensive preparation enabled us to write scenarios that we knew mirrored actual political dynamics, using the same language that respondents used to describe clientelism in their communities. Second, hypothetical responses may be biased by social desirability bias. We work to mitigate this risk in several different ways in our survey experiments: for example, by framing the scenarios in neutral terms and by using a conjoint design to provide plausible deniability. We describe these techniques in more depth in Section 3.2.2.3.

We draw from three different survey experiments in the chapters that follow. In Chapter 4, we present a re-analysis of a conjoint experiment conducted by Mares and Visconti (2019) that enables comparison of candidates who do and do not offer voters public favors, in addition to a range of other characteristics including candidate experience, gender, and party. This experiment was carried out in 2016 with a total of 323 respondents in Romania, each of whom we asked to react to five different pairs of candidate profiles. The sample mirrors the main demographic characteristics of the Romanian population, with respect to age, gender, and urban/rural localities. In Chapter 5, we present an analysis of a second survey experiment in which we asked 518 respondents in ninety localities in three Romanian counties to react to one of three scenarios describing no welfare-based clientelism, welfare favors, or welfare coercion. In Chapter 7, we discuss the findings of a final survey-based experiment in which 695 respondents in the same set of ninety localities were asked to assess a candidate who used one of two different forms of vote buying or a candidate who used no clientelism.

In all of the survey experiments that we discuss, we test two primary hypotheses.

First, we test whether the average respondent perceives candidates who use various forms of clientelism differently to candidates who do not engage in it. To do this we calculate the average treatment effect (ATE) of the clientelism scenarios.[2]

Second, we test whether voters with certain characteristics, particularly different social policy characteristics, differ in how they evaluate forms of clientelism. To do so we test for heterogeneous treatment effects and estimate the effects of the clientelism scenarios for different groups of voters.

3.2.2 Using multiple methods to measure the incidence of clientelistic strategies

Measurement difficulties affect both the incentives of voters and of brokers and politicians to provide truthful answers about levels of clientelism. Voters' incentives to report clientelistic strategies truthfully are affected both by considerations of social desirability and by fears of retaliation. Both considerations are likely to depress reports of occurrences of various clientelistic practices. As a result, efforts to measure clientelistic strategies using direct survey questions is likely to produce biased estimates. Similarly, politicians or brokers engaged in clientelistic exchanges are also likely to misrepresent such practices. Commenting on these incentives to misrepresent clientelistic practices, Kitschelt and Wilkinson noted that "politicians may treat direct questions about clientelism or corruption as valence questions on which they suspect most citizens and observers to be on one side of the issue (against). Hence, they present their own practices as devoid of clientelism, but may attribute such practices to their competitors and opponents" (Kitschelt and Wilkinson 2007: 326).

Before we discuss our empirical strategy, let us briefly consider alternative approaches to measuring patronage or clientelism. One empirical strategy for the study of patronage and clientelism has attempted to proxy these phenomena using measures of the size of the state administration or the total expenditures devoted to partisan spending. Consider some of the empirical proxies used in existing studies. Remmer (2007) measures clientelism as the percentage of total expenditures allocated to personnel spending; Brusco et al. (2004) estimate it using municipal spending on personnel; O'Dwyer (2004, 2006) uses the increase in the total number of positions in the state administrative personnel; and Grzymała-Busse (2003) uses the share of employment in the public administration out of total employment to proxy party patronage.

Such proxies may be only weakly correlated with the phenomenon of interest and therefore are likely to be quite problematic. Public employment is an imperfect proxy of patronage appointments. First, the size of public sector may be determined by a variety of other factors besides patronage. Such factors include international influences, such as World Bank or International Monetary Fund requirements, demands from domestic interest groups or business associations, and so on. Alternatively, patronage may occur in the absence of a change in the size of the public sector, when politicized appointments are made to replace existing appointments. The intensity of the political pressure that politicians place on employees of the local administration may also increase in conditions when public sector employment declines. As such, the relationship between these measures and the theoretical concept remains very weak.

A second empirical strategy seeks to capture electoral clientelism using expert coding. In a number of comparative studies examining the incidence of patronage practices in Eastern and Western Europe, Petr Kopecký and several co-authors have used expert coding to measure the politicization of the state administration across different ministries (Kopecký et al. 2012). These studies rely on interviews with current or retired civil servants, analysts in NGOs, or journalists to collect systematic information about the extent of bureaucratic patronage. These studies use this information to develop various indicators that capture the level of party patronage, the motivations for patronage appointments; and the characteristics of people who are appointed to patronage positions (Kopecký et al. 2012). In recent years, Herbert Kitschelt and his collaborators have carried out the most extensive cross-national study of electoral clientelism that relies on expert coding (Kitschelt 2011). The survey on citizen–politician linkages developed by Herbert Kitschelt and his collaborators draws on interviews with party experts to measure the incidence of a large number of non-programmatic strategies pursued by political parties in over one hundred countries.

Efforts to measure clientelism by relying on small panels of experts are more promising than earlier empirical strategies. This approach has several advantages. First, this strategy allows researchers to harness the wealth of insider knowledge such participants offer, while at the same time structuring the information and exploiting its comparative implications. This approach also allows researchers to obtain information on practices that are often illicit and, thus, hard to assess. But the reliance on expert coding has also disadvantages. The objectivity of some respondents in providing this information might, at times, be questionable, and such imperfections in objectivity might pose challenges for the validity and reliability of the research (Putnam 1973: 18). These measurement problems may be amplified by the low number of participants in such panels. Second, while expert panels might be reliable in creating cross-sectional snapshots of clientelistic measures in a particular context, this method is less amenable to examining changes in illicit practices after a dramatic shock to the system or identifying variation in clientelism at a local level.

Our empirical strategy to the study of clientelism departs from existing approaches in several ways. The main goals of our study are to document several different non-programmatic strategies and to assess how the experience of these strategies affects voters' evaluations of different candidates and their political choices. To examine these questions, our empirical strategy needed to measure voters' experiences of clientelistic practices as well as their assessment of different forms of clientelism. Obtaining valid measures of these phenomena is extremely challenging, due to the illicit nature of clientelistic transactions.

We use three primary strategies to overcome these measurement difficulties. In the qualitative interviews, we rely on trust built over time between the local researchers and the respondents. In the locality survey, we primarily use list experiments, which allow us to obtain an estimate of the incidence of clientelism without requiring respondents to directly report experiences that make them look like bad citizens or criminals. Finally, in the individual-level survey experiments, we use a variety of methods including a conjoint experiment to reduce the pressure of social desirability bias. Our decision to use these three methods, each of which has its own drawbacks and advantages, reflects Tarrow's argument that "triangulation [between multiple methods] is particularly appropriate in cases in which quantitative data are partial and qualitative investigation is obstructed by political conditions" (Tarrow 1995: 473). We discuss each of these methods in turn.

3.2.2.1 Establishing trust in qualitative interviews

We trained our qualitative research team to elicit truthful information through three primary methods. First, we relied on local researchers affiliated with universities without histories of activism in the communities in our study. These researchers, mostly PhD and masters students at universities including the National University of Political Studies and Public Administration in Romania and the Central European University in Hungary, introduced themselves as students and as research assistants working for researchers at Columbia University in the United States, where both of the authors were affiliated at the time of the study. When applicable, they also introduced themselves based on their ties to the area (i.e., as having grown up in a neighboring locality).

Second, the researchers established trust in the interviews by explaining the procedures that would be taken to protect the respondents' confidentiality. They obtained consent both to do the interview and to record it, asking the respondent not to mention their name or the names of the locality or other residents in the recording. They also explained how we would handle the recording, particularly that it would be transcribed and completely anonymized.

Finally, we built trust through the conduct of the interviews. The researchers were trained to react to respondents with expressions of interest, including more specific follow-up questions and verbal cues. In particular, they were trained not to express any judgments that would reinforce the respondent's beliefs about what the researcher wanted to hear. Before and after the interview, they explained to the respondent that the purpose of the research was to understand how things work in the locality, and expressed gratitude to the respondent for helping them build that understanding. After each interview, the researcher wrote notes, including reflections on how trusting and truthful the respondent was, and what they could do to better build trust in the subsequent interviews. They also provided a first analysis of the credibility of the information provided by each interviewee that we took into account during our comprehensive analysis.

3.2.2.2 Indirect methods of measuring clientelism in surveys

The second component of our empirical strategy attempted to measure the incidence of different forms of electoral clientelism in recent elections. This poses critical and well-known challenges. Traditional survey methods are of little use in assessing sensitive phenomena, such as offers of money and favors in exchange for the vote, or the threat to withhold access to a benefit. While voters may have experienced some of these illicit electoral strategies, they may be reluctant to admit these experiences. Their reluctance may have different sources: social desirability bias, fear of retaliation from the agent who has engaged in such behavior, or fear of prosecution by the state.

One research strategy that has grown in importance in recent years and that mitigates these measurement problems is the list experiment (Sniderman and Grob 1996). Traditionally, list experiments were used and developed to elicit unbiased answers about sensitive political attitudes, such as racism or anti-Semitism. In recent years, scholars of electoral clientelism have increasingly used list experiments to study the incidence of illicit political phenomena, such as electoral fraud or vote buying (Gonzalez-Ocantos et al. 2012; Ahlquist et al. 2014). In an extremely creative application of the list experiment to the study of political patronage, Oliveros measures illicit political activities performed by employees of several local administrations in Argentina (Oliveros 2013).

In list experiments, respondents are presented with a list of items and asked how many (as opposed to which) items are true. To capture the incidence of the sensitive behavior, respondents are randomly divided into two groups. Respondents that are assigned to the control group are given questionnaires that include only the non-sensitive item. By contrast, respondents in the treatment group are presented the same list of non-sensitive items given to the control group and an additional item that seeks to measure the sensitive behavior. We can infer the magnitude of the incidence of the sensitive behavior in the population by taking the difference in the mean number of items chosen by respondents in the treatment and control group, respectively.

In both countries included in our study, we used list experiments to measure the incidence of the four types of electoral irregularities discussed in Chapter 2. As our study is the first effort to measure illicit electoral strategies in both countries, we took a number of additional steps to ensure the validity of our survey instruments. In Romania, we conducted several focus groups in a small locality located in the eastern part of the country to develop the wording for the illicit strategies that corresponded to the experiences of voters. In both Romania and Hungary, we consulted with experts on electoral politics and experts on ethnic minorities to develop the survey instruments.[3] We then pre-tested both the instruments measuring the sensitive behavior and the control items that were included in our list in a number of pilot surveys. In each country, we conducted three rounds of pre-tests, with sample sizes between 100 and 150 voters. One goal of the pre-test was to design the control items on the lists such that most control respondents would select one to avoid "ceiling" and "floor" effects (Glynn 2013). We believed this move was likely to increase the confidence of respondents in reporting the sensitive behavior truthfully, while also reducing the variance in the means estimate for the treatment and control groups.

In order to assess the validity of the list experiments, we carried out several diagnostics. First, we ran simple tests of balance to check that the versions of the survey were correctly randomized. These tests are presented in Appendix B3. We find no indications that the list experiments had been randomized incorrectly.

Second, we ran a test formalized by Blair and Imai (2012) for "design effects," or evidence that the inclusion of the sensitive item changed how participants responded to the control items on the list. This test looks for evidence that the inclusion of the sensitive item either decreased or increased the number of items that respondents reported by more than one, both of which are impossible if respondents are answering honestly. In general, this test is not very sensitive because the changes in the responses to the control items would have to be quite large to meet either threshold. However, because the estimated prevalence of clientelism in our case is relatively low, the tests have higher sensitivity. We find no evidence of design effects in any of our list experiments, and the results of these tests appear in Appendix B4. Finally, we look at the distribution of the control items to assess whether respondents are likely to suffer from ceiling or floor effects. Ideally, list experiment control responses should be tightly centered on one so that respondents don't worry that their answer reveals agreement with the sensitive item. Appendix B4 shows that the control means on our list experiments are between 0.97 and 1.15, with fewer than 10 percent of control group respondents reporting either zero or three items. This suggests that the lists indeed provide plausible deniability to respondents who have experienced clientelism.

3.2.2.3 Framing and plausible deniability in survey experiments

The final component of our research strategy examines how voters evaluate candidates who use different non-programmatic strategies. Social desirability bias, or the potential for respondents to tell surveyors what they think is the morally acceptable answer, is a primary concern in these experiments. To reduce the potential for this bias, we use two different methods: framing and plausible deniability.

We begin by discussing the strategy for reducing social desirability bias in the conjoint experiment presented in Chapter 4. In conjoint designs, respondents are presented with two profiles that vary along a number of dimensions. In our case, respondents are given information on past legislative experience, business experience, gender, party, and clientelism for two different candidates. Because respondents are presented with so many characteristics, they can often come up with multiple justifications for choosing a candidate who is socially undesirable along one of the dimensions (Wallander 2009; Hainmueller et al. 2014). In other words, they can reveal their socially undesirable preference while maintaining the ability to plausibly deny that they actually prefer the candidate because of his socially undesirable trait. Empirically, we find that in 43 percent of the candidate pairs that respondents were presented with, the respondent said that they would prefer to vote for the clientelistic candidate. This high rate of reported support for clientelistic candidates suggests that the risk of social desirability may be relatively small.

In the scenario experiments that we use to study policy coercion and vote buying, we rely primarily on framing to reduce social desirability bias. To frame the policy coercion scenario, in the introduction and in the control scenario we mention factors that might make it socially acceptable for candidates to bend the rules in the allocation of social policy. In the introduction to the scenario, for example, respondents are reminded that some low-income residents are currently excluded from the main welfare program. In the control scenario, respondents are told that the candidate refused to give social assistance to anyone who could not document their eligibility. Thus, the scenario sets up a murkier ethical situation in which respondents could feel ethically justified in saying that candidates who engage in clientelism are breaking the rules for the right reasons, and those who do not are hurting deserving constituents.

3.3 Conclusion

In this chapter, we have provided the necessary context for the empirical chapters that follow. First, we provided an overview of the structure of political competition during the post-communist period in Hungary and Romania. We argued based on the existing empirical literature that clientelism has played an increasingly important role in the strategies of the main political parties in the region. Along with investments in party structures and ideological positioning, the development of clientelistic linkages with voters has been noted in the literature on politics in the region as a major element of inter-party competition since the mid-1990s. However, to date there has been little empirical work rigorously documenting this illicit strategy or analyzing how and where it occurs.

We developed a mixed methods research design to address this gap in the literature on politics in the region and the gap in the broader theoretical literature on clientelism that we discussed in Chapter 2. A mixed methods design is particularly appropriate for the study of clientelism for several reasons. First, it allows us to iteratively test our theory at different levels. This is particularly important in our case because our theory has observable implications at the individual and locality level. In addition, because so little micro-level empirical work has been done on this topic in the region, the qualitative case studies, locality surveys, and survey experiments provided us with critical information that we used to itera-tively inform and improve later stages of our research design. Finally, because this illegal, socially undesirable behavior is particularly hard to measure, using mul-tiple methods allows us to triangulate sources that are potentially subject to different forms of bias.

Notes

1. Because in some cases we selected 100 percent of the localities in a stratum, we do not use inverse propensity sampling weights to back out a representative sample. As such, our results should be interpreted as representative of the sample, but not necessarily of the administrative units from which we drew our sample.
2. In the case of the conjoint experiment, the ATE is commonly called AMCE (Hainmueller et al. 2014).
3. For a list of these expert interviews in both countries, see Appendix A1.

4

Policy Favors

Building on the Status Quo

Existing studies examining the use of policy resources of the state to influence voters' electoral choices suggest that such strategies are likely to occur in two different contexts characterized by very different types of political endowments. One set of studies suggests that clientelistic strategies are likely to occur in contexts where parties control an abundant set of resources that can be exploited electorally. Aristide Zolberg's study of postcolonial states in Africa characterizes clientelism as the "politics of inflationary demand expectation" (Zolberg 1968). In Zolberg's account, political elites manipulate a diverse menu of policy resources, while also managing citizens' rising demands for goods and favors in exchange for their votes. Judith Chubb's landmark study of clientelism in postwar Italy also depicts an environment characterized by abundant resources. This study concludes that the clientelistic strategies pursued by the Italian Christian Democracy party were made possible by "the tremendous expansion of state intervention in the postwar period and the progressive interpenetration of the DC and the state administration" (Chubb 1982: 174). Finally, Grzymała Busse's study of political patronage in the first decade after the fall of communism also conjures up the image of resource abundance. In this unique environment, the abundance resulted from the fact that all the resources held by the state were up "for sale" (Grzymała-Busse 2002).

However, clientelistic strategies using state resources are also likely to occur in contexts where parties control a much more limited range of policies that can be deployed for electoral mobilization. In an early contribution, Wolfinger argued that clientelistic behavior is more likely to be found in smaller welfare states, rather than extensive ones due to the intense competition for benefits one encounters in the former (Wolfinger 1972: 384). In most countries, neoliberal reforms adopted in recent decades have reduced the scope of state presence, limiting also the repertoire of policies available to parties for clientelistic mobilization. As the rapidly growing literature on electoral clientelism has documented, however, such scarcity of policy resources does not eliminate the presence and importance of electoral clientelism (Stokes et al. 2013; Weitz-Shapiro 2014). Political environments characterized by scarce policy resources whose benefits are meager and residualized create different opportunities for the use of clientelism as compared to the contexts of resource abundance. Resource scarcity increases the value of policy resources controlled by candidates, while also intensifying distributional conflict over its allocation among voters.

The resource environment in both Hungary and Romania is one of scarcity. The market-oriented reforms adopted by successive governments during the post-communist transition have limited the scope and size of state intervention in the economy. As a result, mayors who act as brokers for candidates competing in parliamentary or presidential elections control a limited menu of resources that can be deployed to influence voters' electoral choices. The most significant programs controlled by mayors are anti-poverty or workfare programs. However, high levels of poverty and labor market exclusion raise the value of these workfare benefits to voters. In many communities, workfare benefits represent the only long-term stream of benefits that can be accessed by those who have no other employment opportunity. At the same time, unfavorable labor market conditions increase the salience of distributional conflicts over access to the program between different low-income voters. As discussed in Chapter 2, variation in the intensity of such distributional conflicts pitting "poor against poor" voters conditions, in turn, which clientelistic strategy candidates favor.

This chapter begins with a discussion of the strategies by which politicians have exploited the state's policy resources for clientelistic mobilization in recent elections in Hungary and Romania. Here, we focus on the use of welfare resources to establish positive electoral incentives. We draw on interviews conducted with mayors, brokers, and voters in rural communities to document such strategies and show that they unfold during both the pre-electoral and the electoral period. Between elections, mayors seek to establish norms of reciprocity that can be later exploited electorally. They attempt to consolidate their political monopoly over the allocation of policy benefits, shape expectations about the scarcity of the resources, personalize the distribution of benefits, and encourage expectations that turnout or vote-choices are monitored. Such strategies set the stage and increase mayors' abilities to incentivize voters during elections.

We next discuss the strategies that politicize state resources or that involve state employees as brokers during the electoral period. At this time, mayors and other brokers in the locality activate the norms of reciprocity established during the pre-electoral period. In parliamentary or presidential elections, parties rely on mayors to coordinate the electoral efforts of all local administrators. State employees who are mobilized as brokers may include tax assessors, administrators of social policy programs, teachers, and, in some rare instances, policemen or other law enforcement officers. These brokers mobilize voters to the polls, observe their turnout, and exploit imperfections in voting technology to monitor vote choice. After ballots have been cast, these brokers attempt to ascertain the actual electoral choices made and to punish voters for incorrect choices.

The use of clientelistic strategies premised on favors violates fundamental democratic norms. We conjectured that candidates choosing between clientelistic strategies will attempt to counter voters' disapproval of such practices by choosing a strategy that signals a policy position that is in line with voters' preferences. In the case of policy favors, we surmised that candidates use favors to signal positive personal characteristics like generosity and policy positions that favor low-income voters. In Section 4.3, we examine the results of a survey designed to examine how voters evaluate candidates that deploy clientelistic strategies premised on favors. Using a conjoint design, we test whether income, and by extension preferences over redistribution, conditions the way that voters evaluate candidates who offer policy favors and the propensity to vote for such candidates. Consistent with the theoretical hypotheses formulated in Chapter 2, we find that low income voters do not view candidates who offer policy favors in exchange for votes as less desirable in terms of their personal characteristics or policy positions, in stark contrast to their higher income peers. Indeed, very poor voters actually view candidates who offer policy favors as more likely to help the poor. These results lend support to the conjecture that candidates can use the programmatic signals of different forms of clientelism to avoid being punished for subverting democratic norms.

In the final section of the chapter, we draw on survey-based evidence to examine the variation across localities in the use of non-programmatic strategies. We draw on the post- electoral surveys administered in Romania and Hungary that use list experiments to measure the incidence of clientelistic strategies premised on policy favors. As discussed in Chapter 2, we conjectured that the use of policy favors would be conditioned by two factors. First, the use of this strategy should be higher in localities where mayors enjoy greater political control in allocating the resources of the state. Such increased control may be facilitated by a long-term incumbency, co-partisanship with the national party, and a low fragmentation of the municipality. Second, the use of policy favors should be more likely in places where the intensity of social conflict over the allocation of social policy benefits is low. Our findings from Hungary lend support to this hypothesis.

4.1 Mayors' Pre-Electoral Strategies: Expectations of Scarcity and Norms of Reciprocity

To gain a better understanding of the allocation of workfare jobs and of the process by which mayors seek to establish clientelistic ties to workfare beneficiaries, members of our research group lined up one morning in the small square located in front of the city hall in FM., a locality in northeastern Hungary.[1] On the evening before, one respondent had shared the news that ten new workfare jobs would become available over the next few days. When we arrived at the city hall in the morning, fifty people were waiting in the square, holding identity papers and other documents in their hands. The atmosphere was tense, as people shouted, quarreled about the timing of their arrival, and boasted about having a special relationship to the mayor. The mayor's son and his friends were also present in the square, smoking, and observing the crowd.

Employees of the city hall who were present in the square played no role in processing the applications for workfare jobs; they directed all applicants to the mayor. The mayor met each of the applicants and addressed their requests in a paternalistic and decisive manner. He also found the time to meet with us in his office, which was covered in red velvet and decorated with a mix of football trophies and religious paintings. In his brief discussion with us, the mayor asserted his determination to oversee the distribution of workfare jobs in the locality personally (FM., Interview 7, July 29, 2015). We met with other employees of the city hall and they also commented on the mayor's personalistic management style. "The mayor is very energetic," one city hall employee asserted; "He wants to solve everything. He is everywhere, all the time" (FM., Interview 1, July 27, 2015). Another employee of the local administration echoed similar views: "The mayor tries to deal with everything, wants to make the process faster without often knowing how it actually works. He knows who should be offered a workfare job and sometimes does illegal things to employ persons in the workfare program" (FM., Interview 6, July 29, 2015).

Like many other mayors we encountered during our fieldwork, the mayor of FM. carefully calibrates the strategies used in the distribution of workfare benefits to create a context that enables clientelistic transactions during elections. Consider the interrelated strategies deployed by this mayor seeking to transform applicants for workfare benefits into future political clients. First, he attempted to shape citizens' perceptions of the scarcity of the workfare jobs or, in other words, to manufacture expectations of scarcity. In this case, he enhanced the perception of scarcity by making workfare applicants queue for extended periods of time in front of the city hall. Such expectations about scarcity drive up the "price" of the goods distributed by the mayor and are likely to make voters more willing to enter clientelistic exchanges with him in order to access the workfare program.

Interviews with voters in multiple sites demonstrate that mayors' efforts to shape expectations of scarcity are effective. One respondent in D., a locality in eastern Romania, remarks, "It is hard to obtain social assistance benefits. The mayor resists and one needs to break this resistance" (D., Interview 1, October 22, 2015). Another voter in K., an urban locality in western Romania, believes that it is extremely difficult to obtain a workfare job. "Workfare jobs are obtained with high difficulty and rewarded with a vote" (K., Interview 9, November 28, 2015). For many voters across the region, scarcity is a familiar category, evoking the experience of the communist period when economic survival required the management of multiple forms of scarcity for economic survival.

Second, the mayor in FM. devotes significant efforts to concentrate discretion over the allocation of workfare jobs. The accumulation of responsibilities allows mayors to claim personal credit for the distribution of all benefits or favors distributed by the municipality. Other studies of clientelism have also discussed the importance of the concentration of discretion in political environments characterized by resource scarcity. Judith Chubb noted that "clientelism can survive in resource scarce environments as long as politicians can succeed in convincing voters that they control access to resources [...] In a situation of scarcity, in one in which the margins of survival, already minimal, have been reduced by the economic crisis, [...] the vote is a vote for a concrete connection to the powerful and the possibility of access to the resources that connection represents" (Chubb 1982: 248).

Such mayoral strategies to cumulate obligations also occur in many of the localities in our study. Mayors are eager to micromanage all interactions with voters in an effort to project the image of gate-keeper to the state's resources. One mayor we encountered in T., Romania, proudly asserted his intention to "take care of every decision in the city hall" (T., Interview 1, September 15, 2015). In other localities, mayors choose to tightly monitor the work performance of workfare employees in order to influence beliefs that their continuous presence in the program can be attributed to mayoral discretion.

The third strategy deployed by the mayor in FM. while our team was observing the workfare distribution involved the personalization of benefits. Early scholarship on clientelism highlighted the importance of personalization. In a seminal contribution, Powell notes that "the development and maintenance of a patron–client relationship rests heavily on face-to-face contact between the two parties, the exchanges encompassed in the relationship being somewhat intimate and highly particularistic and dependent on such proximity" (Powell 1970: 412). Mayors use the process of allocation of social policy benefits to shape voters' expectations that access to social policy benefits is not determined on the basis of abstract policy criteria, but, rather, solely attributable to their personal goodwill.

In many of our fieldwork sites, the central component of the pre-electoral strategy pursued by mayors is to establish and cultivate expectations of reciprocity with voters. Such expectations imply that continuing access of workfare benefits not only must be but actually should be reciprocated at the time of elections. On many occasions, mayors directly emphasized these norms of reciprocity during their interactions with social policy beneficiaries or with citizens who requested some administrative approval from their office. In Q., a locality in southern Romania, the mayor reminds all workfare employees that his personal intervention is of decisive importance in making access to benefits possible and that reciprocity is expected. As one respondent in this municipality recalled, the mayor reminds workfare employees, "I will do you a favor and you will return it to me" (Q., Interview 13, September 9, 2015). In FJ., a locality in Hungary, the mayor also seeks to shape expectations of workfare employees, by informing voters that access to workfare employment is not an abstract right but that one that results from "the personal invitation" of the mayor. As one respondent from this locality remarks, "People like to be invited because it matters whether they receive 20,000 HUF, 50,000 HUF or, in better cases, 80,000 HUF" (FJ., Interview 1, October 10, 2015). This respondent also commented on how voters linked their access to workfare benefits to the mayor's personal intervention:

> Roma people were coming to us. And we were talking. And I asked them whom they will vote for. Most of the people considered that we need to vote for N., because a large number of voters receive workfare benefits. And this is what really counts. And everybody said to vote for him, because he offers workfare jobs to people, so he is the driving force.   (FJ, Interview 1, October 10, 2015)

In other cases, mayors formulate their expectations more directly. In FB., another locality in Heves county, Hungary, the mayor used much sharper rhetoric to remind workfare employees that they needed to vote in the correct way if they expected to receive employment in the workfare program. One of our respondents in this locality recalls having been told by the mayor that he needs to "join the party line to access a workfare job" (FB., Interview 2, July 22, 2015).

If such norms and expectations are reinforced during successive interactions between the mayor and social policy beneficiaries, those beneficiaries become an important constituency at elections. One mayor in M., a locality in Teleorman county, Romania, commented cynically on the political use of the workfare program:

> I know cases of other mayors who use the social policy beneficiaries as a mass of voters who can be easily manipulated. To this end, mayors intend to have as many welfare recipients as possible in their locality. In some localities, about four or five hundred persons receive benefits of law 416. This is an important mass of voters that has consequences at elections. If those four hundred voters are on the side of the mayor, he needs to 'hook' two hundred other voters and then he is done.   (M., Interview 5, July 24, 2015)

In addition to facilitating access to the workfare program, mayors in the region retain the monopoly for the distribution of a variety of administrative licenses, which include locality IDs, land titles, and so on. Mayors also serve as the interface between voters and higher-level state institutions, which are perceived by many low-income voters as impersonal and intimidating. In a context of resource scarcity, such administrative resources also become important tools that mayors can use to activate expectations of political reciprocity. In interview after interview, voters recognized the power of mayors to resolve any issue they encountered in their interactions with the state. As one respondent in a Romanian locality noted, "All issues in the locality are solved with the help of the mayor, because he has all the power. If he does not sign, things will not be resolved" (M., Interview 6, July 24, 2015).

Mayors leverage their ability to distribute these administrative resources by transforming routine services provided by the city hall into personalized favors provided by the mayor, which require reciprocation by voters at the ballot box. In the words of one mayor in a southern Romanian locality, "the person will understand that I helped him when he was in need of help and will continue to be close to me" (P., Interview 1, August 21, 2015). As such, mayors treat every single interaction with voters as an opportunity to cultivate loyalty that can be activated at elections. In the words of this mayor, "Everything counts. Everything adds up over time. This is how we transform them into a loyal voter" (P., Interview 1, August 21, 2015).

In neighboring Hungary, mayors also attempt to transform interactions with voters into a source of future political advantage. Here, respondents also considered that administrative decisions made by the mayor involved the "principle of reciprocity" (P., Interview 4, August 21, 2015). A respondent in another locality noted that the cultivation of these expectations of reciprocity throughout the mandate paid off at elections: many voters did not vote "proactively, to enact changes, but to reciprocate for the favors received from the mayor. After you receive favors from the mayor for four years, you place the stamp on the ballot to reward this. The mayor did not coerce people to vote in a particular way, but he told them, 'If I will be mayor I will take care of you just like I have taken care until now'" (T., Interview 4, September 16, 2015).

In addition to these strategies of personalized credit claiming, mayors use their control over the allocation of policy benefits to modify the program's design or to introduce explicit biases in the distribution of benefits. Such biased allocation of benefits results from a variety of decisions, which can either be small in scope or can transform the very design of the program. This strategy has two distinct goals. Its first goal is to strengthen the political loyalty of the narrow groups of voters who benefit from such largesse. But politicized allocation of policy benefits also has a second political audience: the broader community of local voters. Mayors seek to signal to these voters that they retain significant discretion over the allocation of benefits and that a personal and political connection to the city hall is required to access such benefits in future.

Mayors can also bias the allocation of benefits by segmenting access to services or by differentiating the speed with which social policies can be accessed. In using such differentiation, mayors seek to impress on voters the belief that political support is required to access even the most basic services of the local administration. In interview after interview, voters commented on mayors' efforts to segment access to basic services. One voter in FJ., a locality in northern Hungary, remarked that some people obtain licenses and services with no delays, while others experience continuous delays and are told that it is impossible to obtain anything from the city hall (FJ., Interview 2, October 10, 2015). Another form of segmentation results from the decision to allow political supporters to access the workfare program for a longer time period. Several respondents in RM., a locality in Borsod, commented on such a differentiation undertaken by RM.'s mayor: "it is visible that those [who] supported the mayor can be employed in the workfare program for longer periods of time, while those who do not support the mayor cannot access the workfare program for more than two months" (RM., Interview 5, August 22, 2015).

One additional strategy by which mayors personalize the distribution of administrative favors is to maintain a fluid boundary between official policy resources and personal favors. Scholars of clientelism in other political contexts have analyzed such strategies of personalization. Chubb discusses such personalization of services by Christian Democratic politicians competing in southern Italy, by noting that "an able administrator can transform a routine bureaucratic procedure into a personal favor, just as the policeman can exploit the slightest infraction of the law, real or imaginary to create a network of personal obligations" (Chubb 1981: 120).

The mayor of P., the locality in southern Romania, pursued such a strategy of blurring the public–private boundary. The mayor, nicknamed "the American" by the voters in this locality, described the services provided by his administration as follows: "Some voters may need a tractor, some may need sand. You may help them during old age, you may give the correct form to those who receive social assistance and you take it to them in your car. This is how we win their support" (P., Interview 1, August 21, 2015). Here the mayor refers to the practice of this municipality to allow citizens that have experienced a death in their family to use, at no charge, tractors owned by the city hall. In addition, this mayor boasts of giving citizens private loans. If beneficiaries of such favors are late in repaying, the mayor recuperates his money taking the outstanding debt from social assistance benefits. The mayor expects voters to reciprocate by voting for his party in the upcoming parliamentary elections (P., Interview 1, August 21, 2015).

Interviews with voters in localities where mayors blur the distinction between public and private favors show that voters hold such mayors in high esteem. One voter in this locality is extremely grateful to the mayor for "helping with money when he is in need and for distributing social wood during the winter" (P., Interview 2, August 21, 2015). In FJ., a locality in Borsod county, one respondent recalls with gratitude that on the day he was hospitalized the mayor offered his wife 5,000 HUF as a source of extraordinary aid (FJ., Interview 2, October 10, 2015). In blurring the boundary between private and public benefits, mayors seek to create a sense of personal obligation on the part of voters and to counter some of the negative perceptions of their requests for electoral support.

Other respondents in these localities considered that such an electoral strategy premised on the cultivation of loyalties based on personalized favors can be a double-edged sword. The main drawback of this strategy is that voters expect favors from every interaction with the mayor and are quick to punish politicians who do not distribute such favors. As one mayor commented on the riskiness of such strategy, "People come to you and ask you for a favor and you cannot give it, but not because you don't want to. People punish you. You do so much good for them for ten years and then one time you cannot help them and then they punish you" (P., Interview 4, July 24, 2015).

Scholars of clientelism in other contexts have also noted the importance of strategies premised on personal favors. In a study of clientelism in the Philippines, Wurfel noted that politicians widely used individual favors with the goal to "create personal obligation of clients" (Wurfel 1963, cited in Scott 1972b: 109). Examining the functioning of clientelistic exchanges in southern Italy, Pizzorno noted that "the critical element for understanding clientelism is not the concrete exchange relationship, but rather the more general bond that underlies it" (Chubb 1982: 167). According to Pizzorno, this personal link, often institutionalized in the form of *comparaggio* ("ritual kinship") is independent of any specific act of material exchange. Voters continue to vote for a politician even in the absence of immediate material benefits because of their recognition of the future utility of this personal bond" (Chubb 1982: 167). More recent quantitative work involving incentivized games also provides evidence that norms of reciprocity underlie clientelistic exchanges involving positive inducements (Finan and Schechter 2012; Lawson and Greene 2014; Gottlieb 2017).

Mayors direct state policy resources not only to individual voters, but also to informal leaders in the locality, in an effort to induce them to act as brokers and mobilize voters during elections. The most prominent informal leaders in many communities are religious leaders, such as priests or pastors. Mayors direct public resources to churches in the hope of incentivizing their leaders to offer electoral support during elections. Referring to these offers, one candidate competing in D., a locality in eastern Romania, suggested that "such favors generate deep bonds of loyalty between the local priest and the mayor. The mayor needs the priest to mobilize voters, while the priest needs the mayor for a continuous stream of small favors" (D., Interview 4, October 22, 2015).

Romanian mayors grant financial support from the local budget both to the dominant Orthodox Church and to the newly entered Protestant churches. Discussing his support for a church, one former mayor in Romania commented: "The mayor does not finance the activity of priests, but the activity of the parish. The church needs renovations, repainting or a new fence. One can find room in the budget of the locality for these expenses" (O., Interview 7, August 14, 2015). In Q., a locality in southeastern Romania, the mayor also used tax resources to build a house for the priest (Q., Interview 7, August 24, 2015). And the mayor of D., a locality in eastern Romania, used a large amount of money from the local budget to incentivize the leader of the Pentecostal church to act as broker. This community experienced a "religious awakening" between 2009 and 2012, when many voters in the locality joined the newly established Protestant church. At the time of our research, the Pentecostal church in this locality had around 1,800 members, which represented 60 percent of the population of the locality. Around 70 percent of Roma voters in this community left the Orthodox Church and joined the Pentecostal church.

The pastor of the Protestant church confirms that his congregation benefitted from generous support from the city hall (D., Interview 2, October 22, 2015). One employee in the municipality recalled that the mayor helped the church by finding both sponsors and construction materials (D., Interview 3, October 22, 2015). Other respondents pointed also to personal advantages provided by the mayor to the Pentecostal pastors. The pastors were given parcels of land and additional funds to build their private residences (D., Interview 1, October 22, 2015).

The Pentecostal pastor in this locality acknowledges that the church's relationship to the municipality is premised on expectations of political reciprocity: "Yes, it is an advantage to have a good relationship to the mayor and we often help each other. I also ask the mayor for help on many occasions. Afterward, we feel obliged to reciprocate. We know this person has helped us, we need to help him as well and give him our vote. Yes, the church allows us to honor the authorities and to pray for them. This is, of course, not mandatory. But if you want God to welcome this community, you have to pray for the mayor, for the police and for the president of the country" (D., Interview 2, October 22, 2015).

Given that the Romanian legislation prohibits open electoral engagement by leaders of the Church, such support is, in the words of one respondent, "softer" and more concealed.

INTERVIEWER: Are priests influencing how people vote? Do they have such power?

RESPONDENT: They have power, but you know, it is a form of theft.

INTERVIEWER: Meaning?

RESPONDENT: They exert it softly. "So and so would be good for mayor." But they say it in a, you know, religious (*bisericesc*) way.

INTERVIEWER: And they say this during mass or...?

RESPONDENT: No, no, no, the mass is public. They are not allowed to.

INTERVIEWER: Then, when? During the requiem?

RESPONDENT: He comes at times when we pay respects to the dead. At that time, people ask him "What should we do, father?" On these occasions, he would reply. "So and so would make a good mayor." (O., Interview 5, July 24, 2015)

Voters are cognizant of the political exchanges that mayors strike with the local priest in the community. As one voter in this locality describes these exchanges, "The pastor from the church and people from the city hall talk among themselves and then they gather all the voters in the church. And then voters are mobilized with words. I wouldn't say that voters are convinced on the basis of resources, but such resources are used to convince the pastor" (D., Interview 3, October 22, 2015).

The above discussion establishes that clientelistic strategies such as favors rely on very elaborate pre-electoral strategies that unfold during the period between elections. These strategies manufacture the perception that valuable resources are extremely scarce, project the image of mayoral discretion over the distribution of benefits, and cultivate norms of reciprocity amongst voters. Mayors implement these strategies both around the workfare program, as well as other benefits and administrative policies. Yet despite the cultivated perception that mayors have high personal discretion over all policy, the implementation of these strategies requires the cooperation of the broader municipal administration. We next examine how mayors instrumentalize the employees of the local administration for their electoral purposes.

4.2 State Employees as Electoral Brokers

"To be an employee of the city administration you need to know how
to run."   (O., Interview 7, August 14, 2015)

Candidates politicize not only the policy and administrative resources of the state, but also the state apparatus, the employees of the local administration. Potentially, every member of the local administration—accountants, tax collectors, welfare officers, mailmen, policemen, or teachers—can be incentivized to operate as brokers.

The deployment of state employees as brokers is a common occurrence across our fieldwork sites. One of our respondents in V., a locality in southeastern Romania, described the network of such state employees as follows: "The large majority of people who try to influence the choices of voters are employees of the city hall. These include the accountant, the economist, the secretary of the city hall, and the drivers who work for the municipality" (V., Interview 7, October 1, 2015). Discussing the advantages of controlling such a large network of state employees for electoral mobilization across a range of other elections, a school teacher in D., a locality in Romania (who himself operated as a broker), stated, "When you have a large winning team after the local elections, it is very easy for you to compete in the national election. Such competition is easy because you can obtain support of all the local councilors in the community. You cannot imagine how extensive our electoral mobilization can be. Without having these critical people in the local administration, the opposition has to work ten times harder" (D., Interview 4, October 23, 2015).

Candidates and voters across the sites of our fieldwork believe that an implicit part of the public employment contract is the provision of political support. Consider the statement of one former mayor in O., a locality in southern Romania: "Those who submit an application to become part of the local administration know that they will have to participate in the campaign. If you want to become a member of the local administration, you need to know how to run" (O., Interview 7, August 14, 2015). Another respondent in V., Romania, expresses similar views on the mayors' expectations. Employees of the state, this respondent considers, are "obliged, by the terms of their contract, to perform these services, otherwise they will be laid off" (V., Interview 7, October 1, 2015).

Positions in the local administration can come through a variety of forms. Some of these positions are administrative appointments, which are unilaterally controlled by the mayor. Other appointments, such as the teachers, are made at higher administrative levels (such as the county), but can be overturned by mayors. Finally, some positions in the local administration are elected positions in the city council. Here candidates have some control over the selection of the candidates on the list, but not full control over the final selection.

The appointment to these administrative positions is both a reward for past support and payment for anticipated future political assistance. Candidates reserve such positions for past brokers who have performed good services. This was the case in SZ., Hungary, where the incumbent mayor promised access to local employment to the heads of households that offered him public electoral support. After the mayor lost the 2014 election, the newly elected mayor used the same political tactic, by appointing the most loyal and efficient brokers to the municipality (SZ., Interview 7, July 31, 2015).

Similarly, when choosing the list of candidates for positions in the local city council, officials consider the possible advantages of using certain candidates as future brokers and distribute the jobs to those who can maximize the vote share (holding expenditures constant). This echoes Gosnell's considerations about the selection of precinct captains by political machines in Chicago during the 1930s. Gosnell considered that the "roster of precinct captains in a typical ward organization in an American city is made up of persons who in some way have demonstrated their ability to win votes" (Gosnell 1968 [1937]: 53). Discussing patronage machines in Pennsylvania during the same period, V. O. Key also notes that "jobs are distributed to leaders or nominees of leaders, of geographical or functional groups in an effort to the party whatever control these leaders have over their followers" (Key 1934: 37). Our interviews in Romania also suggest that the size of the network that can be mobilized is a crucial consideration for candidates selecting their intermediaries. One broker in a Romanian locality characterized the criteria affecting the final list of city council employees as follows:

> It is very important to appoint members of the local city council who have credibility. Who do we put on the list? Should we put "Mr. X," the one who owns the local store and is a relative of the candidate? And "Mr. X" will accept, because he is interested that his store will work well in future and it is a question of prestige, he will want his relative to be mayor. Who else should we put on the list?

The nephew, because he has a photo camera, he goes to weddings and baptisms and he spreads the word. Who else? The deputy mayor because he was the president of the local agricultural cooperative and he helped many people in the campaign and he comes from a large family."

(D., Interview 4, October 23, 2015)

As brokers, state employees provide political services at all stages of the campaign and the election. During the campaign, they are deployed to persuade voters. On election day, state employees are deployed to bring voters to the polls, to monitor turnout, and to attempt to pierce the secrecy of the ballot. And even after elections are over, employees of the state are deployed to obtain information about the electoral choices of voters and to reallocate policy benefits based on that information.

Consider first the involvement of state employees as brokers during the campaign. One such employee of the local administration who can play a decisive role is the school teacher. We encountered one teacher-turned-broker in E., a locality in central Romania. This teacher had been initially elected to the local city council as a representative of the National Liberal Party, but migrated to the Social Democratic Party after the elections. This teacher recalls with great pride the political services he provides to the mayor during elections: "The school is like an appendix of the city hall," this teacher boasted: "Through my own personal engagement, I help the mayor. I accomplish a lot by talking to parents. But in addition to this, I am responsible for going to various neighborhoods. As messenger of the mayor, I contact a variety of voters" (E., Interview 5, November 5, 2015). This broker explains his political involvement by invoking the advantages it affords his school: "The school has a lot to gain from my friendship with the mayor. The previous mayor did not provide me with the same opportunities as the current mayor" (E., Interview 5, November 5, 2015).

Campaigning in small communities involves finding out about the voting intentions of a large number of people. One such broker recalled how he spent countless hours in public spaces, trying to learn about voters' political preferences: "We knew who votes for the Liberal Democratic Party [i.e., the party of the mayor in this locality], we knew who votes for what councilors, we knew everything." This information played a critical role during the first campaign of the mayor in this locality in 2004, when a challenger defeated the Social Democratic incumbent with a margin of only eighteen votes. The broker takes pride in this victory, but also comments on its downside: "I helped him become mayor. I helped both the mayor and the deputy mayor, an illiterate person with only seven years of schooling" (P., Interview 3, August 21, 2015).

One of the most important roles played by state employees as brokers is the electoral mobilization of voters. V. O. Key's observation about such electoral mobilization (discussing electoral campaigns in the United States during the

1930s) aptly characterizes electoral practices in post-communist eastern Europe: "The will of the people does not rise as a miasma from a swamp. There must be a dissemination of information and now and then downright begging to pace the voters through the tricks of democracy" (Key 1934: 19). State employees play a significant role in this process of "pacing voters through the tricks of democracy." This mobilization can take very elaborate forms. In Z., a locality in southern Romania, employees of the local administration are asked to patrol the street in teams, one taking the left side of the street and the other the right. They approach every household and bring voters to the polling place (Z., Interview 1, November 8, 2016). In R., Romania, employees of the municipality organize a very sophisticated system to pick voters up and bring them to the polls. Coordinators schedule these pickups and let voters know the exact time that employees of the city hall will arrive. Inside the cars, voters are shown a ballot and told how to vote (R., Interview 13, August 21, 2015). Such practices are common in other Romanian localities. As one former mayor of another Romanian locality recalled, "I went with my people and took the elderly voters with me in the car. I had a ballot with me in the car and showed them where they had to vote" (O., Interview 7, August 14, 2015).

Finally, candidates place trusted state employees either as observers in the voting station or even in an official capacity as presidents of the polling section. This in itself in an important asset for the party affiliated with the mayor, who can control the allocation of these responsibilities at the time of the vote. As one former mayor in Romania explained, "The party of the incumbent mayor always wins because they have the majority of persons stationed at the voting place. And they always win because they have the right persons present [at] the voting place" (O., Interview 7, August 14, 2015). When asked whether this initiative is a local one, the mayor reports that such initiative comes from higher levels in the party organization: "The directions to do this come from the top. You can see what is happening to Dragnea [leader of the Social Democratic Party who was being investigated for electoral irregularities committed during the 2014 referendum]. And then those mayors who are more active and more cunning (*isteţ*) find a way to implement these recommendations (*indicaţii*). And those who find a way of doing so are compensated" (O., Interview 7, August 14, 2015).

State employees stationed at the voting place have three distinct responsibilities. The first is to monitor the turnout of their supporters. In FB., a locality in Heves county, Hungary, brokers supporting Fidesz candidates monitored turnout using a booklet that had a list of all known Fidesz supporters (FB., Interview 1, July 21, 2015). The second responsibility of these brokers is to prevent opposition voters from voting. One broker in P., a locality in southern Romania, recalled: "I had a big fight with the Social Democratic Party and the candidate who lost. I told them, 'Don't come to this particular voting section, because I will not let you vote.' My people from the Liberal Democratic Party surround the voting section and we kept track of how everybody voted" (P., Interview 4, August 21, 2015). The third responsibility of such brokers is to exert last-minute pressure on opposition voters to change their voting intentions. One voter commented on this pressure exerted by employees of the local administration as follows:

> Around 70 percent of the people present in the voting station are employees of the local administration who observe how voters vote. These employees observe the different ways in which voters fold their ballot. Those who voted for change [i.e., voted against the mayor] felt they had something to hide and, as a result, they folded the ballot multiple times. One could also see that those who collapsed under pressure did not fold the ballot.   (V., Interview 9, September 29, 2015)

4.3 How Do Voters Evaluate Welfare Favors? Evidence from a Conjoint Experiment

As discussed in Chapter 2, informational theories of clientelism posit that in addition to the direct effect that they have in shaping the material incentives of targeted voters, clientelistic strategies may also fulfill a signaling role. In other words, the use of particular forms of clientelism may allow candidates to send signals about their personal attributes and policy positions on issues that are distributionally divisive in the locality. While clientelistic strategies are normatively undesirable and generally sanctioned by voters, such signals may enable candidates to offset some of this normative undesirability for a subset of ideologically aligned voters.

In Chapter 2, we developed two broad sets of predictions about the use and consequences of signaling strategies. First, we have conjectured that different clientelistic strategies allow candidates to send different signals about their competencies or policy positions. Our theoretical expectation is that the use of policy favors allows candidates to signal a "pro-poor" concern and a commitment to the continuous allocation of social policy resources, rather than reallocation of benefits. By contrast, the use of coercive clientelistic strategies signals that the candidate favors a disciplinary approach towards the poor and supports social policy retrenchment.

As discussed in Chapter 2, we expected to find significant heterogeneity in the assessment of clientelistic practices by different voters. Previous studies have shown that voters' willingness to condone various forms of corruption is affected by their level of income. One possible interpretation for this differential relationship between income and the tolerance threshold for different illicit strategies is that low-income voters may attach a higher weight to the material benefits that are associated with the clientelistic exchanges as compared to high-income voters. We have conjectured that social policy preferences condition voters' evaluations of non-programmatic strategies because clientelism sends informational signals about candidates' social policy platforms. In our view, poorer voters who prefer more extensive benefits view such signals more positively and thus are less willing to sanction clientelistic strategies premised on favors.

Standard survey techniques are generally not an adequate method to investigate voters' attitudes toward different illicit strategies. Considerations about social desirability are likely to affect respondents' incentives to provide truthful answers to such questions. In this chapter, we rely on an experimental choice-based conjoint design to obtain a comprehensive view of how citizens evaluate different clientelistic strategies, while limiting the potential of desirability bias. While conjoint analyses have been used widely in other social science disciplines, they have become an important research strategy in the political science tool-kit only in recent years (Hainmueller et al. 2014, 2015; Carlson 2015). In the conjoint experiment, respondents are presented with realistic portraits of different candidates in which certain attributes, including their use of clientelistic strategies, are exogenously varied. The conjoint thus mimics the context that citizens face at times of elections, which asks candidates to choose one of two candidates, rather than to report their preferences for a single candidate to an enumerator. Respondents are asked to make choices among candidates who are not ideal on every single attribute and thus by design force respondents to prioritize different attributes (Mares and Visconti 2019). Finally, because the two candidates differ along a number of different dimensions, respondents do not have to directly admit to socially undesirable preferences. In this way, conjoint designs can reduce social desirability bias. As such, a conjoint design provides us with the opportunity to evaluate the impact of clientelistic strategies on voters' decision-making, even on sensitive topics like clientelism.

In the experimental set-up of our survey, respondents were presented with descriptions of five pairs of hypothetical candidates. The profiles of the candidates included information on five different attributes: partisanship (ALDE, PNL, PSD, PMP, or USR), prior legislative experience (no legislative experience or legislative experience), experience in the private sector (no private sector experience, private sector experience, or private sector experience and corruption investigation), gender (male or female), and the use of clientelistic strategies (offered voters social policy benefits in exchange for their votes or has *not* offered voters social policy benefits in exchange for their votes).

The survey participants were read the following introduction:

Using your help, we are trying to understand the political preferences of Romanian voters. We will present information that include profiles about some persons who could compete during the parliamentary elections that will be held in December. We present information about two hypothetical candidates whose names could be placed in important positions in two different electoral lists and some information about these candidates. We will ask you some questions about these candidates and ask you to choose one of the candidates, by offering your vote.

Table 4.1 presents an example of two randomly generated profiles of candidates that were included in our survey.

Table 4.1 Experimental design: example of a pair of candidates

Candidate 1	Candidate 2
Candidate has prior legislative experience	Candidate does NOT have prior legislative experience
Candidate has prior experience in the business sector, but is currently investigated	Candidate does not have prior experience in the business sector
Male	Female
National Liberal Party	Social Democratic Party
The candidate has offered voters social policy benefits in exchange for their votes	The candidate has NOT offered voters social policy benefits in exchange for their votes

After the enumerator presented the profiles of the two candidates, each respondent was asked about their intention to vote for a particular candidate and to evaluate the candidates along a number of dimensions based on their personal characteristics and policy positions. These questions allow us to assess whether the clientelistic offer of policy benefits in exchange for electoral support modifies voters' perceptions of the policy positions and personal attributes of candidates who engage in such strategies. In Appendix C1, we provide supplementary information about the demographic characteristics of our sample.

Following Hainmueller et al. (2014), we analyze our data using ordinary least squares with standard errors clustered at the respondent level to take into account the fact that each respondent evaluated multiple pairs of candidate profiles. Our analysis focuses on two quantities of interest: the average marginal component effects (AMCE) and the heterogeneous treatment effects (HTE). The AMCE corresponds to the average difference in the probability of selecting a candidate when comparing two different attribute values (e.g. a candidate who has offered voters social policies benefits in exchange for their votes versus a candidate who has not made such offers). By contrast, the heterogeneous treatment effects evaluate whether the effect of the candidate attributes vary across voters with different individual characteristics.

While clientelistic strategies premised on positive inducements may be considered normatively undesirable by most voters, we expect that the "tolerance thresholds" (Mares and Visconti 2019) for irregularities will vary across voters. As discussed in Chapter 2, income may shape voters' tolerance for clientelism through their social policy preferences. Building on insights of informational explanations of clientelism, we have conjectured that different non-programmatic strategies may carry information about candidates' personal attributes and policy positions. If voters selectively interpret clientelistic strategies as signals of positive personal characteristics or policy positions that correspond with their preferences, they may be less likely to punish candidates who have engaged in this clientelistic strategy.

We test these informational arguments in this chapter by examining whether low-income voters are less likely than high-income voters to negatively evaluate candidates who offer policy favors. Because poor voters generally prefer more redistributive social policy, we expect that they will view candidates who use offer policy favors more positively than wealthier voters do. We examine whether the use of clientelism contributes to a change in the perception of such voters along two dimensions: the candidate's personal attributes and their policy positions. Informational explanations suggest that candidates use clientelistic strategies to affect voters' perceptions of personal attributes, such as their magnanimity. We also conjectured in Chapter 2 that clientelistic strategies premised on positive inducements may signal a candidate's policy position, for example a commitment to policies that redistribute more resources to low-income voters. We test these informational hypotheses by asking respondents to assess different candidate attributes (such as their honesty and their managerial capacities) as well as candidates' willingness to help low-income voters or to help voters in cases of emergency.

In Table 4.2, we present both the average marginal component effects and the heterogeneous treatment effects of the candidate characteristics. Although our main characteristic of interest is the effect of policy favors, we also show the coefficients on the other four dimensions that we vary: the candidate's gender, party affiliation, past political experience, and past business experience. These coefficients are interesting in their own right (and discussed in much more depth in Mares and Visconti 2019) and are presented here to give some context to the magnitude of the effects of policy favors.

In addition to the average effect of policy favors, we are interested in whether voters with different characteristics have distinctive ways of evaluating candidates who use this clientelistic strategy. In particular, in this section we investigate whether poor voters evaluate this positive, public form of clientelism more positively than wealthier voters do. To test for the presence of such heterogeneity, we look at the interaction between voters' self-reported income, inverted such that higher values indicate poorer individuals, and the indicator for being assigned to a profile where the candidate offered policy favors.

We interpret poverty as primarily shaping voters' reactions to clientelism through their social policy preferences, although it is possible that it works through another channel. It is reasonable to assume that poorer voters such as the unemployed and the marginalized Roma minority would like to keep the benefits that they receive under the workfare program. In Appendix C3 we empirically assess whether poverty is a reasonable proxy for pro-welfare

Table 4.2 Income and the social policy signals of policy favors

	Dependent variable		
	Help Low Income (1)	Help in Emergency (2)	Give Jobs (3)
Clientelism: Policy favors	−0.008	−0.037[*]	−0.048[***]
	(0.020)	(0.019)	(0.019)
Clientelism: Policy favors × Poor	0.078[***]	0.054[***]	0.063[***]
	(0.020)	(0.019)	(0.018)
Poor	−0.040[***]	−0.029[***]	−0.031[***]
	(0.011)	(0.011)	(0.010)
Political experience: Legislative	0.034[*]	0.061[***]	0.064[***]
	(0.018)	(0.018)	(0.018)
Business experience: No corruption	0.084[***]	0.060[**]	0.143[***]
	(0.023)	(0.024)	(0.023)
Business experience: Corruption	−0.054[**]	−0.074[***]	0.023
	(0.022)	(0.022)	(0.023)
Gender: Female	0.041[**]	0.041[**]	0.013
	(0.018)	(0.018)	(0.019)
Party: PMP	−0.119[***]	−0.108[***]	−0.086[***]
	(0.029)	(0.029)	(0.029)
Party: PNL	0.014	−0.019	0.001
	(0.028)	(0.028)	(0.029)
Party: PSD	0.103[***]	0.045	0.079[***]
	(0.028)	(0.029)	(0.028)
Party: USR	−0.004	−0.017	−0.038
	(0.029)	(0.030)	(0.029)
Constant	0.469[***]	0.499[***]	0.447[***]
	(0.033)	(0.032)	(0.032)
Individual Controls	✓	✓	
Observations	3,220	3,220	3,220
R^2	0.043	0.033	0.039

*p<0.1; **p<0.05; ***p<0.01

Standard errors clustered by respondent in parentheses.

Models are estimated using OLS. The outcome is a dummy variable indicating that the respondent thought that the candidate profile was better on the dimension under question than the alternative profile with which it was presented. Data is analyzed at the level of the candidate profile such that the full data frame of 3,220 includes ten observations (two from each of five pairs) per respondent. The base case for Clientelism is no policy favors. The base case for Business Experience and Political Experience is no experience. The base case for Party is the ALD. Individual controls include gender, age, education, and a dummy indicating that the respondent supports the PSD.

preferences using the data from our other survey experiments in Romania. We find that income is a strong negative predictor of support for existing welfare programs.

Table 4.2 presents the analysis of these characteristics and the interaction of policy favors with poverty on three different outcomes, all of which measure perceptions of candidates' social policy platforms. The specific outcomes are measured with the following questions:

Help Low-Income: Which of these candidates would help low income people?
Help in Emergency: Which of these candidates would help a person like you if you had an emergency?
Give Jobs: Which of these candidates could create jobs in your district?

The results presented in Table 4.2 lend strong support to the informational hypotheses presented in Chapter 2. First, for the voter at the mean level of poverty (which takes a value of zero on our standardized scale), policy favors generally send negative signals about a candidate's welfare policy platform. The average voter perceives that candidates who offer policy favors in exchange for votes are less likely to help them in an emergency and less likely to create jobs for people in their area. The exception, importantly, is in beliefs about how likely it is that the candidate will help the poor. On this outcome, the average voter does not perceive candidates who offer policy favors as any more or less likely to help the poor than those who do not engage in this form of clientelism. Given the tendency to view clientelistic candidates as worse candidates across the board, the fact that they are not seen as less likely to help the poor suggests that policy favors may carry a strong informational signal of pro-redistributive social policy that cancels out the generally negative signal sent by electoral corruption.

In general, the magnitudes of the coefficients on policy favors are small compared to other characteristics. The effect of business experience (as long as the experience doesn't involve illicit activities), for example, is viewed positively on all three welfare policy dimensions, with magnitudes of 0.06 to 0.14 compared to 0.04 to 0.05 for candidates who offer policy favors. Party affiliation has a much stronger effect on welfare policy perceptions than policy favors. These results suggest that voters logically view clientelism as one of several ways to assess a candidate's social policy platform.

Turning to the heterogeneous effects of policy favors, we find that poverty has large and significant effects on how voters evaluate policy favors. The interactions between policy favors and poverty are all significant at the 1 percent level, and their magnitudes are larger than the main effect of policy favors. Figure 4.1 presents the marginal effects of policy favors at different levels of poverty. The estimated marginal effect of policy favors with poverty as a continuous variable is presented as a gray line with 95 percent confidence intervals shaded in gray, and the estimated marginal effect of policy favors at each of the four categories of poverty are presented as black points with 95 percent confidence intervals.[2] The bar plot on the x-axis presents a histogram of the moderating variable, poverty.

Figure 4.1 shows that the effects of policy favors on perceived welfare policy are much more negative at low poverty levels than at high ones. Importantly, for the 26 percent of respondents with incomes below the poverty line, the effect of policy favors is actually positive, although significantly so in only in a scenario when the candidate will help the poor. The estimates based on the categorical version of the

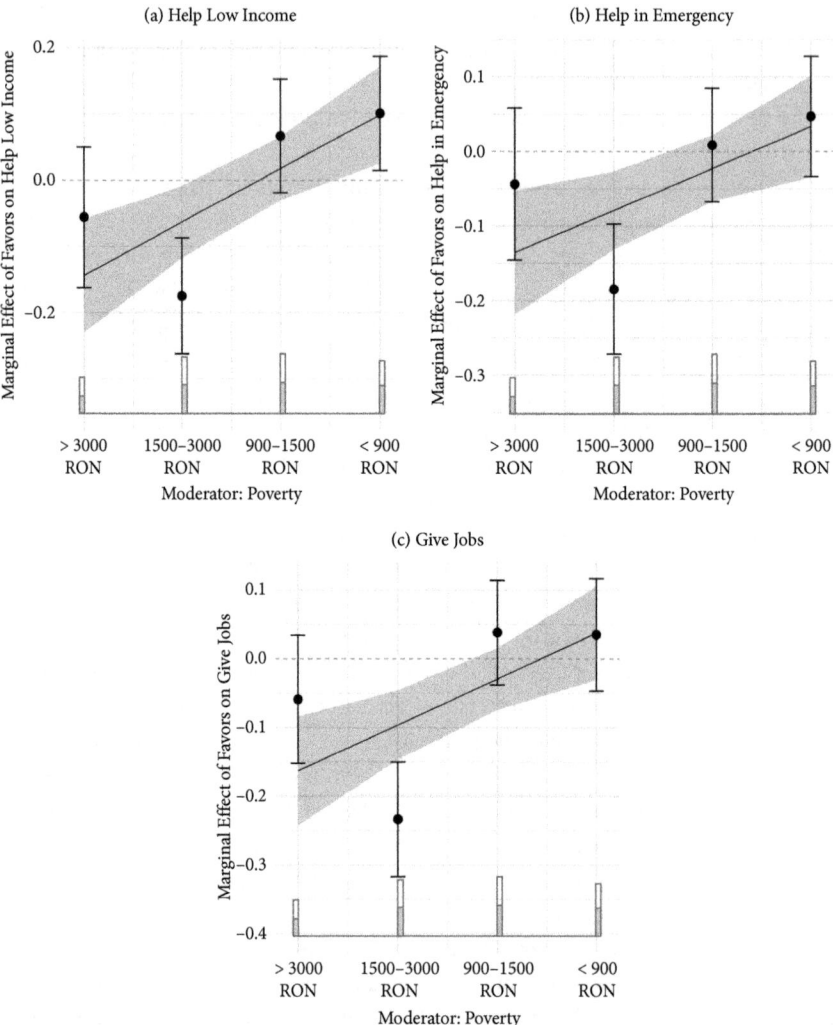

Figure 4.1 The marginal effect of policy favors on perceptions of the social policy positions of candidates at varying levels of poverty

poverty variable show that the effect of the clientelism attribute is not monotonically increasing: specifically, for people in the lowest category of poverty the effects of policy favors are less negative than for people in the second-lowest. However, we do not find this to be a major cause for concern because this very well-off group is relatively small. The results are robust to a binary coding of poverty, as shown in Appendix C6.

Next, we look at the effect of policy favors on voter perceptions of personal candidate qualities. We measure these outcomes with the following questions:

Honesty: Which of the two candidates is likely to be more honest?

Management: Which of these candidates is likely to be a better administrator?

Table 4.3 presents the results of the analysis of the average marginal component effects and the heterogeneous effects on perceptions of these two measures of general candidate quality. The results presented in this table again show that candidates who use policy favors are viewed less favorably by the average voter in terms of these personal characteristics. Profiles of candidates who offer policy favors are 6.4 percentage points less likely to be viewed as the better administrator,

Table 4.3 Income and the personal quality signals of policy favors

	Dependent variable	
	Management (1)	Honesty (2)
Clientelism: Policy favors	−0.064***	−0.129***
	(0.019)	(0.019)
Clientelism: Policy favors × Poor	0.064***	0.077***
	(0.019)	(0.019)
Poor	−0.030***	−0.033***
	(0.010)	(0.010)
Political experience: Legislative	0.058***	0.026
	(0.018)	(0.017)
Business experience: No corruption	0.103***	0.028
	(0.025)	(0.023)
Business experience: Corruption	−0.048**	−0.166***
	(0.023)	(0.023)
Gender: Female	0.037**	0.035*
	(0.018)	(0.018)
Party: PMP	−0.124***	−0.118***
	(0.028)	(0.028)
Party: PNL	−0.033	−0.016
	(0.028)	(0.029)
Party: PSD	0.025	0.052*
	(0.029)	(0.028)
Party: USR	−0.005	-0.013
	(0.029)	(0.029)
Constant	0.499***	0.605***
	(0.035)	(0.033)
Individual Controls	✓	✓
Observations	3,220	3,220
R^2	0.041	0.067

*p < 0.1; **p < 0.05; ***p < 0.01

Standard errors clustered by respondent in parentheses.

Models are estimated using OLS. The outcome is a dummy variable indicating that the respondent thought that the candidate profile was better on the dimension under question than the alternative profile with which it was presented. Data is analyzed at the level of the candidate profile such that the full data frame of 3,220 includes ten observations (two from each of five pairs) per respondent. Individual controls include gender, age, education, and a dummy indicating that the respondent supports the PSD.

and 12.9 percentage points less likely to be viewed as the more honest candidate. Again, these effects vary significantly by poverty status. The interaction of the policy favors treatment indicator and the respondent's poverty status is statistically significant at the 1 percent level and is similar in magnitude to the main effect.

Figure 4.2 again presents the marginal effects at different levels of poverty graphically. The black line indicates the estimated marginal effect from a linear specification, with a 95 percent confidence interval represented in gray. The black dots indicate the estimated coefficients when we treat poverty as a categorical variable, again with 95 percent confidence intervals represented as black bars. The histogram along the x-axis indicates the distribution of the moderating variable poverty, with the number of respondents in each poverty category who were assigned to the control version of the policy favors characteristic in white and the number of respondents assigned to the treatment version (in which the candidate did offer policy favors) in gray.

Figure 4.2 plots the marginal effects of policy favors on perceived personal characteristics at different levels of poverty. Again, there is strong evidence of heterogeneity, both in the linear and categorical specifications. While the poorest respondents are no less likely to think that the candidate using policy favors is honest or a good administrator, those who are less poor are increasingly likely to view candidates using policy favors more negatively on these dimensions.

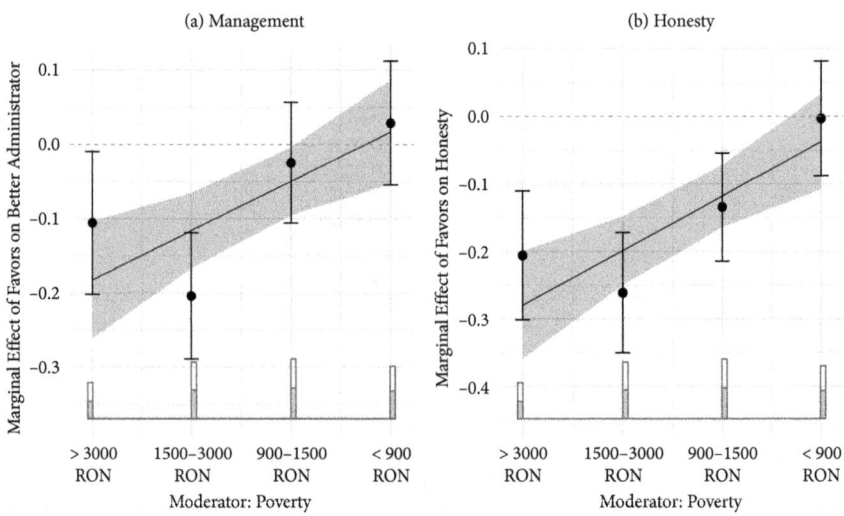

Figure 4.2 The marginal effect of policy favors on perceptions of the personal characteristics of candidates at varying levels of poverty

Finally, we test for the effect of policy favors on voting intentions. We measure voting intentions in this hypothetical scenario by asking respondents the following question:

Vote choice: Which of these two candidates would you prefer for the position of legislator?

Table 4.4 presents the results of this analysis.

Table 4.4 Income, policy favors, and vote choice

	Dependent variable
	Preferred Candidate
Clientelism: Policy favors	−0.109***
	(0.019)
Clientelism: Policy favors × Poor	0.087***
	(0.019)
Poor	−0.041***
	(0.010)
Political experience: Legislative	0.042**
	(0.018)
Business experience: No corruption	0.062***
	(0.022)
Business experience: Corruption	−0.116***
	(0.022)
Gender: Female	0.035**
	(0.018)
Party: PMP	−0.114***
	(0.029)
Party: PNL	0.008
	(0.030)
Party: PSD	0.089***
	(0.028)
Party: USR	−0.003
	(0.029)
Constant	0.547***
	(0.033)
Individual Controls	✓
Observations	3,220
R^2	0.062

*p<0.1; **p<0.05; ***p<0.01

Standard errors clustered by respondent in parentheses.

Models are estimated using OLS. The outcome is a dummy variable indicating that the respondent preferred to vote for the candidate profile than the alternative profile with which it was presented. Data is analyzed at the level of the candidate profile such that the full data frame of 3,220 includes ten observations (two from each of five pairs) per respondent. The base case for Clientelism is no policy favors. The base case for Business Experience and Political Experience is no experience. The base case for Party is the ALD. Individual controls include gender, age, education, and a dummy indicating that the respondent supports the PSD.

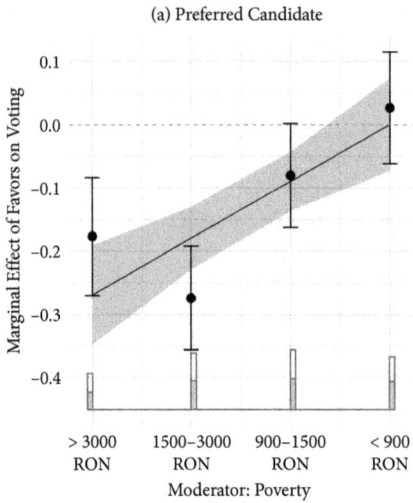

Figure 4.3 The marginal effect of policy favors on the intention to vote for a candidate at varying levels of poverty

Table 4.4 shows that, while the average respondent reports being about 11 percentage points less likely to vote for a candidate who uses policy favors, the effect is significantly smaller for poor voters. Figure 4.3 shows that the poorest voters are no less likely to vote for candidates who offer policy favors in exchange for votes.

In summary, we find evidence of strong differences in the ways that high- and low-income voters evaluate candidates who use policy favors at elections. Consistent with the theoretical predictions formulated in Chapter 2, low-income voters understand policy favors as a signal of a more redistributive policy orientation. Candidates who use policy favors are viewed by the poorest survey participants as being slightly more likely to help low-income voters, but by other respondents with higher incomes as less likely to help low-income voters. We also find that low- and high-income voters differ in their evaluation of the personal attributes of candidates who use clientelistic strategies. High income voters judge candidates who offer policy favors to be worse administrators and less honest people, while low income voters do not update their beliefs about these personal characteristics when candidates use this form of clientelism.

The design of this conjoint experiment also enables us to rule out several alternative explanations for these patterns. First, we can compare the effect of policy-based clientelism to that of corruption not based on public funds and not explicitly tied to political campaigns. In Appendix C6, we compare how low-income voters evaluate electoral clientelism relative to another illicit behavior, namely corruption in business dealings. Respondents to our survey were also asked to evaluate candidates "with prior experience in the business sector but who are currently investigated for irregularities." As the results reported in Appendix C6 indicate, low-income voters do not evaluate candidates that engage in this illicit strategy more positively, especially in comparison to candidates with non-corrupt business experience. Moreover, we find little evidence that corruption in business carries signals of candidates' competence or of their policy position on social policy issues. This suggests that poor voters are not just more tolerant of any kind of corruption, but are specifically more tolerant of state-based, positive clientelism. Second, we can test whether the poor are simply less sensitive to all of the characteristics in the conjoint, perhaps because they are less attentive during the survey. We find little evidence that this is the case: the poor are equally if not more responsive to the other characteristics, including party affiliation, private sector experience, and gender.

In addition to the survey-based evidence, we also found ample evidence that voters located on different sides of the eligibility threshold of the workfare programs evaluate clientelistic strategies that use favors differently. Interviews in FB., a locality in Hungary, can illustrate this systematic variation among voters in their evaluation of policy favors, in this case promises of access to workfare benefits in exchange for policy support. In this locality, the mayor who won during the 2014 local election was a former employee of the social policy administration and relied heavily on his interaction with program beneficiaries to win the election. Many recipients of social assistance benefits (or persons anticipating future access to this program) spoke of the mayor's strategies in very favorable terms. One brigade leader in the public works program considered that new mayor was elected because "he solved many problems of the workfare employees" and that workfare employees "trust him and they think that he will solve every one of their problems as mayor too" (FB., Interview 11, July 23, 2015). By contrast, voters who could not qualify for the workfare program were more critical and hostile to the strategy of the mayor. One of our respondents, who worked as a janitor at the local house of culture criticized the mayor for extending the scope of the workfare program: "he obtained the votes but there is not enough for them to do in the locality and they have a bad working morale" (FB., Interview 13, July 23, 2015).

These findings lend support to the informational explanations of clientelistic strategies presented in Chapter 2. Clientelistic strategies such as the use of policy favors are normatively undesirable. However, such strategies present opportunities for candidates to obfuscate this normative undesirability by signaling a policy concern for low-income voters or their personal positive attributes. Consistent with prior studies, we find evidence of heterogeneity among low- and high-income voters in their evaluation of this clientelistic strategy. In particular, we find that low-income voters evaluate this clientelistic strategy as signaling a more redistributive policy position. These results suggest that positive forms of state clientelism may be a particularly effective strategy for candidates trying to win the votes of large numbers of poor voters who are happy with the status quo distribution of policy benefits. We explore this implication at the local level in the following section.

4.4 Variation across Localities in the Use of Policy Favors

Where do candidates use non-programmatic strategies premised on favors? What are the main social, economic, and political factors that account for the variation in the use of such strategies? In Chapter 2, we conjectured that variation across localities in the incidence of different non-programmatic strategies should be driven by local political and economic conditions that enable clientelism, on the one hand, and by social conditions that influence the signaling opportunities presented by those strategies, on the other hand. In this section, we draw on our survey-based evidence to examine the cross-sectional variation in the use of these strategies.

We proposed two hypotheses about which local conditions might prompt candidates to choose policy favors over other non-programmatic electoral strategies. First, we conjectured that candidates are more likely to use favors in localities where they can access the state's policy resources. The higher availability of such state resources also lowers the costs of favors relative to other non-programmatic strategies. Such "control" over state resources can be facilitated by a variety of political conditions in the locality, including incumbency, co-partisanship between the candidate and the national level party, and representation in local institutions.

Second, we conjectured that the desirability of clientelistic strategies premised on positive inducements, as opposed to coercion, depends on the underlying social conditions in the locality. The allocation of social policy benefits by the mayor and the clientelistic use of these policies is distributionally divisive: many low-income voters who cannot meet the eligibility conditions for workfare benefits are likely to resent the beneficiaries of workfare programs. This latent distributional conflict between persons who are eligible to access the social policy benefits and those who cannot meet the eligibility criteria conditions the attractiveness of clientelistic strategies premised on favors. The use of positive inducements is likely to be an attractive electoral strategy in localities where the underlying electoral coalition favoring social policy expansion is large and where the presence of distributional conflict over the allocation of social policy benefits is small.

4.4.1 Research design

To test these hypotheses, we operationalize local political control (LOCAL CONTROL) using a standardized additive index of three variables, which measure whether a locality has an incumbent mayor, a mayor who is a co-partisan of the national executive, and a united city hall (meaning that the mayor's party also holds a majority in the city council). For all the localities included in our sample, we code these variables using results for the 2010 local election in Hungary and the 2012 local election in Romania. The sources of this data are publications of the Hungarian Electoral Office (*Nemzeti Választási Iroda*) and the Central Electoral Bureau (*Biroul Electoral Central*) in Romania. Appendix B2 presents descriptive information about the variation in these locality level conditions across the localities included in our sample.

We use two variables to operationalize unfavorable local economic conditions. The first variable measures the proportion of residents in poverty (LOCALITY POVERTY). We construct this variable using information provided by the national statistical authorities in both countries that assesses the quality of the stock of houses in each locality (Központi Statisztikai Hivatal 2013a, 2013b, 2013c, Table 4.3.4.3; Institutul National de Statistica 2011). Our second measure of poverty is the proportion of residents who report having debt (DEBT). We construct this variable using responses to the surveys we administered in these localities.

To test our second hypotheses which links distributional conflict over social policy benefits and the incidence of welfare favors, we construct a variety of measures that capture the size of the coalitions favoring social policy expansion and retrenchment, respectively, and the likelihood of distributional conflict over social policy benefits. We use locality-level demographic characteristics collected by the national statistical authorities as part of the most recent census. Given that the distribution of workfare benefits is the most significant divisive issue, we operationalize the coalition favoring policy retrenchment (RETRENCHMENT COALITION) to include both the employed and retirees. In rural areas, retirees rely on noncontributory pensions with very low benefit levels and are likely to be resentful of workfare beneficiaries who can access much higher benefits. We construct the measure of the coalition favoring social policy expansion (EXPANSION COALITION) as including both unemployed and Roma voters. A third variable (SOCIAL CONFLICT) measures the likelihood of locality-level conflict over the allocation of social policy benefits. This variable is constructed using the interaction of the retrenchment and expansion coalition. As such, social conflict takes higher values in localities where the two other coalitions are high. We expect to find a negative relationship between this variable and the incidence of clientelistic favors. We measure the likelihood of social conflict using the interaction of the size of the two electoral coalitions. This interactive measure takes higher values in localities where both electoral coalitions are large. We expect to find a negative relationship between this measure and the incidence of favors.

We also hypothesized that the intensity of social conflict over the allocation of welfare benefits would influence the relative attractiveness of positive and negative forms of clientelism in the eyes of candidates and their brokers. To test this hypothesis, we examine whether the size of demographic groups that benefit or are excluded from the workfare program influences the incentives of candidates to use clientelistic favors.

In Chapter 3, we discussed the empirical difficulties associated with the measurement of clientelism. We also presented our empirical strategy to assess the incidence of these phenomena using list experiments. To measure the incidence of clientelistic strategies premised on favors, we fielded two post-electoral surveys in Romania and Hungary. As discussed in Chapter 3, the Hungarian survey was fielded in the immediate aftermath of the 2014 parliamentary election in ninety communities with a population lower than 10,000 voters. The Romanian survey was fielded in December 2015 and seeks to assess the use of this non-programmatic strategy during the presidential election held in November of the same year. We refer the reader to Chapter 3 and Appendix B for additional details about how the survey was fielded and respondents were sampled within each locality.

In designing our surveys, we pre-tested a variety of items that characterized the brokers deployed by candidates and the goods and favors provided by mayors in exchange for political support in order to phrase the wording of the sensitive question on the survey. We relied on information from qualitative interviews and a list of terms recommended by experts on electoral politics in the two countries to establish a list of possible ways to phrase the sensitive items. We also fielded several pre-tests in each country to choose the control items on the lists. Our pre-tests included, on average, between 100 and 150 respondents.

The lists that included the sensitive questions measuring the incidence of favors were worded as follows.

Hungary

I am going to read some statements of events that happened or could have happened during elections. Please recall the elections of 6 April 2014, and tell me how many of these events happened in your locality. You do not need to tell which ones happened exactly, only how many.

- There were Fidesz posters in my neighborhood.
- None of the parties had posters in my neighborhood.
- I got into a fight over politics.
- (*Sensitive Item*) I expected a favor from the mayors' men in case I voted well.

Romania

I will read a number of statements that refer to the recent presidential elections held in November 2014. For each of these statements, I would like you to tell me how many of these events happened here, in this community. You do not need to tell me which of these happened, but only how many.

- At the polling place, I saw observers from Germany who came to see how the elections are administered.
- When I arrived at the polling place, the polling place was already open.
- Traian Băsescu visited our locality on the day of the elections.
- (*Sensitive Item*) To serve me also in the future, a person employed in the city hall told me how to vote.

In Table 4.5, we report the aggregate results of our surveys. For each country, we present descriptive information on the mean response chosen by respondents who were presented with the version of the survey that included only non-sensitive items ("Control Mean") and of the mean response of respondents who received the version of the survey that also included the sensitive question ("Treatment Mean"). The difference between these two quantities allows us to assess the incidence of the illicit strategies. Slightly more than 5 percent of Hungarian voters have experienced the non-programmatic strategies premised on offers of favors during the 2014 parliamentary election. By contrast, in Romania, during the presidential election held during the same year, 7 percent of voters have experienced non-programmatic strategies premised on favors.[3]

Table 4.5 Estimated incidence of policy favors

Country	N	Control Mean	Treatment Mean	Estimated Incidence	p-value
Hungary	1,817	0.97 (0.95, 0.99)	1.03 (1.01, 1.05)	5.3% (1.4%, 9.1%)	0.01
Romania	1,494	0.99 (0.98, 1)	1.05 (1.03, 1.07)	6.7% (3.8%, 9.6%)	0.00

We analyze the variation across localities in the incidence of these non-programmatic strategies in the following section.

In Figure 4.4, we a map of the estimated incidence of clientelistic favors across the different localities included in our Romanian and Hungarian surveys. Each dot on the map represents a locality where we conducted our survey and is constructed as an average of twenty individual survey responses. Darker dots indicate higher estimated incidences of clientelistic favors, which in the Hungarian sample ranges from no clientelistic favors (which includes some localities where because of random chance the estimate was negative) to a maximum incidence estimate of 60 percent. We have added a small amount of random noise to (or "jittered") the locality coordinates in order to prevent identification.

Figure 4.4 shows that, although there are some visible trends across counties in the incidence of clientelistic favors, the strategy is not strongly geographically concentrated.

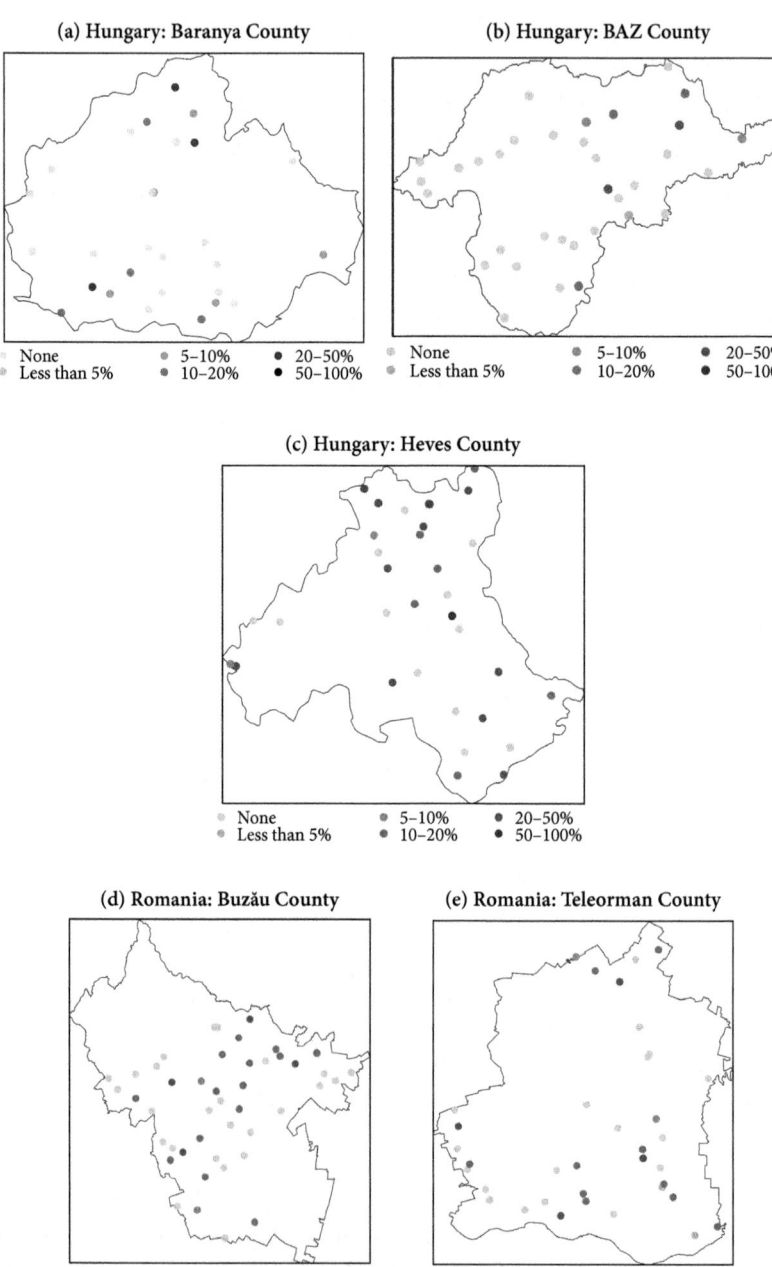

Figure 4.4 Geographic distribution of welfare favors

4.5 Results

We now turn to the analysis of the variation across localities in the incidence of the provision of clientelistic favors that use state resources. We take advantage of the nested nature of our data and use the following specification to estimate the incidence of different non-programmatic strategies for each of the lists in our experiment using mixed models (Gelman and Hill 2007). Let j subscript the different municipalities in our study and i the individual respondents.

$$Y_{ij} = \beta_0 + \beta_1 TREATMENT_{ij} + \beta_2 X_j + \beta_3 X_j \times TREATMENT$$
$$+ \beta_4 Z_i + \beta_5 TREATMENT \times Z_i + a_j + \epsilon_i$$
$$\text{where } a_j = N(0, \sigma_j)$$

The dependent variable Y_{ij} represents the list response for each treatment, subscripted ij for different individuals (i) in different localities (j). $TREATMENT_i$ is a variable that takes the value of 1 for those individuals that have received the version of the questionnaire that includes the sensitive item for each of the sensitive behaviors we are attempting to assess empirically. X_j is a vector of locality-level variables. Z_i is a battery of individual-level characteristics. ϵ_i are the error terms. In this specification, β_2 is the estimated relationship between the variables X_j and the incidence of the control items on the list, while β_3 is the estimated relationship between the variables X_j and the sensitive item of interest.

Table 4.6 presents the results of our multivariate analysis of the incidence of clientelistic favors in both countries. For each of the two countries, we present three different models. The first model represents the central test of our hypotheses outlined above. The second model adds additional locality-level controls. For each country, the third model adds individual-level characteristics of the respondent.

Table 4.6, which presents the results for Hungary, shows that there is little support for our hypotheses about the role of economic and political factors as enablers of positive forms of state clientelism. We find no relationship between the Local Control Index and the incidence of favors. Figure 4.5 presents the coefficients on each of the binary subindicators that make up the local control index. Contrary to our expectations, in Hungary co-partisanship with the national executive is actually related to a statistically significant decrease in the use of favors. The rest of the coefficients are small and indistinguishable from zero. Similarly, favors are not more likely in localities with higher poverty rates or rates of indebtedness.

On the other hand, in Hungary we find evidence of a relationship between the political characteristics that we argued should condition the costliness of positive forms of clientelism for candidates and the incidence of favors. The size of the coalitions favoring the retrenchment and expansion of the workfare program,

Table 4.6 Correlates of policy favors in Hungary and Romania

| | *Dependent variable* | | | | | |
| | **Policy Favors** | | | | | |
	(1)	(2)	(3)	(4)	(5)	(6)
Retrenchment Coalition	0.09***	0.09***	0.09***	−0.002	0.004	0.004
	(0.03)	(0.03)	(0.03)	(0.02)	(0.03)	(0.03)
Expansion Coalition	0.05*	0.05*	0.06**	0.02	0.02	0.01
	(0.03)	(0.03)	(0.03)	(0.02)	(0.02)	(0.02)
Retrenchment × Expansion (Social Conflict)	−0.03**	−0.03**	−0.03*	−0.004	−0.01	0.01
	(0.02)	(0.02)	(0.02)	(0.03)	(0.03)	(0.03)
Local Control	−0.01	−0.01	−0.01	−0.01	−0.01	−0.01
	(0.02)	(0.02)	(0.02)	(0.02)	(0.02)	(0.02)
Poverty Rate	−0.04	−0.05	−0.07	−0.01	−0.004	−0.003
	(0.20)	(0.20)	(0.20)	(0.02)	(0.02)	(0.02)
Debt Rate	0.02	0.02	0.02	0.01	0.01	0.004
	(0.02)	(0.02)	(0.02)	(0.02)	(0.02)	(0.02)
Mayor Margin		0.005	0.01	0.01	0.002	0.004
		(0.02)	(0.02)	(0.02)	(0.02)	(0.02)
Population		−0.004	−0.002		0.01	0.01
		(0.02)	(0.02)		(0.02)	(0.02)
Roma			−0.04			0.04
			(0.04)			(0.04)
Female			0.05			−0.02
			(0.03)			(0.03)
Education						−0.02*
						(0.01)
Age			0.01			−0.01
			(0.03)			(0.02)
Employed			−0.11*			−0.07

			(0.06)			(0.14)
Unemployed			−0.06			−0.14
			(0.06)			(0.14)
Retired			−0.09			−0.05
			(0.08)			(0.15)
Direct Effects	✓	✓	✓	✓	✓	✓
Observations	1,777	1,777	1,669	1,439	1,439	1,424
Akaike Inf. Crit.	1,258.95	1,287.12	1,190.75	594.36	626.80	723.02
		Hungary			Romania	

*p<0.1; **p<0.05; ***p<0.01

Standard errors in parentheses.

Models are estimated using a multilevel model with intercepts varying by locality. The coefficients shown are from interactions with the list treatment indicator. Local Control is an additive index of indicators that take a value of 1 if the locality has a mayor who is an incumbent, a co-partisan with the national executive, or from the same party as the plurality in the city council. Retrenchment Coalition is the average of the standardized proportions of the anti-workfare constituency: the employed and retirees. Expansion Coalition is the average of the standardized proportions of the pro-workfare constituency: the unemployed and Roma. Retrenchment X Expansion is the interaction of the pro- and anti-workfare constituencies. Poverty Rate is the proportion of inhabitants who are below the poverty line. Debt Rate is the proportion of survey respondents by locality who reported being in debt. Mayor Margin is the margin of victory of the mayor. Population is the population size. Roma, Female, Age, Employed, Unemployed, Retired, Debt and Poor are individual-level variables coded from our surveys. All but Age and Poor are binary. All continuous variables are standardized.

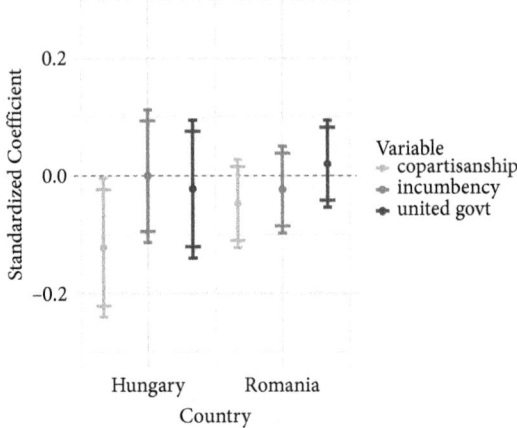

Figure 4.5 Coefficients on sub-indicators of the local control index

respectively, are both positively associated with policy favors. The interaction of the size of the retrenchment and expansion coalitions, our proxy for social conflict, is negatively and significantly associated with the incidence of policy favors. Figure 4.6a plots the marginal effect of a one standard-deviation increase in the size of the expansion coalition at varying levels of the retrenchment coalition in Hungary to illustrate this interaction term. The gray shaded area represents 95percent confidence intervals for the linear estimate of this marginal effect, and the black dots and vertical lines represent estimated marginal effects when the retrenchment coalition is split into five equally sized bins. The gray histogram on the x-axis plots the distribution of the moderating variable, Retrenchment Coalition. Although the estimate is noisy, this figure shows that in Hungary an increase in the size of the Expansion Coalition is associated with an increase in the incidence of Mayor Favors, and that the size of this relationship decreases as the Retrenchment Coalition gets larger. Substantively, these results imply that increases in the size of the workfare expansion coalition are associated with large differences in the incidence of policy favors when the workfare retrenchment coalition is small, but these effects disappear when more of the electorate is made up of groups that oppose the existing distribution of social policy.

In contrast to Hungary, our hypotheses fail to explain the variation in the incidence of favors in Romania. There are no systematic relationships between the social, political, or economic variables and the incidence of policy favors in Romania. Figure 4.6b also demonstrates this visually: there is no apparent relationship between the size of the Expansion Coalition and the incidence of Policy Favors, regardless of the size of the Retrenchment Coalition, in the data from Romania.

These null results could be caused by either of two scenarios. First, it's possible that the test we ran in Romania was less sensitive than the test we ran in Hungary.

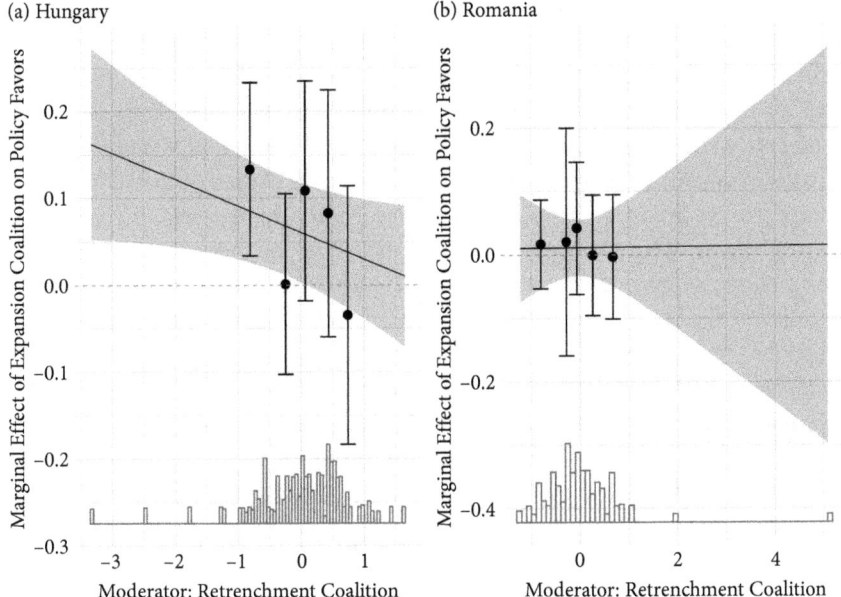

Figure 4.6 Marginal effect of a one standard-deviation increase in the Expansion Coalition at varying levels of the Retrenchment Coalition on Mayor Favors

This could mean that the true effect is not zero, but our tests nevertheless have failed to detect it. List experiments are notoriously noisy outcome variables. In Romania we have a smaller sample of individuals (around 1,400 versus almost 1,800 in Hungary) that covers fewer localities (86 versus 94 in Hungary). The smaller number of localities is particularly important because our main explanatory variables of interest are at the locality level. In general, however, there are signs that the statistical power of our tests on the two different samples is comparable. As shown in Appendix B4, the control items on the lists in Romania and Hungary are similarly centered around 1 and have similar standard errors, which influences the precision of the lists (Glynn 2013). There is more variation on most of the locality-level demographic variables in our Romanian sample than in Hungary, which should make the test slightly more sensitive in Romania. One important exception is the data on the share of Roma residents by locality: our Romania data has less variation than in Hungary and is known to grossly underestimate the Roma population. Nevertheless, the estimates of our main coefficients of interest shown in Table 4.6 are similarly "noisy," meaning that their standard errors are similarly wide, across Hungary and Romania. Thus, we think that it's unlikely that the null effects in Romania are only caused by a lower-sensitivity test.

The second explanation for these null results is that the true relationship between these locality-level variables could be close to zero in Romania but not in Hungary. If this is the case, it may also be an idiosyncratic feature of the 2014 election, given that our survey was fielded in the weeks after this election and our questions asked specifically about exposure to clientelism during the last campaign. At the micro level our evidence shows that voters in Romania are sensitive to the policy signals of positive versus negative manipulation of state resources. However, Romanian politicians may nevertheless have chosen not to tailor their strategies to variation in voter coalition sizes at the local level. The extreme competitiveness of the race, which was eventually won by the outsider candidate Klaus Iohannis, may have created unique incentives for all mayors to use resources of the state to appeal to voters. In addition, vote buying was heavily and publicly prosecuted before this election, creating an incentive to substitute out of vote buying into strategies that leverage public resources. Our later chapters will show that Romanian politicians did not use private forms of clientelism in this election. We suspect that these electoral considerations attenuated some of the locality-level variation in the use of favors, thereby equalizing mayoral incentives to use this strategy.

4.6 Conclusion

This chapter has documented the use of clientelistic strategies that politicize the resources of the state in recent elections in Hungary and Romania. We began by situating the cases in the comparative literature examining the electoral use of state resources. The policy environment in both Hungary and Romania, we argue, is not one of resource abundance but one of resource scarcity. Political parties and their brokers in different localities can exploit only a limited amount of policy resources of the state to incentivize the electoral choices of voters. Among such resources, the most significant program is the anti-poverty program or workfare.

Using a wide range of interviews with mayors, brokers, and voters in both countries, we documented the most significant strategies used by candidates and brokers that politicize state resources to influence voters' electoral choices. We began by documenting crucial pre-electoral strategies used by candidates to establish norms of reciprocity to voters which can then be exploited at elections. Such strategies include personalizing the distribution of policy benefits and creating expectations that future access to policy is dependent on personal connections to the mayor. At the time of an election, candidates rely on a variety of state employees to mobilize voters to the polls, observe their turnout, and exploit imperfections in voting technology to monitor vote choice.

Using a conjoint experiment administered in Romania, we tested the micro-level predictions of our informational explanation of this clientelistic strategy. We find that voters with different levels of income evaluate candidates that use state resources in exchange for electoral support very differently. While higher-income voters are likely to punish candidates that use this clientelistic strategy, lower-income voters seem generally indifferent to offers of policy favors. More significantly, we find that low-income voters evaluate clientelistic strategies that use state resources as a signal of pro-poor concern of such candidates. While higher-income voters view candidates who offer policy favors as worse across a range of characteristics, low-income voters have much higher "tolerance thresholds" for this form of electoral corruption, and in some cases view candidates who offer policy favors more positively than those who do not. These findings provide strong support for the weak form of the informational argument, which posited that certain types of voters should be less likely to view candidates who use clientelism as less desirable. It also finds support for the strong form of the informational argument, which posits that acts of clientelism can actually make candidates look more desirable in the eyes of some voters.

In the concluding section of the chapter, we drew on post-electoral surveys administered in Romania and Hungary that make use of list experiments to document the use of clientelistic strategies that involve policy favors. We find evidence supporting our distributional explanation of clientelism in Hungary, but not in Romania. Consistent with our hypothesis, in Hungary mayors are less likely to offer favors in localities where the potential for social conflict is lower. In Romania, however, we find that favors are used at a fairly equal rate across the types of localities that we study, perhaps because in the 2014 election the incentives to politicize state resources rather than buying votes with private resources were particularly strong. In the following chapter, we turn to the analysis of a related non-programmatic strategy that uses social policy benefits not as positive inducements but as a form of coercion. In contrast to favors, we conjecture that the political incentives to use coercion are higher in localities characterized by a strong distributional conflict over the allocation of policy benefits.

Notes

1. Throughout this book, we give pseudonyms to individuals who participated in our qualitative interviews in order to protect their privacy. All of our quantitative surveys were anonymous. Because the small number of local officials in rural municipalities implies that individuals could be identified by their locations, we denote localities where we conducted quantitative or qualitative interviews using one or two-letter codes that were randomly assigned.

2. Presenting binned estimates helps assess whether the linear relationship that is forced upon the data by interacting the treatment indicator with a continuous moderator is actually justified (Hainmueller et al. 2016). In our case, the binned estimates suggest that a linear specification is generally an appropriate fit for the data.

3. In related research, we have collected data on the incidence of policy favors at election time in urban areas in Bulgaria and Romania. These results allow us to benchmark the results of the survey fielded in a large number of rural localities. The Bulgarian survey was fielded in June 2013, in the aftermath of the parliamentary election held in May of the same year. The Romanian survey was fielded in 2013 and measures the incidence of non-programmatic strategies that took place during the 2012 parliamentary election. In both cases, we measured the incidence of favors using questions that are worded very similarly to the questions fielded during the 2014 surveys. The results of these initial surveys provide a useful benchmark and comparison to the results discussed in this chapter. For the Romanian case (for which we have data across multiple elections), we found that 6 percent of voters in our urban sample (N = 3,576) experienced an offer of a favor from the mayor's office. In Bulgaria (N = 2,768) we found an estimated incidence of favors of 13 percent. These results suggest that the incidence of non-programmatic strategies premised on favors is similar across rural and urban communities.

5

Policy Coercion

Social Conflict and Control

Angela is a 55-year-old woman living in V., a rural locality in southern Romania. She recalls with nostalgia the Communist period, when she worked at the mechanical station of the local agricultural cooperative. At the time we met her, in the fall of 2015, Angela was without employment. Her only source of income was the benefit she received from the social assistance program, an amount that did not exceed 80 RON [approximately 20 dollars] per month. Angela yearns for a regular job to end her dependency on the social assistance program: "I have hands and feet and would like to work to receive the minimum wage, but there are no jobs in this locality" (V., Interview 1, September 30, 2015).

Angela is not happy with the performance of her political representatives, but she does not voice her dissatisfaction at the ballot box. Angela's economic dependence on social assistance benefits makes her vulnerable to coercive threats at the time of elections. On a recent parliamentary election day, employees of the city hall rounded her up in a car and took her to vote, even though she was sick and expressed her desire not to vote. She doesn't remember what candidate or party she voted for, but only remembers she "followed the instructions of those who work in the city hall." We asked what would have happened if she had refused to vote: "I would have lost all my benefits," she replied (V., Interview 1, September 30, 2015). Another respondent in the locality reaffirms the extensive threats made by the mayor in this locality: "The mayor threatened beneficiaries of the social assistance program to cut their benefits if they do not vote for this or that candidate" (V., Interview 2, September 30, 2015).

In this chapter, we examine the conditions in which politicians use social policy benefits to coerce beneficiaries to change their voting behavior. The politicization of the welfare state is a powerful form of clientelism not only because it expands the resources available to politicians, but also because it is easy to use coercively. Mayors who act as political brokers for candidates competing in parliamentary or presidential elections may threaten voters who depend on access to the workfare program or on public employment in the municipality with interruption of future income streams if they do not vote for the candidate supported by the mayor. Voters who expect this continuous stream of future benefits perceive such threats as losses. Given the importance of such benefits—such as the 140 RON that one receives for basic income support—voters believe that they have no choice but to comply.

Social policy programs in the region have been designed to grant mayors an important role over the allocation of important social benefits. This enables politicians to structure incentives as threats to take away vital benefits on which voters depend. Such politicization of the welfare state can incentivize voting behavior even when monitoring is weak. In both Hungary and Romania, workfare programs represent the main public policies used by mayors who engage in coercive electoral strategies. In Chapter 3 we discussed the origin of these programs and reasons that post-communist governments are increasingly conditioning benefits on work participation. Such changes in the design of social programs are not unique to these two countries, but are instead part of a broader policy shift across the region. These measures were adopted alongside legislation that increased mayors' discretion over the distribution of social policy benefits and made anti-poverty benefits conditional on work requirements. These changes established the preconditions for the coercive use of the workfare program at elections.

Chapter 2 formulated two families of hypotheses about the factors that affect the cost–benefit calculations of candidates and brokers towards different non-programmatic strategies. Theories focused on the supply side of clientelism predict that the choice between clientelistic strategies that deploy public versus private resources should be affected by the relative availability of such policy resources in the locality. We predicted that access to the policy resources of the state should be more likely in localities where local political conditions provide candidates with control over the allocation of policy benefits.

On the other hand, we argued that different forms of clientelism send signals about candidates' programmatic positions that can offset the electoral costs associated with clientelism. While clientelistic policies premised on positive policy inducements may signal pro-poor concern or a commitment to a further expansion of social programs, coercive clientelistic strategies allow candidates to signal their policy opposition to the current distribution of social policy benefits and support for retrenchment of existing programs. We have conjectured that the value derived by candidates from these coercive strategies is higher in localities where access to social policy benefits is a source of conflict. Social policy programs that offer highly valuable political resources to a narrow subgroup of policy beneficiaries are likely to engender conflict between those who are eligible for the benefits and those who are not. We refer to this conflict as pitting poor against poor voters. We conjecture that mayors will find non-programmatic strategies premised on coercion particularly attractive in localities where such conflict over the allocation of social policy benefits is high. In these conditions, coercive forms of clientelism are less likely to be punished by voters who are opposed to the current distribution of social policy because threatening to remove policy benefits from the "undeserving poor" is in line with their policy preferences.

In this chapter, we present three forms of evidence on electoral coercion that, taken together, illustrate how and where candidates use electoral strategies premised on welfare coercion when competing in low-income communities. First, we present qualitative evidence from interviews with candidates, brokers, and voters in forty communities in both Hungary and Romania that illustrates in rich detail how welfare coercion is carried out. Our qualitative research documents the variety of "micro-strategies" used by mayors during the pre-election period to create the potential for electoral coercion, and their efforts to incentivize individual voting behavior during elections. Second, we present evidence from a survey experiment showing that voters receive signals of candidates' policy positions and personal characteristics from the forms of clientelism that they use. Finally, we use evidence from surveys with a total of 3,300 citizens that use list experiments to measure the prevalence of welfare coercion in 180 localities across Hungary and Romania during the parliamentary (Hungary) and presidential (Romania) elections held in 2014.

Altogether, the evidence presented in this chapter suggests that demand-side factors that shape the electoral costs of clientelism are an important predictor of where and how clientelism is used. We first document the use of clientelistic policies that are much more exploitative than assumed in the dominant political economy literature on clientelism. Consistent with the predictions of our signaling theory, voters with anti-workfare preferences are less likely to perceive candidates who use coercion as having undesirable policy positions and personal characteristics. Finally, we find that the use of coercive strategies is higher in localities where a sizable political constituency opposing the current allocation of welfare benefits exists. In such communities the use of welfare coercion allows mayors to expropriate the votes of vulnerable voters, while getting away with the politicization of policy benefits by signaling to anti-workfare voters a willingness to use an authoritarian management style to reallocate social policy to the "deserving" poor.

5.1 Welfare Coercion in the Menu of Non-Programmatic Strategies

Beginning with research by René Lemarchand (1972) and James Scott (1972b), scholars have recognized the importance of coercion in clientelistic relationships. However, most scholars of clientelism have not differentiated between the use of positive and negative inducements to motivate voters. This is particularly true in the recent political economy literature on clientelism, which has focused heavily on vote-buying transactions that each party enters into willingly (Mares and

Young 2016). Positive inducements, a category that includes vote buying, involves offers of rewards such as money, goods, or favors. Negative inducements include the threat of economic or physical sanctions for an individual's voting behavior. Such negative inducements include cutting voters off from benefits on which they depend, removing them from their land, or firing them from jobs that are their livelihoods.

As discussed in Chapter 2, coercive strategies differ from inducement-based strategies in fundamental ways. First, these strategies place voters in the domain of losses. In using coercion, brokers threaten to take away a good or a stream of income that voters expect to receive, and on which recipients depend for basic survival. In this way, coercive strategies worsen the baseline condition of a voter. In contrast to offers to buy a vote, coercive strategies are not transactions into which voters can enter freely. Therefore, strategies premised on coercion have more severe normative implications than illicit but consensual exchanges of positive inducements for votes.

More recent approaches to the study of clientelism downplay the importance of coercion in the menu of non-programmatic strategies. The theoretical justification for this omission provided by existing studies is that clientelistic exchanges can be understood as an infinitely repeated exchange between brokers and voters. Coercive strategies are the grim trigger strategy in this infinitely repeated game (Stokes 2005). The implication of such a conceptualization of clientelistic exchanges is that there is no need to study coercion as a separate strategy from the provision of positive inducements. In this framework, both machine operatives and weakly opposed voters find themselves in a Prisoner's Dilemma, wherein one player's defection triggers the brokers' decision to cut the voter off from all future benefits.

We argue that such results rest on two assumptions that can be reconsidered and should be relaxed. One assumption concerns the symmetry in the response of voters to positive inducements versus coercion. In the example discussed above, voters react in similar ways to gains and losses, as both gains and losses enter the utility of voters linearly. As we pointed out earlier, however, findings from behavioral economics suggest that the change in voter utility differs across the domain of gains and the domain of losses such that voters lose more utility from losses than they gain from commensurate gains. If brokers anticipate this asymmetric response, they may try to exploit this loss aversion.

Second, we must reconsider the assumption that the electoral costs incurred by candidates who engage in positive clientelistic inducements and coercion are symmetrical. A variety of studies suggest that politicians may incur differential costs for pursuing positive or negative strategies. One source of asymmetrical costs is voters' normative beliefs. Using experimental survey-based methods, several studies have shown that voters punish more severely candidates who engage in coercive clientelistic strategies than those who engage in vote buying (Mares and Visconti 2019; Mares and Young 2016; Mares and Young 2019).

At the same time, differences across voters may condition the extent to which inducements and coercion are perceived as violating norms. In particular, voters' economic or social characteristics, or their ideological predispositions, may condition the extent to which voters punish politicians who use inducements and coercion. In many communities, social assistance programs with particular target populations result in conflict between eligible and ineligible citizens. In these contexts, voters may punish candidates who offer highly desirable goods to a particular group if they anticipate that their own likelihood of accessing these goods is low. On the other hand, they may be less likely to punish politicians who threaten to retrench these benefits by cutting beneficiaries from these programs. Such considerations are important in explaining the relative costs politicians face in using social policy resources either as favors or as coercion. In short, candidates will have stronger incentives to rely on non-programmatic strategies premised on coercion in localities with large constituencies of voters who are ineligible for the workfare program and especially where social conflict over benefits is strong.

5.2 Welfare Coercion in Contemporary Elections

James C. Scott noted that there is hardly any linguistic shortage when it comes to expressing the notion of exploitation (Scott 1990: 187). The same can be said about coercion. While welfare and economic coercion are pervasive non-programmatic strategies across the region, respondents use a wide range of terms to describe their experiences. During our first focus group, conducted in Focșani, a town in Vrancea county, Romania, we distributed blank pieces of paper and asked participants to write down various illicit strategies used by candidates at elections and to rank them according to their prevalence. The majority of respondents in this focus group ranked "psychological intimidation" as the most pervasive non-programmatic strategy they experienced. Other voters referred to coercive strategies such as intimidation, harassment, pressure, or subjugation.

Such diversity in language points to the wide heterogeneity in the types of coercive strategies used. We begin with a brief presentation of the variety of coercive strategies that involve state policy resources as part of the exchange between candidates, brokers, and voters. In Chapter 6, we turn to a discussion of strategies of economic coercion. In the case of this strategy, brokers are economic actors (such as landholders, employers, or moneylenders) who threaten voters with worsening the terms of the ongoing economic exchange if voters' electoral behavior is undesirable. Our discussion draws on qualitative interviews with candidates, brokers, and voters conducted between May 2015 and October 2016 in Hungary and Romania. To protect the confidentiality of our respondents, we anonymize the names of the localities and of the respondents.

The modal form of welfare coercion consists of threats used by mayors and brokers operating on their behalf that access to policy benefits will be cut if voters do not support a particular candidate or if they decide to abstain. Let us consider some examples that illustrate the use of this strategy. Simona is a 54-year-old woman of Roma origin living in V., the locality in southeastern Romania. At the time of our interview, Simona received social assistance benefits from the city hall. The situation was different a few years ago. At the time, Simona recalls that both she and her husband came into conflict with the mayor after complaining about irregularities in the distribution of assistance benefits in the locality. The mayor retaliated by cutting their social assistance benefits. For Simona and her family, this was a hard lesson. After this event, she decided that the only solution for survival is "to do what the other Roma people in the locality are doing, show less resistance and 'shut up' in order to receive social assistance benefits. There are a few Roma people who have voted for Johannis [the candidate for presidential election not supported by the mayor], but they have lost access to social policy benefits because of this." She concludes that "there is nobody in the locality who can stand up to the mayor. He controls everything, the police and the priests" (V., Interview 2, September 30, 2015).

One way that mayors make coercion more socially acceptable and effective is by justifying it through claims of voters' failure to adhere to program rules. This is important because, as survey evidence has shown, voters have strong normative preferences against coercive strategies (Mares and Visconti 2019; Mares and Young 2017). We call this form of coercion blackmail because it exploits misconduct by voters to incentivize specific behavior. Mayors implement electoral strategies based on blackmail in two steps. First, during the pre-electoral period, mayors create situations that permit the use of blackmail by engaging in forbearance, or decisions to forgo the enforcement of laws (Holland 2016). Such irregularities may include non-compliance with tax obligations, irregularities in accessing policy benefits, or other violations of the law, such as theft. In the case of workfare coercion, the most common type of forbearance is the non-enforcement of the requirement that recipients work. This forbearance increases the future vulnerability of voters who have committed some irregularity to blackmail.

Second, at election time, candidates and their brokers exploit the vulnerabilities that they have helped create. The use of blackmail involves threats to expose these irregularities and therefore end voters' ability to engage in the illicit activity, and to oblige them to make repayments or face other punishments for previous offenses. Mayors or state employees remind voters that their past irregularities have been duly recorded and will be punished in future. One such example of blackmail we encountered during our fieldwork is the threat that voters who have avoided their fiscal obligations will owe their entire unpaid tax bill if they vote for an undesirable candidate (R., Interview 4, October 23, 2015). Another example of this strategy is the threat that future access to social policy benefits will be rescinded for voters who have committed irregularities in accessing them.

To illustrate the electoral use of blackmail, consider the example of Q., a locality in Teleorman county, Romania. At the time of our fieldwork, 500 people, or 16 percent of the locality's population, received workfare benefits. This high number of workfare beneficiaries resulted from the decision of workfare officials to implement only very loosely the work requirements that were demanded by the Romanian workfare legislation. The Romanian workfare legislation (law 416) requires workfare beneficiaries to clean public spaces and help with the renovation of official buildings, such as the school or the kindergarten. The deputy mayor was responsible for monitoring the work performance of social assistance beneficiaries. One former employee of the municipality commented, however, that such verification of work was rare: "The deputy mayor usually gathers around sixty workfare employees in the morning for a project, checks their presence and lets them disappear on the way to work." This respondent maintained that the decision to grant social assistance benefits without requiring work was a deliberate strategy of the mayor to increase the continuing dependence of workfare employees on the city hall: "It is a form of slavery, a way in which the city hall keeps these persons under control" (Q., Interview 15, April 9, 2015). During elections, the mayor of this locality exploited this vulnerability by reminding workfare employees of the irregularities they had committed in accessing policy benefits. Several respondents commented on the use of such a strategy and reported that the mayor campaigned "based on influence and fear" and that "social assistance beneficiaries are particularly fearful of the mayor" (Q., Interview 1, April 9, 2015).

5.2.1 Pre-electoral strategies

To deploy welfare coercion effectively, a mayor uses a variety of strategies during his mandate. Such strategies seek to deepen the sense of vulnerability of social policy beneficiaries and the belief in their complete dependence on the goodwill of the mayor. In the following, we discuss three such pre-electoral strategies. These strategies seek to increase voters' perceptions of the arbitrariness of the mayor, which is likely to facilitate submission and weaken political resistance.

Other strategies deepen the economic dependence of workfare recipients on mayors, which contributes to the formation of quasi-feudal relations of dependency. Finally, mayors pursue a variety of strategies that lay the groundwork for the electoral use of blackmail. Such strategies include tolerating or actively encouraging activities that violate legal provisions with the goal of blackmailing offenders at the time of the election.

5.2.1.1 Projecting external power

Coercive threats are more credible if voters believe that mayors have unlimited discretion over the allocation of workfare jobs and other employment opportunities in the locality. To establish and cultivate this perception, mayors find it advantageous to project an image of capriciousness, arbitrariness, and, often, ruthlessness. Following Scott, we refer to these pre-electoral strategies as efforts to "project external power" (Scott 1990). In Scott's insightful analysis, coercion rests on the systematic personal humiliation of persons situated in a relationship of dependence (Scott 1990: 112). This weakens voters' sense of self-efficacy and lowers their propensity to resist. Such systematic humiliation of voters in their everyday interactions with local officials is a common occurrence in many of the rural localities where we conducted our fieldwork.

One way that mayors project external power is by inflicting arbitrary acts of punishment on voters who come into contact with the local administration. Voters of HN., in Borsod county, Hungary, refer to the mayor of the locality as tyrannical and arbitrary. One voter in this locality recalls having been dismissed from the public employment program with no prior justification (HN., Interview 8, July 26, 2015). In this locality, we also witnessed a violent verbal exchange between the mayor and a workfare employee triggered by the mayors' objection to an insignificant detail in the behavior of the workfare employees; this dispute resulted in the dismissal of this person from the workfare program (HN., Interview 5, July 23, 2015). In SZ., in Heves county, Hungary, one retired voter recalls a similarly capricious decision of the mayor: "My wife had five days left before retiring from her job. The mayor called her telling her that she had to complete these remaining days of work. She requested to maintain her job as a cook at the community kitchen, but was instead sent to the potato fields and asked to work there for the remaining five days" (SZ., Interview 5, July 18, 2015). These arbitrary punishments create a perception that mayors have enormous personal power over voters.

Another component of these attempts to project external power is the verbal humiliation of welfare beneficiaries and other people who come into contact with the city hall. The use of abusive language by local politicians in Hungary has been the object of research by Hungarian sociologists in recent years (Zolnay 2012; Szombati 2016). In a recent study of local discrimination in northeastern Hungarian localities, Janos Zolnay has shown that local politicians systematically use aggressive racist terms in referring to social policy beneficiaries (Zolnay 2012). Kristóf Szombati's study of right-wing political mobilization in rural Hungarian communities also documents the abusive racist language used by welfare officials during their day-to-day interactions with Roma voters (Szombati 2016).

Respondents whom we encountered in our own research also reported the use of abusive language by public authorities. One workfare employee in SZ., in

Borsod county, Hungary, described interactions with authorities in the city hall as "repressive and humiliating" (SZ., Interview 1, July 16, 2015). The mayor of this locality addressed workfare employees using highly charged racist language. In HN., a locality in northern Hungary, one respondent reported that the mayor systematically showed "verbal disrespect" to him and other workfare employees. Another respondent in this locality considered that the mayor intentionally humiliated all workfare employees who come into contact with the city hall (HN., Interview 5, July 23, 2015). We witnessed one such scene of verbal humiliation of workfare employees during our fieldwork in this locality. At the time, one employee of the workfare program complained to the mayor about the "inhumane working conditions," including the lack of water and the disrespectful attitude of the brigade leaders who were monitoring their work. He informed the mayor of his intention to report these abusive practices to labor authorities. The mayor responded dismissively to these accusations. He referred to workfare employees as "beggars for work," and threatened to dismiss them from the workfare program.

5.2.1.2 Monopsony power

In several fieldwork sites, we encountered mayors employing workfare employees in economic enterprises or farms they own. These situations openly violate the provisions of social policy legislation, which makes lack of employment the precondition of access to social policy benefits, yet have significant advantages for mayors. On the one hand, mayors take advantage of significant opportunities for economic profit created by the workfare legislation. Workfare employees, whose wages are paid by tax revenues, are a reservoir of free labor. In addition to these economic gains, mayors also reap political benefits from illegally employing workfare employees: the outside options of workfare employees who enter this illegal employment relationship are significantly worsened. If such irregularity in employment is detected, these employees cannot reapply to the workfare program for two years. As such, a mayor's decision to hire persons employed in the workfare program is part of a broader political strategy that seeks to worsen the outside options of workfare employees and increase their economic and political dependency on political authorities. These decisions create quasi-feudal relationships of dependency in these localities by reinforcing the perception that the mayor is the only local source of employment.

Consider several examples of this neo-feudal dependency. In V. in southern Romania, the mayor employed workfare employees on his farm. The mayor here is reported to have dismissed from the workfare program people who refused such offers of employment. In HN., a town in Borsod County, Hungary, the family of the mayor owned a cucumber plantation that employed workfare employees from the locality. Workplace conditions on the farm were very harsh, and employees were required to work in very high temperatures and without water (HN., Interview 6, July 26, 2015). One of our respondents in HN., who is a Roma minority representative on the city council, considers that the mayor does not give employees in the workfare program the alternative to turn down an offer of employment on the farm. Rather, workfare employees consider work on the farm as an obligation to ensure continuing access to social policy benefits (HN., Interview 7, July 26, 2015).

In NO., a locality in Nógrád county, Hungary, the mayor is the owner of a pheasant farm that employs many local workfare employees. One respondent in this locality considers that people who are employed on the pheasant farm are "trapped" due to their dependence on the mayor (NO., Interview 1, July 15, 2015). This respondent argues that the economic dependence of these voters on the mayor also creates a political dependence: "People were told that they had to vote for the mayor because of their employment on the farm. If you work on the farm, you will not vote for anyone else because you are living off the mayor" (NO., Interview 1, July 15, 2015). Another respondent in this locality restated the theme of dependency. He maintained that "workfare employees are likely to vote for the mayor because he pays them every day" (NO., Interview 7, July 17, 2015).

5.2.1.3 Forbearance as the precondition of blackmail

The pre-electoral period is of special importance to mayors who seek to pursue clientelistic strategies premised on blackmail. These mayors turn a blind eye to a variety of illegal actions throughout their mandates. Possible violations of the provisions of the social policy legislation may include decisions to take up illegal employment or not to perform the work required for social assistance benefits. Other legal violations that are not prosecuted include minor theft or the non-payment of taxes. Mayors pursuing strategies premised on blackmail not only tolerate but often encourage these irregularities to exploit voters' enhanced vulnerability during elections.

Mayors in several localities where we have conducted fieldwork chose to selectively ignore the eligibility rules of social assistance legislation. In D., a locality in Buzău County, Romania, employees of the city hall systematically turned a blind eye to people who maintained employment while claiming social policy benefits. According to the figures reported to us by officials of this municipality, 1,700 persons (or 35 percent of the population) benefit from the workfare program. However, many of these persons also maintain part-time employment in other neighboring localities while drawing social assistance benefits. The result of a decision not to enforce the provisions of the social policy legislation creates a high number of "captive" workfare employees who are vulnerable to blackmail.

Another irregularity that some mayors choose to tolerate is the nonpayment of taxes. In D., the locality discussed above, local authorities turn a blind eye to the evasion of taxes owed to the municipality. Such noncompliance with fiscal obligations was higher among Roma families. According to employees of the municipality, only twenty-seven out of the 400 Roma families in this town paid water and electricity charges. At election time, city hall employees who operated as brokers were deployed to remind voters about their previous noncompliance with tax obligations. As one broker in this locality explains, "voters know that the current mayor has not asked them to pay their tax obligations in full." The mayor thus uses the threat that the selection of his political opponent will result in the punishment of previous noncompliance and increase voters' retrospective tax obligations. This broker contends that this strategy lowers the cost of electoral mobilization. He considers that "Voters in this locality are not very expensive because they understand the indirect payments that have been made on their behalf" (D., Interview 4, October 22, 2015).

A final strategy based on blackmail involves theft. In locality T., where several voters complained about the high rates of theft, the mayor told us that he kept detailed records of legal transgressions (T., Interview 1, September 17, 2015). In fact, this mayor had installed an expensive camera system to monitor and deter acts of theft. However, despite its high costs, the mayor rarely used the system to prosecute theft. In the eyes of a political candidate who had challenged the incumbent mayor, the cameras "have been established to blackmail people. If the people caught stealing vote correctly, they are forgiven. The mayor only checks up on acts of theft that matter for the vote" (T., Interview 6, September 15, 2015).

5.2.2 Electoral strategies

These pre-electoral strategies enhance opportunities for the use of workfare coercion or blackmail as electoral strategies. We now turn to a discussion of the electoral use of coercion. We examine the use of threats and coercion to incentivize voters to turn out and vote for a candidate as well as on post-electoral efforts to verify that voters did not support the "correct" candidate.

Workfare employees are an important constituency that can be mobilized during campaigns. Mayors often require workfare employees to participate in campaign events supporting their candidacy and condition their future access to workfare benefits on the participation in such events. To illustrate this strategy, consider events occurring in the most recent local election in ZS., a locality in Vrancea County in Romania. The election was an extremely competitive contest: the incumbent Socialist mayor faced challenges from two other candidates with roughly equal levels of electoral strength. An electoral event scheduled by the deputy mayor during the campaign brought in Marian Oprişan, a prominent national figure of the Social Democratic Party and one of Romania's most powerful "regional barons." To increase participation in this event, the mayor issued a "public invitation" to the meeting. The statement (Figure 5.1), invited all voters to this event, but included a special note warning that access to social assistance benefits would be cut for people who chose not to attend the meeting.

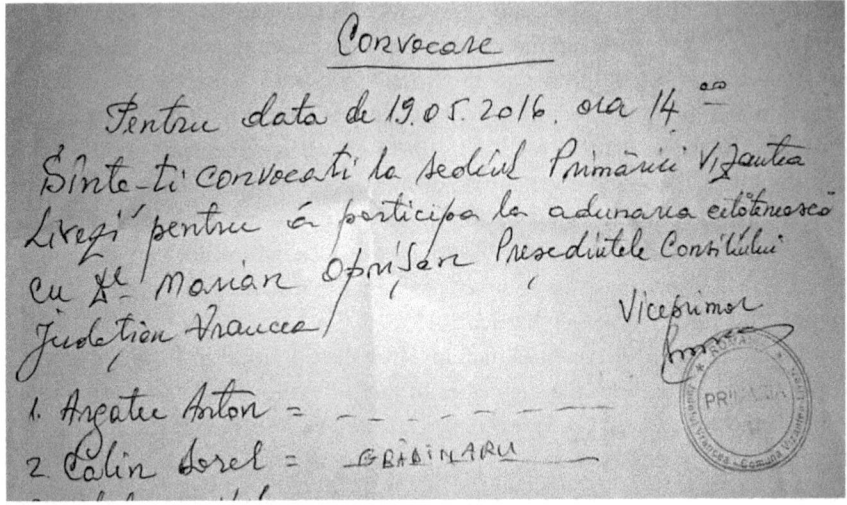

Figure 5.1 Letter from a deputy-mayor threatening the loss of social assistance
(*Source*: http://www.justitiecurata.ro)

This publicly voiced threat backfired in this locality: the Socialist candidate for mayor lost the race. In our discussion with him, the outgoing mayor defended the deputy mayor's decisions and contended that "the deputy mayor could have invited them to do other things, such as clean up the building of the city hall. He used, however, this unfortunate wording and those in the media used it against him" (ZS., Interview 6, July 13, 2016). The candidate refused to comment on whether the coercive mobilization of workfare employees was an important factor contributing to his defeat.

However, the electoral use of welfare coercion often seeks to accomplish more than just participation in electoral events. Its main goal is to induce workfare employees to turn out and vote for the candidate who controls their future participation in the program. We find ample evidence of such welfare coercion in both Romania and Hungary. The mayor of OK., a town in Baranya County, Hungary, relied on the use of coercion during the parliamentary elections in April 2014 and the local elections in 2015. A former member of the city council of the locality recalled that during the 2014 parliamentary election, workfare employees were called in by the mayor and threatened that they would lose access to workfare benefits if they did not support the Fidesz candidate. This respondent considered that as a result, "people who had only the income from social assistance knew how to vote. Campaigning is not only about what I can give you, but also what I can take away. This also makes campaigns cheaper" (OK., Interview 6, July 13, 2015).

Such threats are particularly effective in localities where the workfare program presents the only viable employment opportunity. This is the case for many communities where we conducted fieldwork and can be illustrated using the example of FB., a locality in Heves County, Hungary. The locality can be accessed only with great difficulty on small roads. The main employer, a local agricultural collective enterprise, closed down nearly a decade ago. The only remaining employers are a water company, a local power station, and the local municipality. In this community, the workfare program offers the only viable source of new employment.

This lack of employment opportunities made it possible for the mayor of FB. to use coercive threats to mobilize voters during elections. Before the 2014 local elections, the mayor convened around 200 workfare workers to a gathering publicized as a work-safety meeting (FB., Interview 1, July 21, 2015). As one participant in the meeting recalled, "All persons who were present were informed that if they want to continue to hold on to their workfare job, they have to vote for the actual mayor" (FB., Interview 1, July 21, 2015). Commenting on this mobilization strategy, the respondent noted that workfare workers acted as "multipliers." "Communicating the threat to workfare employees was a very effective strategy, as they passed on the threat to their families, multiplying this support for the candidate of the mayor" (FB., Interview 1, July 21, 2015). Another respondent also confirmed this account of workfare employees as multipliers. According to this respondent, "The mayor won with the support of employees in the municipality and of employees in the workfare program who were bringing people in" (FB., Interview 2, July 21, 2015).

Another respondent in FB., currently a city council member in the municipality, considered that such strategies premised on the inducement of fear were electorally effective. Workfare employees, this respondent argued, responded to threats not by rebelling, but by complying with the mayor. We probed further, by asking how the mayor knows who is on her side, given the secrecy of the vote. The respondent answered that the mayor could learn the voting intentions of voters because she "has established a spy system like Rákosi used to have. They are tracking who is talking to whom and where. Lots of people complained that they will not get a workfare job, and the mayor even made the comments that the ones who will not join the party line will not receive employment in the workfare program" (FB., Interview 2, July 21, 2015).

We also found evidence of the use of welfare coercion in HK., a locality in Borsod county with a nominally independent mayor. As in many other communities located in this struggling economic region, the workfare program offers the main opportunity for employment. One of our respondents described the importance of this program for the economic situation in this community: "If this public works program did not exist, then revolution would break out or food riots would happen" (HK., Interview 7, September 24, 2015). At the time of our research, only eighty people were employed in the workfare program, leaving a large portion of the demand for workfare jobs unmet. According to one informant who was employed in the local municipality, around 200 people were in need of employment in the workfare program. Due to their scarcity, workfare jobs were intensely desired. "People fight to access public workfare jobs," this respondent stated (HK., Interview 1, September 21, 2015). This situation created an opportunity for the mayor to exploit the vulnerability of workfare employees by threatening that those who supported the opposition candidate would lose their employment in the program.

Several respondents in this locality commented on the use of welfare coercion during the 2014 local election. One respondent considered that "workfare employees supported the incumbent mayor out of fear of losing their jobs." This respondent added that the mayor exploited the belief of workfare recipients that their current and future employment opportunities were entirely conditional on mayoral discretion (HK., Interview 2, September 21, 2015). One of our respondents in this community also competed during the 2014 local elections, but lost the race (HK., Interview 5, September 23, 2015). His discussion of the electoral strategies used by the incumbent mayor extensively details the use of welfare coercion. "The mayor," this challenger argued, "did not compete on the basis of a clearly articulated platform. The main element of her campaign was to threaten workfare employees that they will lose their employment if they do not vote for her. She could influence voters because they are vulnerable" (HK., Interview 5, September 23, 2015). The mayor also threatened workfare employees that their employment in the program would be terminated if they signed any documents supporting the candidacy of her challenger. This challenger believed that these strategies played a decisive role in accounting for the victory of the mayor. "I think that people employed in the workfare program elected her. They voted for her in order to maintain their workfare job" (HK., Interview 5, September 23, 2015).

As we discussed above, a complementary coercive strategy involves blackmail. Electoral events in T., a locality in southern Romania, provide an illustration of the use of blackmail. Here, the mayor laid the foundations for the electoral use of blackmail by permitting blatant violations of social policy legislation, which could be then exploited. During the pre-electoral period, the mayor turned a blind eye to people who engaged in black market employment while also drawing access to social policy benefits. Many people in T. combined participation in the workfare program with temporary jobs in neighboring urban localities. At the same time, the mayor allowed workfare employees to draw their social assistance benefits without performing work for the community. As one respondent in this locality commented on the use of workfare employment, "there are 330 people who receive social assistance benefits and need to perform work for the community. But only ten people perform this work every day. The rest of the beneficiaries receive money without working. However, at the time of the vote, these persons are reminded that they have not performed the work" (T., Interview 3, September 15, 2015). The mayor himself acknowledges that these decisions violate the provisions of the legislation, but regards these strategies as a necessary quid pro quo with voters in conditions of extreme poverty. He refers to such forbearance as a "way to reach our little agreements" (T., Interview 1, September 17, 2015).

This forbearance during the mayor's mandate created opportunities for electoral blackmail during the election. One former opponent recalled that the mayor relied on fifteen to twenty people to mobilize voters during elections. Their mission, the challenger recalls, was "to make people afraid and to remind social assistance beneficiaries that they have access to the social benefits because of the mayor and that they would lose access if they didn't vote as told" (T., Interview 3, September 15, 2015). Workfare beneficiaries were also reminded that they had received the benefits without working. The mayor also disapproved of workfare employees' participation in the electoral events of opposition candidates. As his opponent recalls, "When I go campaigning and talk to people, they tell me that they cannot be seen talking to me. They tell me, you know, I will vote for you [lasă că tot cu tine merg] but I don't want them to see me with you. If they do so, they will cut my assistance benefits" (T., Interview 4, September 15, 2015).

Candidates combine threats of future employment losses with the electoral (and post-electoral) monitoring of workfare employees to ensure that they support the correct candidate. In several Romanian localities, candidates deployed brokers who attempted to "lock in" the promise of workfare employees, by making them swear on a Bible. The additional strategy sought to increase the perceived costs of defection from the initial promise to vote for a candidate. As one broker describes the strategy, "if you swear on the Bible and then you break your promise, you are dead" (S., Interview 6, September 15, 2015).

Brokers, often employees of the municipality, also use their presence at the voting place to gather information about voters' preferences and voting intentions. One such broker, who was present at the polling station in this locality, recalls that he used to advise voters to "come and talk to him" when they are voting (P., Interview 4, August 21, 2015). But he admits that as president of the voting section, he used significant discretion to try to identify the vote choices made by individual voters. Sometimes, brokers seek to influence voters using harsher and sometimes brutal strategies. One voter we encountered in V., Romania, recalls his voting experience during the 2016 local Romanian election as follows:

> I was not able to put my ballot in the urn before leaving. He [referring to an employee in the municipality] put my ballot in his pocket then he showed it to the mayor. I know that I am finished and I have no future.
>
> (V., Interview 10, September 29, 2016)

Such monitoring of voters at the time they cast their ballots is a much less frequent occurrence in Hungary, as compared to Romania. Nevertheless, we encountered cases in which candidates sought to pierce voting secrecy and observe individual votes. In RM., a locality in Borsod county, the mayor relied on his representatives at the polling station to monitor voters' choices when they cast their ballot. The specific excuse used by these candidates was that these monitors would help voters who were illiterate make the correct political choice. One respondent in this locality commented on this pressure from the mayor: "If I refused the person accompanying me into the polling place and voted unattended, then my vote would not count" (RM., Interview 3, August 22, 2015). Another respondent countered this interpretation, arguing that such efforts also occurred with voters who were not illiterate and that these voters were urged to support the mayor (RM., Interview 7, August 24, 2015). In NM., a locality in Baranya county, voters also reported that mayors used the pretext of "ballot complexity" to accompany voters inside the voting booth and "help" them cast the ballot (NM., Interview 2, March 23, 2014).

Mayors also deploy city hall employees in the immediate aftermath of elections to collect additional information about voter's choices. We asked a mayor in P., a locality in southern Romania, how he could ascertain whether voters that were granted favors throughout his administration had reciprocated, given the secrecy of the ballot. He answered, "We know and we also know those who betray us. They talk, we can hear. The boy who goes from house to house to collect taxes and other fees talks to them and asks them, Who is in the race for mayor? Will this mayor be re-elected? If they say he will not be re-elected, then one can be sure they will not vote for us." His assistant concurred: "We know those who betray us very well" (P., Interview 1, August 21, 2015).

5.3 The Programmatic Signals of Welfare Coercion

In Chapter 2, we conjectured that different clientelistic strategies may vary in their costliness to candidates because they signal different programmatic policies to voters. Despite the fact that most voters dislike candidates who use clientelism, voters are much less likely to actually punish, or will even possibly reward, candidates for employing this tactic if it comprises a form of clientelism that signals programmatic priorities in line with their interests. In this section, we present the results of a survey experiment testing how different forms of clientelism affect the way that voters perceive the policy positions and general qualities of candidates. We test whether voters with anti-workfare preferences evaluate candidates who use coercion more positively, and those who use policy favors more harshly, than voters with pro-workfare preferences evaluate them.

In Section 2.3.3, we also distinguished between strong and weak versions of arguments about the informational signals of clientelism. The strong version of the information story posits that the informational signals sent by clientelism are actually positive for some or all voters, and thus provide benefits on top of the material incentives offered in clientelistic exchanges. The weak version of the informational argument is that certain forms of clientelism may have smaller negative effects on how candidates are perceived than others, particularly with voters who have policy preferences that are aligned with a specific type of clientelism. In the last chapter, we found strong evidence for the weak informational argument, and some evidence for the strong informational argument, for the strategy of policy favors. In this section, we adjudicate between the strong and weak informational arguments in these Eastern European cases for coercive forms of clientelism.

We test our hypotheses about the policy signals of clientelism using survey experiments in which we randomly assign voters to candidate descriptions and ask them to assess those candidates on a number of dimensions. In this chapter, we present the results of comparisons of vignettes in which mayoral candidates perform favors involving social assistance for voters in exchange for their votes, to those in which the mayoral candidates do not engage in clientelism. The introduction to the scenarios describes the social assistance program and asks the respondent to imagine a locality that is "similar to your locality" with many low-income people, some of whom are Roma. In the control scenario, the mayor of that locality does not politicize access to the social assistance program. In the favor scenario, the mayor makes access to the social assistance program conditional on political support. In the coercion scenario, the mayor threatens to cut people from the workfare rolls if they do not vote for him. The full text of the three vignettes appears below.

Introduction (everyone)

I would now like to have a general discussion about the social assistance program. As you probably know, under the law guaranteeing minimum income, persons with low incomes can receive social assistance benefits. In exchange, they need to work for a number of hours in the interests of the community. Although they have low income, both the elderly and persons employed with formal contracts cannot benefit from the provisions of the law guaranteeing minimum income. Imagine now a place very similar to your locality. There are many low-income people living in this locality. Many of these people are Roma.

Control Scenario

Despite receiving a very large number of requests for social assistance benefits, the mayor of this locality decided to offer guaranteed minimum income benefits only to people who can prove that they meet the requirements of the law.

Favor Scenario

The mayor of this locality makes access to social assistance conditional on political support. He encourages people who want to get these benefits to vote for him in local elections and vote for his party in parliamentary elections.

Coercion Scenario

The mayor of this locality conditions access to social assistance benefits on political support. He has punished people who did not vote for him during the local elections or who did not support his party during the parliamentary election, by cutting their access to social policy benefits and leaving them without any means of subsistence.

We tested our informational explanation with a total sample of over 500 Romanian respondents in ninety localities in the three counties of Giurgiu, Constanţa, and Olt. Giurgiu and Olt border Teleorman county, one of the two counties where we collected the data for our locality-level tests, and have similar demographics.

We begin by examining how voters use the information in the different clientelistic scenarios to draw inferences about the different social policy positions of the respective candidates. In this section, we present an analysis of five different outcomes that relate to how a candidate would spend social policy resources. We aggregate individual survey questions into two indices that measure different dimensions of a candidate's perceived welfare policy.

Workfare Retrenchment Index
- *Against Laziness*: Do you think that this mayor tries to limit the number of people living off state money to avoid paying people to be lazy?
- *Help Elderly*: Do you think this mayor reduces the number of persons receiving social assistance in order to help the elderly?

Help Deserving Poor Index
- *Help Poor*: Does this mayor help poor people?
- *Help Emergency*: Would this mayor help persons in your locality in cases of emergency?
- *Job for You*: How likely is it that this candidate would give a job to people like you?

The first two questions ask directly about reducing and limiting social assistance in order to allocate it to other groups. Voters who are opposed to the workfare program should prefer candidates who score high on the Workfare Retrenchment Index, while voters who favor the workfare program should prefer candidates who score low on this index.[1] The second three questions ask about generally helping deserving groups with social assistance. We expect that all voters—those who support and those opposed to the workfare program alike—should prefer candidates who score higher on this index. In these poor localities, most voters who support retrenchment of current social policy benefits are not voters who do not want any welfare, but rather voters who wish that social policy were reallocated to benefits members of the "deserving" poor like retirees and the unemployed. Thus,

they prefer candidates who will give jobs to "people like you [the respondent],"
will help in emergencies, and will help those who they believe are truly suffering
from economic deprivation. Similarly, voters who favor the expansion of the
workfare program should also prefer candidates who will give jobs to people
like them, help in emergencies, and help the poor.

Table 5.1 presents the results of our evaluations of these hypotheses. For each of
the two outcome indices, we present two different specifications: first, the effect of
the clientelism scenarios interacted with the respondent's anti-workfare preferences; and second, the interaction specification with a set of individual-level
controls such as ethnicity, gender, and occupation. Because the continuous
variables are standardized with a mean of zero, the main coefficient on the

Table 5.1 Anti-workfare ideology and the social policy signals of policy favors and
coercion

	Dependent variable			
	Workfare Retrenchment Index		Help Deserving Poor Index	
	(1)	(2)	(3)	(4)
Clientelism: Policy favors	−0.47***	−0.46***	−0.70***	−0.67***
	(0.11)	(0.11)	(0.10)	(0.10)
Clientelism: Policy coercion	−0.56***	−0.53***	−0.97***	−0.99***
	(0.11)	(0.11)	(0.10)	(0.10)
Clientelism: Policy favors × Anti-Workfare Ideology	−0.25**	−0.26**	0.05	0.09
	(0.10)	(0.11)	(0.09)	(0.09)
Clientelism: Policy coercion × Anti-Workfare Ideology	−0.12	−0.08	0.21**	0.27**
	(0.12)	(0.12)	(0.10)	(0.10)
Anti-Workfare Ideology	0.11	0.09	−0.11	−0.14**
	(0.08)	(0.08)	(0.07)	(0.07)
Constant	0.38***	−0.15	0.59***	0.67**
	(0.07)	(0.32)	(0.07)	(0.29)
Individual Controls		✓		✓
Observations	413	390	424	401
R^2	0.09	0.10	0.21	0.25

*p<0.1; **p<0.05; ***p<0.01

Standard errors clustered by respondent in parentheses.

Models are estimated using OLS. All outcomes are standardized. Favor Treatment is a dummy
indicating that the respondent was randomly assigned to the vignette in which the mayor offered a
policy favor; Coercion Treatment is a dummy indicating that the respondent was randomly assigned to
the vignette in which the mayor threatened to take away policy benefits; the residual category is the
vignette in which the mayor refrains from clientelistic offers or threats. Anti-Workfare Ideology is a
standardized continuous measure of the respondent's opposition to the existing state welfare programs.
Individual controls include gender, age, income, ethnicity, education, and workfare eligibility.

treatment variables can be interpreted as the effect of the treatments when the interaction term is at its average value.

Table 5.1 shows first that respondents perceive both candidates who offer clientelistic favors and those who threaten electoral sanctions lower on both policy dimensions. On average, candidates who offer clientelistic favors are perceived as 0.5 to 0.7 standard deviations lower in terms of how much they would prevent lazy people from accessing welfare, help the elderly, help the poor, and help people during emergencies. Those who threaten sanctions are perceived as 0.5 to 1 standard deviations lower on these policy traits. These across-the-board negative results are reflective of the normative attitudes that voters hold against clientelism, which appears to color their views of candidates along a wide range of dimensions.

Whether these perceived policy positions are good or bad for the candidates, however, depends on the policy preferences of the voters. For voters who favor cutbacks of existing social policies, a higher score on the Workfare Retrenchment index should make a candidate more desirable, because she is perceived as more likely to implement policies in line with those voters' preferences. For voters who support the workfare program, by contrast, candidates who score higher on the Workfare Retrenchment index should be less desirable. By contrast, we phrased the questions that go into the Help Deserving Poor index to capture policies that all voters should support, such as giving a job to "people like you," helping people after emergencies, and helping the poor, a subjective and implicitly deserving group. Thus, for all voters, regardless of their position on the Anti-Workfare Ideology scale, candidates who score higher on the Help Deserving Poor index should be more desirable.

We find evidence that the negative effects of clientelism on perceptions of candidates are conditional on the policy preferences of the respondent. Respondents who disapprove of the current distribution of social policy benefits view candidates who use favors as much less likely to reform the workfare program—which should make candidates who use policy favors particularly undesirable for these voters. These anti-workfare voters also view candidates who use coercion as more likely to help the more deserving poor, relative to pro-workfare voters. For voters who are supportive of the workfare program, there is virtually no negative effect of policy favors on perceptions that the candidate will retrench the workfare program. By contrast, the negative effect of coercion is significantly larger than for anti-workfare voters.

Figure 5.2 shows that the marginal effects of the favors scenario depend on the strength of respondents' anti-workfare attitudes. The black line shows the estimated marginal effect with 95 percent confidence intervals shaded in gray based on the specification presented in the third and sixth columns of Table 5.1. The black coefficients are estimates based on a three-category categorical version of the

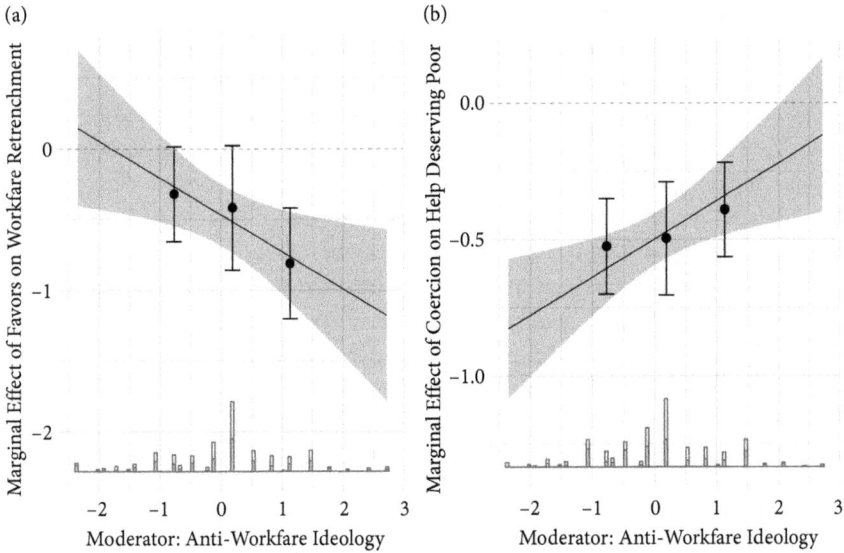

Figure 5.2 The marginal effects of policy-based clientelism on perceptions of the social policy positions of candidates at varying levels of anti-workfare ideology

moderator. The histogram along the *x*-axis shows the distribution of the moderating variable.

As shown in the left panel of Figure 5.2, the favors scenario has the biggest negative effect on perceptions of the candidate's welfare policy for people who hold strong anti-workfare preferences. For such respondents, a candidate who offers favors is perceived as particularly out of line with their policy preferences on this key distributional issue. For voters who are pro-workfare (more negative on the Anti-Workfare Ideology scale), the negative effect of favors is much smaller and basically indistinguishable from zero. By contrast, the right panel of Figure 5.2 shows that the negative effect of the coercion scenario on perceptions of how much the candidate would help the "deserving poor" is significantly smaller for people who rank high on Anti-Workfare Ideology. Because we expect that all voters prefer a candidate who will provide jobs to voters like them and help people after emergencies, this heterogeneity implies that the negative effect of policy coercion is attenuated for anti-workfare voters.

Importantly, there do not appear to be any positive signaling benefits to candidates regardless of voters' positions on the current social policy benefits. This result is also consistent with weak signaling explanations of clientelism. For most voters the effects of policy coercion and policy favors are decidedly negative. However, these results suggest that when candidates use a form of clientelism that is in line with a voter's policy position, the voter no longer judges the candidate as being more out of line with her policy preferences because of the clientelistic exchange.

In Chapter 2, we have hypothesized that voters also draw inferences about the personal attributes of candidates who engage in clientelistic transactions. To examine these hypotheses, we consider the effects of the scenarios on perceptions of candidates' general qualities. In this section, our dependent variables are four indices measuring different aspects of the personal qualities of politicians that might affect how they carry out their programmatic priorities. We examine, first, an index of management quality; second, an index measuring how honest vs. corrupt the politician is; third, an index of personal characteristics measuring perceptions about the politician's private behavior; and finally, a competitiveness index that measures voters' perceptions of the likelihood of the candidate winning office. The indices are constructed using the following questions:

Management Index
- *Good Manager*: How good a manager do you think this candidate is?
- *Law and Order*: How capable is this candidate of ensuring law and order in the locality?
- *Solve Problems*: Would this candidate be able to solve problems in town?

Corruption Index
- *Honest*: How honest do you think this candidate is?
- *Fight Corruption*: How much would this candidate fight against corruption?

Personal Qualities Index
- *Good Christian*: How good a Christian do you think this candidate is?
- *Family Man*: How good a family man do you think this candidate is?
- *Treats People Well*: How well do you think this candidate knows how to treat people?

Competitiveness Index
- *Win Others' Vote*: How likely is it that he would have the votes of some people in the locality?
- *Win Election*: How likely is it that he would win the election?

The Management Index is based on three questions that ask about perceptions of the mayor's ability to manage the locality, including his ability to generally ensure law and order and to solve local problems. The Corruption Index is based on two questions on respondents' perceptions of how honest or corrupt the mayor would be in office. The Personal Qualities Index is based on three questions about the personal qualities, like whether the candidate is good by the standards of his religion or family. Finally, the Competitiveness Index is constructed from two questions that measure the expectation that the candidate will win the election. For all of these outcomes, if our theoretical predictions are correct, then we would expect that voters opposing the workfare program would judge mayors who use positive forms of clientelism more harshly on these policy characteristics, and those who use negative inducements less harshly.

The results, presented in Table 5.2, show again that candidates who use favors are perceived as less desirable along a range of positive characteristics relating to management practices and corruption. The effects are largest on the perceived corruption of the candidate, with magnitudes of around 1.1 standard deviations on the favors treatment and 1.25 standard deviations for the coercion scenario, and smallest on perceived competitiveness of the candidate.

For some of these outcomes, there is also evidence that the effects vary significantly across respondents with different social policy attitudes. The negative effects of coercion on perceptions of management quality are significantly smaller for respondents with anti-workfare preferences. Figure 5.3 shows that the marginal effect of the coercion scenario on perceptions of management quality is significantly smaller for respondents with anti-workfare preferences. These effects are also consistent across the three sub-indicators, as shown in Appendix C4.

On the other hand, there is no significant interaction between either of the treatments and perceptions of corruption, personal qualities, and competitiveness. This suggests that even when respondents are ideologically aligned with the policy signals that a type of clientelism sends, they still perceive it as a form of corruption and that it reflects poorly on personal attributes of the candidate.

Finally, we analyze three outcomes that directly ask respondents to assess how they would vote if they were living in the locality described in the vignette. We caution that measuring propensity to vote for clientelistic candidates is difficult because of the strong potential for social desirability effects. Ultimately, we interpret these effects as indicative of what respondents think they should do rather than an accurate reflection of their behavior. Nevertheless, we include them because we are still interested in whether there is variation by ideology in how respondents think they should vote.

We measure hypothetical voting behavior using questions that ask respondents to rate their propensity to vote in three different ways on a five-point likelihood scale:

Electoral Punishment Index
- *Win Your Vote*: How likely is it that you would vote for this mayor?
- *Abstain*: How likely is it that you would not vote at all?
- *Lose Your Vote*: How likely is it that you would vote for another candidate?

Table 5.3 presents the results of the analysis of these voting propensity outcomes. We test this hypothesis using an index of self-reported propensity to punish the candidate at the ballot box where higher values indicate less likely to win the respondent's vote, more likely to abstain, and more likely to lose the respondent's vote.

Table 5.2 Anti-workfare ideology and the personal quality signals of policy favors and coercion

	Dependent variable							
	Management Index		Anti-Corruption Index		Personal Index		Competitiveness Index	
	(1)	(2)	(3)	(4)	(5)	(6)	(7)	(8)
Clientelism: Policy favors	−0.73***	−0.78***	−1.15***	−1.15***	−0.33***	−0.34***	−0.20**	−0.20**
	(0.10)	(0.10)	(0.10)	(0.10)	(0.09)	(0.10)	(0.10)	(0.10)
Clientelism: Policy coercion	−1.02***	−1.02***	−1.29***	−1.28***	−0.46***	−0.48***	−0.28***	−0.30***
	(0.10)	(0.10)	(0.10)	(0.10)	(0.09)	(0.09)	(0.10)	(0.10)
Clientelism: Policy favors × Anti-Workfare Ideology	0.02	0.05	0.09	0.13	−0.01	0.02	0.05	0.05
	(0.09)	(0.10)	(0.09)	(0.10)	(0.09)	(0.09)	(0.10)	(0.10)
Clientelism: Policy coercion × Anti-Workfare Ideology	0.19*	0.23**	0.11	0.14	−0.02	−0.001	0.09	0.12
	(0.10)	(0.11)	(0.10)	(0.11)	(0.10)	(0.10)	(0.11)	(0.11)
Anti-Workfare Ideology	−0.09	−0.10	−0.13*	−0.14*	0.01	0.02	−0.07	−0.09
	(0.07)	(0.07)	(0.07)	(0.07)	(0.06)	(0.07)	(0.07)	(0.07)
Constant	0.67***	0.43	0.92***	0.67**	0.31***	0.23	0.17**	0.04
	(0.07)	(0.29)	(0.07)	(0.30)	(0.06)	(0.28)	(0.07)	(0.30)
Individual Controls		✓		✓		✓		✓
Observations	426	404	415	393	435	413	397	374
R^2	0.23	0.25	0.34	0.35	0.06	0.08	0.02	0.05

*$p<0.1$; **$p<0.05$; ***$p<0.01$

Standard errors in parentheses.

Models are estimated using OLS. All outcomes are standardized. Favor Treatment is a dummy indicating that the respondent was randomly assigned to the vignette in which the mayor offered a policy favor; Coercion Treatment is a dummy indicating that the respondent was randomly assigned to the vignette in which the mayor threatened to take away policy benefits; the residual category is the vignette in which the mayor refrains from clientelistic offers or threats. Anti-Workfare Ideology is a standardized continuous measure of the respondent's opposition to the existing state welfare programs. Individual controls include gender, age, income, ethnicity, education, and workfare eligibility.

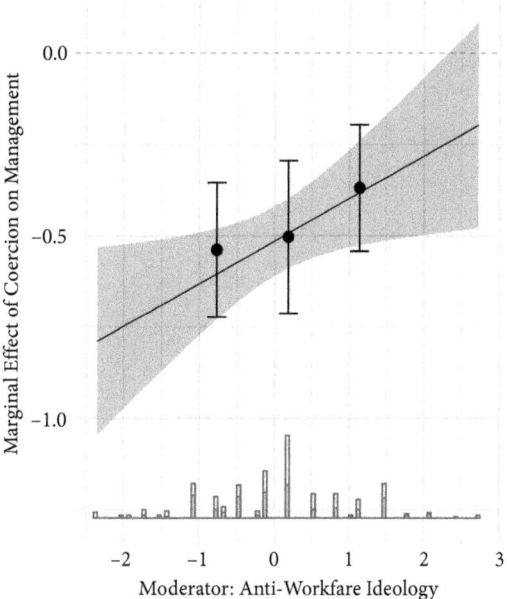

Figure 5.3 The marginal effect of policy clientelism on perceptions of the management capacity of candidates at varying levels of anti-workfare ideology

The results in Table 5.3 show first that respondents report being much less likely to vote for candidates who use clientelistic favors and coercion. To put this into real terms, while almost 60 percent of respondents in the control scenario say that it is very likely or sure that they would vote for the incumbent, just 10 percent fall into this category in the favors condition and 7 percent in the coercion condition.[2]

Taken together with other pieces of evidence, these results suggest that the potential for electoral punishment may be a serious consideration for candidates considering whether or not to use policy clientelism. The magnitude of these effects should be interpreted with some caution given that social desirability bias might lead respondents to say that they would punish corrupt candidates even if they would not in a real election. However, we find similarly negative electoral effects on policy favors in the conjoint design presented in Chapter 4, and on perceptions of how other citizens will vote in Columns 7 and 8 of Table 5.2. Taken together, these results suggest that the use of policy in clientelistic transactions carries significant electoral costs for candidates with many voters. If these electoral costs are high enough, such electoral costs may be a more important consideration for candidates than variation in the availability of clientelism resources.

Second, counter to our findings on perceptions of candidates' policy positions, there is little evidence that revealing hypothetical voting support for clientelistic

Table 5.3 Anti-workfare ideology and propensity to punish candidates who use policy favors and coercion

	Dependent variable	
	Electoral Punishment Index	
	(1)	(2)
Clientelism: Policy favors	0.74***	0.72***
	(0.07)	(0.07)
Clientelism: Policy coercion	0.80***	0.77***
	(0.07)	(0.07)
Clientelism: Policy favors × Anti-Workfare Ideology	0.01	−0.02
	(0.07)	(0.07)
Clientelism: Policy coercion × Anti-Workfare Ideology	0.01	−0.01
	(0.07)	(0.08)
Anti-Workfare Ideology	−0.01	0.01
	(0.05)	(0.05)
Constant	−0.50***	−0.60***
	(0.05)	(0.21)
Individual Controls		✓
Observations	457	433
R²	0.27	0.26

*p<0.1; **p<0.05; ***p<0.01

Standard errors in parentheses.

Models are estimated using OLS. All outcomes are standardized. Favor Treatment is a dummy indicating that the respondent was randomly assigned to the vignette in which the mayor offered a policy favor; Coercion Treatment is a dummy indicating that the respondent was randomly assigned to the vignette in which the mayor threatened to take away policy benefits; the residual category is the vignette in which the mayor refrains from clientelistic offers or threats. Anti-Workfare Ideology is a standardized continuous measure of the respondent's opposition to the existing state welfare programs. Individual controls include gender, age, income, ethnicity, education, and workfare eligibility.

candidates is conditioned by ideology. Respondents with social policy preferences that are supportive of the workfare program are no more or less likely to say that they would vote for candidates who use favors than those with attitudes opposed to the programs. Respondents opposing the workfare program are no different in their propensity to punish candidates who use coercion. We suggest two ways of interpreting the fact that these voting outcomes are not conditioned by ideology in light of the differential results on attitudes. First, it is possible that although clientelism has differential results on perceptions of candidates, the dimensions that they affect are not important factors in voters' decisions of whether or not to support a candidate. For instance, anti-workfare voters may perceive mayors who use clientelistic favors as much less likely to scale back the workfare program, but they may nonetheless decide not to vote for those candidates because the workfare program is less important to them than the general level of corruption that the candidate engages in. We find this unlikely in this case given the importance of the workfare program in the economies of the localities in our study.

The second possible interpretation is that there are differential effects on voting behavior, but that these are masked in this analysis by very strong social desirability effects. In other words, while there is no variation in what respondents think they should do when confronted with a clientelistic candidate, there may still be variation in what they would actually do in a real election. This interpretation is bolstered by the fact that we find differential propensity to punish candidates who offer policy favors in the conjoint experiment presented in Chapter 4. In the conjoint design, which provides a more realistic choice to respondents by presenting two candidates who differ on multiple dimensions, we found that voters who earn less than 1,500 RON were no less likely to vote for candidates who offer policy favors.

In this section, we have tested whether different forms of clientelism not only provide material inducements to voters who are directly targeted, but also signal candidate's positions on a range of important programmatic policies and personal characteristics to voters who observe the clientelistic transaction. In this experiment, voters evaluate candidates who use clientelism more negatively across a range of important characteristics, with coercion generally causing even more negative effects than favors. However, some of these negative effects are conditioned by voters' social policy preferences. While voters across the board view candidates who use clientelism as more corrupt, less ethical in their personal life, and less competitive, the effect of policy clientelism on perceptions of the candidates' position on social policy, propensity to help the deserving poor, and management capacity are conditioned by the voters' social policy preferences. For these important outcomes, voters with social policy preferences that are aligned with the form of clientelism that the candidate uses do not view the candidates who use clientelism less favorably. If these evaluations are important to voters, these results suggest that politicians may be able to reduce the electoral costs of clientelism by using forms that are aligned with voters' social policy preferences.

Additional qualitative evidence corroborates these findings by demonstrating how voters' views about which low income residents deserve help from the state influence how critical they are of candidates who use policy coercion. In HN., a locality in Borsod county, the mayor engaged in repression and public humiliation of workfare employees. Yet elderly voters who were opposed to the workfare programs were less likely to sanction him for using these strategies. A 60-year-old respondent who also served as member of the city council in the locality did not object to such strategies, considering that "workfare recipients are neither reliable nor responsible" (HN., Interview 2, July 22, 2015). In V., a locality in southern

Romania, elderly respondents also approved of mayors' coercive strategies. Here, one respondent considered that "receiving social assistance benefits by the state is not a good situation; young people wait for social assistance benefits rather than working." This voter did not disapprove of the abusive and disrespectful attitude of the mayor in his interaction with the workfare employees: "The mayor is a good man," this respondent considered, and "it is good, from time to time, to teach a lesson to the social assistance beneficiaries (*asistații sociali*)" (V., Interview 4, July 30, 2015). These respondents, critical of the current social policy distribution because it excluded groups like the elderly whom they viewed as more deserving of state support, illustrate how voters who oppose the workfare program can excuse mayors who personalize and politicize access to it because they view its beneficiaries as undeserving.

The results presented here suggest that these heterogeneous effects are important for perceptions of candidates' policy positions and management style, but not for their personal characteristics or electoral viability. These results suggest that the manipulation of policy benefits is a very direct signal of how a candidate will administer social policy. They suggest that voters with anti-workfare preferences know that policy coercion is unethical and thus are equally likely to interpret it as a signal that the candidate is more corrupt and less ethical in his personal life. Nevertheless, they are not critical of the management style of coercive candidates, their commitment to helping the "deserving" poor, or their propensity to reallocate welfare priorities. In other words, voters process the informational signals of clientelism in a sophisticated and nuanced manner. In addition, the material incentives of clientelistic transactions are tightly integrated with voters' evaluations of the policy positions of candidates.

If welfare policy positions and management abilities are important factors in actual vote choice, these heterogeneous effects suggest that the costs of clientelism for candidates should vary depending on the ideological makeup of the voters in their districts. In places with large populations of voters who are dissatisfied with the current social policy distribution, candidates who use welfare favors will be perceived much less favorably than those who do not. By contrast, in this type of locality, the costs of using welfare coercion in terms of programmatic perceptions are relatively small. In the following section we test whether these individual-level findings scale up into meaningful variation across localities in the use of welfare coercion.

5.4 Variation across Localities in the Use of Welfare Coercion

Does the use of welfare coercion vary systematically across localities? If so, what are the main factors that explain this variation? We turn to the analysis of these questions next. In the theory section we argued that explanations for the incidence of clientelism at the local level can be separated into theories focused on the supply of clientelism, and those focused on the electoral costs. In this section we analyze the extent to which locality-level conditions associated with both of these explanations are associated with variation in the incidence of policy favors across localities.

5.4.1 Research design

We measure the incidence of coercive strategies in different localities by using the results of post-electoral surveys fielded in both Hungary and Romania in the aftermath of recent elections. For Hungary, we report the result of the survey fielded in May 2014, which sought to measure a variety of illicit strategies deployed during the parliamentary election held during the previous month. For Romania, we report the results of a survey fielded in December 2014, which attempted to measure the incidence of this non-programmatic strategy during the presidential election held in November 2014. The Hungarian survey was fielded in a sample of over ninety communities located in three provinces: Heves, Borsod, and Baranya. The Romanian survey was fielded in seventy communities located in Teleorman and Buzău, two counties located in eastern and southeastern Romania. We refer the reader to Chapter 3 and Appendix B for additional details about the survey.

In both countries, we sought to estimate the incidence of welfare coercion using questions with similar wording. The questions measuring the incidence of welfare coercion included in our survey were embedded in the following lists.

Hungary

I am going to read some statements of events that happened or could have happened during elections. Please recall the elections of 6 April, 2014, and tell me how many of these events happened in your locality. You do not need to tell which ones happened exactly, only how many.

- Several candidates visited our locality.
- One of the candidates promised to protect animal rights.
- None of the candidates visited our locality.
- (*Sensitive item*) I was worried that a family member would lose employment in the public works program if I voted for the wrong candidate.

Romania

I will read you a number of statements that refer to the recent presidential elections held in November 2014. For each of these statements, I would like you to tell me how many of these events happened here, in this community. You do not need to tell me which of these happened, but only how many.

- I waited in line in order to vote.

Table 5.4 Estimated incidence of policy coercion

Country	N	Control Mean	Treatment Mean	Estimated Incidence	p-value
Hungary	1,819	1.02 (1.01, 1.03)	1.08 (1.06, 1.1)	5.8% (2.3%, 9.3%)	0.00
Romania	1,495	1.15 (1.12, 1.18)	1.27 (1.24, 1.3)	11.5% (6%, 17%)	0.00

- When I went to vote, I saw several persons who were drunk.
- In our locality, the campaign unfolded without any incidents of violence.
- (*Sensitive item*) I was afraid to lose social assistance benefits from the city hall, if I voted for the wrong candidate.

The implementation of our survey was successful. In Appendices A1–A3 we present summary statistics about the distribution of different respondents across the versions of the questionnaires in the surveys administered in Hungary and Romania, respectively. We do not find any statistically significant differences in observable characteristics of respondents across the two versions of the questionnaire.

Table 5.4 presents the results of our surveys estimating the incidence of welfare coercion in our sample. The third column ("Control Mean") presents the average responses to the version of the questionnaire that includes only the control items, while the fourth column ("Treatment Mean") presents the average responses to the version of the questionnaire that includes the sensitive question. By subtracting the mean number of items of respondents who received the treatment version of the questionnaire from the mean items of respondents who received the control version of the questionnaire, we obtain the list experiment estimate of the incidence of the particular electoral irregularity measured in the survey.

The survey allows us to document the incidence of clientelistic strategies premised on welfare coercion in both countries. In Hungary, we estimate that around 6 percent of voters in our survey area have experienced the threat of losing access to the workfare program if they do not support the mayor's preferred candidate. In Romania, the number of voters who have experienced this strategy is significantly higher at 11 percent.

Figure 5.4 presents the geographic distribution of welfare coercion in the five counties in Hungary and Romania that are included in the analysis. Dots on the map represent localities in which we conducted our survey. Each dot on the map represents a locality where we conducted our survey and is based on twenty individual survey responses in the case of Hungary, or on an average of seventeen individual survey responses in the case of Romania. Darker dots indicate higher estimated incidences of welfare coercion. We have added a small

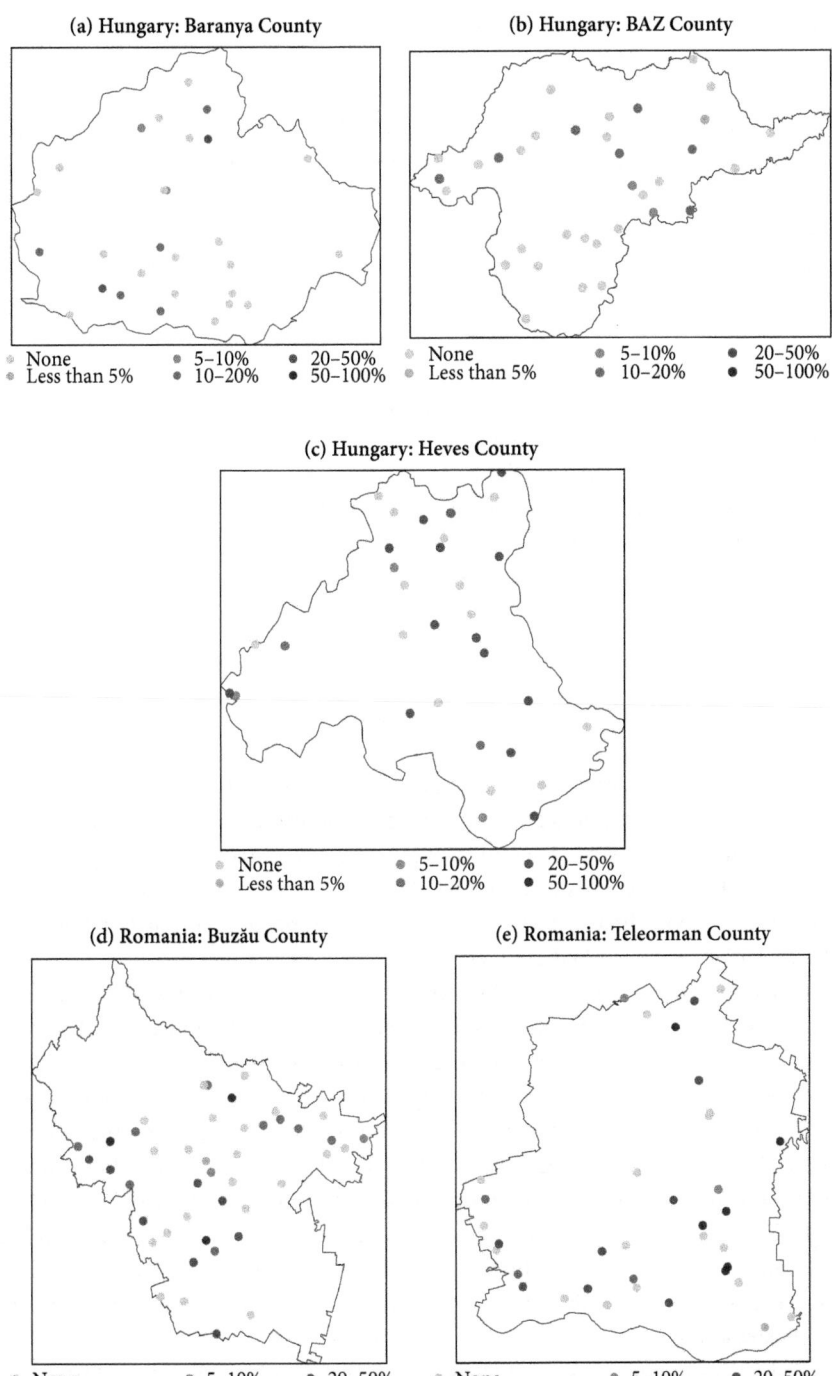

Figure 5.4 Geographic distribution of policy coercion

amount of random noise (or "jittered") the locality coordinates in order to prevent identification.

Figure 5.4 shows that, although there are some visible trends across counties in the incidence of welfare coercion, the strategy does not appear to be geographically concentrated. We discuss a number of tests of the validity of our survey design in Chapter 2 and Appendix B. As shown in Appendix B, there are no signs that randomization was carried out incorrectly in tests of balance across treatment assignments for the lists. We also use the Blair and Imai (2012) method to test for design effects, or evidence that responses to the control items on the list change systematically when the sensitive item is present. There is no evidence that the lists are biased by design effects.

We are now ready to examine the correlates of the variation in the use of these coercive strategies across municipalities and across individuals. As discussed in Chapter 3, we take advantage of the nested nature of our data and use a multilevel model to estimate the effect of both locality- and individual-level characteristics on the incidence of welfare coercion (Gelman and Hill 2007). We refer the reader to Section 4.5 of Chapter 4 for a presentation of the equation used to estimate these models.

5.4.2 Results

In Chapter 2 we conjectured that incidence of state coercion was more likely in localities where local political control enables the use of clientelism, and where local social conditions create conflict over welfare resources. Specifically, first we predicted that state coercion should be higher when local political institutions are more tightly controlled by local elites through incumbency, co-partisanship with the executive, and a unified city hall.

Our second prediction is that the incidence of state coercion should be higher in localities characterized by high levels of polarization and intense distributional conflicts over the allocation of employment or workfare benefits. In such localities, the use of coercion allows candidates to capture the votes of low-income voters, while also signaling "toughness" and disrespect for the rights of those being coerced. In communities characterized by intense distributional conflicts, candidates who use coercive strategies expect to incur very low electoral costs from right-leaning voters. While this prediction also applies to forms of coercion involving non-state actors (which we call "economic coercion"), the effects may be particularly strong with state coercion because it is even more obviously linked to welfare conflict.

To test this hypothesis we use measures of local distributional conflict based on demographic conditions. Given that the distribution of workfare benefits is the most significant divisive issue, we operationalize the coalition favoring policy retrenchment (RETRENCHMENT COALITION) to include both employed and low-income retirees. By contrast, the coalition favoring the expansion of the workfare programs (EXPANSION COALITION) is likely to include the unemployed and Roma voters. The signaling argument presented in Chapter 2 generates two hypotheses about the correlation between these coalitions and the use of coercive strategies. First, we expect that the use of coercive strategies will be higher in localities with a larger political coalition favoring retrenchment. Second, we predict that the incidence of state coercion is likely to be higher in localities with by higher incidence of social conflict. We measure the likelihood of social conflict using the interaction of the size of the two electoral coalitions. The interaction takes higher values in cases when both electoral coalitions are high. We expect to find a positive relationship between this measure and the incidence of coercion.

Table 5.5 presents the results of our analysis of the variation in the incidence of welfare coercion across Hungarian and Romanian municipalities. We estimate three different models with each sample. The first model examines the relationship between the locality-level variables of interest and the incidence of welfare coercion. The second model adds two additional locality-level controls, and the third includes individual-level controls. These covariates include variables that measure the gender, age, and ethnicity of the respondent, and in the case of Romania, the respondent's education. Columns 1 through 3 present the results for Hungary, and 4 through 6 for Romania. In all specifications, the continuous variables are standardized for ease of interpretation.

We first discuss the relationship between the variables that we hypothesized would increase the ability of local actors to influence voters by politicizing state resources. First, we hypothesized that the index of local political control would be positively related to state-based forms of clientelism including welfare coercion. Table 5.5 shows little support for that hypothesis in both the Hungarian and Romanian cases. Figure 5.5 breaks down the Local Control index into its sub-indicators using the specification in columns 2 and 5 of Table 5.5. When looking at these disaggregated results, we find some evidence that incumbency is associated with welfare coercion in Romania. The coefficients on co-partisanship with the national executive are consistently positive but statistically indistinguishable from zero, and the coefficients on united local government (having the same party in control of a plurality of the city council and the mayor's office) are very close to zero. Taken together, the disaggregated results also suggest that local political control has little effect on state coercion.

On the other hand, we find some support that poor local economic conditions are associated with higher state coercion, at least in the Hungarian case. Localities in Hungary that are one standard deviation higher in the proportion of their

Table 5.5 Correlates of policy coercion in Hungary and Romania

	(1)	(2)	(3)	(4)	(5)	(6)
			Dependent variable			
			Policy Coercion			
Retrenchment Coalition	0.07**	0.07**	0.07**	0.07*	0.08	0.09*
	(0.03)	(0.03)	(0.03)	(0.04)	(0.05)	(0.05)
Expansion Coalition	0.03	0.03	0.03	0.005	0.003	−0.02
	(0.03)	(0.03)	(0.03)	(0.04)	(0.04)	(0.04)
Retrenchment × Expansion (Social Conflict)	0.02	0.02	0.02	−0.05	−0.05	−0.03
	(0.02)	(0.02)	(0.02)	(0.06)	(0.06)	(0.06)
Local Control	0.004	0.01	0.002	0.04	0.04	0.04
	(0.02)	(0.02)	(0.02)	(0.03)	(0.03)	(0.03)
Poverty Rate	0.27	0.26	0.28	−0.02	−0.03	−0.03
	(0.19)	(0.19)	(0.19)	(0.03)	(0.03)	(0.03)
Debt Rate	0.03**	0.04**	0.04**	0.002	0.004	−0.01
	(0.02)	(0.02)	(0.02)	(0.03)	(0.03)	(0.03)
Mayor Margin		−0.001	−0.01		−0.03	−0.02
		(0.02)	(0.02)		(0.03)	(0.03)
Population		−0.01	−0.01		−0.01	−0.01
		(0.02)	(0.02)		(0.04)	(0.04)
Roma			−0.04			0.20**
			(0.04)			(0.08)
Female			0.02			0.04
			(0.03)			(0.06)
Education						−0.0002
						(0.02)
Age			−0.02			−0.003
			(0.03)			(0.04)
Employed			−0.08			−0.07
			(0.06)			(0.26)
Unemployed			−0.04			−0.19
			(0.06)			(0.27)
Retired			−0.03			−0.14
			(0.08)			(0.28)
Direct Effects	✓	✓	✓	✓	✓	✓
Observations Akaike Inf. Crit.	1,779	1,779	1,672	1,440	1,440	1,425
	1,190.02	1,219.50	1,170.15	2,424.48	2,451.94	2,487.35
		Hungary			Romania	

*p<0.1; **p<0.05; ***p<0.01

Standard errors in parentheses.

Models are estimated using a multilevel model with intercepts varying by locality. The coefficients shown are from interactions with the list treatment indicator. Local Control is an additive index of indicators that take a value of 1 if the locality has a mayor who is an incumbent, a co-partisan with the national executive, or from the same party as the plurality in the city council. Retrenchment Coalition is the average of the standardized proportions of the anti-workfare constituency: the employed and retirees. Expansion Coalition is the average of the standardized proportions of the pro-workfare constituency: the unemployed and Roma. Retrenchment X Expansion is the interaction of the pro- and anti-workfare constituencies. Poverty Rate is the proportion of inhabitants who are below the poverty line. Debt Rate is the proportion of survey respondents by locality who reported being in debt. Mayor Margin is the margin of victory of the mayor. Population is the population size. Roma, Female, Age, Employed, Unemployed, Retired, Debt, and Poor are individual-level variables coded from our surveys. All but Age and Poor are binary. All continuous variables are standardized.

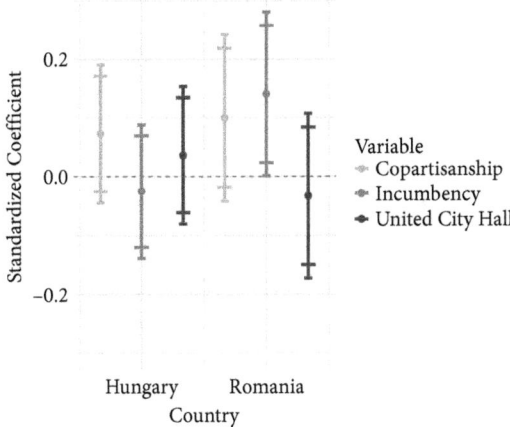

Figure 5.5 Coefficients on sub-indicators of the local control index

residents who have some kind of debt are almost four percentage points higher in their incidence of welfare coercion. The proportion of residents below the poverty line in Hungary is also associated with higher welfare coercion, although this relationship is not statistically significant. There is little evidence that poor economic conditions are associated with higher welfare coercion in Romania.

Next we turn to the variables that we predicted would weaken the public's propensity to punish candidates and mayors for engaging in coercive clientelistic strategies. Here we find that the size of the Retrenchment Coalition, composed of the retired and employed population, is positively and significantly associated with the incidence of welfare coercion in both cases. In both cases, a one-standard-deviation increase in the size of the Retrenchment Coalition is associated with an increase in the incidence of welfare coercion of seven to nine percentage points.

Interestingly, there is no significant relationship between the size of the Expansion Coalition and Retrenchment Coalition, our proxy for social conflict over welfare benefits. This may be because welfare benefits are so politicized that even in areas with relatively small unemployed and Roma populations, welfare coercion is not punished by members of the Retrenchment Coalition such as retirees or the employed. Figure 5.6 plots the marginal effect of a one standard deviation increase in the size of the Retrenchment Coalition at varying sizes of the Expansion Coalition.

Figure 5.6 visualizes the results of the coefficients on social conflict presented in Table 5.5. The figure on the left presents the marginal effect in Hungary, and that on the right in Romania. The light gray area represents 95 percent confidence intervals for the linear estimate, while the black dots are the estimated marginal effects of the Retrenchment Coalition when the Expansion Coalition is analyzed as

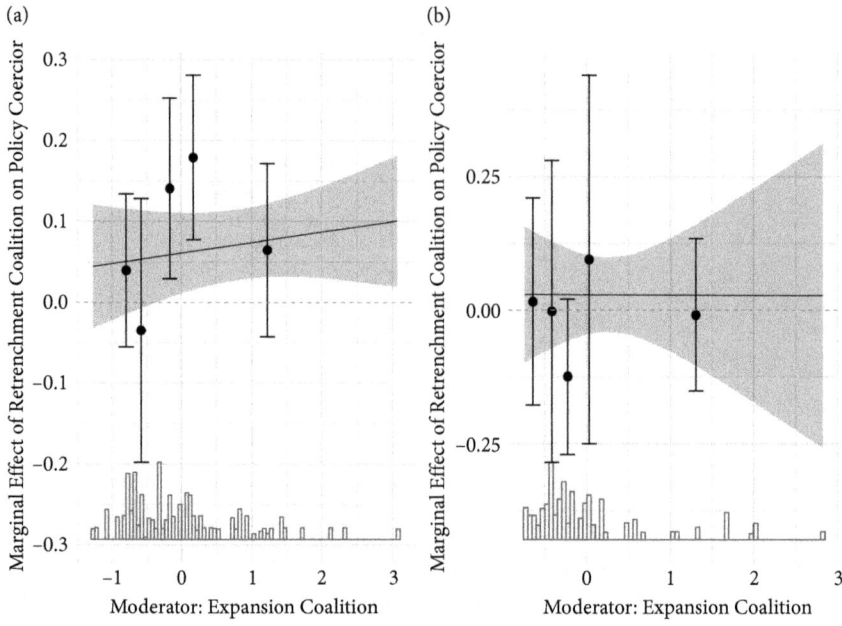

Figure 5.6 The marginal effects of a one standard-deviation increase in the Retrenchment Coalition at varying levels of the Expansion Coalition on Policy Coercion

a five-category variable. The grey histogram on the x-axis shows the distribution of the moderating variable. The Hungary plot shows that at almost all levels of the Expansion Coalition, an increase in the size of the Retrenchment Coalition is associated with a higher use of welfare coercion. The effect does get larger as the size of the Expansion Coalition increases, but as Table 5.5 shows this interaction is not statistically significant. In the Romanian case, the marginal effect of the Retrenchment Coalition is positive at most values of the Expansion Coalition and there is no apparent interaction effect between the sizes of the two coalitions.

5.5 Conclusion

Drawing on qualitative interviews with voters, candidates, and brokers in rural communities and on the analysis of new survey data, this chapter has documented the existence of non-programmatic electoral strategies premised on coercion. We have illustrated a variety of pre-electoral and electoral strategies that allow candidates and their brokers to use social policy benefits to engage in coercion and blackmail at elections.

We also presented two levels of quantitative tests of our hypotheses in this chapter. First, we tested the micro-foundations of our argument that different forms of clientelism send programmatic signals to voters. We found strong evidence that voters are staunchly opposed to candidates who use policy resources in clientelistic transactions, and view them as less desirable on a range of personal and policy dimensions. The large negative effect of policy clientelism on our respondents' voting intentions suggests that the electoral costs of clientelism may be a significant consideration for candidates seeking to win elections. In addition, we found that these electoral costs might vary across voters. Specifically, voters with anti-workfare preferences view coercive candidates more permissively on some policy and personal qualities, and these same voters view candidates who offer favors more harshly. These programmatic signals affect the extent to which voters expect candidates to effectively represent their interests once in office, particularly on the key local policy issue of the workfare program.

Finally, we tested the extent to which locality-level characteristics, including the size of demographic groups that hold pro- and anti-workfare preferences, relate to the incidence of welfare coercion at the locality level in both Hungary and Romania. As in Chapter 4, we found little support for theories based on the availability of resources to engage in clientelism. Indicators of local political control are largely unrelated to the incidence of policy coercion. We do find, however, that electoral strategies premised on welfare coercion occur in localities with residents who are opposed to the current welfare distribution and therefore less likely to judge candidates who use policy coercion harshly. This is in stark contrast to the results in Chapter 4, where we find that candidates and their brokers in Hungary are more likely to offer policy favors when demographic conditions reduce social conflict between groups of poor voters. These results lend support to the proposition that clientelistic strategies premised on positive versus negative inducements are driven by different political logics. These logics, in turn, seem to be shaped more by the propensities of voters to negatively update their beliefs about candidates who use various forms of clientelism than the availability of resources that can be used in clientelistic transactions.

These results provide important insight into how clientelism persists, despite its apparent unpopularity with most voters. Our results show that although most voters judge clientelistic candidates harshly, in localities where there is conflict over policy resources, those who are unhappy with the current distribution of social policy benefits are willing to overlook even a strategy as noxious as welfare coercion if they interpret it as a signal that a candidate will act in their interests once in office. As a result, welfare coercion can be used without strong electoral sanctions in localities where demographic conditions create social conflict over social policy spending between the "working" and "nonworking" poor.

Notes

1. However, it is important to note that the questions do have a normative tone ("to avoid paying people to be lazy" and "in order to help the elderly") that might prevent even pro-workfare voters from seeing them in a very positive light.
2. The substantive interpretations of the other voting outcomes are similar. In the control condition only 11 percent of respondents say they would be very likely or sure to abstain and 24 percent very likely or sure to vote for a different candidate compared to 23 percent and 66 percent in the favors condition.

6

Economic Coercion

Conflict and Forbearance

Chapter 5 documented the existence of strategies premised on welfare coercion, where brokers condition future access to social policy on political support. In this chapter, we examine coercive strategies executed by brokers who control a variety of economic resources that are not state-owned. Such economic resources may include loans, land, employment, and wages. Brokers controlling such resources may use threats to worsen the terms of their ongoing exchange with voters to induce them to support a candidate. We refer to these electoral strategies as economic coercion.

Economic coercion takes a wide variety of forms. Tenant farmers may threaten people who lease their land to return their land or to lower the amount of in-kind goods that are offered in exchange for their land. Employers may threaten their employees with a worsening of the terms of the employment relationship or layoffs, an even more severe economic punishment, of voters who make an undesirable political choice. Finally, moneylenders may threaten their clients that the terms of their exchange may worsen if they support the incorrect candidate. In all of these cases, such brokers condition voters' continued access to a particular economic resource or the continuation of the current exchange on electoral support.

Economic coercion is one of the oldest non-programmatic electoral strategies. Electoral intimidation of workers by their employers was a widespread political phenomenon in all European countries in the decades following the adoption of mass suffrage (Anderson 2000; Mares 2015; Mares and Zhu 2015). In Germany, the country where this phenomenon was most pervasive, employers intervened at all stages of the electoral campaign—from the announcement of a candidacy to the casting of ballots (Mares and Zhu 2015). Employers waged aggressive campaigns among their employees in support of particular candidates and confiscated the electoral materials of opposition candidates. On voting day, employers regimented their workers in columns, marched them to the voting place, and monitored them as they cast their ballots. Employers also engaged in systematic post-electoral harassment of voters who supported opposition candidates, reduced the wages of such employees, and even dismissed individuals or groups of workers (Anderson 2000; Klein 2003). In Britain, large firms in industrial constituencies made "party allegiance one of their hiring terms" (Hanham 1959: 68), thus ensuring the dominance of Liberal candidates in their districts. Similarly, in France, electoral coercion by employers persisted throughout the Third Republic (Charnay 1964; Garrigou 1992). Such forms of economic coercion were documented as late as 1914. At the time, urban employers threatened workers with layoffs, if the "factory" candidate was not elected (Journal Officiel de la République Française, Débats Chambre des Députés 1914: 31).

Economic intimidation is, regrettably, not an extinct political phenomenon, but one that persists in contemporary elections in recent European democracies (Mares, Muntean and Petrova 2018). In this chapter, we document the existence of electoral practices premised on economic coercion in recent elections in Hungary and Romania. We begin by drawing on interviews with candidates, brokers, and voters to illustrate the incidence of electoral strategies involving economic coercion. We document the existence of different types of economic brokers used by candidates, including moneylenders and tenant farmers.

Next, we report the quantitative results of surveys that attempt to measure the incidence of coercive strategies using non-obtrusive survey techniques and analyze the variation across localities in the incidence of strategies of economic coercion. Consistent with the theoretical predictions formulated in Chapter 2, we show that such strategies of economic coercion are more salient in localities where poor economic conditions give brokers leverage to use over voters, and where social conditions are so polarized that candidates face lower electoral sanctions for the use of coercion. In the remainder of the chapter, we examine the use of coercive strategies where the main brokers deployed to influence voters' choices are employers and informal moneylenders.

Taken together with the evidence about the divergence in the interpretation of clientelistic strategies between right- and left-wing voters presented in Chapter 5, the evidence presented in this chapter helps explain how candidates who rely on at least some popular support can obfuscate such electoral strategies that strongly violate normative practices. Our findings suggest that politicians and brokers operating on their behalf are able to exploit voters' economic vulnerabilities in environments where poor versus poor conflicts are pervasive. In such environments, less vulnerable voters who resent the very poor are less likely to negatively update their perceptions of politicians who use electoral coercion.

6.1 Economic Coercion: Candidates, Brokers and their Strategies

6.1.1 Moneylenders as brokers

The previous two chapters have documented that candidates competing in parliamentary elections rely on employees of the local administration to cultivate electoral loyalties throughout their mandates, to mobilize voters at elections, and to attempt to pierce the secrecy of the vote. State employees who are selected to perform these strategies usually share the partisanship of the candidate or of the mayor of the locality. The degree of integration of such brokers with the party organization varies, however, across different parties. Romanian parties that have a strong infrastructure have strongly integrated partisan brokers within their organization. By contrast, Hungarian parties, which have a much weaker organizational reach than Romanian parties do, compete by co-opting nominally independent brokers as coordinators of local political activities.

In addition to state employees, candidates can deploy brokers who control economic resources that constitute significant economic streams for voters. As this chapter will document, the term economic brokers encompasses a heterogeneous mix of "characters" that includes employers, tenants, and moneylenders. Due to the diversity among these brokers, we find significant heterogeneity in the relationship between such candidates and brokers. Some of these brokers may be integrated internally within the party organization and provide electoral support in exchange for goods or political advancement within the party organization. Other brokers may be in a very loose relationship to the candidate. Some of these brokers are engaged in illicit activities, and their continued operation may be contingent on candidates' willingness to turn a blind eye. In such cases, candidates incentivize brokers at elections by exploiting this initial forbearance. On other occasions, brokers may exploit their economic strength within the locality to exert power over their politician patrons.

Moneylenders are an example of the economic brokers one encounters in many low-income communities in northern Hungary. We also encountered these practices in small rural Romanian communities, though they are less pervasive there. In both Romania and Hungary, moneylending or usury is an economic activity that is prosecutable under the penal law. Often this illicit activity persists only because local authorities decide not to prosecute such offenses. Even in cases where local law enforcement authorities attempt to eradicate such exploitative economic arrangements, their efforts may be stymied by officials' unwillingness to denounce such illicit activities. One of our respondents in NO., a Hungarian locality in Borsod county, commented on the difficulties of prosecuting such illicit activities as follows:

> My husband is a policeman in a neighboring locality. He is an investigator in the department prosecuting criminal activities. And even he could not denounce the moneylender. People were not willing to come and testify against the moneylender and this is why we could not denounce him at the police.
>
> (NO., Interview 11, July 27, 2015)

In BF., another locality in Borsod, we learned about the presence of five prominent moneylending families and about the strong competition among them (BF.,

Interview 4, July 27, 2015). After 2006, the locality and some neighboring settlements experienced higher than usual suicide rates. The police began investigating the activities of moneylenders due to suspicions that they were involved in these deaths (BF., Interview 2, July 21, 2015). This investigation was followed by a number of arrests of moneylenders, who were then released shortly thereafter. After this initiative by the police, moneylenders shifted to more informal activities. A former mayor of the locality commented on the changes resulting from this initiative:

> These days, moneylending appears to be a hidden thing. But it is a very serious problem. There was a time when it was wide in the open, unbelievably so. What I mean is, one could find a BMW waiting in front of the Savings Bank and [...] ninety people waiting in front of the car. Next to the car, one could see five powerful men waiting. And people went to these men, one by one. On one occasion, a local government official placed a camera that recorded a similar scene. A man took out money from the bank, came out and one could see that [he] gave twenty thousand Forint to the moneylender who returned two thousand Forint. And when the police started to go after these moneylenders ... I saw more and more news about moneylenders getting caught. So I think that's when they realized [...] that they couldn't do it this openly. They are still doing it, but it is more hidden. But no one prosecutes them, because they are afraid to do it.
>
> (BF., Interview 14, July 23, 2015)

Questions about moneylenders were arguably the most sensitive part of our interviews, and as a result, it was significantly more difficult to document this clientelistic practice than the other non-programmatic strategies we examine in our book. Spending multiple days in each locality, using skilled local researchers, and promising that not only individual respondents' names but also the locality names would be anonymized were important factors that persuaded some respondents to provide information on this sensitive dynamic. To illustrate the difficulties in reaching these brokers, consider the field notes of one member of our research team:

> I built trust with my constant presence; I spent full days in the village, trying to speak with as many people as I could. I also told some information, my opinion on the research. I spoke about my other field experiences, comparing their village with others. Generally speaking it was not hard to get access to the main actors of the village or find the key informants; however, after certain number of interviews and conversations the openness of the field ceased to exist, they started to repeat narratives I already heard. They did not give further names, such as the names of moneylenders.   (Field notes, BF., July 23, 2015)

Moneylending practices differ significantly across localities. In one locality in Romania, moneylenders use well-specified legal contracts that are formulated by a lawyer (S., Interview 6, September 15, 2015). In many other localities, the contracts between lenders and borrowers are agreed to only informally. Sometimes voters borrow only small amounts of money that are necessary to purchase food or other everyday consumables. In other cases, personal emergencies such as sickness lead people to turn to moneylenders for larger amounts. The interest rates on loans vary considerably and can be as high as 100 percent (NO., Interview 11, July 27, 2015). The penalties for not repaying can be also very high. In one Romanian locality, the lender requires creditors who fall behind in repaying their outstanding debt to pay 2 percent of the outstanding debt every day. If borrowers cannot make these payments, moneylenders take possession of their valuable goods and sometimes evict them from their homes.

In most cases, moneylenders prey on the most impoverished and vulnerable persons. One respondent in RM., a locality in northern Hungary, characterized borrowers as "very poor families, who often lack access to electricity. They often do not have money even to buy bread. Then they need to go to the moneylender to beg him for money. There are some families who have five children and go to the moneylender to borrow money for food" (RM., Interview 4, August 22, 2015). Another respondent in BF., commented on the poverty of persons turning to moneylenders: "these persons don't have shoes, don't have clothes and don't have food" (BF., Interview 14, July 23, 2015). In this locality, moneylenders exploited the inability of many impoverished people to pay for the school bus for their children. Many children in this locality take a bus to attend school in a neighboring locality located ten kilometers away. On the days when passes for the school busses were on sale, moneylenders make their appearance in bus stops, offering parents high interest-rate loans to parents so they can purchase these passes (BF., Interview 14, July 23, 2015).

Finally, we encountered cases when moneylenders used violence against clients who could not repay their debts. One moneylender we encountered in Romania reported that he used to lock up people who defaulted in the basement of his building. Here, victims spent days without food or water. The moneylender casually referred to these clients as his "slaves." He also reported that he forcefully employed persons who could not repay their debt as a means of repayment (S., Interview 6, September 15, 2015).

Our interviews suggest that relationships between moneylenders and local elected officials take two common forms. In the first, moneylenders are able to operate because they can exert some personal power over the local political system. In some cases, this power stems from the fact that moneylenders themselves hold political office, are close relatives of the mayor, or are so powerful that they can intimidate local officials. In the second, the mayor and moneylenders have a symbiotic relationship in which the mayor facilitates the moneylenders' financial operations through forbearance and the moneylenders support the mayor by mobilizing their clients around elections. The power dynamic in this relationship may shift over time: sometimes, the mayor may be able to use the threat of prosecution to strongly motivate the moneylenders, while at others, moneylenders can exert disproportionate influence over political decisions because the mayor owes his electoral victory to their political intervention.

We focus primarily on the latter arrangement, in which moneylenders and mayors exchange electoral influence for forbearance, because the former is less relevant for electoral clientelism. Political developments in NO., a locality in northern Hungary, illustrate this type of interaction between the candidate and brokers. Here, the presence and thriving economic activity of the moneylenders can be attributed to the decisions of a long-term incumbent mayor, who tolerated such illicit activities in order to extract the moneylenders' services at elections. One respondent explains:

> I think that this has been going for a long time. For sure there are three or four cycles since he the mayor collaborates with the moneylender. It should be known that this man was confronted with the law on many occasions. He was in pre-trial detention and the mayor always paid bail and brought him out of jail. So he owes a lot to the mayor. The mayor does not hinder the activities of the moneylender in the locality. He can do things as freely as he wants. The moneylender can go and obtain wood whenever he wants [refers to free wood found on the locality's common grounds] and he can sell anything he wants. He can lend money, sell drugs and do anything he wants because the mayor protects him. The mayor lets him do his business. (NO., Interview 5, July 16, 2015)

In other cases, forbearance takes the form of decisions to tolerate tax evasion by the moneylender. One such broker we interviewed in S., a locality in southern Romania, reported that the promise to "forgive" the non-payment of taxes is used not just by mayors, but by politicians competing for parliamentary and senate elections. Such politicians, this moneylender reported, "came to me and told me that they will help with my taxes if I help them obtain a certain number of votes in the locality" (S., Interview 6, September 15, 2015).

Mayors often combine forbearance with offers of immediate material benefits to the moneylender and to members of their family. One respondent in NO., a locality in Borsod county, recalls that members of the family of the moneylender benefit from public housing from the municipality (NO., Interview 11, July 27, 2015). Another respondent points to material inducements offered by the mayor of the locality to the moneylender:. "I asked the moneylender: Why do you go against your own people? What are ten trucks of wood?" (NO., Interview 2, July 15, 2015).

In other cases, tolerance of illicit moneylending is facilitated by close personal connections between moneylenders and political officials. In RM., a locality in Borsod county, Hungary, the deputy mayor is engaged in illicit moneylending. Together with his large "influential family," he owns several stores in the locality and also acts as an informal moneylender. His loans allow his clients to purchase durable consumer goods and also basic foodstuffs. Discussing the role of this family in the municipality, one respondent noted: "This family is very influential in terms of the economy, but also in politics. They lead the entire village and they have a very good relationship with the mayor" (RM., Interview 7, August 24, 2015).

In other localities, the relationship between moneylenders and politicians are more closely connected. In RM, the deputy mayor acted also as informal money-lender. Here, the deputy mayor owned a local store that sold small household items and food. Employees of the public works program were his most significant customers, and he offered employees of the public works program loans at the time these employees were paid by the municipality. At the time the employees receive their salaries in cash, the deputy mayor offers them loans for household consumables. One respondent recalls that "employees receive their salaries in an envelope in cash. If a person receives 55,000 HUF as salary, then the family of the mayor allows him to take a loan up to 50,000 HUF." Both the notary and the mayor generally consent to this transaction (RM., Interview 10, August 25, 2015).

In BF., a locality in northern Hungary, respondents feel that moneylenders exert disproportionate influence in the locality. The situation became especially acute after 2010, when a new mayor won with their strong backing. Many respondents in this locality think moneylenders exert a decisive influence over this mayor. One statement that came up in repeated interviews was that money-lenders chose a mayor who could be their puppet. As a result, moneylenders are the true "rulers" of the locality. "In my humble opinion, illegal creditors exert a high influence on the mayor. They want people who owe them money to remain employed in the workfare program so that they continue making their monthly payments. They point to people and the mayor employs them. They lead and control the village" (BF., Interview 8, July 22, 2015). Another respondent expressed similar considerations about the power of moneylenders. Moneylenders "see their interest in everything and they want to increase their power. There are growing accusations that moneylenders tell employees of the local administration who should be employed in workfare" (BF., Interview 3, July 20, 2015).

S., in southeastern Romania, is one such place where moneylenders exert disproportionate influence over the mayors' political activities. We had a unique opportunity to gain insights into the informal politics of this locality, because a moneylender in S. consented to discuss the political situation with us. We corroborated the information shared by the moneylender with former mayors and candidates for local office. The moneylender of this locality met with us and openly discussed his illicit electoral strategies. The meeting took place in the moneylender's compound, a place known locally as The Castle.

The moneylender owned several construction companies in the locality and several enterprises in Bucharest. These considerable economic resources gave him the clout to become the main "coordinator" of all local political activities. Due to his remarkable economic strength in this locality, the moneylender is the de facto king-maker; his influence allows him to choose the winner in local and parliamentary elections. He also operates as the informal arbiter of legal disputes: "There is no police left and I have to make my own justice," he informed us (S., Interview 6, September 15, 2015). The moneylender takes great pride in his ability to influence the number of candidates in a race. If the likely outcome of a race appears to tilt toward an unfavorable candidate, the moneylender intervenes, by creating the "political opportunity" for a new candidate to enter the race. He also claims to play a personal role in selecting the candidates who run for different offices. The mayor of this locality—who had been elected in 2010 thanks to "support" from the moneylender—resigned before completing his mandate. Over time, the moneylender had grown increasingly disappointed with the mayor's unwillingness "to fulfill his obligations" toward those who made this political victory possible. "He did not want to adapt, he did not steal, he was stupid," the broker commented: "I have helped him personally at elections. When somebody appoints you as mayor, you have certain obligations toward those who have helped you and brought you to office." After the resignation of this mayor, the moneylender supported another "familiar" candidate. He characterized the current mayor as someone who "had previously worked for me and was employed in my company" (S., Interview 6, September 15, 2015).

Across the different sites of our study, moneylenders perform a range of political activities on candidates' behalf, including electoral mobilization. Such mobilization consists in persuading their clients to turn out and vote and bringing them to the polls. The moneylender we interviewed in southeastern Romania referred to these mobilization efforts quite casually: "I put some cars in place and help the candidates with cars" (S., Interview 6, September 15, 2015). In NO., Hungary, a respondent also recalled that the "moneylender brought people to vote in a Ford Transit bus" (NO., Interview 11, July 27, 2015).

In other localities, the electoral mobilization involves more violent threats. In NO., an ethnically segregated town in northern Hungary, the mayor deployed the moneylender to mobilize voters from a remote Roma settlement located on a hill, outside the locality. Voters described the moneylender as the mayor's "right-hand man" or as the "soldier" of the mayor (NO., Interview 2, July 15, 2015). Moneylenders sought to mobilize voters using violent language, threats of extortion, and threats of physical violence. Our respondents recalled:

RESPONDENT: Here, in our county, there is a person having power and authority in many fields. So it is an open secret that the mayor looked for this person and sent him to the hill and to the other settlement where Roma people live. And he said that you have to vote for the mayor. If not, there will be problems.
INTERVIEWER: In 2014?

RESPONDENT: In 2014 and also before. He threatened voters that it will be the end for all of them if the mayor does not win. (NO., Interview 2, July 15, 2015)

RESPONDENT: There is a man who is the mayor's right hand. He is serving the mayor's wishes. So if the mayor asks something than he (this man) goes and does it. It can be anything, such as threats or even acts of violence. During the last elections, when I was also campaigning, I witnessed this man threatening people verbally. He threatened voters that they will encounter problems if they do not vote for the mayor.

INTERVIEWER: What kind of problems?

RESPONDENT: It can be anything. I saw him hitting voters. This man is a street-fighter champion. He had a lot of troubles with the law and he is a drug dealer and moneylender in the locality. This man also has illegal duties. The mayor found a person that can help him reach out and mediate with Roma voters. This man is employed by the mayor at elections and so far it has been working. (NO., Interview 5, July 16, 2015)

Such electoral mobilization goes hand in hand with efforts to persuade voters to support a particular candidate. In discussing the electoral influence of money-lenders, several respondents in BF., a locality in northern Hungary, observed that soft pressure was sufficient to persuade voters to support a particular candidate. One respondent stated: "People who owed money followed the commands made by moneylenders. Violent threats were unnecessary. The only thing that money-lenders had to do was to tell them whom to vote for" (BF., Interview 12, July 23, 2015). Another respondent explained that voters could not turn down requests made by moneylenders to support particular candidates: "The client system works like a big family where the one who has capital rules all those who owe them. If the lenders ask you for a favor, you cannot refuse" (BF., Interview 10, July 23, 2015). Similarly, the pastor of this locality characterized the electoral pressure exerted by moneylenders on voters as silent and "natural." "Things like this happen in every election. The moneylender persuaded their clients to vote for the current mayor. These events are a natural part of the elections" (BF., Interview 11, July 23, 2015).

In RM., a locality in northern Hungary, moneylenders exert pressure on voters by using threats that the terms of their economic exchange will otherwise deteri-orate. On many occasions, such influence involves threats that loans will not be available if they support a particular candidate. The moneylender in RM., for example, was, in fact, the deputy mayor. As elections approached, this lender pressured voters to support his candidacy: "The moneylender told voters to vote for him. Many voters believe they he will really know that they did not vote for him. And later, if they want to get a loan, they are afraid that they will not have this possibility. Do you understand? If they run out of money on the fifth of the month and they have to obtain a loan, they are afraid that the lender will not give it to them because the lender knows that they did not vote for him" (RM., Interview 4, August 22, 2015).

The moneylender we interviewed in Romania prides himself on having developed cunning strategies to ensure that voters vote "correctly." This moneylender asks voters to place their hand on the Bible and swear to support a particular candidate. While this is a strategy we encountered in other Romanian localities, this broker prides himself on having found a way to reduce the likelihood of voters' defection. "If voters swear they will vote for candidate X," he explains to us, "then they could vote for other candidates and then cancel their vote." For this reason, he asks voters to swear that they will "vote for candidate X and only for candidate X." When asked whether the strategy is effective, he conjectures that only 5 percent of the voters may break their promise. "The threat is more effective if voters have a child in their arms," he explains. "Then they do not break their promise. There were other cases of people who changed their vote, then they went to the priest to ask to be liberated from their promises." At the voting place, this broker selects additional helpers who monitor voters at the time they cast their ballot. "Some of the ballots are transparent and one can see through them. I hire people who help you see how people are voting. These are people who take the ballot from the hand of the voter and put it in the urn after looking at it. Then they nod, if the person had voted correctly" (S., Interview 6, September 15, 2015).

6.1.2 Social polarization and the use of economic coercion

As this evidence indicates, moneylenders thrive in localities characterized by high levels of poverty and unemployment. We have also conjectured that candidates are likely to find coercive strategies more attractive in localities characterized by high levels of local distributional conflict or polarization. In such localities, candidates seek to extract two distinct electoral gains from using coercive strategies. On the one hand, they hope to capture the votes of coerced voters. On the other hand, in using repressive and exploitative electoral strategies, candidates seek to convey a signal of "toughness" and disrespect for the rights of those coerced. In polarized localities, such signals are of value to candidates who court the electoral support of voters who themselves disregard the coerced voters. At the least, these policy signals mitigate the negative effects of clientelism on how voters view candidates that use it. At best, they may even boost support for these candidates with voters who are strongly against the existing distribution of social spending.

To illustrate the interplay of both considerations in accounting for the use of coercive strategies, we consider their use in BF., a locality in Borsod county, Hungary. BF. is a small locality with a population of 2,500 persons which also experiences a high politicization of the ethnic conflict between ethnic Hungarians and Roma. According to the results of the 2010 Hungarian census, 35 percent of the population belongs to the ethnic Roma minority. Ethnic Hungarian voters in this locality perceive, however, that the share of Roma voters is significantly higher and that the "ongoing struggle" over the future of this community hangs in a fragile balance (BF., Interview 8, July 22, 2015). Tensions escalated during a festival held in 2014. At the end of this festival, which had been organized with the goal of bringing the community together, members of the two ethnic groups found themselves on opposite sides of the main road, throwing stones at each other (BF., Interview 1, July 21, 2015).

Between 2006 and 2010, the mayor of BF. won office with electoral support from ethnic Hungarians. When we asked who his main supporters were, the mayor indicated that his main constituency was the elderly ethnic Hungarian voters. "Basically the older people," he replied, "people who want the security, peace and quiet. That's all" (BF., Interview 14, July 23, 2015). When the mayor discusses the situation of the ethnic Roma voters in the locality, he shares the racially charged views of other ethnic Hungarians: "The problem is [. . .] that integrating the people is a really good, really righteous goal. Integration should have happened over 500 years ago. But it failed. The problem is, the majority that cannot integrate. But in a village like this, the majority cannot integrate because the majority is actually a minority. And I don't know what will happen to localities like ours. Localities like Taktaszada, Taktaharkány, Taktakenéz, Báj. There are unbelievably many localities that are in a similar position" (BF., Interview 14, July 23, 2015).

The ethnic conflict in this locality between Roma and Hungarians is linked to and reinforced by economic conflict. As in other Hungarian localities, the distributional issue that is most divisive is the scope of the workfare program and the allocation of workfare benefits. The mayor of the locality between 2006 and 2010 opposed the workfare program. In his words, the program "does not create any economic value, but only waste" (BF., Interview 14, July 23, 2015). The mayor signed the "Taktaharkány proposal," a policy document that called for the dramatic overhaul of the workfare program. He explains his opposition to the workfare program:

When I was mayor, I signed the proposal of the Taktaharkány mayor. So we wrote down that we wanted jobs instead of welfare support. We only wanted four or six hours of daily work and a salary that is not higher than half the minimal wage, because it would create competition to the private sector. And this is exactly what happened. Nowadays, 16-year-old children are taken out of school and sent to the public work because that way they bring home more money. And the people who were working for the contractor for 110,000 forints, they say they won't do it anymore. Because they prefer to work as public sector workers for 70,000 forint, because they don't have to do anything to earn the money from the workfare program.   (BF., Interview 14, July 23, 2015)

In this highly polarized locality, the mayor competed by enlisting moneylenders as brokers. The choice of this electoral strategy can be attributed to several factors. On the one hand, his opposition to the workfare program and his unwillingness to expand the policy, deprived the mayor of important clientelistic instruments. On the other hand, due to electoral uncertainty, some Roma votes were necessary to the mayor. The mayor discussed his strategy to mobilize Roma voters using moneylenders in language that was highly racially charged: "With these people [sic], a person who graduated from the university is not considered a good person. A good person is the person who spent most time in prison, whose arm is the strongest from whom they can borrow money. These things have influence over them. I think it's pretty clear...America in the twenties. The clans, who are pushing the people in front of them, influencing them, existed even then. This is natural. And unfortunately this will get to the point, I dare to say that this is happening right now" (BF., Interview 14, July 23, 2015).

At the same time, one electoral calculation made by this mayor was that "capturing" the Roma voters using coercive strategies was unlikely to reduce his electoral support among his core constituency, of ethnic Hungarians. In ethnically divided localities, such as BF., the use of coercive strategies is less likely to be punished electorally and candidates using such strategies also expect to derive electoral advantage from using repressive strategies against members of an outsider group. Our discussions with the supporters of this mayor in BF. provide indirect support for this conjecture. While many supporters were aware of the mayor's reliance on moneylenders, they were unwilling to punish this strategy. "The struggle over the fate of the locality," as one supporter of the mayor put it, "is still undecided," which justifies strategies to protect the narrow electoral majority of ethnic Hungarians (BF., Interview 8, July 22, 2015). Other voters' views on the use of coercion is also strongly colored by their hostility toward the Roma. Another voter in this community, who was married to the local pastor and who taught Bible school on Sundays, also expressed support for the mayor. Her support was unaffected by the widespread knowledge of coercive strategies: "The mayor wanted to introduce a sustainable public works program, for people who work and deserve it. Roma do not like to work for money; they want the money but do not want to do anything in exchange. The moneylender persuaded clients to vote for the mayor, but these things are a natural part of elections" (BF., Interview 12, July 23, 2015).

The electoral strategy which allowed this mayor to win office on repeated occasions broke down in recent years. This breakdown is not attributed to the political dissatisfaction of voters, but to the dissatisfaction of moneylenders with the current economic arrangements in the locality. As in other districts, moneylenders pushed for an expansion of employment in the workfare program and were dissatisfied by the current mayor's decision to limit the number of workfare employees. During the 2010 local elections, moneylenders switched sides and supported the challenger, a candidate who promised to expand employment in the workfare program. The former mayor attributes his electoral loss to the switch in political allegiance by the moneylenders: "These people practically joined forces, so I lost the elections" (BF., Interview 14, July 23, 2015).

6.1.3 Land and employment: Other forms of economic coercion in rural communities

Moneylenders are not the only actor exerting influence over the electoral choices of voters through economic coercion. Other brokers leverage a variety of alternative economic resources to influence votes. Rural employers may take advantage of their privileged economic position to influence the vote choice of voters. In contexts where land-leasing is important, agricultural enterprises or corporate tenants may threaten small land-owners with the loss of their holdings if they exhibit the wrong political loyalties.

The relationship between such economic agents and political actors can vary. On some occasions, the political and economic power in the locality may be fused, as incumbent mayors may also own large agricultural enterprises in the area. On other occasions, the economic and political power may be separated: owners of large agricultural enterprises may attempt to leverage their economic power to challenge incumbent mayors or the candidates supported by these incumbents.

In some cases, mayors accumulate both economic and political power. In R., a Romanian locality with 3,000 inhabitants, the mayor owns the largest local agricultural enterprise, holding leases of more than 1,200 hectares of land. Somewhere between 300 and 400 families are in a tenancy relationship with the mayor. In exchange for the right to use their land, the mayor offers these landholders a share of the harvest (*retribuție*). For a long period of time, the share the mayor has repaid to croppers was set at 500kg of harvest/hectare. In recent years, the mayor increased the share to 700kg/hectare in order to pre-empt the activities of competitors.

The mayor exploits his powerful economic situation by pressuring sharecroppers to support him electorally and to support his party's candidates in parliamentary elections. He exerts ample political pressure on many of the area landowners. One local respondent characterizes the economic pressure exercised by the mayor thus: "He tells people, I hold your land, be careful, the elections are coming. Many tenant farmers think that the mayor gives them the food so they need to vote for him" (R., Interview 10, August 19, 2015). Reflecting on his relationship to the mayor, another respondent in this locality explains that it is built on both favors and threats. On the one hand, this voter considers the land-leasing arrangement as a personal favor: "He holds my land, he gives me food and other things, so I will vote for him." But at the same time, the mayor warned him that the terms of their exchange may worsen if the landowner does not show electoral support. As this voter recalls, the mayor often chooses to formulate the threat in the form, "if you don't vote for me, I will not take your land to farm it" (R., Interview 10, August 19, 2015).

Due to his powerful economic position in this area, the mayor can control a large block of voters. This has established his reputation within the Social Democratic Party as one of the most powerful mayors in the county. The principal of the local school characterizes his reputation as follows: "He can mobilize 2,000 voters for anyone competing in any other type of election, either parliamentary, European, presidential or local. He goes to the county, he negotiates with them and tells them: 'I can deliver 2,000 votes out of 2,100 people who are registered to vote.' When one looks at the total share of voters he can mobilize, he is stronger than any of the other mayors in the county" (R., Interview 13, August 21, 2015).

We encountered a similar situation of economic coercion in W., a locality in Teleorman county, Romania. Here, economic pressure is exerted through an agricultural association that employs many of the working-age people. Liviu Dragnea, the current leader of the Social Democratic Party, holds significant shares in this association. As a result of this connection to high-ranking Social Democratic politicians, the agricultural association becomes a central node in the party's electoral machine. Several current and former employees of the agricultural association reported that its managers pressured them to vote for Socialist candidates in local, parliamentary, or presidential elections: "Everybody votes for the Social Democrats," one former employee recalls. "They are afraid to lose their employment. And everybody holds on to their jobs by their teeth. If you don't vote as told, you are out and they will hire another person" (W., Interview 2, October 13, 2016). Another respondent argued that such pressures originate at high levels in the Socialist Party organization: "This is exactly what happens in the enterprise: the orders come from above, you vote as told, if not you lose your job. I have also worked there and I know: if you don't vote how you are told, the next day you can lose your job" (W., Interview 4, October 13, 2016).

The use of economic pressure to incentivize voters is also present in Hungary. In NO., a locality in the north of the country, economic and political power were again fused. The mayor is also the main local employer: he owns a large farm that provides seasonal employment to a significant number of people (NO., Interview 7, July 27, 2015). Employment on the mayor's farm is highly desirable and offers an income of between 4,000 and 5,000 HUF daily (NO., Interview 2, July 15, 2015). Control of voters employed on the farm guaranteed this nominally independent mayor a comfortable political majority and allowed him to win election after election.

The electoral mobilization of workers employed on the farm was particularly pronounced during the 2014 election. At the time, the mayor experienced strong electoral competition from an ethnically Roma candidate. The race ended with the victory of the incumbent mayor, who succeeded in securing his win by a narrow margin of 170 votes. The farm became a site of campaigning during elections. All employees were convened several times in a public place and asked to vote for the mayor (NO., Interview 12, July 27, 2015). One voter recalls that farm employees were told to vote for the mayor in order to maintain employment on the farm (NO., Interview 2, July 15, 2015). Another voter recalls that employees on the farm had no choice but to support the mayor: "If you work on the farm, you will not vote for anybody else, because you 'live from the mayor.' This is a form of dependency" (NO., Interview 1, July 15, 2015).

In other places, actors that control significant economic resources may leverage their economic power to vie for political power. In Q., a locality in southern Romania, the owner of an agricultural enterprise that leases land from a variety of small landowners defeated the long-term incumbent mayor during the 2016 local election. Reflecting on the race, this mayor said: "It is hard to unseat an incumbent, because they pay people, they invite them to meals. It is hard if you don't have your own people" (Q., Interview 18, September 27, 2018). To compete against the incumbent, the challenger drew on the economic resources he controlled. One strategy available to this challenger was to exert pressure on families that leased their land and to warn them that their tenancy agreement would be terminated unless they supported his candidacy. A related strategy used by this mayor was to increase the duration of the tenancy contracts. As a voter recalls: "The tenancy contracts used to be for a period of two or three years. Now, they are for a period of ten years (Q., Interview 19, June 27, 2018).

6.2 Variation across Rural Localities in the Incidence of Economic Coercion

How pervasive is economic coercion compared to other non-programmatic strategies? What explains the variation across localities in the use of this strategy? We turn now to an analysis of these questions, based on the post-electoral surveys we fielded in both Romania and Hungary.

As with the other forms of sensitive electoral behavior we examine in this study, we embedded the survey question measuring the incidence of economic coercion in a list that included other non-sensitive questions and randomized the distribution of questionnaires that included this sensitive question. The two lists that included the sensitive question measuring economic coercion were worded as follows:

Hungary

I am going to read some statements of events that happened or could have happened during elections. Please recall the elections of 6 April, 2014, and tell me how many of these events happened in your locality. You do not need to tell which ones happened exactly, only how many.

- Most people rushed to vote at very early hours of the morning.
- People went to vote at different times of the day.
- The election commission did not have enough ballots for every person who wanted to vote.
- (*Sensitive item*) I worried that I would owe money to my creditor if I voted badly.

Romania

I will read a number of statements that refer to the recent presidential elections held in November 2014. For each of these statements, I would like you to tell me how many of these events happened here, in this community. You do not need to tell me which of these happened, but only how many.

- During the campaign, I met both Victor Ponta and Klaus Johannis.
- In order to vote, the people in the electoral commission at the voting place asked for my ID.
- I waited in line for a few hours in order to vote.
- (*Sensitive item*) A person to whom I owe money told me that I would owe more money if I don't vote for the right candidate.

Table 6.1 presents the aggregate results of the two surveys fielded in both countries. The results presented in this table provide an empirical estimate of the magnitude of electoral strategies premised on economic coercion in both countries. The second row in this table presents the mean number of items reported by respondents who received the control version of the questionnaire, while the following row presents the mean number of items reported by respondents who received the version of the questionnaire that included the sensitive item. The final row reports the difference between these two quantities, which represents the estimate of the incidence of economic coercion in rural settings. In Appendix B, we present additional empirical tests that demonstrate that the respondents who received the treatment and control version of the questionnaire, respectively, did not differ in other observable characteristics. We also present the results of a test for design effects formulated by Blair and Imai (2012). These results reported in the

Table 6.1 Estimated incidence of economic coercion

Country	N	Control Mean	Treatment Mean	Estimated Incidence	*p*-value
Hungary	1,834	1.08 (1.07, 1.09)	1.13 (1.11, 1.15)	5.6% (2.2%, 9%)	0.00
Romania	1,495	1.03 (1.02, 1.04)	1.02 (1.01, 1.03)	−1.2% (−4%, 1.5%)	0.38

appendix show that the inclusion of the sensitive item did not change the list response in illogical ways, and thus indicate that the sensitive item nevertheless caused people to misreport their experiences.

Our survey allows us to identify the presence of economic coercion perpetuated by moneylenders in Hungary. Our findings suggest that around 5 percent of the respondents have experienced economic coercion by moneylenders. We find that the prevalence of economic coercion is similar to that of other non-programmatic strategies such as policy favors and welfare coercion. By contrast, we do not find evidence of economic pressure exerted through moneylenders in the survey fielded in Romania. Our estimate of the overall incidence of economic coercion in Romania is statistically indistinguishable from zero. As a result, going forward we only use the data from Hungary to test our hypotheses about the conditions that give rise to economic coercion.

Figure 6.1 displays the variation in the incidence of moneylender pressure across the Hungarian and Romanian localities included in our study. Darker marks represent localities where over 20 percent of the respondents have experienced moneylender pressure. As displayed in this figure, we find evidence of moneylender pressure across all three Hungarian counties included in our study.

In Chapter 2 we laid out two families of predictions about when forms of clientelism based on economic coercion should be more prevalent. Resource-based theories suggest that the use of economic coercion should be more likely when local political control enables the use of clientelism. Signaling or demand-side theories suggest that economic coercion should be prevalent when local social conditions create conflict over welfare resources. Specifically, we predicted first that economic coercion should be higher when local political institutions are more tightly controlled by local elites through incumbency, co-partisanship with the executive, and a unified city hall.

Our second prediction is that the incidence of economic coercion is higher in localities characterized by high levels of polarization and intense distributional conflicts over the allocation of employment or workfare benefits. In such localities, the use of coercion allows candidates to capture the votes of low-income voters, while also signaling "toughness" and disrespect for the rights of those that are coerced. In communities characterized by intense distributional conflicts, candidates who use coercive strategies expect to incur very low electoral costs from right-leaning voters.

To test this hypothesis—and to allow for comparability to results presented in previous chapters—we use similar measures of distributional conflict in the locality. Given that the distribution of workfare benefits is the most significant divisive issue, we operationalize the coalition favoring policy retrenchment (RETRENCHMENT COALITION) to include both employed and low-income retirees. By contrast, the coalition favoring the expansion of the workfare programs (EXPANSION COALITION) is likely to include the unemployed and

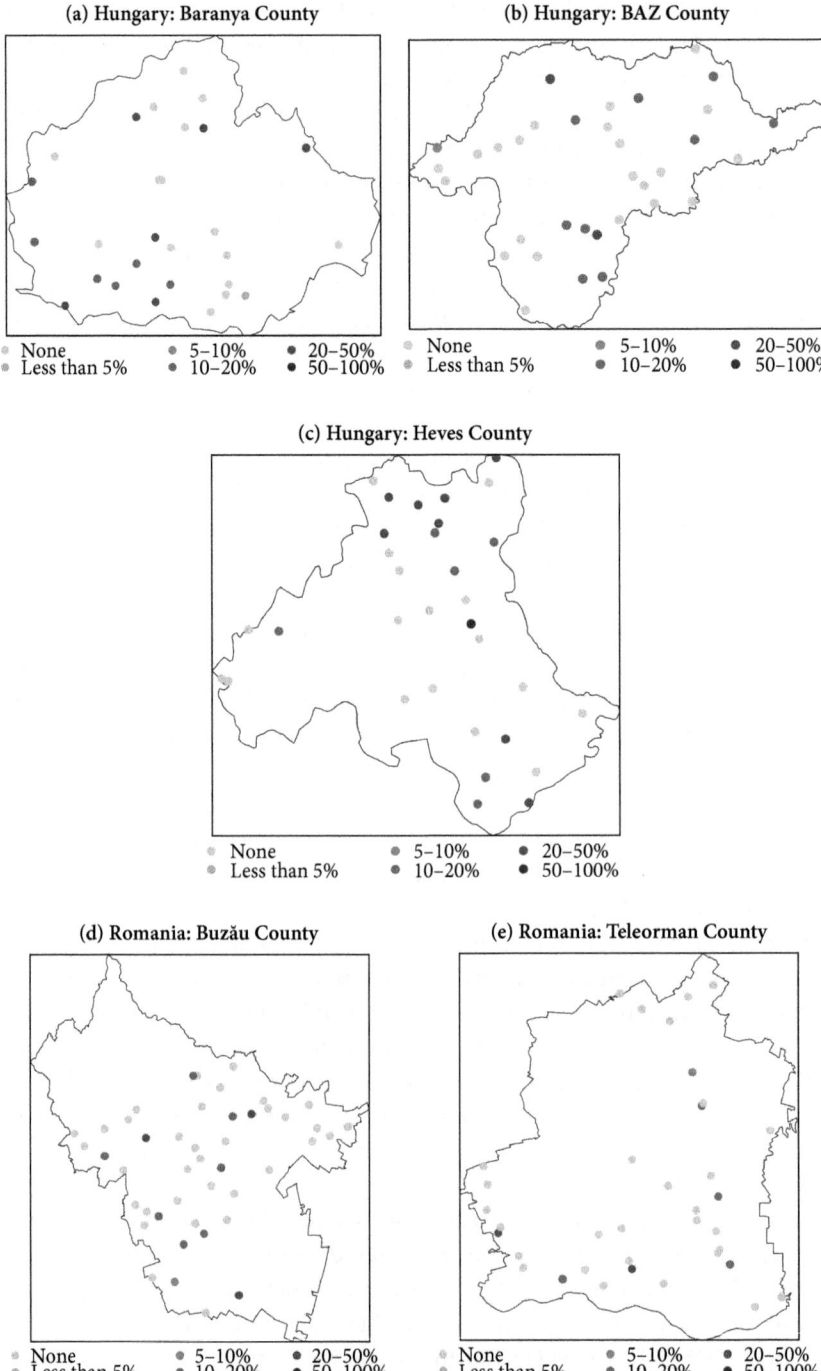

Figure 6.1 Geographic distribution of economic coercion

Roma voters. The signaling argument presented in Chapter 2 generates two hypotheses about the correlation between these coalitions and the use of coercive strategies. First, we expect that the use of coercive strategies will be higher in localities with a larger political coalition favoring retrenchment. Second, we predict that the incidence of economic coercion is likely to be higher in localities characterized by higher incidence of social conflict. We measure the likelihood of social conflict using an interactive term of the size of the two electoral coalitions. Such an interactive measure takes higher values in cases when both electoral coalitions are high. We expect to find a positive relationship between this measure and the incidence of coercion.

Similar to the analysis presented in other chapters, we examine the locality-level variation in the incidence of this strategy using multilevel models. We refer the reader to Section 4.5 of Chapter 4 for a presentation of the equation used to estimate these models. The results presented in Table 6.2 provide strong support for our hypotheses about the variation in the incidence of this strategy. We turn first to the conditions that enable economic coercion. First, we find little support for the hypothesis that local political control would be associated with greater economic coercion. There is a positive coefficient on Local Control, but it is very small in magnitude and the coefficient does not achieve statistical significance at conventional levels. On the other hand, there is consistent evidence that poor economic conditions are associated with higher levels of economic coercion. In places where the 2014 census found a higher poverty rate, and where our survey found a higher proportion of respondents were in debt, more people experience economic coercion. A one-standard-deviation increase in the poverty rate (which translates into a poverty rate increase of about nine percentage points), and the rate of indebtedness (an increase in the proportion indebted of about twenty-one percentage points), are both associated with an increase of three percentage points in the proportion of respondents who experienced economic pressure.

We next turn to the factors that we hypothesize reduce the electoral costs of negative forms of clientelism. We do not find support for the first observable implication of the signaling argument, which suggests that incidence of this strategy is higher in localities with a larger underlying coalition favoring retrenchment. The measure of the coalition favoring retrenchment is negatively correlated with the incidence of economic coercion (when holding the competing coalition favoring expansion at its mean level). We do, however, find empirical support for the second signaling hypothesis, suggesting that the incidence of economic coercion is higher in localities characterized by higher levels of social conflict. The correlation between a measure of the size of the two coalitions and the incidence of economic coercion is positive and reaches statistical significance at the 5 percent level. At higher than average levels of the right coalition, increases in the size of the left coalition are associated with increases in the level of economic coercion.

Table 6.2 Correlates of economic coercion in Hungary

	Dependent variable		
	Economic Coercion		
	(1)	(2)	(3)
Retrenchment Coalition	−0.01	−0.02	−0.01
	(0.03)	(0.03)	(0.03)
Expansion Coalition	−0.01	−0.02	−0.02
	(0.03)	(0.03)	(0.03)
Retrenchment × Expansion (Social Conflict)	0.03**	0.03**	0.03*
	(0.02)	(0.02)	(0.02)
Local Control	0.01	0.01	0.01
	(0.02)	(0.02)	(0.02)
Poverty Rate	0.37*	0.34*	0.37*
	(0.19)	(0.19)	(0.19)
Debt Rate	0.03*	0.03*	0.03
	(0.02)	(0.02)	(0.02)
Mayor Margin		0.001	−0.004
		(0.02)	(0.02)
Population		−0.02	−0.01
		(0.02)	(0.02)
Roma			0.09**
			(0.04)
Female			0.03
			(0.03)
Age			−0.04
			(0.03)
Employed			0.08
			(0.06)
Unemployed			0.07
			(0.06)
Retired			0.14*
			(0.08)
Direct Effects	✓	✓	✓
Observations	1,794	1,794	1,688
Akaike Inf. Crit.	1,228.51	1,259.72	1,185.86
		Hungary	

$^*p<0.1$; $^{**}p<0.05$; $^{***}p<0.01$

Standard errors in parentheses.

Models are estimated using a multilevel model with intercepts varying by locality. The coefficients shown are from interactions with the list treatment indicator. Local Control is an additive index of indicators that take a value of 1 if the locality has a mayor who is an incumbent, a co-partisan with the national executive, or from the same party as the plurality in the city council. Retrenchment Coalition is the average of the standardized proportions of the anti-workfare constituency: the employed and retirees. Expansion Coalition is the average of the standardized proportions of the pro-workfare constituency: the unemployed and Roma. Retrenchment X Expansion is the interaction of the pro- and anti-workfare constituencies. Poverty Rate is the proportion of inhabitants who are below the poverty line. Debt Rate is the proportion of survey respondents by locality who reported being in debt. Mayor Margin is the margin of victory of the mayor. Population is the population size. Roma, Female, Age, Employed, Unemployed, Retired, Debt, and Poor are individual-level variables coded from our surveys. All but Age and Poor are binary. All continuous variables are standardized.

In the third model reported in Table 6.2, we add several individual-level covariates. While these individual patterns are not direct tests of our hypotheses about locality-level conditions, they do provide some insight into the mechanisms driving the locality-level patterns. In particular, the data show that Roma respondents are nine percentage points more likely to experience economic coercion by moneylenders as compared to ethnic Hungarians.

A second individual-level variable that is correlated with the incidence of economic coercion is the retirement status of the respondent. Specifically, compared to the base category of people who are permanently out of the workforce (students and homemakers), retirees are fourteen percentage points more likely to experience economic coercion. This difference is statistically significant at p < 10 percent. However, the difference between retirees and those active in the work force (employed or unemployed) is much smaller and statistically insignificant, suggesting that the result is driven more by the lower prevalence of economic coercion among homemakers than a higher prevalence for retirees.

6.3 Conclusion

In this chapter, we have documented the use of electoral strategies premised on economic coercion in recent elections in Hungary and Romania. In the case of these non-programmatic strategies, brokers exploit their control over a variety of economic resources that are valuable to voters and condition the terms of ongoing or anticipated economic exchanges on voters' electoral support. As this chapter has documented, one finds a variety of such economic brokers in the current Eastern European electoral landscape. Such brokers include moneylenders, tenant farmers, and employers. These private brokers enter into exchanges with political actors, particularly mayors, in which they deliver votes, often in exchange for a policy benefit such as forbearance that allows them to continue illicit economic activities such as illegal moneylending. Drawing on interviews with voters, candidates, and brokers, we have documented the range of coercive strategies used by these actors to influence voters' political decisions. These include a variety of threats about ways in which private economic actors can worsen the terms of ongoing or anticipated economic exchanges. Moneylenders in particular can threaten to increase interest rates, refuse to give future loans, or even use the extrajudicial enforcement systems they have set up to deal with defaults to incentivize voters.

Finally, we documented that the incidence of these strategies varies across localities in ways that are predicted by the theoretical predictions that we outlined in Chapter 2, particularly the implications of supply-side or signaling theories. We find that two different conditions increase the incidence of the use of electoral strategies premised on the use of coercion. First, such strategies are more prevalent in places where economic conditions create a deep economic need that can be manipulated by economic brokers like moneylenders. These unfavorable economic conditions include high levels of poverty and high debt burdens. By contrast, we find no evidence that control of local institutions, which resource-based theories predict should enable local actors to engage in clientelism, is related to the incidence of economic coercion.

Finally, as in the case of policy coercion, we find that private coercive strategies are more prevalent in localities characterized by high levels of distributional conflict between constituents who do and do not benefit from the dominant welfare transfers, the workfare program. The incidence of economic coercion is most common in localities where large constituencies mobilize both in support of and in opposition to the workfare program. We argue that opponents of the ongoing distribution of social policy benefits are less likely to sanction the use of coercive strategies directed towards voters that they perceive as being lazy or excessively dependent on welfare. We find that economic coercion by money-lenders is targeted against Roma ethnic voters and is more pervasive in localities where both the coalition favoring retrenchment and the coalition favoring expansion are large.

7

Vote Buying

Non-Targeted and Unmonitored

The previous two chapters have analyzed non-programmatic strategies that deploy state resources. In addition to these strategies, candidates in Eastern European elections seek to mobilize and sway voters to support a particular candidate, by offering them small material rewards. The all-encompassing term "vote buying" captures such practices.

What forms does vote buying take in Eastern Europe? What goods are offered to voters as part of vote-buying exchanges? We begin by mapping the heterogeneity in the type of vote-buying strategies. One commonly encountered strategy comes in the form of offers of non-targeted goods, which include meals, drinks, or other public entertainment. A second form of vote buying comes in the form of goods such as money or gifts that are targeted and expressly contingent on the voter's behavior.

We draw on informational and resource-based explanations of clientelism to examine the variation in the use of these different strategies that fall under the encompassing category of vote buying. As discussed in Chapter 2, resource-based explanations suggest that differences in the relative endowments of candidates account for the variation in the use of non-programmatic strategies. By contrast, informational explanations suggest that candidates use various non-programmatic strategies to send voters signals about their policy positions and personal characteristics. Resource-based explanations are largely unable to account for the decision of many candidates to devote campaign resources for the distribution of electoral handouts without putting mechanisms in place to monitor and punish voters who defect at the polling station. Informational approaches, by contrast, suggest that vote buying is deployed to signal candidates' electoral qualities relative to their competitors.

In this chapter, we begin by documenting the variety of goods that are offered as part of vote-buying exchanges, the type of brokers distributing such goods and the strategies developed by these brokers to monitor the choices of voters and to increase voters' perceptions that their electoral choice is observable. Our qualitative evidence documents the co-existence of targeted and non-targeted vote-buying strategies. In the following section, we use survey experimental evidence to examine how voters assess these different strategies and test predictions from informational explanations of vote buying. Finally, we draw on our locality-level surveys to analyze how the incidence of this strategy varies across districts.

Overall, our evidence suggests that while vote buying (particularly in its unconditional forms) is common, there is little evidence that it is strategically targeted by candidates relative to the other forms of clientelism we study. First, while we find evidence that vote buying does signal some positive personal characteristics to pro-workfare voters, the overall effects on perceptions of candidates are almost entirely negative, and we find no effects of vote buying on perceptions of policy platforms. This suggests that the overall informational content of vote buying is low compared to policy coercion or policy favors. Second, we find little evidence that candidates strategically target vote buying in particular localities or amongst types of voters. Again, this suggests that vote buying may be relatively unimportant compared to other forms of clientelism. These results are particularly important in light of the strong focus on vote buying in the literature on clientelism, and the strong signaling effects that it seems to have in other contexts where social policy is less prevalent.

7.1 Targeted and Non-Targeted Vote-Buying Strategies

7.1.1 Festivals, meals, and entertainment

Nineteenth-century British electoral law made the important distinction between "bribing" and "treating." Treating referred to offers of meals and alcohol and entertainment, and we find legislative efforts to regulate "excessive" treating as early as 1677. According to the provisions of the Treating Act, a person could be found guilty of treating if it "by himself/by any other persons/either before during or after an election/directly or indirectly gives/provides/pays wholly or in part the expense of giving or providing meat, drink entertainment, provision to or from any person for the purpose of corruptly influencing that person or any other person to give or refrain from giving his vote at election" (Rogers 1906: 334).

Bribing, by contrast, referred to more involved offers of goods and money, gifts, or loans. According to the 1854 Corrupt Practices Prevention Act (17 & 18 Vict c. 102), a person was deemed guilty of bribing if he "agreed to give/lend/agree to give/agree to lend/offer/promise/promise to procure/promise to endeavor to procure any money or monetary considerations to or for any voter/to or for any person on behalf of any voter to induce any voter to vote or refrain from voting" (Rogers 1906: 296).

"Bribing" and "treating" were considered distinct types of electoral irregularities, as the interpretation of the election regulations suggested: "There is a wide difference in the nature of the two offenses, both as regards the candidate and the voter. In bribery, a corrupt contract between the voter and the candidate for the purchase of a vote usually exists; but not so in treating. Bribery is directed to obtain the adverse or fix the doubtful voters; treating is resorted to confirm the good intentions and keep up the party zeal of those believed to be already in the interest of the candidate" (Rogers 1906: 332). As a result, the two different offenses were treated with different levels of stringency. For a long time bribery was considered an indictable offense while treating was merely illegal, and the penalties imposed on candidates who engaged in treating were only half those attached to bribing.

As discussed in Chapter 2, studies of electoral clientelism in other political contexts have also noted the heterogeneity in the use of vote-buying strategies. Electoral practices during the French Third Republic were characterized by the simultaneous use of treating and of offers of money and gifts (Pilenco 1928). In a study of electoral clientelism in Brazil, Alan Rouquié also noted the coexistence of "gregarious vote-buying" with more targeted clientelism where candidates offer goods or money in exchange for political support (Rouquié 1978).

In both Romania and Hungary, candidates deploy both treating, also called "electoral handouts" in recent work by Eric Kramon (2016), and vote buying as part of the mix of non-programmatic strategies. Consider first the use of treating. Treating of voters—through meals or public festivals—is a common phenomenon in the countries included in our study. Such festivals are general events, which are open to all (or most) voters in the respective locality. Candidates who make use of this strategy do not attempt to monitor participation in such events. As attendance in these events is unsupervised, participants are not reminded that the participation in such events increases their obligation to support a particular candidate.

We found evidence of such non-targeted or "gregarious" vote buying across multiple sites of our research. Respondents in many localities reported that offers of free food or drinks were a regular and routine occurrence at elections (OK., Interview 2, July 7, 2015). One respondent in BF., a locality in Heves county, characterized treating as "a natural part of elections. Things like this happen on every election. The mayor slaughtered a pig in 2010 and gave it to the Roma. There is nothing illegal in these practices" (BF., Interview 11, July 23, 2015). A voter in FJ., another locality in Heves county, expressed a similar view: "Things like this happen here like in other localities. A bit of goulash soup and other offers to voters" (FJ., Interview 2, August 21, 2015). Such non-targeted vote buying coexists alongside clientelistic strategies that deploy state resources and also alongside more targeted vote-buying strategies where candidates offer voters money and goods.

Treating comes in many colorful forms. Let us consider some examples. In RM., a locality in Heves county, candidates organized meals for voters on several Saturdays prior to the election. Here several respondents reported that candidates offered voters "a shot of *palinka* and beer" at these events (RM., Interview 1, August 21, 2015). The most important meal occurred on the day of the election. At this time, the mayor invited voters to a banquet held in the city center in the proximity of the polling station. One participant at this party described the event:

"They cut a up a pig and set up a big cauldron at the end of the street. They gave free food or drink for everybody. Immediately after this, voters went to vote" (RM., Interview 10, August 25, 2015). Mayors approach participants with various types of recommendations or requests for electoral support. One voter recalls that "the mayor organized one event in the garden of one of the representatives to the city hall. On the day of the election, he invited people in the garden, saying, come and drink a shot of *palinka*, but you know where to put the X" (RM., Interview 4, August 22, 2015).

Respondents in FB., in northern Hungary, reported that public meals during campaigns were common and that such events were organized by all candidates (FB., Interview 4, July 23, 2015). As one voter recalled, "Fidesz candidates prepared a special meal for public workers to thank them for their efforts and involvement in the campaign" (FB., Interview 2, July 22, 2015). Another respondent recalls these events as follows: "There was a strong campaign and of course this was required from the government (…) The candidate was actively present, visiting the community (…). Also there was a cooking event organized in the cultural center. This event was timed ideally during the campaign" (FB., Interview 6, July 24, 2015). In MN., another locality in Borsod county, one of the mayoral candidates who was affiliated with Fidesz "slaughtered pigs and chicken and served wine and *palinka* to voters. The entry to this event organized by the mayor included also free tickets to a raffle, which gave participants the chance to win expensive prizes, such as television sets and mobile phones (MN., Interview 3, October 24, 2015).

NO., a community in Nógrád county, has a long-term incumbent mayor who has held four terms of office. Here, as we discussed in Chapter 5, we found evidence of extensive use of coercive clientelistic strategies. The mayor of this locality combines repressive strategies with treating—prior to the 2014 local election, he organized a vintage ball whose purpose was to appease ethnic conflict. He invited both ethnically Roma and Hungarian voters to this event and incentivized electoral participation by offering alcohol and food (NO., Interview 2, July 15, 2015; Interview 7, July 17, 2015). Although informal brokers referred to as "mayor's men" reminded participants at the banquet to vote for the mayor in the upcoming election, the pressure they exerted on voters was gentle, and brokers lacked any serious mechanisms to monitor voters' choices.

During the 2014 local election in FM., in central Hungary, an ethnically Roma candidate who was backed by the ruling Fidesz party defeated the incumbent mayor in a very narrow race. The losing candidate attributed the victory of the Roma candidate to the use of clientelistic strategies that involved "treating" by the latter. Using strongly ethnically charged language, this former mayor recalls: "Roma voters need to be entertained. They need food and drinks. He brought Kis Grofo and Nagy Grofo (two famous Roma singers) to this locality. He gave everybody a plate of *goulash* and a bottle of beer. When he introduced himself on the stage of the cultural house, the audience did not deal with the contents of his speech, but with Bunyos Pityu, another famous Roma singer, who was standing there next to the stage" (FM., Interview 9, July 30, 2015). All respondents we encountered in this locality, including critics of the new mayor, stressed that such "acts of kindness" and favors were offered to all voters who were present and that there were no instances of favoritism. As one participant remembers: "He gave food to everybody and the concert was for everybody" (FM., Interview 10, July 30, 2015). The candidate did not monitor participation at such events. The interaction between candidates, brokers, and voters was minimal, giving brokers few opportunities to shape voters' expectations that reciprocity was required.

Festivals that involve non-targeted and non-contingent vote buying are also common in rural Romanian communities. One voter in S. estimates that candidates in the 2014 campaign spent thousands of RON on entertainment and food (S., Interview 2, September 9, 2015). In C., a locality in Buzau county, voters remember that the mayor "opened some barrels of wine" at every election, be it local, parliamentary, and presidential (C., Interview 8, October 16, 2015). Another voter in this locality recalls that "drinks and chicken meals" were commonly offered during elections (C., Interview 6, October 16, 2015). In R., another community in southeastern Romania, respondents report that the four-term incumbent mayor organized banquets during the weeks leading up to the elections: "He organized parties and gives people to eat and drink" (R., Interview 10, August 19, 2015). The deputy mayor of F., a locality in Buzau county, reports that he organized a banquet where voters were offered both wine and food during the 2010 election. When asked how such campaign expenses were financed, he became elusive and feigned forgetfulness about the source for the funds that made such generous treating possible (F., Interview 4, November 6, 2015).

According to our respondents in Romania, representatives of all political parties organize such events. Commenting on the practice of treating voters, one former mayor of a town in southern Romania recalls that "both major parties, such as the Socialists (PSD) and National Liberals (PNL) offer drinks and meals to voters. This is how every party attracts its followers and I cannot say that one particular party is different. The party that does not do this can say good-bye to the prospect of winning the elections. They will not be able to elect a single city councilor" (O., Interview 7, August 14, 2015). Several respondents in Romania noted, however, that practices of treating underwent significant changes in the most recent election cycles. One such change is the growing involvement of leaders from regional party organizations. Meals and banquets are now organized by party leaders and occur in close temporal proximity to the party conference. Such events are thus part of the carefully orchestrated campaigns by which parties seek to define their distinctive "political brand."

Practices of treating involving offers of money and food occupy an important place in the menu of non-programmatic strategies in both Romania and Hungary.

Our qualitative results suggest that such non-targeted vote buying is a more important strategy in Hungary than in Romania. As discussed in Chapter 2, informational explanations of vote buying hold that non-targeted vote buying is a strategy through which candidates signal information about their competence in managing the affairs of the community. When asked about the reasons why he organized generous banquets at times of elections, one Romanian mayor gave reasons very close to the signaling argument. According to him, the main goal of these events is to "communicate to voters that I am a good administrator of the community and that I am a good manager (*gospodar*) who is attentive to people's needs." In Section 7.2, we will provide a more systematic test of the signaling logic in explaining both targeted and non-targeted vote buying.

7.1.2 Targeted vote buying: Offers of money and in-kind goods

A second type of vote-buying strategy is targeted vote buying. Unlike with meals and banquets, offers of in-kind goods or money are accompanied by efforts to monitor the electoral participation and sometimes the electoral choice of the recipients. As we will document below, candidates rely on a heterogeneous group of brokers to approach voters. In small urban and rural localities, such brokers may include people hired by the candidate in an ad hoc fashion, close relatives of the candidates, or party representatives.

The goods offered as part of targeted vote-buying exchanges are typically of low monetary value. They include bags of flour or potatoes, buckets of oil or sugar, or clothes. In W., in Veszprém county, Hungary, brokers offered voters "backpacks and bicycles" (W., Interview 1, July 29, 2015). In D., a locality in eastern Romania, voters report being offered more durable goods. Here politicians distributed, "cement and metal sheets" (D., Interview 3, October 22, 2016) or "wood and bricks" (D., Interview 1, October 22, 2015).

Brokers can offer the identical in-kind goods using either targeted or non-targeted strategies. Consider events that occurred during the 2014 local election in MN., a locality in Borsod county. As one voter recalls, one of the candidates who competed with the support of the ruling Fidesz party "slaughtered pigs and chicken and served voters with wine and *palinka*. His competitor in the race for mayor, who ran as an independent offered the same good—*palinka*—but after the election and only to voters who could provide proofs of their votes. The price for one vote delivered for this candidate was one liter of *palinka*" (MN., Interview 1, October 23, 2015).

In-kind goods are offered in both local and national elections. During the 2014 parliamentary elections in NO., Hungary, candidates offered voters such goods. One voter recalls: "It is typical that in this village at times of national elections, both the MSZP and Fidesz go house to house mostly to very poor voters. And there are examples in this locality that these people voted for the candidate they were told to support for one kilo of chicken [...]. It happened during the last local election as well. It happened that people were brought to vote for 1,000 HUF" (NO., Interview 11, July 27, 2015).

In addition to in-kind goods, candidates offer voters money. In many places, voters know the "common price" of a vote. When asked about the "going rate" for a vote, a mayor in P., Romania, considered that "the price of a vote is 100 RON, approximately 25 dollars." He implied that this was a "good deal" for many low-income voters. "There are very poor families in this locality, families for which 100 RON means a lot" (P., Interview 1, August 21, 2015). In C., another locality in Romania, the price of a vote was 50 RON. In N., the price of a vote was estimated at between 30 and 50 RON (N., Interview 7, September 15, 2015). By contrast, in V., the price of a vote was 30 RON, but voters were offered "a bucket of flour or sugar in addition to this amount" (V., Interview 6, October 1, 2015). In NO., a locality in Nógrad county, one respondent recalls that "during the last local election, people were brought to vote for 1,000 HUF" (NO., Interview 11, July 27, 2015). In other places, voters reported higher offers for their vote. In FB., a locality in Heves county, voters reported that the going rate for a vote was 3,000 HUF, which was offered either in cash or in the form of a voucher for grocery goods (FB., Interview 1, July 21, 2015).

Interviews with brokers, candidates, and election officials indicate that these funds come from the regional party organization. The deputy mayor of HN., a locality in Borsod county, who is affiliated with Fidesz confirms that the money originates with the party: "I know that the money to buy votes was ensured by Fidesz. The party supplied a certain amount of money at elections" (HN., Interview 8, July 25, 2015). One of our respondents in C., a locality in eastern Romania, is the daughter of a long-term incumbent mayor. She confirms that the regional party organization financed campaign expenditures in the locality. Recalling events of the 2012 election, another voter in this locality reports that "at the time, there was a push from above for the National Liberal Party to win. The president of the regional organization of the National Liberal Party came from the regional council to bring the bag of money [sacul cu bani]" (C., Interview 5, October 16, 2015). This respondent believes that such infusion of cash determined the outcome of that election: "Money spoke."

In many cases, vote-buying brokers target one voter by offering her both in-kind goods and money. Surprisingly, voters perceive a hierarchy among the two offers and that brokers offer monetary inducements to "better-known" voters, while targeting "less important people in the community" with in-kind goods. One respondent, a 75-year-old retiree, recalled being offered either "two liters of oil or two kilos of flour, depending on what people at the city hall consider best." She has not been offered money and considers that "only those held by the mayor in high esteem receive money" (V., Interview 4, September 30, 2015).

Our qualitative evidence finds that both incumbents and challengers turn to vote-buying strategies. In RM., a locality in Hungary, the incumbent mayor encountered very strong competition and offered money to persuade undecided voters. As one voter recalls, "there was another non-Roma voter candidate running at elections. But the mayor realized that she would not have enough votes. Because she knew where people stood. Mayors know at every election who is voting with whom. And then she went to the people who were not supporting her and she gave them envelopes with money" (RM., Interview 10, August 25, 2015).

In BF., another locality in northern Hungary, the incumbent mayor turned to vote buying to create an electoral advantage in an extremely competitive race. Throughout his mandate, this mayor had expressed his opposition to a public works program and kept the number of participants in the program at a very low number. This decision to limit employment in the public works program deprived him of a very important non-programmatic strategy and opened up opportunities for another candidate to enter the race and compete on the basis of promises to expand employment in this program. Lacking state policy resources and facing strong electoral competition, the mayor turned to vote-buying strategies. As one voter here commented on the use of vote buying:

> The use of vote buying is a fact. Everybody knows it. How else could he have obtained so many votes? When he was mayor he did not do anything, he was so selfish and arrogant with his ranks and diplomas. During the last election, people from Fidesz were going around and paying people. Everybody knows it, nobody would have supported him anyway. Even among Roma, a lot of people voted for him, even though it is against their interest. He did not want to provide enough places for public workers, the interest of the Roma is public work and not his autocratic way of ruling the village.   (BF., Interview 12, July 23, 2015)

This example illustrates that in competitive environments mayors who lack alternative non-programmatic strategies to influence voters' choices turn to vote buying. In other localities, candidates turn to vote buying as a complement to and not a substitute for other non-programmatic strategies. For example, the mayor of P., in southern Romania, has actively used favors and other state resources throughout his mandate. In his discussion with us, he explained his decision to also distribute money and goods to voters before the election, by invoking the extremely competitive nature of the local race. This strategy allowed him to win the race by a very narrow margin of less than 100 votes (P., Interview 1, August 21, 2015). Yet according to this mayor, vote buying is an extremely risky strategy. To make vote buying work, "one has to give the voter the highest amount of money and also one has to be the last person who gives voters money." This mayor described his attempt to be "the last" person who came into contact with voters before they cast their ballots.

MAYOR: You just take the ID of the voter one week before the election. Then, you offer him to eat and to drink for one week. You tell him to take 100 RON for brandy and another 100 RON for cognac. On the day of the election you go to the voter and tell him, I have your ID, come into my car and let us go and vote.

INTERVIEWER: But how do you know how the voter has voted and whether he will keep his promise?

MAYOR: You are never sure about this. You never know what he will do when he votes. (P., Interview 1, August 21, 2015)

In localities characterized by high levels of competition, vote-buying strategies are used by both the incumbent and the challenger. Consider the example of an extremely contested local election in HN., a locality in Borsod county, during the spring of 2014. The two competitors in this race were the incumbent mayor, who competed as an independent candidate and a challenger, who was backed by Fidesz. The challenger won by a very narrow margin of about twenty-five votes. In this election, both candidates offered money and in-kind goods to voters—taking advantage of his incumbency, the mayor also offered promises of access to the workfare program. One respondent recalls: "There were some families who received money, while others received promises for work possibilities" (HN., Interview 6, July 23, 2016). In several public statements after the election, the mayor attributed his victory to the use of vote buying, despite the illegality of such practices. Defying his challenger who lost the race, the mayor stated: "I had the money to buy people. Why did you not use money to buy voters?" (HN., Interview 9, July 26, 2015).

The challenger competing in HN. also made widespread promises of monetary rewards in exchange for political support. One of our respondents, an employee in the local administration, described the campaign of the challenger as follows: "He bribed people. He bribed poor people and those who drink, by offering *palinka* and money. One person associated with his campaign was present at the time of voting. He gave voters money to put the X next to the correct name" (HN., Interview 8, July 25, 2015). This respondent, who was also affiliated with the ruling party and a member of the local city council, attributed the source of these funds to the party organization: "I know that the money for votes was ensured by Fidesz. The party supplied elections with a certain amount of money" (HN., Interview 6, July 23, 2015). Other respondents in this locality noted that the challenger offered voters 5,000 HUF in exchange for support and an additional 5,000 HUF if he won the race (HN., Interview 2, July 22, 2015). However, after his victory, he did not keep his promise, which created considerable outrage among voters. As an expression of their dissatisfaction, voters drew graffiti on the wall of the school that stated, "This is not what you promised, [mayor first name]" (HN., Interview 2, July 22, 2015).

Contrast these situations characterized by very high levels of competition with localities where long-term incumbents encounter only a weak competitor. If the threat faced by such an incumbent is low, he may tolerate some vote-buying practices by his competitor. We encountered such a situation where vote-buying practices were allowed and even tacitly encouraged by a secure incumbent mayor in R., a locality in Romania. In this district, the deputy mayor reported that the mayor preferred to "manage" competition, by "allowing" his opponents to rely on vote-buying strategies at elections. This deputy mayor recalls: "The mayor allows them to give out gifts. This is also good for us. This is how we get along with all parties" (R., Interview 11, August 21, 2015). This strategy of accommodating the opposition, by granting a green light to illicit vote-buying practices generated political payoffs for this mayor, allowing him to switch across a variety of parties. Throughout his four terms in office, this mayor transitioned across all political parties in the Romanian political landscape: first the Socialists, then the Liberals, and then back to the Socialists. At the time of our fieldwork, the mayor was affiliated with the Liberal splinter party, the Alliance of Liberals and Democrats for Europe (ALDE) (R., Interview 11, August 21, 2015).

While vote buying has been a common non-programmatic strategy in both countries included in our study, the incidence of this practice was significantly more pronounced in Romania during the first decades of the post-communist transition. Post-electoral reports collected by non-governmental associations in Romania after 2000 indicate a very high incidence of this strategy. A survey measuring perceptions of the incidence of vote buying conducted by the Pro-Democracy Association, a Romanian NGO, in 2009 found that 70 percent of respondents considered that vote buying was a commonly used strategy in Romanian elections (Asociatia ProDemocratia 2009). While this survey measured perceptions of the electorate and not the actual incidence of vote-buying strategies, it is nevertheless indicative of broad public concern about vote-buying practices. Interviews with election observers during the period 2002–12 also confirm the widespread use of vote-buying strategies during these elections (Expert Interview, Romania, March 16, 2013).

In recent years, Romanian authorities have launched an unprecedented assault to limit the incidence of vote buying at elections. These efforts intensified after the referendum to impeach Romania's president, Traian Băsescu. Such initiatives resulted in the prosecution and indictment of a number of prominent Romanian politicians on accusations of vote buying. The list of indicted politicians or those facing ongoing prosecutorial investigation includes Adrian Nastase, Romania's prime minister who served a prison sentence for irregularities in campaign spending; Vasile Blaga, Romania's interior minister; and Liviu Dragnea, the president of the Socialist Party. The investigation of vote-buying strategies by the anti-corruption agencies has extended deeply into Romania's rural localities and has influenced candidates' incentives to employ them in recent elections.

Our qualitative fieldwork and the fielding of our post-electoral surveys took place at the time this prosecutorial campaign was unfolding. While we lack systematic survey data on the incidence of vote buying in Romania prior to

2012 that would allow us to measure the effects of this campaign on the 2014 election, interviews with observers and members of Romanian NGOs monitoring Romanian elections suggest the incidence of vote buying has declined strongly in the years immediately preceding our data collection. It is possible that this decline in the incidence of vote buying was associated with an increase in the incidence of non-programmatic strategies that deployed state resources, such as favors or coercion.

The vigorous prosecutorial investigation of vote-buying practices has contributed to the decline in the use of this non-programmatic strategy in Romanian elections in recent years. As we will show in Section 7.4, while using non-obtrusive survey techniques, we were unable to find evidence of vote buying during the most recent presidential election. This offensive also changed incentives of brokers to hide and dissimulate such practices. Brokers attempted to minimize the risk of being caught by taking higher precautionary actions. One such strategy of obfuscation used by vote-buying brokers consisted in the distribution of in-kind goods, such as oil or sugar, only at night-time. We encountered this pervasive practice in a variety of localities. One respondent in V. reported that brokers delivered in-kind goods such as "four to five liters of oil, two or three kilograms of sugar and four kilograms of flour" to his house at night (V., Interview 7, October 1, 2015). In another locality, a voter recalls having found in his courtyard three of four bags of potatoes that had been delivered there during the night" (S., Interview 1, September 9, 2015). In N., one voter recalls that during the 2014 election brokers "came at night-time, in hiding. They brought us gifts at night-time. Money. Sugar. (…). There are cars who come at two or three in the morning and throw bags of flour, wheat in the garden. If you are asleep, you do not receive the goods." "This implies," this voter conjectured, "that those voters who received the goods had been told, in advance, by the broker to stay awake" (N., Interview 15, August 28, 2015).

7.1.3 Vote-buying brokers

Who are the brokers that distribute these in-kind goods and services? How do candidates incentivize these brokers to exert effort on their behalf? Do such vote-buying brokers monitor the vote choices of voters, and if so, how? Our qualitative evidence allows us to shed some light on these questions.

The brokers deployed by candidates to offer in-kind goods or money to voters are very heterogeneous in their socio-economic background and their connection to the candidate. On some occasions, candidates deploy members of their extended families as vote-buying brokers. On other occasions, candidates hire brokers through on-the-spot markets and incentivize them using amounts that only barely exceed the offers made to voters. Finally, some candidates, especially incumbent mayors, use state employees as brokers.

In small communities, candidates turn to members of their extended family to distribute goods and money to voters during the campaign. We asked one former mayor in Romania what it takes to be elected in this locality. His answer was that one needs to have an extended family. This mayor recalled the first time he ran for mayor, in 1996. In that election, he competed against twelve other candidates and all of them deployed members of their extensive families to contact voters and offer them various gifts and money. In F., another Romanian locality, one respondent recalls that the mayor's relatives went from house to house and distributed "buckets full of things. They also went to the other localities and brought voters to vote in their car." These relatives agreed to serve as brokers because they expected post-electoral rewards, by way of employment in the municipality (F., Interview 3, November 6, 2015). Once elected, this mayor delivered on his promise.

In rural Hungarian communities, mayors also employ members of their extended families as vote-buying brokers. In NO., a locality in Nógràd county, the mayor's son was the most significant broker in his father's campaign. One respondent recalls that "the mayor's son went from house to house. He talked to voters and offered them money. This is the Hungarian mentality. Chicken meat, 2,000 HUF and Fidesz" (NO., Interview 2, July 15, 2015). In SZ., a locality in northeastern Hungary, the wife of the mayor, who owned a restaurant in the district, was the most significant broker. She was known for her attempts to create a "loyal entourage" for the mayor, by offering "free beer, wine and brandy" (SZ., Interview 5, July 18, 2015; Interview 6, July 18, 2015). The mayor's loyal entourage, we were told, consisted of a number of low-income families who "were given free drinks and meals at the local pub. She built this relationship with these families over a long period of time (SZ., Interview 7, August 20, 2015). During elections, the owner of the pub sent voters envelopes with a list that included the names of candidates for various offices. She circled the names of the "recommended" candidates (SZ., Interview 5, July 18, 2015).

On other occasions, candidates hired brokers on the spot to distribute goods or money to voters. Several respondents in V., Romania, reported that the mayor paid some people twenty to thirty RON and asked them to "mobilize the Roma to come out and vote." Another voter confirms the existence of these practices, suggesting that the pool of candidates for brokers consists of people with lower levels of education: "They are not using the teacher or the mailman for such jobs, but people who have not yet finished eight years of school" (V., Interview 8, October 1, 2016).

A similar situation exists in C., a locality in southern Romania. According to one respondent in this district, one employee in the local administration who was responsible for Roma issues "betrayed" the mayor. As a result, the mayor had to hire some people "to do the job." He hired brokers to distribute money to voters, who were integrated in an already established network of brokers ("supervisors").

One broker, an employee of the local agricultural association, recalls: "The mayor could [give] 10,000 RON to distribute to everybody in the locality. I could take some of the money and not share it with others, but he has his own people to watch" (C., Interview 8, October 16, 2015).

As the preceding statement illustrates, candidates who use on-the-spot brokers construct a hierarchy among these brokers to facilitate electoral monitoring. The brokers hired in this way are incentivized by small monetary rewards to provide electoral services to the mayor. Two of the brokers we encountered in Q., Romania, were retired employees. While they did not want to divulge the identity of the candidate they supported, they claimed that they acted out of "pleasure and boredom." When pressed further that nobody provides electoral services for free, they admitted that "they get a small monetary gain and that in this way people in the community will get to know them better" (Q., Interview 5, September 27, 2015).

The types of vote-buying brokers used by candidates vary between national and local elections. In national elections, brokers may be representatives of political parties, who distribute goods that are financed from the coffers of those parties. One respondent in R., Romania, distinguished between such party representatives and brokers who were part of the mayor's regular entourage: "The people who were distributing the buckets at elections were coming from the parties, from the regional office. They were different from the brokers who brought people to vote in cars. Relatives of the mayor and people employed at the city hall brought voters to the voting place in their car" (R., Interview 14, August 21, 2015).

R. is the Romanian locality discussed above, whose mayor has migrated across all major political parties. At the time of the 2014 Romanian parliamentary election, the mayor had a particularly close relationship to ALDE, a splinter party of the Liberal Party led by Romania's former Prime Minister Călin Popescu-Tăriceanu. ALDE backed the candidacy of the Social Democratic candidate Victor Ponta. As a result of this alliance, the municipality benefited from additional help from the Social Democratic Party. As an employee in the municipality explained: "We are now with Tăriceanu, so we are with Ponta, because they are a team. We voted with Ponta during the presidential elections." This respondent discussed the electoral involvement of such partisan brokers as follows:

> They go from door to door and distribute: a bucket of sugar or oil. Poor people are extremely grateful for a kilogram of oil and for a kilogram of sugar and thank them profusely. This comes from the party, not from the candidate. Party operatives distribute the buckets, the oil, the sugar.
>
> (R., Interview 9, August 18, 2015)

Finally, candidates can also rely on employees of the local administration to distribute money or in-kind goods to voters, a situation that slightly blurs the distinction between vote buying and other clientelistic strategies that deploy state resources. To illustrate this complementarity between favors and targeted vote buying, consider events that occurred during the most recent election in HN., Hungary. Here candidates and members of the city councils distributed 3,000 HUF vouchers to voters. While in previous elections, members of the city council had offered these vouchers to all voters over 60 years of age, during the 2014 election the mayor decided to offer the vouchers only to known Fidesz supporters (HN., Interview 2, July 2, 2015). While the mayor was distributing these vouchers, the deputy mayor accompanied him, promising voters "social wood," an in-kind social assistance benefit financed by the municipality. "This means a lot for those who are left behind in this locality," one respondent stated (HN., Interview 2, July 22, 2015).

On many occasions, state employees accompany partisan brokers who distribute in-kind goods. They use their knowledge of the local population to create detailed records of the transactions that have taken place. One voter in S., Romania, recalls such interaction with an employee of the locality: "There is one person in the city hall who writes down whether you have taken goods. Then this person told me, watch out, you have taken the oil and the cornmeal, now you know how to vote, no?" (S., Interview 1, September 9, 2015).

Candidates rely on the brokers they trust most to monitor both turnout and the electoral choices of voters. In V., Romania, the mayor used city hall employees to distribute money to voters on the night before the vote. The following day, he placed these city hall employees near the voting place to monitor vote choice. One respondent maintained that the mayor chose close collaborators in the city hall to perform this task "because he could not trust anyone else" (V., Interview 2, October 30, 2015).

In other cases, brokers try to make voters comply with their offer by exploiting the traditionalism that is pervasive among rural Romanian voters. One broker we encountered in R., a locality in southern Romania, considered that it was relatively straightforward to obtain such compliance: "You give voters 10 RON, you make them kiss the cross and that's that. It is very easy" (R., Interview 13, August 21, 2015).

In Hungary, vote-buying brokers seek to monitor both the vote choice and turnout. During the 2014 parliamentary election, brokers for the Fidesz candidate had a detailed list of local supporters, whose electoral participation was closely monitored (FB., Interview 1, July 21, 2015). In RM., vote-buying brokers accompanied groups of ten voters to the polling station, monitoring their turnout. While these brokers could not pierce the secrecy of the ballot, they could pressure known partisan supporters to turn out during elections (RM., Interview 5, August 22, 2015). In other localities, vote-buying brokers also seek to monitor votes at the time voters cast their ballots. Such brokers usually wait at the voting station and then offer their services to voters to help them "understand" and "decipher" the ballot. In several Hungarian localities, brokers accompanied voters into the booth and explained these breaches of voting secrecy as efforts to help voters understand the ballot paper (NM., Interview 2, March 23, 2014; F., Interview 1, October 23, 2015). However, such instances of this are quite rare.

7.1.4 Hidden transcripts

While we can rely on unobtrusive survey techniques to estimate the share of voters targeted by non-programmatic strategies, such survey results do not allow us to assess the effectiveness of vote buying. How successful are vote buying strategies in swaying voters' decisions? Are the targeted voters likely to comply with brokers' demands or do they retain their autonomy?

Our qualitative evidence allows us to begin to address such questions. One form of qualitative evidence we may use to assess the effectiveness of targeted vote buying comes in the form of the "hidden transcripts" of voters targeted by the strategy (Scott 1990). As James Scott has shown, the analysis of such "hidden transcripts" allows researchers to understand patterns of resistance among vulnerable populations that have been subjected to coercion. Such strategies of resistance, which Scott labels "weapons of the weak," include deference to the demands of the brokers and feigned compliance that is not followed up in practice or in the vote (Scott 1990).

Some of the voters that had been offered money or goods in exchange for their vote openly admitted that such offers were sufficient in swaying their political decisions and making them comply with the request of the broker. For such voters, even small amounts of money were enough to influence their vote. As one 40-year-old voter in Romania declared, "Yes, I would vote for 100 RON. If I am hungry, I have to vote" (D., Interview 1, October 22, 2015).

Other voters, however, have developed quite sophisticated strategies of resistance to offers of money and goods. A generalized sense of skepticism about the effectiveness of vote buying is the first step in this strategy of resistance. One voter in C., Romania, remarked, "I am sick of it, the way they ran around the village with buckets and scarves. Do they think they fool anyone to vote for them for a bucket and a scarf?" (C., Interview 5, October 15, 2015). A voter in another Romanian locality admits having received "a bucket and a pen." She took these goods because she could find a use for them in her household. "I will use the bucket to feed the animals," she said. "Why not take them, when they are free? In the voting booth, I will do whatever I want" (V., Interview 8, October 1, 2015).

Voters' disbelief about the effectiveness of vote buying is surprisingly pervasive. On repeated occasions, voters expressed the view that the money and goods have no real consequences, that they are given "for nothing." A saleswoman at a local store in U., Romania, questioned the purpose of this electoral strategy: "You can give me the money, but it is for nothing [*degeaba*], as you will not know with whom I will vote. You cannot control. Perhaps you can control only the elderly people whom you accompany in the voting place" (U., Interview 7, September 9, 2015). Another voter in the same locality contended that "everybody votes how they want, it is not an obligation, you enter in the voting place and place the stamp, the mayor and secretary do not enter with you" (U., Interview 2, September 9, 2015). After enumerating a long list of goods she received from a broker, a 65-year-old woman in Q., Romania, asserted her independence: "I go and vote with whomever I want. I go to vote because I want to. If I don't want, I don't go. And if I want, I go. And vote" (Q., Interview 17, September 4, 2015).

Much like Romanian voters, Hungarian voters also express skepticism about the effectiveness of vote buying. Discussing his exchange with the brokers, one respondent in RM. recalls: "He gave me the money and paid me in the pub. But in the polling booth, I am alone. How would he know whom I end up casting my ballot for?" (RM., Interview 13, August 26, 2015). Another voter in ZI. remembers having received a plastic bag full of foodstuffs from the Fidesz representative: "However, when I go to the polling booth, nobody knows whom I support" (ZI., Interview 4, October 24, 2015).

The contrast between voters who have been targeted by vote-buying strategies and those who have experienced coercion is striking. Those who had experienced coercion (and even those who had not, but lived in the same locality) displayed fear even when simply approached for discussion. Such respondents often suspected that the mayor of the locality had sent us to verify how they voted. After encountering us, one respondent in Romania rushed to his house to bring back his ID and demonstrate that they had actually voted. Voters who had experienced coercion were silent and subdued. They believed that even the smallest hint of resistance might lead to a permanent loss of their benefits. Stefan, one such voter we encountered in D., a locality in eastern Romania, was permanently blackmailed by the mayor for irregularities in the receipt of social policy benefits. He believed that he was completely at the mercy of the mayor and that his "arrest" was in fact, possible any day: "If they will arrest me, the children will stay behind with my wife." When talking about his relationship to the city hall, he commented that it "goes both easily and hard, depending on how they want it to be." Both the mayor and the city council asked for his vote at elections, and he complied with their demand: "Of course I gave them my vote," he admitted, "because I am afraid and hungry" (D., Interview 1, October 22, 2015).

The hidden transcripts of voters targeted by various non-programmatic strategies differ. Coercive strategies are likely to be more effective than vote buying in generating voters' submission. We leave it to further research to systematically compare the effectiveness of these different strategies.

7.2 Vote Buying as a Selective Policy Signal

Informational approaches to the study of clientelism argue that candidates use vote-buying strategies to send voters signals about their personal attributes, their relative strength vis-à-vis competitors, or their policy position. Early anthropological studies of clientelism highlighted the importance of signaling, noting that "vote buying may serve other functions than the influence of a vote" (Foltz 1977: 243). Bill Foltz, an early proponent of the informational hypothesis, argued that candidates distributed money at elections to "signal their status in a relatively differentiated urban society." Vote buying was, thus, "a patterned process designed to reflect the concern for honor of the giver and not an underhanded and reprehensible attempt to buy support" (Foltz 1977: 247).

In recent years, such informational hypotheses have regained ground in the study of electoral clientelism. This renewed interest to uncover the informational implications of different vote-buying strategies has been motivated by efforts to understand the rationale behind candidate decisions to invest sizable resources in unmonitored clientelistic exchanges. These may include offers of drinks, meals, or other goods without monitoring of the turnout or the vote choice of the recipients (Conroy-Krutz and Logan 2012). Discussing the incidence of unmonitored vote buying in Indian elections, Schneider argues that these strategies represent candidates' efforts to signal their political strength relative to their competitors and not offers to buy votes per se (Schneider 2015). In a similar vein, Kramon's study of vote-buying practices in Kenya argues that the distribution of handouts is an effort to signal competence and to strengthen perceptions that candidates will be able to provide future benefits to the community (Kramon 2016: 463).

The variety of forms of vote buying documented in Section 7.1 provides us with an ideal opportunity to examine such informational explanations in the very different context of Eastern Europe. Our first set of questions is descriptive. How do voters evaluate candidates who use different forms of vote-buying strategies compared to those who do not turn to electoral clientelism? Do voters reward or punish the use of vote-buying strategies? Are there any differences across voters in how they evaluate candidates who use vote buying?

As we discussed in Chapter 2, different clientelistic strategies may create opportunities for candidates to send two different types of signals. First, such strategies may allow candidates to send voters signals about their personal attributes—such as their wealth—or about their strength and electoral viability relative to their competitors. These strategies may also allow candidates to signal different policy positions, such as concern for low-income voters. These signaling opportunities may allow candidates to offset the generally negative evaluations of clientelism and try to turn "a vice into a virtue."

To examine the informational implications of different vote-buying strategies, we use a survey-based experiment that we embedded in a larger questionnaire fielded in rural Romanian localities in October 2016. The survey was administered in forty communities located in three Romanian counties: Constanța, Giurgiu, and Olt. In Appendix C, we present additional information on the sampling of localities and on the selection of respondents within these localities. The appendix also presents information about the sample characteristics and randomization of the different versions of the survey.

Participants in the survey were randomly assigned to three experimental conditions. One-third of the participants were assigned to a control version of the survey. These participants received information about a neutral campaign event that involved no clientelism. The other two-thirds of the respondents received information about one of two common forms of electoral handouts: an in-kind gift of a meal, or a cash handout. We include two different variations of the clientelism scenario (cash and in-kind goods) both to test the generality of the findings across common forms of clientelism and to assess whether different modalities of clientelism have different effects.

Given that this survey-based experiment was administered in the aftermath of the 2016 local election, the information in the vignette referred to possible situations that could occur during a local election. The full vignette that was presented to voters read as follows:

Introduction (everyone)
Now, I would like you to consider a situation that could have happened during the electoral campaign for local elections. Consider that one candidate whom you appreciate very much has organized an electoral meeting in this locality. The candidate has completed a university degree, but preferred to return to his home locality after completing his studies. Here, he started a family and has an orderly [*îngrijit*] household. At this meeting, the candidate presented his plans to develop the locality.

After hearing this vignette, respondents received one of the following three treatments.

Control scenario
At the end of the meeting, the candidate thanked all people who came and encouraged them to vote for him.

In-kind benefits scenario
At the end of the meeting, the candidate offered a meal and drinks to all people who were present.

Cash benefits scenario
The candidate offered fifty RON to all people who were present during the meeting.[1]

After hearing the different scenarios, respondents were asked a number of questions about the candidates. A first set of questions measured perceptions of the policy positions of candidates who buy votes. In a second battery of questions, we measured voters' perceptions of the personal attributes of the candidate, including their honesty, individual qualities, and electoral viability. Finally, we assessed the effectiveness of these strategies on self-reported electoral outcomes, including the intention to vote for the candidate, to vote for his competitor, and to abstain.

In Chapter 2 we posited that the electoral costs of different forms of clientelism vary based on what they signal to voters about candidates' personal characteristics and policy positions. As Chapters 4 and 5 have demonstrated, clientelistic strategies that use state resources allow candidates to signal their positions on key policies related to welfare spending and management competence. In contrast to state-based forms of clientelism, we do not expect that vote buying carries such strong signals of candidates' policy positions, because it conveys very little information about the policy choices made by the candidate in allocating social policy benefits. Instead, because vote buying involves personal gifts or payments from candidates to voters, we expect to see stronger effects on perceptions of personal characteristics. In other words, the informational model should imply that vote buying is a signal of personal qualities rather than policy positions.

In Chapter 2 we laid out two variations of the informational or signaling theory. In general, signaling theories of clientelism argue that voters glean some information about candidates from their use of clientelism. As a result, the vote choices of citizens who are directly and indirectly exposed to clientelism take into account not only the material incentive offered in a clientelistic transaction, but also their updated beliefs about how well the candidate will deliver public goods and services valued by the voter once in office. The strong version of the signaling theory argues that these informational signals are actually positive for all or some voters. The weaker version of this theory suggests that these informational effects simply attenuate clientelism's negative effects, and therefore make it less costly for candidates to use.

For each set of outcomes, we present two specifications. The first specification presents the estimates of the effects of the two clientelistic treatments compared to the control scenario. It also tests whether the respondents' social policy preferences condition their evaluation of vote-buying strategies using an interaction term. The second specification includes additional controls for the gender, age, and ethnicity of the respondent to increase the precision of the estimates.

We begin by presenting the results of the vignettes on the perceived policy positions of candidates described as using clientelistic favors. In this section, we present an analysis on outcome related to how a candidate would spend social policy resources. We aggregate individual survey questions into an index that measures a candidate's perceived social policy position.

Help Deserving Poor Index
- *Help Poor*: Does this mayor help poor people?
- *Help Emergency*: Would this mayor help people in your locality if they faced an emergency?
- *Job for You*: How likely is it that this candidate would give a job to people like you?

Table 7.1 Anti-workfare ideology and the social policy signals of vote buying

	Dependent variable	
	Help	Deserving Poor Index
	(1)	(2)
Vote Buying: In-kind	-0.37***	-0.39***
	(0.08)	(0.09)
Vote Buying: Cash	-0.80***	-0.80***
	(0.08)	(0.09)
Vote Buying: In-kind × Anti-Workfare Ideology	-0.13	-0.10
	(0.08)	(0.09)
Vote Buying: Cash × Anti-Workfare Ideology	-0.07	-0.01
	(0.09)	(0.09)
Anti-Workfare Ideology	-0.01	-0.02
	(0.06)	(0.06)
Constant	0.39***	-0.03
	(0.06)	(0.25)
Individual Controls		✓
Observations	585	551
R^2	0.14	0.17

*p<0.1; **p<0.05; ***p<0.01

Standard errors in parentheses.

Models are estimated using OLS. All outcomes are standardized. Vote Buying: In-kind is a dummy indicating that the respondent was randomly assigned to the vignette in which the candidate offered a meal; Vote Buying: Cash is a dummy indicating that the respondent was randomly assigned to the vignette in which the candidate offered cash; the residual category is the vignette in which the candidate offers nothing. Anti-Workfare Ideology is a standardized continuous measure of the respondent's opposition to the existing state welfare programs. Individual controls include gender, age, income, ethnicity, education, and workfare eligibility.

These questions ask perceptions of respondents about the willingness of the candidate to help deserving groups with social assistance. In the welfare survey experiment presented in Chapter 5, we also asked welfare-specific questions about the scenarios. These include questions about whether the candidate (in that case, an incumbent mayor) would try to avoid "paying people to be lazy" and would reallocate social assistance to the elderly. In the vote-buying scenario, we did not ask these follow-up questions because during pre-testing many respondents reported that they did not have enough information to answer them.

The results of our analysis, presented in Table 7.1, use the Help Deserving Poor index as our dependent variable. As in the analysis presented in Chapter 5, the main effects of the treatment variables Vote Buying: In-kind and Vote Buying: Cash denote the effect of the treatments for the average respondent. The interaction of the treatment variables with the respondents' social policy attitudes, denoted by the variable Anti-Workfare Ideology, test whether respondents with different social policy preferences interpret the informational signals of vote buying differently.

The results in Table 7.1 show that offers of money or in-kind goods are understood as signals that candidates have little concern for low-income voters. In other words, there is no support for the strong version of the signaling theory, as clientelism makes respondents perceive the candidate as less effective in helping groups of citizens who most agree are deserving of support All respondents perceive candidates who engage in these clientelistic exchanges as being less likely to help low-income voters compared to the candidate in the baseline scenario. On average, candidates who offer meals at rallies are perceived as 0.4 standard deviations lower in terms of how much they would help the poor and help people during emergencies compared to the candidate in the baseline scenario. Those who offer money are perceived as 0.8 standard deviations lower on these policy traits.

In addition, these negative perceptions of vote-buying practices are not conditioned by the social policy preferences of the respondents. The interactions of the index measuring opposition to workfare and the vote-buying scenarios are not statistically significant and are small in magnitude relative to the main effects. Table C15 in Appendix C presents these effects for each of the questions that make up the Help Deserving Poor Index.

Next we examine whether offers of vote buying or in-kind goods affect perceptions of the candidate's more personal qualities. These include management style, corruption, personal comportment, and likelihood of winning the election. To investigate these questions, we construct four additional indices using responses to the following questions.

Management Index
- *Good Manager*: How good a manager do you think this candidate is?
- *Law and Order*: How capable is this candidate of ensuring law and order in the locality?
- *Solve Problems*: Would this candidate be able to solve problems in town?

Corruption Index
- *Honest*: How honest do you think this candidate is?
- *Fight Corruption*: How much would this candidate fight against corruption?

Personal Qualities Index
- *Good Christian*: How good a Christian do you think this candidate is?
- *Family Man*: How good a family man do you think this candidate is?
- *Treats People Well*: How well do you think this candidate knows how to treat people?

Competitiveness Index
- *Win Others' Vote*: How likely is it that he would have the votes of some people in the locality?
- *Win Election*: How likely is it that he would win the election?

The first set of three questions asks about perceptions of the mayor's ability to manage the locality, including his ability to generally ensure law and order and to solve local problems. The second set of two questions asks for respondents' perceptions of how honest or corrupt the mayor would be in office. The third set, called the Personal Qualities Index, asks about perceptions of how the candidate behaves in his private life, including whether he adheres to religious standards, and treats his family and personal relations well. Finally, the fourth index is constructed of two questions measuring how competitive respondents perceive the candidate to be.

For all of these outcomes, we expect that voters opposed to redistribution would judge mayors who use vote buying more harshly on these dimensions.

The results, presented in Table 7.2, show again that candidates who engage in vote buying are perceived as less desirable along a range of positive characteristics. The negative effects are largest on the perceived corruption of the candidate, with magnitudes of around 1.2 standard deviations for candidates who give out cash and 0.6 standard deviations for those who give out meals. In general, these negative effects are larger for cash gifts than in-kind gifts with a similar value.

We find some evidence that the responses to these scenarios are conditioned by the social policy preferences of respondents. Respondents who are more opposed to the distribution of social policy benefits are likely to view the personal characteristics of candidates that distribute in-kind benefits less favorably compared to voters that hold more left-leaning social policy views. However, for seven out of eight coefficients, there is no significant interaction between Anti-Workfare Ideology and the treatments. Thus, despite these suggestive patterns, we conclude that there is insufficient evidence that heterogeneity in voters' preferences condition the interpretation of vote buying as signal of a candidate's personal characteristics such as honesty, management skills, and competitiveness. Figures 7.1–7.3 displays the marginal effect of the two treatments at varying levels of Anti-Workfare Ideology.

Finally, we analyze self-reported propensity to support a clientelistic candidate at the polls. We measure hypothetical voting behavior by asking respondents to rate their propensity to vote in three different ways on a five-point likelihood scale:

Electoral Punishment Index
- *Win Your Vote*: How likely is it that you would vote for this mayor?
- *Abstain*: How likely is it that you would not vote at all?
- *Lose Your Vote*: How likely is it that you would vote for another candidate?

As discussed in Chapter 5, we caution that these outcomes are the most likely to be biased by social desirability and thus interpret them more as an indication of how respondents think they *should* vote than how they actually *would* vote.

Table 7.3 presents the results of the analysis of these voting propensity outcomes. We test this hypothesis using an index of self-reported propensity to punish the candidate at the ballot box where higher values indicate that the candidate is less likely to win the respondent's vote, more likely to abstain, and more likely to lose the respondent's vote.

Table 7.2 Anti-workfare ideology and the personal quality signals of vote buying

	Dependent variable							
	Management Index		Anti-Corruption Index		Personal Index		Competitiveness Index	
	(1)	(2)	(3)	(4)	(5)	(6)	(7)	(8)
Vote Buying: In-kind	-0.44***	-0.47***	-0.58***	-0.61***	-0.43***	-0.44***	-0.25***	-0.29***
	(0.08)	(0.09)	(0.08)	(0.09)	(0.08)	(0.08)	(0.09)	(0.09)
Vote Buying: Cash	-0.85***	-0.85***	-1.21***	-1.21***	-0.88***	-0.88***	-0.48***	-0.51***
	(0.08)	(0.09)	(0.08)	(0.09)	(0.08)	(0.08)	(0.09)	(0.09)
Vote Buying: In-kind × Anti-Workfare Ideology	-0.05	-0.04	-0.04	-0.02	-0.14*	-0.14*	0.01	0.03
	(0.08)	(0.09)	(0.08)	(0.09)	(0.08)	(0.08)	(0.09)	(0.09)
Vote Buying: Cash × Anti-Workfare Ideology	-0.004	0.04	-0.06	-0.05	-0.07	-0.04	0.11	0.15
	(0.08)	(0.09)	(0.08)	(0.09)	(0.08)	(0.08)	(0.09)	(0.10)
Anti-Workfare Ideology	-0.01	-0.02	-0.01	-0.01	0.01	0.03	-0.10	-0.09
	(0.06)	(0.06)	(0.06)	(0.06)	(0.06)	(0.06)	(0.06)	(0.07)
Constant	0.42***	-0.01	0.62***	0.10	0.44***	-0.15	0.25***	-0.32
	(0.06)	(0.25)	(0.06)	(0.25)	(0.06)	(0.24)	(0.06)	(0.27)
Individual Controls		✓		✓		✓		✓
Observations	595	559	573	539	579	547	621	583
R^2	0.15	0.18	0.28	0.29	0.18	0.20	0.05	0.09

*p<0.1; **p<0.05; ***p<0.01

Standard errors in parentheses.

Models are estimated using OLS. All outcomes are standardized. Vote Buying: In-kind is a dummy indicating that the respondent was randomly assigned to the vignette in which the candidate offered a meal; Vote Buying: Cash is a dummy indicating that the respondent was randomly assigned to the vignette in which the candidate offered cash; the residual category is the vignette in which the candidate offers nothing. Anti-Workfare Ideology is a standardized continuous measure of the respondent's opposition to the existing state welfare programs. Individual controls include gender, age, income, ethnicity, education, and workfare eligibility.

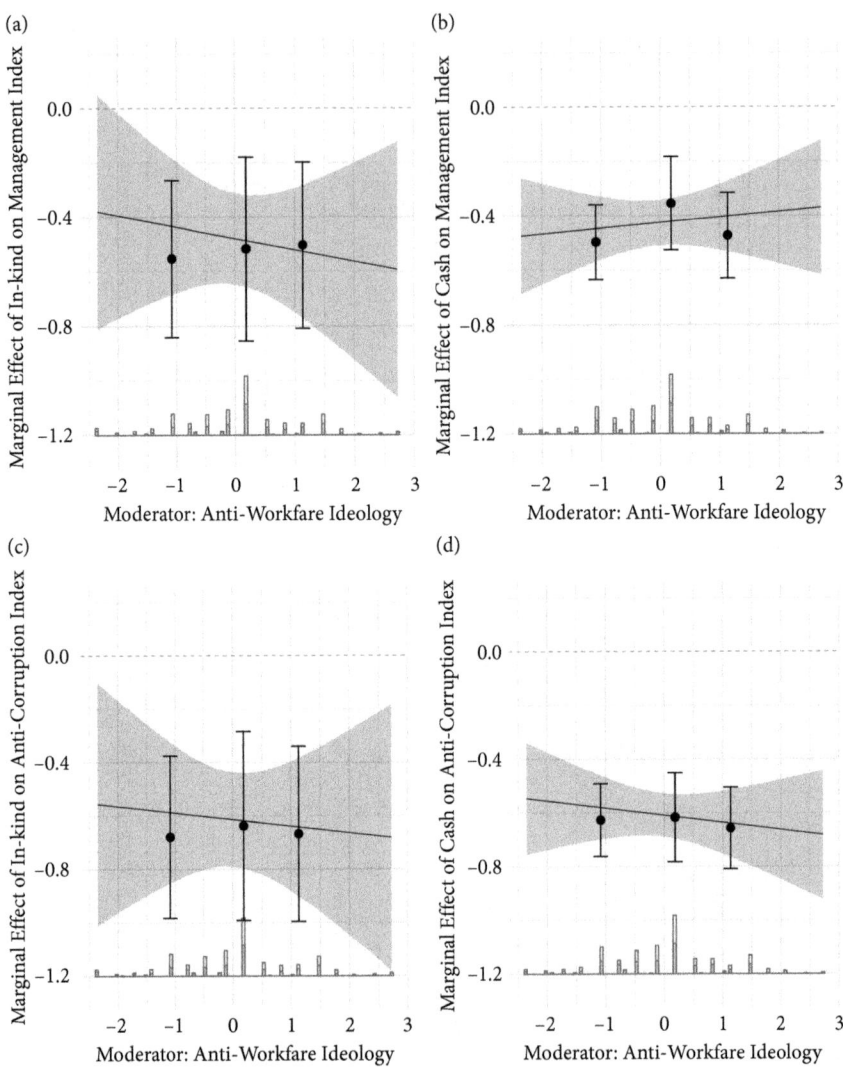

Figure 7.1 The marginal effect of clientelism on perceptions of social policy positions of candidate at varying levels of anti-workfare ideology

The results in Table 7.3 show first that respondents report being much less likely to vote for candidates who hand out cash or in-kind goods at their campaign events. To put this in real terms, while 30 percent of respondents in the control scenario say that it is very unlikely or impossible that they would vote for the candidate, this number jumps to 56 percent in the meals condition and 84 percent in the money condition.

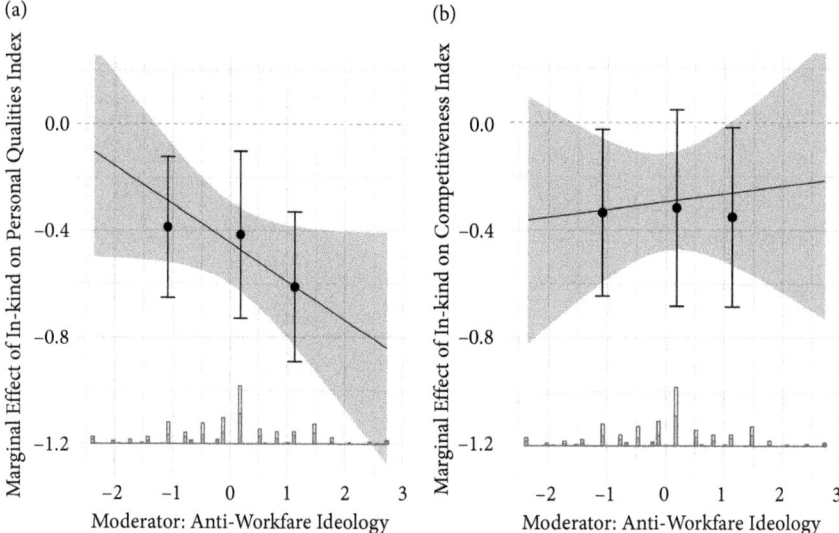

Figure 7.2 The marginal effect of in-kind vote- buying on perceptions of personal characteristics (left) and competitiveness (right) at varying levels of anti-workfare ideology

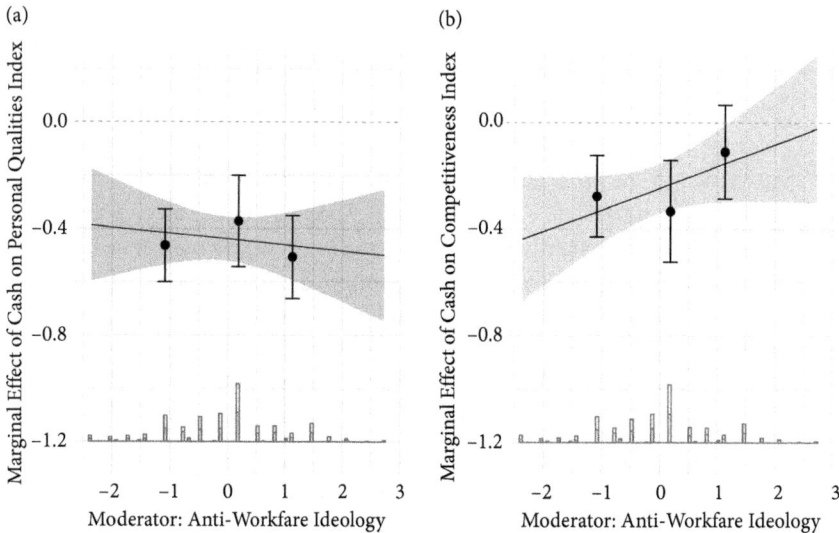

Figure 7.3 The marginal effect of in-kind (left) and cash (right) vote- buying on self-reported propensity to electorally punish candidates at varying levels of anti-workfare ideology

Table 7.3 Anti-workfare ideology and propensity to punish candidates who use vote buying

	Dependent variable	
	Electoral Punishment Index	
	(1)	(2)
Vote Buying: In-kind	0.39***	0.42***
	(0.06)	(0.06)
Vote Buying: Cash	0.81***	0.82***
	(0.06)	(0.06)
Vote Buying: In-kind × Anti-Workfare Ideology	0.05	0.02
	(0.06)	(0.06)
Vote Buying: Cash × Anti-Workfare Ideology	0.10	0.05
	(0.06)	(0.06)
Anti-Workfare Ideology	−0.02	−0.01
	(0.04)	(0.05)
Constant	−0.40***	−0.21
	(0.04)	(0.18)
Individual Controls		✓
Observations	623	585
R^2	0.23	0.25

*$p<0.1$; **$p<0.05$; ***$p<0.01$

Standard errors in parentheses.

Models are estimated using OLS. All outcomes are standardized. Vote Buying: In-kind is a dummy indicating that the respondent was randomly assigned to the vignette in which the candidate offered a meal; Vote Buying: Cash is a dummy indicating that the respondent was randomly assigned to the vignette in which the candidate offered cash; the residual category is the vignette in which the candidate offers nothing. Anti-Workfare Ideology is a standardized continuous measure of the respondent's opposition to the existing state welfare programs. Individual controls include gender, age, income, ethnicity, education, and workfare eligibility.

When we turn to heterogeneous effects, we find patterns similar to those on perceptions of candidates in Tables 7.1 and 7.2. Specifically, voters with anti-workfare preferences are slightly more likely to say they would punish candidates who engage in vote buying, but the interaction terms are not statistically significant and their magnitudes are small compared to the main effects. This implies that even voters with strongly pro-workfare preferences say they would punish candidates who engage in this form of vote buying at the polls.

Taken together, the findings of this vignette experiment suggest that vote buying with private resources sends informational signals to voters that are much more uniformly negative. In other words, there is little evidence in favor of the strong version of the signaling argument in this case with respect to vote buying. This negative result is particularly credible given that the forms of clientelism described in the vignette are perhaps the least odious of those that we identified in our qualitative work, and characterized by the literature across cases. The forms of clientelism described in the vignettes are non-targeted and non-contingent, which our qualitative interviews suggest is viewed as the least harmful form of vote buying. In addition, the large differences in how voters perceive in-kind and cash gifts suggest that voters are sensitive to such variations in the way that vote buying is structured. Thus, if the strong version of the signaling theory were operating, this would perhaps be the easiest test for it. Yet there is no evidence that vote buying actually improves perceptions of candidates on any dimensions, for any groups of voters.

In addition, in the case of vote buying, unlike for clientelism based on state resources, there is little evidence for the weaker form of the signaling theory. The weak version of this theory argues that the policy or personal signals of clientelism counterbalance most voters' general disapproval of electoral corruption. However, we find that vote buying has strong negative effects on perceptions of candidates for all subsets of voters. Voters with almost all types of preferences regarding local social policy view candidates who distribute cash or in-kind goods at their campaign rallies as worse in terms of their social policy, personal characteristics, corruption, and competitiveness relative to challengers. This is in contrast to our findings regarding clientelistic strategies based on state resources.

These findings also differ sharply from the results of similar experiments in Latin America and Africa. The starkest difference is with Kramon (2016), who finds counterintuitive evidence in favor of the strong version of the signaling theory in Kenya. Using a similar experimental vignette, Kramon finds that voters are 40 percent more likely to say they would vote for a candidate who they are told has handed out cash at a political rally (Kramon 2016: 477), although this main effect did not appear in a subsequent replication (Kramon 2016: 485). In addition, he finds evidence that low-income voters perceive candidates who engage in vote buying as more likely to help the poor (Kramon 2016: 486). There are several possible explanations for these differences. First, they could be driven by stronger anti-clientelism norms than in the Eastern European case, which has a shorter democratic history but much higher development and close proximity to strong democracies in the rest of Europe. Second, the signaling value of clientelistic transactions using private resources could be replaced in cases with higher levels of social spending by the politicization of state resources.

Second, we find little evidence that personal characteristics condition how voters interpret vote buying. Our measure of anti-workfare preferences is strongly related to poverty, and we find similar results when we examine heterogeneous effects on income, ethnicity, and welfare eligibility (see Appendix C for additional results). The only group where the effects of clientelism may be consistently different is the Roma, but since the total number of Roma respondents in our vignette sample is very small, we do not want to over-interpret these results. This is again in contrast to Kramon (2016), who finds that income affects how voters interpret parties who engage in vote buying. It is also in contrast to Gonzalez-

Ocantos et al. (2012), who find that education conditions the amount of stigma that voters report against clients in vote-buying transactions in Uruguay and Bolivia (although not Honduras). Finally, it is in contrast to our own results on other clientelistic strategies, namely welfare favors and welfare coercion. The absence of heterogeneous effects in the vote-buying vignettes lends additional support to the interpretation that voters in this context look more towards clientelism based on state resources for signals of candidates' policy positions and personal characteristics.

One limitation to keep in mind with these results is that although we do extend the extant literature by looking at both cash and in-kind electoral handouts, we still examine voter reactions to a fairly limited range of vote-buying strategies. The vote-buying scenarios that we describe involve gifts of a standard but fixed value (around 12 USD) distributed at a campaign rally. They are not explicitly conditioned on voting behavior, and there is no mention of monitoring. Because this is a relatively non-egregious form of vote buying, we suspect that if we do not find positive signaling effects here, then they are also likely to be absent for vote-buying strategies that are more strictly targeted, monitored, and conditioned on voting behavior.

7.3 Variation across Localities in Vote Buying

Our qualitative analysis of vote-buying strategies points to the existence of a significant heterogeneity in the strategies that fall in the encompassing category "vote buying." We find both evidence of what Alan Rouquié (1978) has called "gregarious vote buying" and of more "targeted clientelism," where candidates offer goods or money in exchange for political support. The qualitative results also document a wide heterogeneity in the type of brokers used by candidates to deliver these goods and in the strategies used by these brokers to monitor the turnout and electoral choices of voters and to influence voters' beliefs that their vote is observable.

Does the incidence of vote buying differ in systematic ways across localities? What are the most salient economic and political characteristics of a locality that explain the incidence of this strategy? As discussed in Chapter 2, one encounters two theoretical perspectives that shed light on the variation in the use of vote-buying strategies. One such perspective, which we have labeled the "resource-based" approach, stresses the importance of material resources of candidates and of competitive conditions in explaining the variation in the use of non-programmatic strategies. A second perspective highlights the signaling role of clientelistic strategies. According to this perspective, candidates deploy different clientelistic strategies to send voters signals about their personal attributes, the relative position vis-à-vis their competitor, and, sometimes, their policy positions. These signals are believed to either actually improve voters' views of candidates, or to at least attenuate the overall negative effect of voters' disdain for clientelism on their views of candidates who use it.

The following two sections test our predictions regarding variation in the use of vote-buying strategies across localities derived from resource-based and informational theories. The main empirical analysis comes from two post-electoral surveys conducted in Romania and Hungary that measure the incidence of vote buying. We combine this survey data with a number of locality-level variables, primarily coded from administrative records, that operationalize different factors that the resource-based and informational theories predict should shape the costs and benefits of vote buying.

7.3.1 Research design

As with the non-programmatic strategies examined in previous chapters, measuring the incidence of vote buying is difficult because voters may face social and even legal pressure not to admit that they have sold their votes. We thus assess the incidence of vote buying by embedding a measure of vote buying in a list experiment that includes other non-sensitive items. The lists measuring the incidence of vote buying were included in two surveys fielded in 2014 in Hungary and 2015 in Romania. We provide more detailed information about the survey in Chapter 3 and Appendix C.

We used similar wording for the question measuring vote buying in both surveys. The lists where the sensitive question measuring the incidence of vote buying were worded as follows:

Hungary
I am going to list some more statements in connection with the elections. Please recall the elections of 6 April. How many of these events happened with you, or in your locality?
- I saw some Jobbik posters.
- I did not see any Jobbik posters.
- I met one of the candidates also in person.
- *(Sensitive item)* In the last elections I was offered a gift, drink, or food in return for my vote.

Romania
I will read you a number of statements that refer to the recent presidential elections held in November 2014. For each of these statements, I would like you to tell me how many of these events happened here, in this community. You do not need to tell me which of these happened, but only how many.
- There was a voting place in our locality, so I could vote in our locality.
- At the times of the previous elections, I was abroad and voted in the UK.

Table 7.4 Estimated incidence of vote buying

Country	N	Control Mean	Treatment Mean	Estimated Incidence	p-value
Hungary	1,838	1.04	1.11	6.8%	0.00
		(1.02, 1.06)	(1.09, 1.13)	(3.1%, 10.5%)	
Romania	1,495	0.99	1	1.3%	0.20
		(0.98, 1)	(0.99, 1.01)	(−0.7%, 3.4%)	

- I saw Victor Ponta in our locality on the day of vote for the runoff.
- *(Sensitive item)* During the campaign, someone offered me money or food (*alimente*) in exchange for my vote.

How pervasive are vote buying strategies premised on offers of money or goods? Table 7.4 presents descriptive information about the use of this strategy in both countries. In column 2, we report the mean value of responses for those respondents who received the version of the questionnaire that included only the non-sensitive items. We also report the standard deviation of these responses. In column 3, we report the average responses for those respondents who received the version of the questionnaire that also includes the sensitive question. By subtracting the response of the non-sensitive version of the questionnaire from the mean response of the sensitive version of the questionnaire, we obtain our estimate of the incidence of vote buying.

We find that around 7 percent of voters in Hungary experienced offers of money or goods during the 2014 parliamentary election. This suggests that the incidence of vote buying in Hungary is roughly comparable in magnitude to the other non-programmatic strategies included in our study, such as welfare favors and economic coercion. By contrast, we find that the incidence of vote buying during the 2015 presidential election in Romania was very low. Our survey estimates that only 1 percent of our respondents were offered money or goods. The estimate of vote buying is not statistically distinguishable from zero in the full sample.[2] In the rest of this section, we analyze only the Hungary data, as the low incidence we measure in Romania suggests that vote buying was not an important strategy in this election.

Figure 7.4 presents the distribution of vote buying across Hungary and Romania. Dots on the map represent localities in which we conducted our survey. Each dot on the map represents a locality where we conducted our survey and is based on twenty individual survey responses for Hungary, or on an average of seventeen individual survey responses for Romania. Darker dots indicate higher estimated incidences of welfare coercion. Locality coordinates have been jittered in order to prevent identification.

Figure 7.4 shows that in Hungary, localities with high levels of vote buying are distributed throughout the three counties in our study. In Romania, in all but

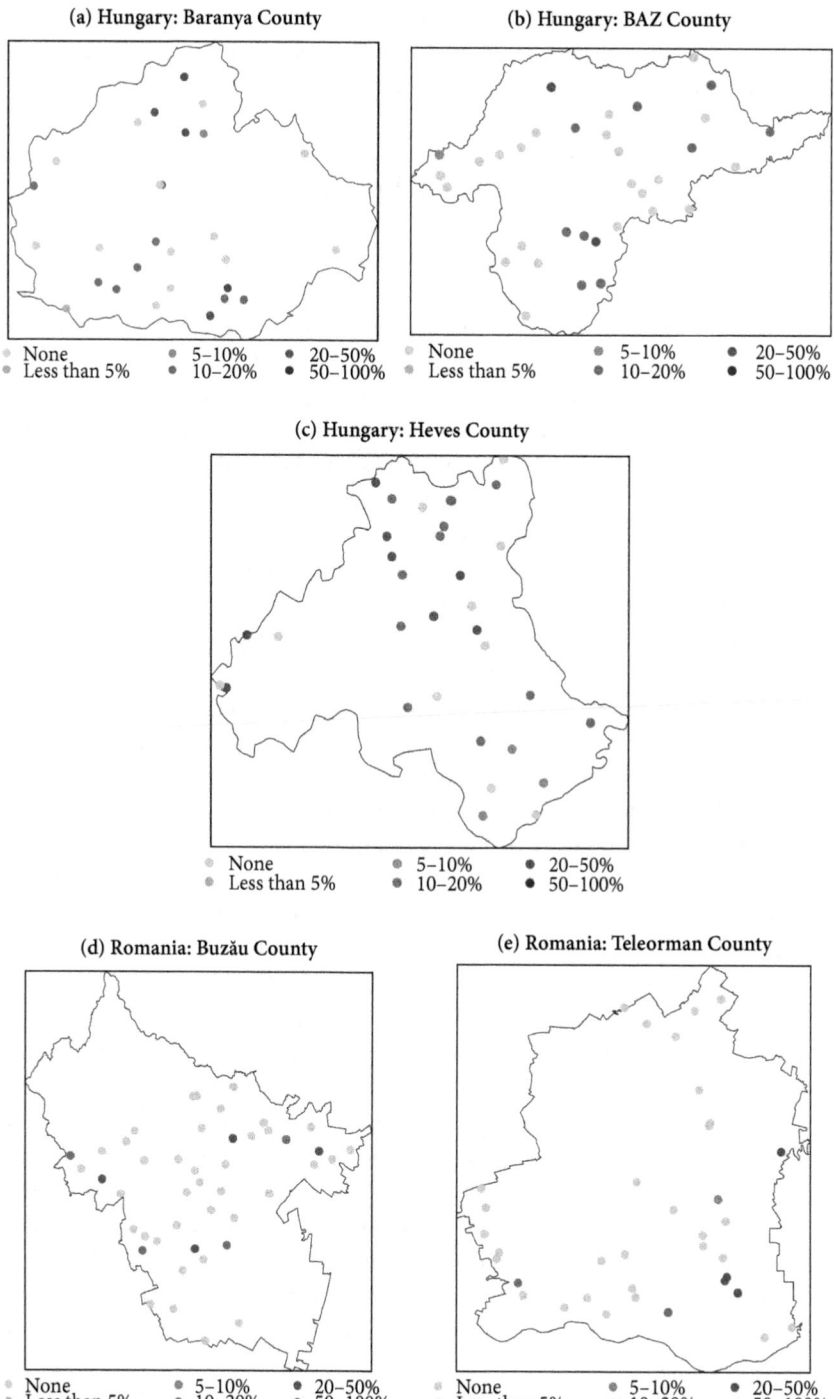

Figure 7.4 Geographic distribution of vote-buying in Hungary and Romania

15 percent of the places we surveyed, the estimated incidence of vote buying is less than 5 percent. By contrast, in Hungary in half of the localities surveyed we estimate an incidence of greater than 5 percent.

7.3.2 Theoretical predictions

What explains the variation in the incidence of vote buying across localities? As discussed in Chapter 2, resource-based explanations point to the importance of specific endowments available to candidates and to differences in electoral competitiveness in explaining the variation in the incidence of particular non-programmatic strategies. More specifically, such explanations point to the importance of locality-level economic and political conditions, electoral competitiveness, and partisanship in explaining the incidence of particular non-programmatic strategies. We begin by using resource-based explanations to derive predictions about the variation in the incidence of vote buying across localities.

As discussed in previous chapters, one important local resource affecting the incidence of non-programmatic strategies that deploy state resources is the length of incumbency. In the case of clientelistic strategies that deploy state resources, the length of political incumbency is likely to be correlated with access to or control over policies that can be mobilized electorally. Can differences in the length of incumbency influence the incidence of vote buying? The main resources that are offered as part of this political exchange, such as money or in-kind goods, are financed by political parties. However, the length of incumbency may influence another political resource that is important for the vote-buying exchange. As the above discussion has pointed out, employees of the local administration are sometimes deployed as brokers distributing the money or in-kind goods and monitoring the voters who have received these offers. This suggests that the length of incumbency may influence the incidence of vote buying by affecting the supply of brokers that may be used in this clientelistic strategy.

We also examine whether one finds partisan differences in the use of vote-buying strategies. As discussed above, our qualitative interviews with voters and brokers suggests that the financing of the goods and money offered as part of clientelistic exchanges often originates with the regional or national party organization. We proxy partisanship with a measure of the partisan orientation of the mayor in the respective locality. In Hungary, our partisan measure estimates whether Fidesz mayors are more likely to turn to vote buying than are independent mayors. For the sake of simplicity and to avoid multiple comparisons, we operationalize these measures of local political control with an additive index of local political control.

Resource-based explanations of clientelism also suggest that candidates have a higher incentive to use clientelistic strategies premised on vote buying in localities with unfavorable economic conditions. A bag of corn flour and a bottle of oil may more effective in swaying the choices of low-income voters than high-income voters, so one expects to find a higher incidence of vote buying in low-income localities. Unfavorable economic conditions, such as high levels of unemployment, are also more likely to make voters more predisposed to support a particular candidate in response to offers of monetary inducements.

As discussed in Chapter 2, informational theories of clientelism suggest that the use of private resources—such as vote-buying—may be signals of pro-poor concern. Thus, the targeted audience of such exchanges is low-income voters in the locality. If this signaling logic is in place, one expects to find a higher incidence of vote buying in localities where the number of low-income voters is large. In contrast to clientelistic strategies that use state resources, politicians that use vote buying are less likely to activate distributional conflicts in the locality over the allocation of social policy benefits. As a result, we do not expect to find correlations between the incidence of vote buying and measures of distributional conflict over the allocation of social policy benefits, such as the size of the RETRENCHMENT COALITION and the measure of social conflict.

We use the same operations of the measures of social conflict as in previous chapters. The standardized index of the RETRENCHMENT COALITION includes the percentage of adults in each locality who are employed and the percentage of adults who are retired. The index of the EXPANSION COALITION includes the percentage of adults who are unemployed and those who identify in the census as Roma. Our measure of SOCIAL CONFLICT is the interaction of the these variables.

7.3.3 Results

As in previous chapters, we estimate the individual- and locality-level covariates in the incidence of coercive strategies by using a hierarchical model. For simplicity, in Table 7.5 we only display the coefficients on the interaction terms with the list experiment treatment because these coefficients indicate the estimated relationship between the independent variables and vote buying. Nevertheless, all specifications also include the direct effects of the characteristics, which should be interpreted as the relationship between the independent variables and the control list responses. We refer the reader to Section 4.5 of Chapter 4 for a presentation of the equation used to estimate these models. Appendix B presents the full models with all coefficients displayed.

The results in Table 7.5 generally suggest that vote buying is not carefully targeted compared to the other illicit electoral strategies we have studied. We first discuss the results on the variables that operationalize theories focused on access to resources. While none of the variables measuring increased access to resources is significantly

Table 7.5 Correlates of vote buying in Hungary

	Dependent variable		
	Vote Buying		
	(1)	(2)	(3)
Retrenchment Coalition	0.003	0.004	0.02
	(0.04)	(0.04)	(0.04)
Expansion Coalition	0.005	0.01	0.01
	(0.03)	(0.03)	(0.03)
Retrenchment × Expansion (Social Conflict)	−0.03	−0.03	−0.03*
	(0.02)	(0.02)	(0.02)
Local Control	−0.02	−0.02	−0.02
	(0.02)	(0.02)	(0.02)
Poverty Rate	0.02	0.01	0.01
	(0.02)	(0.02)	(0.02)
Debt Rate		−0.01	−0.01
		(0.02)	(0.02)
Mayor Margin		0.01	0.01
		(0.02)	(0.02)
Population			−0.01
			(0.05)
Roma			0.01
			(0.04)
Female			0.01
			(0.03)
Age			−0.04
			(0.07)
Employed			0.003
			(0.07)
Unemployed			−0.05
			(0.09)
Retired	−0.10	−0.08	−0.02
	(0.21)	(0.21)	(0.22)
Direct Effects	✓	✓	✓
Observations	1,798	1,798	1,691
Akaike Inf. Crit.	1,592.23	1,620.50	1,549.24
		Hungary	

*p<0.1; **p<0.05; ***p<0.01

Standard errors in parentheses.

Models are estimated using a multilevel model with intercepts varying by locality. The coefficients shown are from interactions with the list treatment indicator. Local Control is an additive index of indicators that take a value of 1 if the locality has a mayor who is an incumbent, a co-partisan with the national executive, or from the same party as the plurality in the city council. Retrenchment Coalition is the average of the standardized proportions of the anti-workfare constituency: the employed and retirees. Expansion Coalition is the average of the standardized proportions of the pro-workfare constituency: the unemployed and Roma. Retrenchment × Expansion is the interaction of the pro- and anti-workfare constituencies. Poverty Rate is the proportion of inhabitants who are below the poverty line. Debt Rate is the proportion of survey respondents by locality who reported being in debt. Mayor Margin is the margin of victory of the mayor. Population is the population size. Roma, Female, Age, Employed, Unemployed, Retired, Debt, and Poor are individual-level variables coded from our surveys. All but Age and Poor are binary. All continuous variables are standardized.

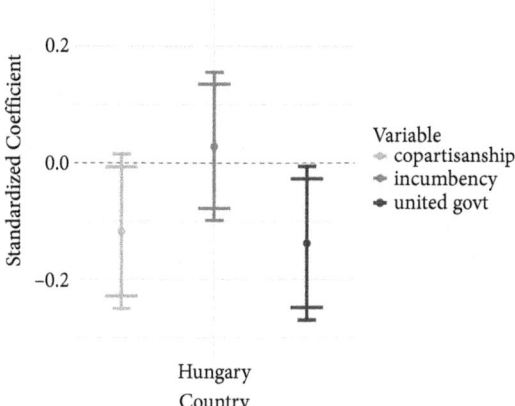

Figure 7.5 Coefficients on sub-indicators of the local control index

related to vote buying, the coefficients are actually negative both for Local Control and Poverty Level, suggesting that vote buying is less likely in places with more local political control and a greater proportion of poor residents.

Figure 7.5 disaggregates the Local Control index into each of its components: a binary variable measuring whether the mayor is a co-partisan of the national executive, a binary variable indicating whether the mayor is an incumbent, and a binary variable indicating whether the mayor's political party also controls a plurality on the city council.

The coefficients plotted in Figure 7.5 reinforce the findings based on the Local Control index: local political control does not seem to have a consistent relationship with vote buying, and if anything, higher levels of local control are associated with lower vote buying. Co-partisanship with the national executive and united government are both negative and significant (at the 10 percent and 5 percent levels, respectively). These negative coefficients could suggest that when politicians have greater local control, they prefer to use less costly forms of clientelism than vote buying based on the politicization of welfare resources. By contrast, we find no detectable relationship between the measure of incumbency and the incidence of vote buying. Overall, while we think these disaggregated results are worth future study, we conclude that local political control has no relationship overall to the incidence of vote buying.

Next we turn to the variables that we use to measure the coalitions that favor and oppose the current social policy distribution and our measure of social conflict. Again, we find little evidence overall that vote buying is strategically targeted in ways predicted by theory. We find no relationship between the welfare expansion coalition and the incidence of vote buying. In conjunction with the individual level evidence presented in the previous section, these findings suggest that in the Hungarian context, politicians do not use vote buying to signal pro-poor concern. The incidence of vote buying is also unaffected by the presence of distributional conflict in the locality. The interaction of the Workfare Retrenchment and Workfare Expansion coalitions is negatively associated with the incidence of vote buying, but is only weakly and inconsistently statistically significant. Ultimately, we conclude that there is no systematic relationship between these variables measuring social conflict and the incidence of vote buying.

Finally, there is little evidence that vote buying is targeted at the individual level based on relevant demographic characteristics. Gender, ethnicity, age, and employment status have little relationship with the incidence of vote buying. These individual-level results are in line with the locality-level evidence that vote buying seems largely untargeted compared to other forms of clientelism.

7.4 Conclusion

In this chapter, we have documented that vote buying comes in two distinct forms: either offers of non-targeted goods, such as meals and other public events or targeted goods, such as offers of money and in-kind goods.

By drawing on a large numbers of interviews with candidates and voters, this chapter documents the wide heterogeneity in the type of vote buying practices one encounters in the region, along with the variety of strategies by which brokers monitor voters' choices. Drawing on James Scott's (1990) analysis of "hidden transcripts," we show that vote buying appears to be less effective than other non-programmatic strategies in actually influencing voters' behavior at the ballot box. Much of the vote buying that informants described during qualitative interviews actually involved little targeting, monitoring, or conditionality. Even when gifts were purportedly handed out with specific conditions, many voters expressed confidence that they could evade attempts at monitoring and enforcement. Overall, the type of vote buying that voters and brokers described in many of our qualitative interviews seems more similar to what nineteenth-century British law called "treating" or contemporary scholars describe as "unconditional electoral handouts" rather than actual quid pro quo transactions.

We next assessed the accuracy of resource-based explanations versus informational explanations in explaining the variation in the incidence of vote buying. When we tested the micro-mechanisms of the informational explanation using a survey experiment administered in Romania, we found little evidence that electoral handouts in cash or in in-kind goods send strong informational signals to any voters. These overall null and negative results are in contrast to the strong, generally positive effects of electoral handouts that Kramon (2016) finds in Kenya. This difference might arise from the fact that the ability to politicize the larger public sector in Eastern Europe provides a much more direct way for politicians to signal their policy positions to voters than with the use of private gifts.

We next tested whether both the resource-based and informational explanations could explain variation in the incidence of vote buying across localities. Because our survey in Romania found very low levels of vote buying overall in the vast majority of individual localities, we focused this analysis on the data from Hungary. We found little evidence that vote buying is targeted in ways that provide support for either resource-based or informational explanations. Furthermore, there is little evidence that vote buying is targeted at the individual level.

Taken together with our qualitative evidence and the findings in previous chapters showing that coercive and state-based strategies are tightly targeted in specific localities and on specific types of voters, we conclude that vote buying using private resources is relatively unimportant in the political calculations of politicians and voters. These null results are particularly interesting given the large role that vote buying has played in most empirical analyses of clientelism. Overall, while conditional and unconditional forms of vote buying are still common, particularly in Hungary, they do not seem to convey significant advantages with any groups of voters and show no evidence of targeting.

Notes

1. 50 RON is worth approximately 12 USD, equivalent to the price of a meal and several drinks.
2. In 2012, we fielded a survey in eight urban localities in Romania, with a total sample size of 3,576 voters. The 2012 survey included a measure of the incidence of vote buying that used similar wording to the question included in the 2015 survey. The results of the 2012 survey found that 6 percent of respondents had been targeted by offers of money or goods in exchange for their vote. The difference between the two surveys could be due to the fact that urban localities have higher vote buying than rural localities, but this explanation is unlikely given that theory generally predicts higher vote buying in small localities where monitoring is easier and norms of reciprocity are stronger. A more plausible explanation is that the incidence of vote buying declined in recent Romanian elections as a result of the intensive prosecution of this illicit strategy. As one voter in ST. commented on the decline in the use of this strategy, "now we no longer go to vote with our pockets full."

8

Conclusion

In November and December 2014, both Hungary and Romania celebrated the twenty-fifth anniversary of the collapse of communism. These celebrations provided ample opportunities for public reflection about the achievements, but also shattered political expectations, that accompanied the post-communist transition.

In contrast to the euphoria of the immediate post-communist transition, the public mood at the time of this anniversary was much more somber. Still, there were reasons for celebration. Citizens in both countries enjoyed their new political freedoms—such as the freedom to travel—and the absence of political surveillance by security forces. Both countries had joined the European Union as part of successive waves of European enlargement—Hungary in 2005 and, against all possible odds, Romania in 2007. In symbolic terms, European accession promised to tear down the iron curtain that had divided the continent since 1945. While membership in the European Union also brought promises of democratic stabilization and economic prosperity, the consequences of European accession were highly disappointing for many citizens. The economic reforms that were implemented during the pre-accession phase aligned the domestic prices of both countries to European prices, even though wage and income-levels were significantly below European levels. As a result of these imbalances, European accession went hand in hand with rising levels of poverty and unemployment.

The political developments experienced by both countries during the post-communist period provided only feeble grounds for euphoria on this anniversary. Over the previous quarter of a century, voters in both countries had experienced increasing disappointment with the ability of their electoral democracies to deliver on a range of expected political outcomes. One of the most painful lessons learned by Hungarian and Romanian voters during this period was that democratic and free elections in themselves provided only very small (or almost no) guarantees of ensuring quality of political representation or of guaranteeing the election of politicians committed to the greater public good. Let us consider several factors that contributed to this generalized disaffection with the quality of democracy.

One such manifestation of the deficiency of the democratic experience is the multiple corruption scandals that have afflicted the elected politicians. These scandals, involving elected politicians, have shaken up the political landscape of both countries on multiple occasions. In Hungary, corruption scandals led to the electoral collapse of the Socialist Party, a party that, not so long ago, was regarded as a success story among the communist successor parties across the region. Corruption continued in different forms under the Orbán administration. Ivan Szelenyi summarized Hungary's recent experience: "the Orbán regime is only slightly more corrupt (if only more corrupt at all) than the previous postcommunist governments" (Szelényi 2015: 646). In Romania, corruption scandals have been endemic in the postcommunist transition. And while recent initiatives by anti-corruption agencies to prosecute various forms of malfeasance have succeeded in indicting hundreds of elected politicians at all levels of government, many Romanians perceive that such indictments represent only the tip of a much larger iceberg. By all standards, Romania's political class is the most venal in Europe.

A second ground for citizens' dissatisfaction with democratic institutions is the realization that elections give voters only very weak tools to sanction politicians who seek to undermine democratic practices. Recent examples of such infringements on democratic practices may include decisions to close down independent media outlets, to limit the ability of courts to fulfill their mandate or decisions, or to close down independent newspapers. Romania has experienced such unsanctioned infringements on democratic practices throughout its post-communist transition. Such post-electoral infringements of democratic norms are now common during Hungary's recent illiberal turn.

Finally, in both countries, citizens' disillusionment with democracy as a political system is grounded in their experience of electoral practices. Despite their legal sophistication, electoral rules in both countries have proved ill-equipped to limit the incidence of different forms of electoral malfeasances. Such irregularities include the intimidation and coercion of voters, the conditioning of access to policy benefits on political support, vote buying, the violation of ballot secrecy, and so on. Such infringements on the autonomy of voters are an important symptom of democratic malaise. At the same time, the persistence of undemocratic practices is, in itself, an important cause for other disfunctionalities of democracies in the region. The existence of these irregularities at elections severely limits the ability of voters to select clean politicians and contributes to the perpetuation of corrupt political elites.

Our book has examined the variety of electoral deficiencies that are present in current Eastern European elections. Our choice is motivated by the consideration that such irregularities are a central element that undermines the quality of political representation in both countries. Clientelistic practices undermine the quality of representation by creating political majorities that do not always fully reflect the political intentions of citizens. To put it in other terms, political majorities formed by counting the votes of free and coerced voters equally are not democratic majorities. The outcomes of several Romanian presidential elections are still mired by accusations that they do not reflect the political will of their citizens. At the time we completed our manuscript, parliamentary investigations of illicit electoral practices used during the 2009 and 2014 presidential elections are ongoing. In Hungary, our study documented the use of significant irregularities during the parliamentary election held in 2014. While it is unlikely that use of clientelistic practices modified the outcome of the 2014 election, such practices aided Fidesz in reaching a two-thirds political majority in the Hungarian parliament. As Kim Lane Scheppele noted, this oversized majority allowed Fidesz to "govern without constraints" during the most recent Orbán administration (Scheppele 2014).

This chapter revisits the argument and findings of the book and discusses additional implications for both academic research into clientelism and for policy interventions designed to limit illicit electoral practices. We begin by reviewing the implications of our findings for the study of clientelism in other political contexts. We review the contributions of our study for several directions of research in the study of electoral clientelism, which include the study of variation among brokers, the signaling opportunities of different forms of clientelism, and the relationship between poverty and different forms of electoral clientelism. We conclude by discussing several implications of our findings for the design of policy interventions that seek to limit opportunities for electoral clientelism and improve electoral accountability.

8.1 Revisiting the Findings

Our study has documented the persistence of electoral practices that violate voters' electoral autonomy in both Hungary and Romania. Our main analytical objective has been to unpack and disaggregate electoral clientelism. Using both qualitative and quantitative evidence, we have described how a highly heterogeneous group of political intermediaries mediate between candidates and voters, using a wide range of illicit strategies to influence voters' electoral choices. Such brokers may include employees of the local social policy administration, teachers, tax collectors, employers, or moneylenders. These electoral intermediaries use their control over a variety of resources to influence voters' electoral choices and seek to incentivize voters to comply with their offers using a combination of positive and negative inducements. Our analysis of the mix of clientelistic strategies has addressed two different themes.

First, we have examined the determinants of the variation in the choice of different non-programmatic strategies across different localities. Does the decision of candidates to choose particular forms of clientelism vary in systematic ways across localities? If so, what are the most significant political and economic variables that influence such choices? Second, we have investigated how voters evaluate and sanction different forms of electoral clientelism. Clientelistic strategies are normatively undesirable and are likely to be sanctioned by voters.

Nevertheless, different forms of clientelism create opportunities for candidates to send voters signals about their personal attributes and their policy position on issues that are distributionally divisive. These signals affect voters' electoral responses to different clientelistic strategies and their willingness to sanction or reward candidates who use such clientelistic strategies to target voters.

Empirically, our study has documented the use of four different non-programmatic strategies in the region. Such strategies differ in the resources used by candidates to incentivize voters and in the choices made by brokers to target voters using positive or negative inducements. We show that variation across localities in the use of different non-programmatic strategies is, in some cases, affected by access or political control of state resources. Access to state resources is, in turn, mediated by several political factors. These include incumbency, co-partisanship with the national party, and the absence of significant political opposition in the local city council. We have shown that higher access to state resources gives candidates a greater ability to rely on clientelistic strategies premised on both favors and policy coercion. By contrast, in localities where the ability of candidates to access state resources is low, we find a higher use of clientelistic strategies that involve private resources, such as vote buying or economic coercion.

Second, we find that the salience and intensity of distributional conflict in the locality affects candidates' willingness to use clientelistic strategies that involve coercion. We find that coercion is an attractive electoral strategy in localities characterized by intense distributional conflict over the allocation of social policy benefits. In such localities, the use of coercion allows candidates to send a signal of support to the working poor and also signals of private competence. By contrast, in localities where such conflict over the distribution is less salient, candidates prefer clientelistic strategies that use positive inducements.

Previous studies examining linkages between candidates and voters consider programmatic and clientelistic linkages as distinct strategies (Kitschelt and Wilkinson 2007). By contrast, we suggest that the distinction between programmatic and clientelistic politics is more blurred. The use of different forms of clientelism creates opportunities for candidates to signal different attributes and policy positions. We document that the use of public policy in the form of positive inducements allows candidates to signal their pro-poor concern and their ability to generate employment in the locality. By contrast, the use of welfare coercion allows candidates to signal policy positions that are ideologically closer to right-wing voters, such as a tough attitude against the lazy, a concern for law and order, and so on.

In addition to contributing to the literature on clientelism, our study provides several findings for understanding the functioning of informal party organizations in Eastern Europe. Existing research examining political parties in the region has focused predominantly on formal organizations and measured their extensiveness, professionalization, and activism (Van Biezen 2003; Enyedi 2006; Enyedi and Linek 2008; Tavits 2013). As Rupnik and Zielonka note, one remarkable gap in the literature on political parties is the absence of studies documenting informal party organizations (Rupnik and Zielonka 2016). Our study responds to this gap and documents the strategies used by candidates at elections in rural and small urban settings where formal party organizations are missing. Strategies of informal party creation involve the capture of the local institutions of the state, the capture of economic brokers, and an on-the-spot creation of networks of vote-buying brokers. In Hungary, where political competition in more limited, we document that the ruling party co-opts both Fidesz mayors and those that are nominally independent as part of its informal party organization. In Romania, where levels of party competition are more robust, we find that all major political parties use similar strategies in developing their informal organizations.

Our research design has methodological implications for the study of informal party organizations in other contexts. Large surveys that include sensitive questions to assess the presence of different types of electoral brokers can be a useful starting point for the measurement of such informal party organizations. These survey results can allow researchers to examine whether strength of informal party organizations varies across different parties and whether parties differ in the types of resources and strategies they employ to appeal to voters.

Finally, our study generates implications for studies examining the relationship between poverty and clientelism. One enduring finding in the literature is that poverty offers a propitious terrain for the use of clientelistic practices. In one of the earliest studies of clientelism, James Scott argued that the "most important quality shared by the mass clientele of machines is poverty. Machines characteristically rely on the suffrage of the poor and, naturally, prosper best when the poor are many and the middle class few" (Scott 1969: 1150). The relationship between poverty and clientelism is at the center of recent research. Stokes (2005) documents that Argentinean brokers are more likely to target low-income voters (see also Stokes et al. 2013). Blaydes also finds a higher propensity of low-income voters in turnouts and attributes this difference to vote-buying practices (Blaydes 2006). Weitz-Shapiro finds that the relationship between poverty and clientelism is mediated by electoral competition. Poverty is conducive to higher levels of clientelism only in more competitive localities (Weitz-Shapiro 2014).

Almost all studies examining the relationship between poverty and clientelism regard the poor as a homogeneous mass of voters. By contrast, we argue that the poor are not a homogeneous group and that communities of low-income voters are deeply divided by distributional conflicts. Existing social policy programs often amplify such conflicts of "poor against the poor." The magnitude of such distributional conflict shapes electoral incentives of candidates to engage in different clientelistic strategies.

In the two countries of our study, anti-poverty programs or workfare programs represent the most important source of this distributional conflict. In many low-income communities, persons who are not eligible to access workfare benefits—such as the low-income elderly or the working poor—are likely to resent workfare employees because the latter can access a very desirable long-term stream of benefits. In localities where the size of the political constituency that is dissatisfied with the allocation of benefits is large, candidates find coercive strategies attractive. The use of coercion allows candidates and brokers to expropriate the votes of workfare employees, while also appealing to the voters that oppose the current allocation of social policy benefits. By contrast, in localities where such distributional conflict is more muted, brokers are likely to find clientelistic strategies based on favors more attractive.

We believe this theoretical logic has broader comparative implications and is likely to "travel" to other political contexts. Such distributional conflict among poor voters is likely to be salient in other political contexts and is likely to shape incentives of candidates to use different types of clientelistic strategies. We leave it to scholars of clientelism in other settings to explore the implications of such poor-against-poor conflict.

8.2 Implications for Electoral Reform and Political Accountability

We conclude by discussing the implications of our study for policy interventions that seek to limit electoral clientelism and improve electoral accountability. What measures can policymakers adopt to limit the incidence of clientelistic practices? What are the main recommendations to improve accountability that result from our study? We believe that our findings generate several implications for electoral reforms that differ from and complement recommendations currently embraced by policymakers and agencies promoting electoral integrity.

8.2.1 Designing policy interventions to limit clientelistic strategies

A central theme of our study has been the multidimensionality of clientelism. Our findings that document the existence of a variety of brokers generate two implications for the design of policy interventions that seek to limit the incidence of clientelism. First, such interventions need to consider not one single strategy, but the full menu of clientelistic strategies that may be available to candidates. Second, to reduce the incidence of all clientelistic practices, policy interventions need to impose punishments of comparable intensity across a broad range of clientelistic strategies to reduce opportunities for brokers to substitute strategies that receive lighter punishment. Let us elaborate on both points.

Similar to scholars of clientelism, policymakers also operate using conceptual blinders that privilege particular clientelistic strategies, while ignoring others. Election monitors consider the full menu of possible clientelistic strategies only on rare occasions. Unsurprisingly, election monitors or other organizations promoting electoral integrity have focused on vote-buying strategies and have attempted to limit the incidence of this particular form of clientelism. This vigorous monitoring of vote buying often leaves a range of additional clientelistic strategies unpunished. A number of such strategies are less likely to be visible to monitors who are present on election day. This is particularly true of clientelistic strategies where the relationship between brokers and voters unfolds over longer periods of time.

The above observation has three implications for the choice of electoral interventions or changes in policy legislation that may attempt to limit the incidence of clientelism. The first, most immediate implication is that interventions designed to eradicate the incidence of electoral clientelism need to consider a wider range of possible forms of clientelistic exchanges. Given that such brokers are unlikely to be found in the immediate vicinity of the polling station, election-day monitoring has to be complemented with other interventions designed to limit these exchanges. To reduce the incidence of clientelism, monitoring the allocation of social policy benefits by mayors may be as important as the presence of election-day monitors.

How should policy interventions that seek to reduce the incidence of clientelism be designed, given the multidimensionality of this phenomenon? And given that candidates can rely on a variety of brokers, how should election observers or electoral authorities structure the punishment for different irregularities? Electoral rules and decisions taken by anti-corruption agencies around the world often consider interventions that impose unequal punishments on different forms of electoral malfeasance. Recent initiatives waged by Romanian anti-corruption agencies to clean up electoral practices provide a good illustration of interventions characterized by high prosecutorial intensity, but a narrow range of targeted types of electoral malfeasance. In recent years, Romanian prosecutors targeted with high levels of intensity two particular forms of electoral irregularities—vote buying and the busing of voters to different locations. The vigorous prosecution of these offenses has led to the prosecution or indictment of a large number of high-ranking Romanian politicians, including Romania's former prime minister Adrian Nastase; Liviu Dragnea, the current president of Romania's Socialist Party; and Vasile Blaga, the former president of the Democratic Party.

Such heavy-handed targeting of vote buying as the quintessential form of electoral malfeasance has had two consequences. Nearly all organizations that have monitored electoral irregularities in recent Romanian elections have concluded that the incidence of vote buying has dramatically declined. Our survey fielded in the aftermath of the 2014 parliamentary election also supports this interpretation. As Chapter 7 demonstrates, we were unable to find survey-based evidence of vote buying during the 2014 presidential election. At the same time, we found evidence of two clientelistic strategies that deployed state resources: favors and welfare coercion.

This example suggests that interventions that target aggressively one form of electoral malfeasance while leaving other forms of clientelistic practices unpunished are likely to be ineffective in reducing the overall incidence of clientelism. Such lopsided interventions are likely to create incentives for candidates and brokers to substitute strategies that are punished less severely. We suggest that the most effective strategies that aim to reduce the overall incidence of electoral clientelism need to minimize opportunities for substitution across strategies, by imposing punishments of equal intensity on all clientelistic strategies.

Our study demonstrates that many clientelistic practices are not election-day exchanges; rather, they originate weeks, even months prior to the elections and are sustained through repeated interactions between brokers and voters. This is the case both with clientelistic strategies involving policy favors, but also of more coercive electoral strategies where brokers control either economic or policy resources. Policy interventions that seek to limit the incidence of electoral clientelism need to consider these differences in the temporal scope and duration of different forms of clientelism. Interventions that focus on election-day exchanges are likely to be ineffective, unless they are complemented by interventions that target brokers' earlier efforts to exploit vulnerabilities of voters and transform economic dependencies into political dependencies.

8.2.2 The limited role of informational campaigns

As we noted at the beginning of the chapter, one of the most important symptoms of the low democratic quality in post-communist societies results from the inability of elections to sanction politicians that have engaged in prior illicit activities. This breakdown of electoral accountability is, of course, not unique to Eastern Europe, but a common problem one encounters in both developed and developing democracies. We conclude our study by offering some reflections on political interventions that are designed to improve electoral accountability.

At the moment, the gold-standard of such interventions is the provision of information about various forms of electoral malfeasance. A recent study summarizes the strong consensus underpinning such interventions: "More informed voters are better able to screen and discipline politicians. Hence, electoral accountability is increasing in voter information" (Pande 2011: 220). This assumption leads both scholars and practitioners to advocate for interventions that disseminate information about different forms of political malfeasance. Summarizing this near-unanimous consensus about the importance of such informational exposures, Pande argues that the "mandatory provision of information about politicians may significantly improve governance in low income countries" (Pande 2011: 217; see also Djankov et al. 2010).

Our findings question the optimism about the provision of information as a panacea for improved electoral accountability that underpins many of these recommendations. Both our theoretical argument and the results of our survey-based experiments suggest that the consequences of such informational campaigns for improving electoral accountability may be much more limited. We depart from the consensus in the literature by arguing that citizens are often unwilling to sanction corrupt politicians because such illicit activities offer voters shortcuts about candidates' personal competence of their policy position.

Our theory and findings provide us with strong reasons to question the effectiveness of interventions premised on the provision of information in improving political accountability. First, we expect that such interventions are likely to have different impacts on different types of voters. In some cases, such interventions may reduce political support for corrupt candidates, but in other cases, they may have the opposite consequences. The willingness of some voters to punish corrupt politicians may increase once voters learn about the particular forms of malfeasance. If voters use such information as a shortcut to understanding the competencies or policy positions of different candidates, then increased information may translate into higher electoral margins enjoyed by corrupt politicians.

To be clear, we do not advocate the wholesale elimination of campaigns raising voters' awareness about various forms of political malfeasance and corruption. However, we suggest that prior to rolling out such extensive interventions, researchers should pay closer attention to the local conditions and salient distributional cleavages that are present in the particular setting. In the presence of such distributional conflict, voters' willingness to condone rather than punish various forms of political malfeasance may increase. As this book has demonstrated, voters' evaluation of political malfeasance is not a binary, but a continuous variable mediated by a multitude of other political and economic considerations. When thinking about how to reduce illicit electoral strategies, political scientists should embrace rather than discount these complexities in voters' calculations.

Qualitative Interviews

A1: List of Expert Interviewees

Country	Locality	Date	Affiliation
Romania	Focşani	16-Mar-13	President NGO
Romania	Focşani	16-Mar-13	Former Senator
Romania	Bucharest	18-Mar-13	Former MP PD
Romania	Bucharest	19-Mar-13	NGO member
Romania	Bucharest	19-Mar-13	NGO member
Romania	Bucharest	19-Mar-13	PSD politician
Romania	Bucharest	20-Mar-13	PDL politician
Hungary	Budapest	17-Mar-14	NGO Political Capital
Hungary	Budapest	20-Mar-14	Journalist
Hungary	Budapest	20-Mar-14	Journalist
Hungary	Budapest	20-Mar-14	K Monitor
Hungary	Budapest	21-Mar-14	Roma Expert
Hungary	Budapest	21-Mar-14	Former Dissident
Hungary	Princeton	15-Dec-15	Expert on Hungarian Politics
Hungary	Budapest	04-May-16	Expert on Regional Politics
Hungary	Budapest	04-May-16	Expert on Regional Politics

A2: List of Locality Interviewees in Romania

Loc.	County	No.	Date	Gender	Age	Ethnicity	Description
A	Alba	1	17/08/16	M	79	Romanian	Voter, retiree
A	Alba	2	17/08/16	M	65	Romanian	Voter, retiree
A	Alba	3	17/08/16	F	73	Romanian	Voter, retiree
A	Alba	4	17/08/16	M	33	Romanian	Mayor
B	Alba	1	18/08/16	M	65	Romanian	Voter, retiree
B	Alba	2	18/08/16	M	65	Romanian	Voter, retiree
B	Alba	3	18/08/16	F	68	Romanian	Voter, retiree
B	Alba	4	18/08/16	M	67	Romanian	Candidate for mayoral position
C	Buzau	1	15/10/15	M	60	Romanian	Voter, retiree
C	Buzau	2	15/10/15	F	68	Romanian	Voter, retiree
C	Buzau	3	15/10/15	F	50	Romanian	Employee of municipality
C	Buzau	4	15/10/15	F	45	Romanian	Employee of municipality
C	Buzau	5	16/10/15	F	30	Romanian	Employer
C	Buzau	6	16/10/15	F	60	Roma	Voter, retiree

Continued

Continued

Loc.	County	No.	Date	Gender	Age	Ethnicity	Description
C	Buzau	7	16/10/15	F	65	Romanian	Self-employed
C	Buzau	8	16/10/15	M	45	Romanian	Voter, employed
C	Buzau	9	14/07/16	F	40	Romanian	Voter, receives social assistance benefits
C	Buzau	10	14/07/16	M	50	Romanian	Voter, seasonally employed
D	Buzau	1	22/10/15	M	45	Roma	Voter, receives social assistance benefits
D	Buzau	2	22/10/15	M	43	Roma	Voter, self-employed, broker
D	Buzau	3	22/10/15	M	55	Romanian	Deputy mayor
D	Buzau	4	23/10/15	M	55	Romanian	Employee of municipality, broker
D	Buzau	5	23/10/15	M	60	Roma	Employee of municipality, broker
D	Buzau	6	23/10/15	M	55	Romanian	Voter, employer
D	Buzau	7	23/10/15	F	30	Romanian	Voter, unemployed
E	Buzau	1	30/10/15	M	25	Roma	Voter, unemployed
E	Buzau	2	30/10/15	F	50	Roma	Voter, receives social assistance benefits
E	Buzau	3	30/10/15	F	65	Roma	Voter, receives social assistance benefits
E	Buzau	4	05/11/15	M	18	Romanian	Voter, self-employed
E	Buzau	5	05/11/15	M	45	Romanian	Employee of municipality
E	Buzau	6	05/11/15	M	50	Romanian	Mayor
E	Buzau	7	05/11/15	F	65	Roma	Voter, unemployed
E	Buzau	8	05/11/15	F	65	Romanian	Voter, retiree
F	Buzau	1	06/11/15	F	65	Romanian	Voter, retiree
F	Buzau	2	06/11/15	M	45	Romanian	Employee of municipality
F	Buzau	3	06/11/15	M	86	Romanian	Voter, retiree
F	Buzau	4	06/11/15	M	50	Romanian	Deputy mayor
F	Buzau	5	06/11/15	M	65	Romanian	Voter, retiree
G	Argeş	1	01/11/16	M	50	Romanian	Voter, employed
G	Argeş	2	01/11/16	F	55	Romanian	Voter, employed
G	Argeş	3	01/11/16	M	67	Romanian	Voter, retiree
H	Gorj	1	24/11/16	F	50	Romanian	Voter, unemployed
H	Gorj	2	24/11/16	F	45	Romanian	Voter, employed
H	Gorj	3	24/11/16	M	55	Romanian	Voter, employed
H	Gorj	4	24/11/16	M	48	Romanian	Voter, manager team of miners
I	Gorj	1	25/11/16	F	60	Romanian	Voter, unemployed
I	Gorj	2	25/11/16	M	50	Romanian	Voter, employed
I	Gorj	3	25/11/16	F	80	Romanian	Voter, retiree
I	Gorj	4	25/11/16	M	65	Romanian	Voter, employed
I	Gorj	5	25/11/16	M	45	Romanian	Voter, employed
I	Gorj	6	25/11/16	F	45	Romanian	Voter, employed
J	Dîmboviţa	1	19/11/15	M	67	Romanian	Voter, retiree
J	Dîmboviţa	2	19/11/15	M	65	Romanian	Voter, retiree
J	Dîmboviţa	3	19/11/15	M	63	Romanian	Voter, retiree
J	Dîmboviţa	4	19/11/15	F	45	Romanian	Employee of municipality
J	Dîmboviţa	5	20/11/15	M	50	Romanian	Priest

J	Dîmbovița	6	20/11/15	M	40	Romanian	Priest
J	Dîmbovița	7	20/11/15	M	55	Romanian	Employee of municipality
J	Dîmbovița	8	20/11/15	F	45	Romanian	Voter, employed
J	Dîmbovița	9	20/11/15	F	60	Romanian	Assistant of candidate
K	Hunedoara	5	27/11/15	F	40	Romanian	Employee of municipality, responsible for social benefits
K	Hunedoara	6	27/11/15	M	70	Romanian	Voter, retired
K	Hunedoara	7	27/11/15	F	55	Romanian	Voter, employed
K	Hunedoara	8	27/11/15	M	52	Romanian	Voter, employed
K	Hunedoara	9	28/11/15	M	55	Romanian	Voter retired
K	Hunedoara	10	28/11/15	M	65	Romanian	Voter, retired
K	Hunedoara	11	28/11/15	F	47	Romanian	Voter, employed
K	Hunedoara	12	20/08/16	M	58	Romanian	Voter, retired
K	Hunedoara	13	20/08/16	M	38	Romanian	Voter, employed
K	Hunedoara	14	20/08/16	M	40	Romanian	Voter, employed
L	Hunedoara	1	21/08/16	M	70	Romanian	Voter, retired
L	Hunedoara	2	21/08/16	F	65	Romanian	Voter, retired
L	Hunedoara	3	21/08/16	M	67	Romanian	Voter, retired
M	Teleorman	5	24/07/15	M		Romanian	Mayor
M	Teleorman	6	24/07/15	F	35	Romanian	Entrepreneur
M	Teleorman	7	24/07/15	F	55	Romanian	Employee of municipality, broker
N	Teleorman	1	21/08/15	M	64	Romanian	Mayor
N	Teleorman	2	21/08/15	M	62	Romanian	Employee of municipality, responsible for social benefits
N	Teleorman	3	21/08/15	M	57	Romanian	Voter, retiree
N	Teleorman	7	27/08/15	M	65	Romanian	Priest, broker
N	Teleorman	8	27/08/15	M	69	Romanian	Employee of municipality
N	Teleorman	9	27/08/15	M	34	Romanian	Employee of municipality
N	Teleorman	10	27/08/15	F	60	Roma	Voter, unemployed
N	Teleorman	11	27/08/15	M	80	Roma	Voter, retiree
N	Teleorman	12	27/08/15	F	67	Roma	Voter, receives social assistance benefits
N	Teleorman	13	24/08/15	M	43	Romanian	Employee of municipality, broker
N	Teleorman	14	24/08/15	M	57	Romanian	Voter, self-employed
N	Teleorman	15	28/08/15	M	58	Romanian	Employee of municipality
N	Teleorman	16	28/08/15	F	48	Romanian	Voter, self-employed
N	Teleorman	17	28/08/15	M	68	Romanian	Voter, retiree
N	Teleorman	18	15/09/15	F	53	Romanian	Employee of municipality
N	Teleorman	19	15/09/15	M	45	Romanian	Voter, self-employed
N	Teleorman	20	15/09/15	F	55	Romanian	Employee of municipality
N	Teleorman	21	15/09/15	F	28	Romanian	Voter, unemployed
N	Teleorman	22	04/09/15	M	41	Romanian	Voter, self-employed
N	Teleorman	23	04/09/15	M	60	Romanian	Employee of municipality
O	Teleorman	1	24/07/15	M	70	Romanian	Voter, receives social assistance benefits
O	Teleorman	2	24/07/15	F	45	Romanian	Voter, self-employed
O	Teleorman	3	24/07/15	M	75	Romanian	Voter, retiree
O	Teleorman	4	24/07/15	F	45	Romanian	Employee of municipality

Continued

Continued

Loc.	County	No.	Date	Gender	Age	Ethnicity	Description
O	Teleorman	5	24/07/15	F	50	Romanian	Employee of municipality
O	Teleorman	6	24/07/15	F	45	Romanian	Employee of municipality
O	Teleorman	7	14/08/15	M	70	Romanian	Former mayor, employer
O	Teleorman	8	14/08/15	F	75	Romanian	Former employee of municipality
P	Teleorman	1	21/08/15	M	60	Romanian	Mayor
P	Teleorman	2	21/08/15	M	41	Romanian	Voter, self-employed
P	Teleorman	3	21/08/15	M	69	Romanian	Broker, retiree
P	Teleorman	4	21/08/15	M	70	Romanian	Voter, retiree
P	Teleorman	5	21/08/15	M	30	Romanian	Voter, in short-term employment
P	Teleorman	6	24/08/15	M	88	Roma	Voter, Retiree
P	Teleorman	7	24/08/15	M	65	Roma	Voter, Retiree
P	Teleorman	8	24/08/15	F	70	Romanian	Voter, Retiree
P	Teleorman	9	24/08/15	M	44	Romanian	Employee of municipality, policeman
P	Teleorman	10	24/08/15	M	70	Romanian	Voter, retiree
P	Teleorman	11	24/08/15	F	40	Romanian	Voter, self-employed
P	Teleorman	12	24/08/15	M	60	Romanian	Farmer
P	Teleorman	13	24/08/15	F	40	Romanian	Voter, unemployed
Q	Teleorman	1	24/08/15	M	65	Romanian	Voter, retiree
Q	Teleorman	2	24/08/15	M	25	Romanian	Employed, gambling house
Q	Teleorman	3	24/08/15	F	55	Romanian	Voter, employed
Q	Teleorman	4	26/08/15	F	45	Roma	Voter, receives social assistance benefits
Q	Teleorman	5	26/08/15	M	40	Romanian	Voter, receives social assistance benefits
Q	Teleorman	6	26/08/15	M	36	Romanian	Voter, receives social assistance benefits
Q	Teleorman	7	24/08/15	M	50	Romanian	Self-employed, broker
Q	Teleorman	8	24/08/15	M	64	Romanian	Voter, receives social assistance benefits
Q	Teleorman	9	24/08/15	M	50	Romanian	Voter, retiree
Q	Teleorman	10	24/08/15	M	45	Romanian	Employee of municipality
Q	Teleorman	11	24/08/15	M	28	Romanian	Voter, unemployed
Q	Teleorman	12	24/08/15	M	50	Romanian	Employee of municipality
Q	Teleorman	13	09/04/15	M	40	Romanian	Priest
Q	Teleorman	14	09/04/15	M	40	Roma	Self-employed
Q	Teleorman	15	04/09/15	M	45	Roma	Former employee of municipality
Q	Teleorman	16	04/09/15	F	35	Romanian	Voter, unemployed
Q	Teleorman	17	04/09/15	F	65	Romanian	Voter, retiree
Q	Teleorman	18	27/09/16	M	43	Romanian	Mayor
Q	Teleorman	19	27/09/16	F	81	Romanian	Voter, retiree
Q	Teleorman	20	27/09/16	F	55	Roma	Voter, receives social assistance benefits
Q	Teleorman	21	27/09/16	F	70	Romanian	Voter, retiree
Q	Teleorman	22	27/09/16	M	55	Romanian	Voter, unemployed
R	Teleorman	1	18/08/15	F	35	Romanian	Voter, self-employed

R	Teleorman	2	18/08/15	F	40	Romanian	Voter, self-employed
R	Teleorman	3	18/08/15	F	45	Romanian	Voter, employed
R	Teleorman	4	18/08/15	M	35	Romanian	Employee of municipality
R	Teleorman	5	18/08/15	F	30	Romanian	Employee of municipality
R	Teleorman	6	19/08/15	F	40	Romanian	Voter, retiree
R	Teleorman	7	19/08/15	M	50	Romanian	Former candidate for mayoral position
R	Teleorman	8	19/08/15	M	40	Romanian	Owner agricultural enterprise, broker
R	Teleorman	9	18/08/15	M	50	Romanian	Employee of municipality
R	Teleorman	10	19/08/15	M	70	Romanian	Doctor
R	Teleorman	11	21/08/15	M	50	Romanian	Deputy mayor, broker
R	Teleorman	12	21/08/15	M	50	Romanian	Employee of municipality
R	Teleorman	13	21/08/15	M	45	Romanian	Employee of municipality, broker
R	Teleorman	14	21/08/15	M	50	Romanian	Voter
R	Teleorman	15	21/08/15	M	70	Romanian	Voter
S	Teleorman	1	09/09/15	M	45	Romanian	Voter, receives social assistance benefits
S	Teleorman	2	09/09/15	M	50	Romanian	Employee of municipality, responsible for social benefits
S	Teleorman	3	15/09/15	M	65	Romanian	Voter, retiree
S	Teleorman	4	15/09/15	F	35	Roma	Voter, receives social assistance benefits
S	Teleorman	5	15/09/15	M	45	Romanian	Former mayor
S	Teleorman	6	15/09/15	M	45	Romanian	Moneylender, broker
T	Teleorman	1	17/09/15	M	55	Romanian	Mayor
T	Teleorman	2	17/09/15	F	40	Romanian	Self-employed
T	Teleorman	3	17/09/15	F	65	Roma	Voter, receives social assistance benefits
T	Teleorman	4	17/09/15	M	36	Romanian	Former candidate for mayoral position, employer
T	Teleorman	5	15/09/15	M	60	Roma	Employee of municipality responsible for Roma issues, broker
T	Teleorman	6	16/9/15	M	55	Romanian	Former employee of municipality, broker
T	Teleorman	7	16/9/15	F	60	Romanian	Former employee of municipality
T	Teleorman	8	28/9/16	M	45	Romanian	Voter, self-employed
T	Teleorman	9	28/09/16	F	60	Romanian	Voter, self-employed
T	Teleorman	10	28/09/16	F	60	Roma	Voter, receives social assistance benefits
U	Teleorman	1	09/09/15	F	50	Romanian	Voter, unemployed
U	Teleorman	2	09/09/15	M	60	Romanian	Voter, unemployed
U	Teleorman	3	09/09/15	F	55	Romanian	Voter, self-employed
U	Teleorman	4	17/09/15	M	30	Romanian	Broker
U	Teleorman	5	17/09/15	F	35	Romanian	Voter, employed
U	Teleorman	6	17/09/15	M	62	Romanian	Voter, retiree
U	Teleorman	7	17/09/15	M	58	Romanian	Voter, employed
V	Teleorman	1	30/09/15	F	74	Roma	Voter, receives social assistance benefits

Continued

Continued

Loc.	County	No.	Date	Gender	Age	Ethnicity	Description
V	Teleorman	1bis	30/09/15	M	30	Roma	Voter, receives social assistance benefits
V	Teleorman	2	30/09/15	F	54	Roma	Voter, receives social assistance benefits
V	Teleorman	3	30/09/15	F	25	Romanian	Voter, receives social assistance benefits
V	Teleorman	4	30/09/15	F	65	Romanian	Voter, retiree
V	Teleorman	5	30/09/15	M	60	Romanian	Deputy mayor
V	Teleorman	6	01/10/15	F	65	Romanian	Voter, retiree
V	Teleorman	7	01/10/15	M	65	Romanian	Voter, employed
V	Teleorman	8	01/10/15	F	70	Romanian	Voter, retiree
V	Teleorman	9	29/09/16	M	45	Romanian	Voter, self-employed
V	Teleorman	10	29/09/16	M	80	Romanian	Voter, retiree
V	Teleorman	11	29/09/16	F	70	Romanian	Voter, retiree
V	Teleorman	12	29/09/16	F	70	Romanian	Voter, retiree
W	Teleorman	1	13/10/16	F	50	Romanian	Voter, retiree
W	Teleorman	2	13/10/16	M	50	Romanian	Voter, employed
W	Teleorman	3	13/10/16	M	65	Romanian	Voter, retiree
X	Teleorman	1	17/10/16	M	50	Romanian	Voter, in short-term employment
Y	Teleorman	1	28/10/16	M	65	Romanian	Voter, retiree
Z	Teleorman	1	30/10/16	M	50	Romanian	Voter, unemployed
Z	Teleorman	2	30/10/16	F	50	Romanian	Voter, employed
Z	Teleorman	3	30/10/16	F	35	Romanian	Voter, employed
Z	Teleorman	4	08/11/16	F	50	Romanian	Employee of municipality
Z	Teleorman	5	08/11/16	M	57	Romanian	Voter, receives social assistance benefits
Z	Teleorman	6	08/11/16	F	35	Romanian	Voter, self-employed
Z	Teleorman	7	08/11/16	F	55	Romanian	Former candidate for mayoral position
BN	Teleorman	1	03/11/16	M	45	Romanian	Voter, employed
BN	Teleorman	2	03/11/16	M	65	Romanian	Employer
BN	Teleorman	3	03/11/16	F	45	Romanian	Voter, self-employed
ZI	Vrancea	1	03/12/15	F	65	Romanian	Voter, retiree
ZI	Vrancea	2	03/12/15	F	30	Romanian	Voter, unemployed
ZI	Vrancea	3	03/12/15	M	35	Roma	Voter, self-employed
ZI	Vrancea	4	03/12/15	M	50	Roma	Voter, unemployed
MO	Vrancea	1	04/12/15	M	40	Romanian	NGO
MO	Vrancea	2	04/12/15	M	55	Roma	Employee of municipality
MO	Vrancea	3	04/12/15	F	50	Romanian	Professor
MO	Vrancea	4	04/12/15	M	65	Romanian	Pensioner
MO	Vrancea	5	04/12/15	M	60	Romanian	Pensioner
ZS	Vrancea	1	12/07/16	F	25	Romanian	Voter, self-employed
ZS	Vrancea	2	12/07/16	F	40	Romanian	Voter, unemployed
ZS	Vrancea	3	12/07/16	F	74	Romanian	Voter, retiree
ZS	Vrancea	4	13/07/16	F	50	Roma	Voter, receives social assistance benefits
ZS	Vrancea	5	13/07/16	F	65	Romanian	Voter, unemployed
ZS	Vrancea	6	13/07/16	M	60	Romanian	Employee of municipality

ZS	Vrancea	7	13/07/16	F	58	Romanian	Voter, receives social assistance benefits
WO	Vaslui	1	12/08/16	M	81	Romanian	Voter, retiree
WO	Vaslui	2	12/08/16	M	65	Romanian	Voter, retiree
WO	Vaslui	3	12/08/16	M	55	Romanian	Mayor
WO	Vaslui	4	12/08/16	F	35	Roma	Voter, unemployed
WO	Vaslui	4bis	12/08/16	F	45	Roma	Voter, unemployed
WO	Vaslui	5	12/08/16	M	46	Roma	Voter, self-employed
TI	Vaslui	1	13/08/16	M	40	Roma	Voter, receives social assistance benefits
TI	Vaslui	2	13/08/16	M	55	Romanian	Voter, received social assistance benefits
TI	Vaslui	3	13/08/16	F	50	Romanian	Voter, receives social assistance benefits
TI	Vaslui	4	13/08/16	M	70	Romanian	Voter, retiree
FY	Vaslui	1	14/08/16	F	65	Romanian	Voter, unemployed
FY	Vaslui	2	14/08/16	F	40	Romanian	Voter, unemployed
FY	Vaslui	3	14/08/16	F	65	Romanian	Voter, unemployed
FY	Vaslui	4	14/08/16	M	70	Romanian	Voter, retiree

A3: List of Locality Interviewees in Hungary

Loc.	County	No.	Date	Gender	Age	Ethnicity	Description
NM	Baranya	1	23/03/14	M	40	Hungarian	Lawyer in NGO providing legal services to Roma minority
NM	Baranya	2	23/03/14	F	40	Roma	Employee local kindergarten
NM	Baranya	3	23/03/14	M	40	Roma	Employee local kindergarten
BF	BAZ	1	07/21/15	F	40	Hungarian	Self-employed, supporter of current mayor
BF	BAZ	2	07/21/15	F	29	Hungarian	Public work employee, supporter of current mayor
BF	BAZ	3	07/27/15	M	30	Hungarian	Son of the former mayor
BF	BAZ	4	07/27/15	F	40	Hungarian	Employee in public administration, supporter of current mayor
BF	BAZ	5	07/27/15	M	50	Hungarian	Tractor driver, supporter of mayor
BF	BAZ	6	07/27/15	F	30	Hungarian	Director of kindergarten, supporter of current mayor
BF	BAZ	7	07/22/15	M	33	Hungarian	Current mayor, Independent
BF	BAZ	8	07/22/15	M	40	Hungarian	Bartender, supporter of former mayor
BF	BAZ	9	07/22/15	M	70	Hungarian	Former employee in cooperative, supporter of former mayor
BF	BAZ	10	07/22/15	M	70	Roma	Former employee in chemical factory in Budapest, supporter of former mayor

Continued

Continued

Loc.	County	No.	Date	Gender	Age	Ethnicity	Description
BF	BAZ	11	07/23/15	M	40	Roma	Leader of public brigade and security guard at municipality, supporter of current mayor
BF	BAZ	12	07/23/15	F	40	Hungarian	Voter
BF	BAZ	13	07/23/15	F	40	Hungarian	Employee at cultural center, broker for current mayor
BF	BAZ	14	07/23/15	M	70	Hungarian	Former mayor between 2006 and 2010, Fidesz supporter
BF	BAZ	15	07/23/15	M	40	Roma	Representative of Roma minority in municipality
BF	BAZ	16	07/24/15	F	40	Roma	Representative of Roma minority in municipality, supporter of current mayor
BF	BAZ	17	07/24/15	M	40	Roma	Representative of Roma minority in municipality, supporter of current mayor minority in municipality, supporter of current mayor
LO	BAZ	1	23/10/15	M	50	Roma	Employee of municipality
LO	BAZ	2	23/10/15	F		Roma	Employee in the public works program
LO	BAZ	3	24/10/15	M	60	Hungarian	Former candidate for mayoral position
LO	BAZ	4	24/10/15	F	50	Roma	Employee in public works program
LO	BAZ	5	24/10/15	M	60	Hungarian	Farmer
HN	BAZ	1	07/22/15	F	50	Hungarian	Employee of local administration
HN	BAZ	2	07/22/15	M	60	Hungarian	Member of village council. Former deputy mayor, former MZSP activist
HN	BAZ	3	07/23/15	F	50	Hungarian	Employee in local administration
HN	BAZ	4	07/23/15	F	30	Hungarian	Head of social policy department in municipality
HN	BAZ	5	07/23/15	M	50	Hungarian	Coordinator of public works program in municipality
HN	BAZ	6	07/23/15	M	55	Hungarian	Former member of city council, Opposition
HN	BAZ	7	07/25/15	M	35	Roma	Member of Roma Minority council
HN	BAZ	8	07/25/15	F	55	Roma	President of Roma Minority Council
HN	BAZ	9	07/26/15	M	40	Roma	Former MZSP activist, former leader of public works program
RZ	Heves	1	07/29/15	F	40	Hungarian	Secretary of agricultural cooperative, former deputy mayor
RZ	Heves	2	07/29/15	M	40	Hungarian	Head of social policy department in municipality

RZ	Heves	3	07/29/15	M	55	Roma	President of Roma Minority Council
RZ	Heves	4	07/29/15	F	40	Roma	Employee in public works program
RZ	Heves	5	07/31/15	F	50	Hungarian	Member of village council
RZ	Heves	6	07/31/15	F	40	Hungarian	Head of social policy department in municipality
RZ	Heves	7	08/1/15	F	45	Hungarian	Mayor of locality
FM	Heves	1	07/28/15	F	30	Hungarian	Employee of municipality, opponent of current mayor
FM	Heves	2	07/28/15	F	40	Roma	Employee in public institution, supporter of mayor
FM	Heves	3	07/28/15	F	50	Roma	Employee in public works Program
FM	Heves	4	07/28/15	F	20	Roma	Employee in public works program, supporter of mayor
FM	Heves	5	07/29/15	M	50	Hungarian	Employee in public works program
FM	Heves	6	07/29/15	F	30	Hungarian	Employee of municipality
FM	Heves	7	07/29/15	M	40	Roma	Mayor of locality
FM	Heves	8	07/29/15	F	30	Hungarian	Employee in public works program, opponent of mayor
FM	Heves	9	07/30/15	M	60	Hungarian	Former mayor
FM	Heves	10	07/30/15	M	40	Hungarian	Employee in agriculture, supporter of mayor
FM	Heves	11	07/30/15	M	50	Hungarian	Employee in agriculture
SZ	BAZ	1	07/16/15	M	30	Hungarian	Employee in forestry
SZ	BAZ	2	07/16/15	M	35	Roma	Employee in forestry
SZ	BAZ	3	07/16/15	M	30	Roma	Member of village council
SZ	BAZ	4	07/16/15	M	60	Roma	Retired, former employee of municipality and former broker of mayor
SZ	BAZ	5	07/18/15	M	70	Hungarian	Retiree, broker for current mayor
SZ	BAZ	6	07/31/15	F	65	Hungarian	Teacher at local school
SZ	BAZ	7	08/20/15	F	65	Hungarian	Retired, former elementary school teacher and representative on local city council
SZ	BAZ	8	08/20/15	R	60	Roma	Representative of Roma minority in municipality, former broker
SZ	BAZ	9	08/20/15	R	60	Hungarian	Retired, former broker for previous mayor
OK	Baranya	1	04/7/15	F	60	Hungarian	Retired
OK	Baranya	2	07/7/15	M	60	Hungarian	Employee in local administration
OK	Baranya	3	07/08/15	M	50	Hungarian	Former council member
OK	Baranya	4	07/10/15	F	50	Hungarian	School teacher
OK	Baranya	5	07/11/15	M	70	Hungarian	Retired, former member of city council,
OK	Baranya	6	07/13/15	M	50	Hungarian	Former member of city council,
OK	Baranya	7	07/13/15	M	60	Hungarian	Former member of city council, Opposition

Continued

Continued

Loc.	County	No.	Date	Gender	Age	Ethnicity	Description
FB	Heves	1	07/21/15	M	60	Hungarian	Former mayor of locality, now broker
FB	Heves	2	07/22/15	F	60	Hungarian	Employee in local city council, broker, opposed to mayor
FB	Heves	3	07/22/15	F	30	Hungarian	Entrepreneur
FB	Heves	4	07/23/15	M	50	Hungarian	President of local water company
FB	Heves	5	07/23/15	M	50	Hungarian	President of local power station, former member of city council
FB	Heves	6	07/24/15	F	40	Hungarian	Employee of local administration, supporter of mayor
FB	Heves	7	07/25/15	F	60	Hungarian	Retired, former school teacher, broker, supporter of mayor
KS	Baranya	1	07/02/15	F	50	Hungarian	Self-employed
KS	Baranya	2	07/03/15	F	80	Hungarian	Retired, active member of MZSP until recently
KS	Baranya	3	07/04/15	F	60	Hungarian	Self-employed
KS	Baranya	4	07/05/15	F	60	Hungarian	Former economist in governmental office, retired
KS	Baranya	5	070/6/15	M	30	Hungarian	Employee in local administration
KS	Baranya	6	07/07/15	F	60	Hungarian	Retired
KS	Baranya	7	07/09/15	M	50	Hungarian	Representative on city council and local leader of MZSP
KS	Baranya	8	07/12/15	M	40	Hungarian	Employee in the municipality, former candidate for mayor, broker
KS	Baranya	9	07/15/15	M	40	Hungarian	Deputy mayor
NO	Nógràd	1	07/15/15	M	30	Hungarian	Activist who has established an NGO in locality
NO	Nógràd	2	07/15/15	M	60	Roma	Representative of Roma minority in municipality
NO	Nógràd	3	07/16/15	F	35	Hungarian	Owner of local store
NO	Nógràd	4	07/16/15	F	40	Hungarian	Former employee in public works program, now unemployed
NO	Nógràd	5	07/16/15	M	30	Roma	Employee in municipality
NO	Nógràd	6	07/17/15	M	35	Hungarian	Priest
NO	Nógràd	7	07/17/15	M	50	Roma	Voter, unemployed
NO	Nógràd	8	07/20/15	F	50	Hungarian	Employee in municipality
NO	Nógràd	9	07/20/15	F	45	Hungarian	Employee in municipality
NO	Nógràd	10	07/27/15	M	65	Roma	Former candidate for mayor
NO	Nógràd	11	07/27/15	F	30	Roma	Voter, president of NGO in locality
NO	Nógràd	12	07/27/15	M	40	Hungarian	Former employee on the mayor's farm
FJ	BAZ	1	10/10/15	M	40	Roma	Representative of Roma minority in municipality
FJ	BAZ	2	10/10/15	M	50	Roma	Former employee in public works program
FJ	BAZ	3	10/11/15	M	50	Roma	Voter, unemployed

FJ	BAZ	4	10/11/15	F	50	Hungarian	Retired
FJ	BAZ	5	10/11/15	F	45	Hungarian	Employee in municipality
FJ	BAZ	6	10/22/15	F	55	Hungarian	Employee in municipality
FJ	BAZ	7	10/22/15	M	30	Roma	Employee in public works program
FJ	BAZ	8	10/22/15	M	40	Hungarian	Local notary
RM	BAZ	1	08/21/15	M	55	Roma	Previously held public position, relative of powerful family who controls economic activity in the locality
RM	BAZ	2	08/21/15	F	60	Roma	Employee in municipality
RM	BAZ	3	08/22/15	M	35	Roma	Employee in municipality
RM	BAZ	4	08/22/15	M	30	Roma	Representative of opposition in municipality government
RM	BAZ	5	08/22/15	F	30	Roma	Teacher at local school
RM	BAZ	6	08/24/15	M	30	Roma	Employee in municipality, relative of powerful family who controls economic activity in the locality
RM	BAZ	7	08/24/15	M	30	Roma	Voter, actively involved in politics
RM	BAZ	8	08/25/15	M	50	Hungarian	Employee in municipality
RM	BAZ	9	08/25/15	M	70	Hungarian	Former mayor
RM	BAZ	10	08/25/15	M	50	Roma	Owner of large agricultural enterprise
RM	BAZ	11	08/26/15	M	65	Roma	Former candidate for mayoral position-
RM	BAZ	12	08/26/15	M	45	Roma	Previously employed in workfare program, now without employment
RM	BAZ	13	08/26/16	M	50	Roma	Pressured voter excluded from social assistance benefits
JU	Veszprém	1	07/29/15	F	50	Roma	Previous employee of municipality
JU	Veszprém	2	07/29/15	M	50	Hungarian	Employee in municipality
JU	Veszprém	3	07/29/15	F	50	Roma	Employee in public works program
JU	Veszprém	4	08/03/15	M	35	Hungarian	Employee in municipality
JU	Veszprém	5	08/03/15	F	60	Hungarian	Employee in municipality
JU	Veszprém	6	08/04/15	M	60	Hungarian	Held public position in municipality during the previous administration
JU	Veszprém	7	08/04/15	M	55	Roma	Employee in municipality
JU	Veszprém	8	08/08/16	M	35	Roma	Employee in municipality
JU	Veszprém	9	08/19/15	F	35	Hungarian	Employee in municipality
JU	Veszprém	10	08/19/15	F	65	Hungarian	Retired
NY	Heves	1	06/30/15	M	50	Hungarian	Leader of local NGO
NY	Heves	2	06/30/15	M	40	Roma	Employee in municipality
GI	Békés	1	06/25/15	M	50	Roma	Coordinator of public works program in the municipality
GI	Békés	2	06/25/15	M	60	Roma	Representative of Roma minority in municipality

Continued on next page

Continued

Continued

Loc.	County	No.	Date	Gender	Age	Ethnicity	Description
GI	Békés	3	06/25/15	M	60	Hungarian	Policeman, active interest in local affairs of municipality
GI	Békés	4	06/26/15	M	45	Roma	Principal of local school
GI	Békés	5	06/26/15	M	50	Roma	Public works employee
GI	Békés	6	06/27/15	M	40	Roma	Public works employee
GI	Békés	7	07/08/15	M	60	Hungarian	Former employee in public works program
GI	Békés	8	07/08/15	M	50	Roma	Roma representative in Roma self-government
GI	Békés	9	07/08/15	M	45	Hungarian	Employee in municipality *Continued on next page*
GI	Békés	10	07/09/15	F	30	Hungarian	Former representative in municipality, also important employer
HK	BAZ	1	09/21/15	M	50	Roma	Employee in municipality
HK	BAZ	2	09/21/15	M	60	Roma	Retired
HK	BAZ	3	09/22/15	M	45	Hungarian	Employee in municipality
HK	BAZ	4	09/22/15	F	65	Hungarian	Employee in municipality
HK	BAZ	5	09/23/15	M	60	Hungarian	Competed as mayoral candidate, holds public position in municipality
HK	BAZ	6	09/23/15	F	45	Hungarian	Director of local organization
HK	BAZ	7	09/24/15	M	40	Roma	Employee in municipality
MN	BAZ	1	10/23/15	M	50	Roma	Employee in municipality
MN	BAZ	2	10/23/15	F	45	Roma	Public works employee
MN	BAZ	3	10/24/15	M	60	Hungarian	Former candidate for mayoral position
MN	BAZ	4	10/24/15	F	50	Roma	Public works employee
MN	BAZ	5	10/24/15	M	60	Hungarian	Farmer

A4: Interview Questions: Qualitative Interviews

Locality:
County:
Date:
Interviewer:

Description of the respondent

[INTERVIEWER: Do not write the name. Please describe the respondent, including age, gender, occupation, and why you are interviewing them. Describe the site of the interview]

1. ECONOMIC CONDITIONS

1.1. GENERAL ECONOMIC CONDITIONS IN THE LOCALITY

How would you characterize the economic situation in the locality? Who are the main employers?

How much money do most people make?

Do people work all year or only part of the year?

1.2. ECONOMIC SITUATION OF THE RESPONDENT

How are you currently supporting yourself?

Do you receive any assistance or help from the mayor/city hall? What kind of assistance? What do you do if the money runs out before the end of the month?

2. ETHNIC RELATIONS

How big is the minority population here? What are the ethnic minority groups?

How well are the minority groups integrated? Where do they live?

How is the relationship between the minority and majority groups?

3. POLITICAL CONDITIONS

3.1. GENERAL POLITICAL CONDITIONS IN LOCALITY

What is the political climate in your locality?

How long has your mayor been in office in this locality? [INTERVIEWER: If the mayor has been in office for less than a year, ask the rest of the questions in this section about the last mayor.]

3.2. MAYOR AND MAYOR NETWORKS

What do you think about the mayor in this locality? Is he doing enough for the locality? Has the mayor done any projects that people are happy with?

How does the mayor obtain funding for such projects?

Who are the most important people that the mayor relies on (e.g. school teacher, priest, relatives in public office)? What are these relationships like?

Does the mayor have bad relations with anyone in the locality? Who helps the mayor the most during elections?

Does the mayor get involved during the elections for other candidates? What does he do to support a candidate?

Does the mayor support one candidate or a party? How does he help them?

Are candidates from all parties free to campaign in this locality? Why or why not?

3.3. CITY HALL AND ADMINISTRATION OF SOCIAL BENEFITS

In the last year or so, did you have any interaction with the people from the city hall (e.g. getting a document or approval from the mayor or city hall)? What was it like? Was it easy to get what you needed?

In general, what do people need to do to get documents or approvals from the city hall? Can this process be different for different people? Does anyone have a hard time getting approvals or documents from the mayor's office?

In general, who receives benefits or social assistance from the mayor's office in this locality? Who has a hard time getting assistance? What do you need to do to obtain assistance benefits?

Do you or someone in your family receive social assistance? How did you get it? Did you have a hard time getting assistance? Did you have to do any unofficial steps to get this assistance?

Has anyone here lost access to public assistance recently (e.g. welfare benefits, public work)? Why did they lose it? Do they think the decision was fair?

Do you know anyone who has gotten assistance even though they were not in need?

4A. CAMPAIGNS AND POLITICAL RELATIONS

What are elections like here?

Are there many posters in your locality during elections? Do candidates come to campaign in your locality?

How do people decide who to vote for? Are there any unofficial ways that voters can be influenced?

What kinds of things are offered?

Do candidates use threats at elections? If so, what threats?

Who are the people who obtain these favors or gifts? Are people who are undecided about which party they like influenced unofficially? Or people who know which party they like? Why?

Can anyone find out how you vote in this locality? If not, how can people find out how you voted?

If your vote is secret, how can people still influence voters with unofficial strategies? Do some candidates benefit from some advantages that help them to win votes?

4B. CAMPAIGNS AND POLITICAL RELATIONS—FOR **BROKERS** ONLY

[Ask these questions to Brokers Only.]

What are elections like here?

Are there many posters in your locality during elections? Do candidates come to campaign in your locality?

During the elections, do you sometimes help the mayor or candidates to win votes? How do you help them?

Do you ever help them in unofficial ways (gifts or favors, threats)? How do you manage to win so many votes?

Do you do it voluntarily or not?

What kind of tools do you use to persuade this many people? How can you convince people? What if the voters are not persuaded by the candidate's qualities?

Can people lose anything based on how they vote?

What kind of people do you try to persuade? People who are undecided about which party they like? Or people whose party you already know? Why?

Do you try to persuade people to vote for a different party? Or to make sure that they actually go to vote?

Can anyone find out how people here voted? If so, how do they know?

5. DEBT

Earlier you told me that it can be hard to get enough money at the end of the month. What can people in this locality do if they run out of money before the end of the month?

Have you heard anything about people lending money in this community?

Can people get money from multiple lenders, or if they have a debt with one is it difficult to take money from anyone else?

What are these people who lend money like?

How can these lenders manage to operate here? Do the local officials know about them? Are any of these lenders close to the mayor?

Locality Surveys

B1: Design and Fielding of Survey

Sampling

In Hungary, we took a random sample of localities with a population below 10,000 inhabitants in three counties: in the south, Baranya, and in the northeast, Heves and Borsod-Abauj-Zemplen. We stratified the sample by unemployment rate (above or below 21 percent), the proportion of the population employed in agriculture (above or below 2.7 percent), whether it has a council representing the minority Roma population (indicating a high Roma population), and whether it has a Fidesz mayor.

In Romania, we chose a random sample of localities with a population below 10,000 inhabitants in two counties: Buzau and Teleorman. We stratified the sample by unemployment, percentage Roma, and the existence of fragmentation in the local city council.

List experiment wording

We used the following lists to measure each of the four types of clientelism that we study. For each list, all participants received the three control items, and a randomly assigned half of the participants received the sensitive item of interest.

Table B1 Wording of list experiments

		Hungary	Romania
State favors	Control	There were Fidesz posters in my neighborhood. I got into a fight over politics. When I arrived at the polling place, the polling place was already open.	None of the parties had posters in my neighborhood. At the polling place, I saw observers from Germany who came to see how the elections are administered. Traian Basescu visited our locality on the day of the elections.
	Sensitive	I expected a favor from the mayors' men in case I voted well.	A person employed in the city hall told me how to vote to serve me also in future.

State coercion	Control	Some candidates visited our locality. None of the candidates visited our locality. When I went to vote, I saw several persons who were drunk.	One of the candidates promised to protect animal rights. I waited in line in order to vote. In our locality, the campaign unfolded without any incidents of violence.
	Sensitive	I was worried that a family member would lose employment in the public works program if I voted for the wrong candidate.	I was afraid to lose social assistance benefits from the city hall, if I voted for the wrong candidate.
Economic coercion	Control	Most people rushed to vote at very early hours of the morning. The election commission did not have enough ballots for every person who wanted to vote. In order to vote, the persons in the electoral commission at the voting place asked for my ID.	People went to vote at different times of the day. During the campaign, I met both Victor Ponta and Klaus Iohannis. I waited in line for a few hours in order to vote.
	Sensitive	I worried that I would owe money to my creditor if I voted badly.	A person to whom I owe money told me that I would owe more money if I don't vote for the right candidate.
Vote buying	Control	I saw some Jobbik posters. I met one of the candidates also in person. At the times of the previous elections, I was abroad and voted in the UK.	I did not see any Jobbik posters. There was a voting place in our locality, so I could vote in our locality. I saw Victor Ponta in our locality on the day of vote for the runoff.
	Sensitive	In the last elections I was offered a gift, drink, or food in return for my vote.	During the campaign, someone offered me money or food [*alimente*] to vote for a candidate.

B2: Descriptive Statistics

In this appendix we present the main locality-level covariates used in our analysis of the results in Hungary and Romania, respectively, and descriptive statistics for these variables in Tables B2 and B3. In Hungary, we use two main sources to construct these variables. For measures of the most significant political variables, we use the results reported by the Hungarian electoral commission. To measure salient economic and social variables, we primarily use results of the 2011 Hungarian census (Központi Statisztikai Hivatal 2013a, 2013b, 2013c).

Table B2 Descriptive statistics on locality-level variables in Hungary

	Mean	Standard.Deviation	N
Employed Percent	0.31	0.07	94
Unemployed Percent	0.08	0.03	94
Retired Percent	0.21	0.05	94
Roma Percent	0.14	0.13	94
Copartisan Mayor	0.41	0.50	94
Incumbent Mayor	0.91	0.28	94
United City Hall	0.53	0.50	94
Debt Percent	0.36	0.21	94
Modern Roof Percent	0.81	0.10	92
Sewage Percent	0.89	0.08	92
Hot Running Water Percent	0.81	0.10	92
Mayor Margin of Victory	0.33	0.29	94
Population	1565.61	1156.22	94

Sources: For political variables: Nemzeti Választási Iroda. Various publications. For economic and social variables: Központi Statisztikai Hivatal. 2013a, 2013b, 2013c; Évi Népszámlálás. Ter√leti adatok. Pecs: Központi Statisztikai Hivatal.

We first discuss the political variables that we think should influence the ability of politicians to use local state resources for clientelistic transactions. The first variable of interest is whether the mayor is part of the national ruling party Fidesz, a dummy variable that we label Co-Partisan Mayor. 41 percent of the localities in our sample have a mayor who ran as part of the Fidesz party, while the majority of the remaining mayors are independents. The second variable that might condition access to state resources is Incumbent Mayor, a dummy variable that takes a value of 1 if a mayor has already served at least one term. 91 percent of the mayors in our sample are incumbents. Finally, we include a dummy variable that takes a value of 1 if the plurality on the city council shares the same party affiliation as the mayor. We label this variable United City Hall, and in 53 percent of the localities in our sample the executive and legislature of the local government are united under the same party affiliation.

The next set of variables included in our analysis is indicators of social conflict over redistribution that we expect to shape voters' reactions to coercive electoral strategies. First, we include the percentage by locality that are employed (Percent Employed) and unemployed (Percent Unemployed) as of 2011, and the percentage that are over 60 years old as of 2001 (Percent Retired). On average, 31 percent of the people in our localities are employed, 8 percent unemployed, and 21 percent retired. Next, we include the percentage of the population that are members of the Roma minority group. On average, our localities are 14 percent Roma.

Last, we include two additional controls in some of our models. These measure factors that could be confounded with social conflict or control of local institutions. First, we include a measure of the margin of victory of the mayor at the time of his last election, Mayor Margin of Victory. The average mayor in our sample won his last election by a large 33-point margin. Second, we include the population size of the locality. Our localities range in size from 410 inhabitants to just over 6,500, with an average population of 1,566.

Table B3 Descriptive statistics on locality-level variables in Romania

	Mean	Standard.Deviation	N
Employed Percent	0.07	0.08	84
Unemployed Percent	0.08	0.08	84
Retired Percent	0.30	0.07	84
Roma Percent	0.04	0.07	86
Copartisan Mayor	0.52	0.50	86
Incumbent Mayor	0.71	0.46	86
United City Hall	0.70	0.46	86
Debt Percent	0.03	0.05	86
Mayor Margin of Victory	0.30	0.26	86
Population	3454.26	1812.91	84

Sources: Institutul National de Statistica 2011; Biroul Electoral Central 2010.

We now turn to the analysis of the variation in the incidence of non-programmatic strategies across Romanian localities. We use a similar set of variables in this analysis, with a few exceptions. Table B3 presents summary statistics on these variables.

As in the Hungarian case, we operationalize co-partisanship, incumbency, and having a united city hall using dummy variables that take a value of 1 for localities where the mayor shares the same party as the national executive, has served at least one prior term in office as mayor, and shares the same partisanship as the plurality of the city councilors, respectively. 52 percent of the Romanian localities in our study have mayors who are co-partisans with the center-left ruling party PSD. 71 percent have mayors who are incumbents, and 70 percent have a united city hall.

We operationalize social conflict using three variables that are salient and available in the Romanian case. As in Hungary, we include locality-level measures of the unemployment and employment rates, and the percentage of the population that is Roma according to the 2011 census. Overall, 7 percent of the total population of our Romanian localities are employed, 8 percent are registered as unemployed, and 30 percent are retired. In our average locality, 4 percent of the population identify as Roma.

We also include the mayor margin of victory in the last local elections and the locality population as controls in some specifications. Our average mayor won his last election by 30 percentage points, and the average population is around 3,400 residents.

B3: Balance Tests

In both Romania and Hungary, the list experiments were randomized across two different versions of a survey. In Hungary, Version A included the treatment versions of the list experiments measuring state coercion and private coercion, while Version B included the treatment versions of the list experiments measuring state favors and vote buying. In Romania, version A included the treatment versions of the lists measuring welfare coercion and vote buying. There are no signs of imbalance across the versions of the questionnaires.

Table B4 Test of balance across list versions in Hungary

	Version A Mean	Version B Mean	Difference	p-value	N
Female	0.60	0.64	−0.04	0.06	1880
Age	53.22	52.89	0.33	0.68	1826
Roma	0.25	0.27	−0.01	0.58	1816
Poor	1.52	1.51	0.01	0.75	1652
Employed	0.25	0.28	−0.03	0.12	1865
Unemployed	0.18	0.17	0.01	0.69	1865
Retired	0.47	0.44	0.03	0.20	1865
Fidesz Voter	0.38	0.38	−0.00	0.93	1880

Table B5 Test of balance across list versions in Romania

	Version A Mean	Version B Mean	Difference	p-value	N
Female	0.50	0.51	−0.00	0.94	1497
Age	50.53	50.18	0.35	0.70	1497
Roma	0.21	0.20	0.01	0.73	1492
Poor	3.50	3.45	0.05	0.23	1403
Education	3.61	3.67	−0.05	0.46	1492
Employed	0.51	0.54	−0.03	0.25	1488
Unemployed	0.12	0.11	0.01	0.60	1488
Retired	0.35	0.34	0.01	0.64	1488
PSD Voter	0.16	0.15	0.01	0.54	1497

B4: Tests of List Validity

We use a method developed by Blair and Imai (2012) to test the validity of our list experiments. Specifically, we test whether the inclusion of the sensitive item changes the responses to the control items in the list. Intuitively, this test assesses whether responses after the addition of the treatment item are larger than responses to the control lists, but by at most one. If either of those conditions is violated, then design effects may drive the difference between treatment and control responses.

We use the standard suggested by Blair and Imai (2012) of setting a rejection criteria of 0.05 in a two-sided test. Because our measured prevalence of the sensitive items is small, the power of the test to pick up negative design effects is quite high. We fail to reject the null hypothesis in the tests for design effects for all of our four list experiments in both Hungary and Romania. Table B6 presents the p-values from these tests for design effects.

The mean responses to the control versions of all four lists are close to 1, which increases the precision of the lists (Glynn 2013). Table B7 shows that in Hungary, the means of the control versions of the list vary between 0.97 and 1.08, with standard deviations of between 0.32 and 0.39. Thus, the ability of the lists to pick up precise estimates of exposure to the sensitive item is high. Furthermore, the risk of floor and ceiling effects is low, as very small percentages of respondents who received the control list experienced either zero or three of the control items: none of the respondents across all four control lists experienced all three control items, and 2–9 percent experienced none.

Table B6 p-values from test for design effects (Blair and Imai 2012)

	Hungary	Romania
Policy coercion	0.15	1.00
Private coercion	0.07	0.28
Policy favors	1.00	0.15
Vote buying	1.00	0.41

Table B7 Control list means and standard deviations in Hungary

	Mean	Standard Deviation
Policy coercion	1.02	0.32
Private coercion	1.08	0.32
Policy favors	0.97	0.39
Vote buying	1.04	0.36

Table B8 Control list means and standard deviations in Romania

	Mean	Standard Deviation
Policy coercion	1.15	0.52
Private coercion	1.03	0.27
Policy favors	0.99	0.21
Vote buying	0.99	0.17

Similarly, in Romania, Table B8 shows that the means of the control items vary between 0.99 and 1.15, with standard deviations ranging from 0.17 to 0.52.

B5: Complete and Disaggregated Results

Policy favors

Table B9 presents the coefficients for all variables included in the specifications used to produce the results in Table 4.6. In Table 4.6 we did not present the estimates of the variables on the control list items for the sake of space. In Table B9, the interactions between the variables and the list treatment indicator, which provide the estimated coefficients for the relationship between each variables and the sensitive item, are presented as "Z X Variable."

Table B10 presents supplementary results from the policy favors section that aim to unpack why, counter to our predictions, the size of the Retrenchment Coalition is associated with increases in the incidence of favors when the Expansion Coalition is not large. We analyze which sub-component of the Workfare Retrenchment Coalition is driving the positive relationship.

Table B9 Correlates of policy favors in Hungary and Romania—all coefficients

	Dependent variable					
	Policy Favors					
	(1)	(2)	(3)	(4)	(5)	(6)
Retrenchment Coalition	0.03	0.04	0.05	−0.01	−0.005	−0.004
	(0.06)	(0.06)	(0.06)	(0.02)	(0.02)	(0.02)
Z × Retrenchment Coalition	0.09***	0.09***	0.09***	−0.002	0.004	0.004
	(0.03)	(0.03)	(0.03)	(0.02)	(0.03)	(0.03)
Expansion Coalition	0.003	0.01	0.01	0.003	0.01	0.004
	(0.05)	(0.05)	(0.06)	(0.02)	(0.02)	(0.02)
Z × Expansion Coalition	0.05*	0.05*	0.06**	0.02	0.02	0.01
	(0.03)	(0.03)	(0.03)	(0.02)	(0.02)	(0.02)
Retrenchment × Expansion (Social Conflict)	0.03	0.02	0.02	−0.01	−0.01	−0.02
	(0.03)	(0.03)	(0.03)	(0.02)	(0.02)	(0.02)
Z × Retrenchment × Expansion (Social Conflict)	−0.03**	−0.03**	−0.03*	−0.004	−0.01	0.01
	(0.02)	(0.02)	(0.02)	(0.03)	(0.03)	(0.03)
Local Control	0.05*	0.05*	0.05	0.01	0.01	0.01
	(0.03)	(0.03)	(0.03)	(0.01)	(0.01)	(0.01)
Z × Local Control	−0.01	−0.01	−0.01	−0.01	−0.01	−0.01
	(0.02)	(0.02)	(0.02)	(0.02)	(0.02)	(0.02)
Poverty Rate	0.06	0.10	0.11	0.01	0.01	0.01
	(0.34)	(0.34)	(0.37)	(0.01)	(0.01)	(0.01)
Z × Poverty Rate	−0.04	−0.05	−0.07	−0.01	−0.004	−0.003
	(0.20)	(0.20)	(0.20)	(0.02)	(0.02)	(0.02)
Debt Rate	0.08***	0.08***	0.09***	−0.003	−0.002	−0.002
	(0.03)	(0.03)	(0.03)	(0.01)	(0.01)	(0.01)
Z × Debt Rate	0.02	0.02	0.02	0.01	0.01	0.004
	(0.02)	(0.02)	(0.02)	(0.02)	(0.02)	(0.02)
Mayor Margin		0.04	0.04		−0.01	−0.01
		(0.03)	(0.03)		(0.01)	(0.01)
Z × Mayor Margin		0.005	0.01		0.002	0.004
		(0.02)	(0.02)		(0.02)	(0.02)
Population		0.04	0.04		0.01	0.01
		(0.03)	(0.03)		(0.01)	(0.01)
Z × Population		−0.004	−0.002		0.01	0.01
		(0.02)	(0.02)		(0.02)	(0.02)
Roma			−0.002			0.04
			(0.03)			(0.03)
Z × Roma			0.04			0.04
			(0.04)			(0.04)
Female			−0.004			0.01
			(0.02)			(0.02)
Z × Female			0.05			−0.02
			(0.03)			(0.03)
Education						0.01
						(0.01)
Z × Education						−0.02*
						(0.01)
Age			−0.04**			0.02
			(0.02)			(0.02)

Z × Age			0.01			−0.01
			(0.03)			(0.02)
Employed			0.10**			−0.05
			(0.04)			(0.11)
Z × Employed			0.08*			−0.02
			(0.05)			(0.12)
Unemployed			−0.11*			−0.07
			(0.06)			(0.14)
Z × Unemployed			−0.06			−0.14
			(0.06)			(0.14)
Retired			0.08			−0.06
			(0.05)			(0.12)
Z × Retired			−0.09			−0.05
			(0.08)			(0.15)
Z	−0.04	−0.05	−0.02	0.06***	0.06***	0.22
	(0.32)	(0.33)	(0.33)	(0.02)	(0.02)	(0.15)
Constant	1.10*	1.16**	1.11*	0.99***	0.99***	0.98***
	(0.56)	(0.56)	(0.61)	(0.01)	(0.01)	(0.12)
Observations Akaike Inf. Crit.	1,777	1,777	1,669	1,439	1,439	1,424
	1,258.95	1,287.12	1,190.75	594.36	626.80	723.02
		Hungary			Romania	

*p<0.1; **p<0.05; ***p<0.01

Standard errors in parentheses.

Models are estimated using a multilevel model with intercepts varying by locality. Z indicates that the respondent was randomly assigned to receive the treatment version of the list experiment. Local Control is an additive index of indicators that take a value of 1 if the locality has a mayor who is an incumbent, a co-partisan with the national executive, or from the same party as the plurality in the city council. Retrenchment Coalition is the average of the standardized proportions of the anti-workfare constituency: the employed and retirees. Expansion Coalition is the average of the standardized proportions of the proworkfare constituency: the unemployed and Roma. Retrenchment X Expansion is the interaction of the pro- and anti-workfare constituencies. Poverty Rate is the proportion of inhabitants who are below the poverty line. Debt Rate is the proportion of survey respondents by locality who reported being in debt. Mayor Margin is the margin of victory of the mayor. Population is the population size. Roma, Female, Age, Employed, Unemployed, Retired, Debt and Poor are individual-level variables coded from our surveys. All but Age and Poor are binary. All continuous variables are standardized.

Table B10 presents the results of the first analysis disaggregating the Retrenchment Coalition into its two sub-components, which represent the standardized proportion of the population that is retired and the standardized proportion of the population that is formally employed. Table B10 only presents the results that are relevant for this analysis, although the specifications include all of the same variables as Columns 1–6 in Tables B9 above and 4.6 in Chapter 4.

Table B10 shows that the positive relationship between the Retrenchment Coalition and the incidence of policy favors is driven by the size of the retired population. A one standard deviation increase in the size of the retired population in a locality is associated with a statistically significant 5–6 percentage point increase in the incidence of mayor favors. By contrast, a one standard deviation increase in the size of the employed population is

Table B10 Correlates of policy favors in Hungary and Romania disaggregating the Retrenchment Coalition

	Dependent variable					
	Mayor Favors					
	(1)	(2)	(3)	(4)	(5)	(6)
Retired Percent	0.06***	0.06***	0.05***	−0.004	0.01	0.01
	(0.02)	(0.02)	(0.02)	(0.02)	(0.02)	(0.02)
Employed Percent	0.01	0.01	0.02	−0.01	−0.01	−0.02
	(0.03)	(0.03)	(0.03)	(0.02)	(0.02)	(0.02)
Retired × Expansion (Social Conflict)	−0.02	−0.02	−0.02	−0.03	−0.03	−0.03
	(0.02)	(0.02)	(0.02)	(0.02)	(0.02)	(0.02)
Employed × Expansion (Social Conflict)	−0.01	−0.01	−0.01	0.06	0.06	0.07*
	(0.02)	(0.02)	(0.02)	(0.04)	(0.04)	(0.04)
Direct Effects	✓	✓	✓	✓	✓	✓
Other Locality-Level Explanatory Variables	✓	✓	✓	✓	✓	✓
Locality Controls		✓	✓		✓	✓
Individual Controls			✓			✓
Observations Akaike Inf. Crit.	1,777 1,282.00	1,777 1,309.54 Hungary	1,669 1,217.28	1,439 621.64	1,439 654.39 Romania	1,424 749.96

*p<0.1; **p<0.05; ***p<0.01

Standard errors clustered by respondent in parentheses.

Models are estimated using a multilevel model with intercepts varying by locality. Coefficients shown are based on the interactions with the list treatment dummy. The models shown here correspond to the same specifications in Tables 4.6 and B.9 except that the variable Retrenchment Coalition has been replaced with its component parts Retired Percent and Employed Percent. Retired Percent is the standardized proportion of a locality's population that is retired. Employed Percent is the standardized proportion of a locality's population that is employed. The coefficients shown are from the interactions with the list treatment indicator. Columns 1-6 also include the other locality-level explanatory variables (Local Control, Poverty Rate, Debt Rate, Workfare Expansion Coalition). Columns 2-3 and 5-6 also include other locality-level controls (Mayor Margin and Population). Columns 3 and 6 also include individual-level controls (Roma, Female, Age, Education (Romania only), Employed, Unemployed, Retired). All but Age and Education are binary, and those are standardized.

associated with an insignificant 1–2 percentage point increase in the incidence of favors. This result is consistent with the higher dependence of retirees than employees on state benefits for their basic income. Consistent with the main results in Tables 4.6 and B9, the interactions of the size of the retired and employed populations and the size of the Expansion Coalition is negative, although in the disaggregated results each interaction is not statistically significant. These results suggest that transfer-dependent retirees may view policy favors positively in the absence of social conflict driven by a large group of workfare beneficiaries.

Policy coercion

Table B11 presents the coefficients for all variables included in the specifications used to produce the results in Table 5.6. In Table 5.6 we did not present the estimates of the variables on the control list items for the sake of space. In Table B11, the interactions between the variables and the list treatment indicator, which provide the estimated coefficients for the relationship between each variables and the sensitive item, are presented as "Z X Variable."

Table B11 Correlates of policy coercion in Hungary and Romania—all coefficients

	Dependent variable					
	Policy Coercion					
	(1)	(2)	(3)	(4)	(5)	(6)
Retrenchment Coalition	0.02	0.03	0.04	−0.08**	−0.07*	−0.07*
	(0.04)	(0.04)	(0.05)	(0.03)	(0.04)	(0.04)
Z × Retrenchment Coalition	0.07**	0.07**	0.07**	0.07*	0.08	0.09*
	(0.03)	(0.03)	(0.03)	(0.04)	(0.05)	(0.05)
Expansion Coalition	0.02	0.03	0.03	0.0002	0.002	0.01
	(0.04)	(0.04)	(0.04)	(0.03)	(0.03)	(0.03)
Z × Expansion Coalition	0.03	0.03	0.03	0.005	0.003	−0.02
	(0.03)	(0.03)	(0.03)	(0.04)	(0.04)	(0.04)
Retrenchment × Expansion (Social Conflict)	0.02	0.02	0.02	0.0001	−0.01	−0.01
	(0.02)	(0.02)	(0.02)	(0.04)	(0.05)	(0.05)
Z × Retrenchment × Expansion (Social Conflict)	0.02	0.02	0.02	−0.05	−0.05	−0.03
	(0.02)	(0.02)	(0.02)	(0.06)	(0.06)	(0.06)
Local Control	0.05**	0.05**	0.05**	−0.01	−0.01	−0.01
	(0.02)	(0.02)	(0.02)	(0.02)	(0.02)	(0.02)
Z × Local Control	0.004	0.01	0.002	0.04	0.04	0.04
	(0.02)	(0.02)	(0.02)	(0.03)	(0.03)	(0.03)
Poverty Rate	0.09	0.10	0.05	0.02	0.02	0.02
	(0.25)	(0.26)	(0.27)	(0.02)	(0.03)	(0.03)
Z × Poverty Rate	0.27	0.26	0.28	−0.02	−0.03	−0.03
	(0.19)	(0.19)	(0.19)	(0.03)	(0.03)	(0.03)
Debt Rate	0.08***	0.08***	0.08***	0.04	0.04	0.04*
	(0.02)	(0.02)	(0.02)	(0.02)	(0.02)	(0.02)
Z × Debt Rate	0.03**	0.04**	0.04**	0.002	0.004	−0.01
	(0.02)	(0.02)	(0.02)	(0.03)	(0.03)	(0.03)
Mayor Margin		0.03	0.04*		−0.01	−0.01
		(0.02)	(0.02)		(0.02)	(0.02)
Z × Mayor Margin		−0.001	−0.01		−0.03	−0.02
		(0.02)	(0.02)		(0.03)	(0.03)
Population		0.02	0.02		0.01	0.01
		(0.02)	(0.02)		(0.03)	(0.03)
Z × Population		−0.01	−0.01		−0.01	−0.01
		(0.02)	(0.02)		(0.04)	(0.04)

Continued

Table B11 *Continued*

	(1)	(2)	(3)	(4)	(5)	(6)
			Dependent variable			
			Policy Coercion			
Roma			0.04			−0.05
			(0.03)			(0.06)
Z × Roma			0.04			0.20**
			(0.04)			(0.08)
Female			0.003			−0.02
			(0.02)			(0.04)
Z × Female			0.02			0.04
			(0.03)			(0.06)
Education						−0.01
						(0.02)
Z × Education						−0.0002
						(0.02)
Age			−0.02			−0.06*
			(0.02)			(0.03)
Z × Age			−0.02			−0.003
			(0.03)			(0.04)
Employed			0.04			−0.15
			(0.04)			(0.15)
Z × Employed			0.03			−0.03
			(0.05)			(0.16)
Unemployed			−0.08			−0.07
			(0.06)			(0.26)
Z × Unemployed			−0.04			−0.19
			(0.06)			(0.27)
Retired			0.04			−0.12
			(0.05)			(0.17)
Z × Retired			−0.03			−0.14
			(0.08)			(0.28)
Z	0.52*	0.49	0.57*	0.13***	0.13***	0.18
	(0.31)	(0.32)	(0.33)	(0.03)	(0.03)	(0.28)
Constant	1.19***	1.20***	1.08**	1.14***	1.14***	1.31***
	(0.42)	(0.42)	(0.45)	(0.02)	(0.02)	(0.17)
Observations	1,779	1,779	1,672	1,440	1,440	1,425
Akaike Inf. Crit.	1,190.02	1,219.50	1,170.15	2,424.48	2,451.94	2,487.35
		Hungary			Romania	

*p<0.1; **p<0.05; ***p<0.01

Standard errors in parentheses.

Models are estimated using a multilevel model with intercepts varying by locality. Z indicates that the respondent was randomly assigned to receive the treatment version of the list experiment. Local Control is an additive index of indicators that take a value of 1 if the locality has a mayor who is an incumbent, a co-partisan with the national executive, or from the same party as the plurality in the city council. Retrenchment Coalition is the average of the standardized proportions of the anti-workfare constituency: the employed and retirees. Expansion Coalition is the average of the standardized proportions of the proworkfare constituency: the unemployed and Roma. Retrenchment X Expansion is the interaction of the pro- and anti-workfare constituencies. Poverty Rate is the proportion of inhabitants who are below the poverty line. Debt Rate is the proportion of survey respondents by locality who reported being in debt. Mayor Margin is the margin of victory of the mayor. Population is the population. Roma, Female, Age, Employed, Unemployed, Retired, Debt and Poor are individual-level variables coded from our surveys. All but Age and Poor are binary. All continuous variables are standardized.

Economic coercion

Table B12 presents the coefficients for all variables included in the specifications used to produce the results in Table 6.2. In Table 6.2 we did not present the estimates of the variables on the control list items for the sake of space. In Table B12, the interactions between the variables and the list treatment indicator, which provide the estimated coefficients for the relationship between each variables and the sensitive item, are presented as "Z X Variable."

Table B12 Correlates of economic coercion in Hungary—all coefficients

	Dependent variable		
	Economic Coercion		
	(1)	(2)	(3)
Retrenchment Coalition	0.06	0.06	0.07*
	(0.04)	(0.04)	(0.04)
Z × Retrenchment Coalition	−0.01	−0.02	−0.01
	(0.03)	(0.03)	(0.03)
Expansion Coalition	0.03	0.03	0.04
	(0.04)	(0.04)	(0.04)
Z × Expansion Coalition	−0.01	−0.02	−0.02
	(0.03)	(0.03)	(0.03)
Retrenchment × Expansion (Social Conflict)	0.004	0.0000	0.01
	(0.02)	(0.02)	(0.02)
Z × Retrenchment × Expansion (Social Conflict)	0.03**	0.03**	0.03*
	(0.02)	(0.02)	(0.02)
Local Control	0.03*	0.03	0.03
	(0.02)	(0.02)	(0.02)
Z × Local Control	0.01	0.01	0.01
	(0.02)	(0.02)	(0.02)
Poverty Rate	−0.05	−0.01	−0.05
	(0.23)	(0.24)	(0.26)
Z × Poverty Rate	0.37*	0.34*	0.37*
	(0.19)	(0.19)	(0.19)
Debt Rate	0.10***	0.10***	0.10***
	(0.02)	(0.02)	(0.02)
Z × Debt Rate	0.03*	0.03*	0.03
	(0.02)	(0.02)	(0.02)
Mayor Margin		0.01	0.01
		(0.02)	(0.02)
Z × Mayor Margin		0.001	−0.004
		(0.02)	(0.02)
Population		0.03	0.03
		(0.02)	(0.02)
Z × Population		−0.02	−0.01
		(0.02)	(0.02)
Roma			0.02
			(0.03)
Z × Roma			0.09**
			(0.04)

Continued

Table B12 *Continued*

	Dependent variable		
	Economic Coercion		
	(1)	(2)	(3)
Female			−0.01
			(0.02)
Z × Female			0.03
			(0.03)
Age			−0.003
			(0.02)
Z × Age			−0.04
			(0.03)
Employed			−0.01
			(0.04)
Z × Employed			0.03
			(0.05)
Unemployed			0.08
			(0.06)
Z × Unemployed			0.07
			(0.06)
Retired			−0.003
			(0.05)
Z × Retired			0.14*
			(0.08)
Z	0.68**	0.63**	0.54*
	(0.32)	(0.32)	(0.33)
Constant	1.00***	1.06***	1.00**
	(0.39)	(0.39)	(0.43)
Observations Akaike Inf. Crit.	1,794	1,794	1,688
	1,228.51	1,259.72	1,185.86
		Hungary	

*p<0.1; **p<0.05; ***p<0.01

Standard errors in parentheses.

Models are estimated using a multilevel model with intercepts varying by locality. Z indicates that the respondent was randomly assigned to receive the treatment version of the list experiment. Local Control is an additive index of indicators that take a value of 1 if the locality has a mayor who is an incumbent, a co-partisan with the national executive, or from the same party as the plurality in the city council. Retrenchment Coalition is the average of the standardized proportions of the anti-workfare constituency: the employed and retirees. Expansion Coalition is the average of the standardized proportions of the pro-workfare constituency: the unemployed and Roma. Retrenchment X Expansion is the interaction of the pro- and anti-workfare constituencies. Poverty Rate is the proportion of inhabitants who are below the poverty line. Debt Rate is the proportion of survey respondents by locality who reported being in debt. Mayor Margin is the margin of victory of the mayor. Population is the population. Roma, Female, Age, Employed, Unemployed, Retired, Debt and Poor are individual-level variables coded from our surveys. All but Age and Poor are binary. All continuous variables are standardized.

Vote buying

Table B13 presents the coefficients for all variables included in the specifications used to produce the results in Table 7.5. In Table 7.5 we did not present the estimates of the variables on the control list items for the sake of space. In Table B13, the interactions between the variables and the list treatment indicator, which provide the estimated coefficients for the relationship between each variables and the sensitive item, are presented as "Z X Variable."

Table B13 Correlates of vote buying in Hungary—all coefficients

	Dependent variable		
	Vote Buying		
	(1)	(2)	(3)
Retrenchment Coalition	0.07*	0.07*	0.09**
	(0.04)	(0.04)	(0.04)
Z × Retrenchment Coalition	0.003	0.004	0.02
	(0.04)	(0.04)	(0.04)
Expansion Coalition	0.01	0.02	0.02
	(0.04)	(0.04)	(0.04)
Z × Expansion Coalition	0.005	0.01	0.01
	(0.03)	(0.03)	(0.03)
Retrenchment × Expansion (Social Conflict)	0.02	0.02	0.02
	(0.02)	(0.02)	(0.02)
Z × Retrenchment × Expansion (Social Conflict)	−0.03	−0.03	−0.03*
	(0.02)	(0.02)	(0.02)
Local Control	0.05**	0.05**	0.05**
	(0.02)	(0.02)	(0.02)
Z × Local Control	−0.02	−0.02	−0.02
	(0.02)	(0.02)	(0.02)
Poverty Rate	0.08***	0.08***	0.08***
	(0.02)	(0.02)	(0.02)
Z × Poverty Rate	0.02	0.01	0.01
	(0.02)	(0.02)	(0.02)
Debt Rate		0.03	0.04*
		(0.02)	(0.02)
Z × Debt Rate		−0.01	−0.01
		(0.02)	(0.02)
Mayor Margin		0.03	0.03
		(0.02)	(0.02)
Z × Mayor Margin		0.01	0.01
		(0.02)	(0.02)
Population			0.01
			(0.03)
Z × Population			−0.01
			(0.05)
Roma			−0.004
			(0.03)
Z × Roma			0.01
			(0.04)

Continued

Table B13 *Continued*

	Dependent variable		
	Vote Buying		
	(1)	(2)	(3)
Female			−0.03
			(0.02)
Z × Female			0.01
			(0.03)
Age			0.03
			(0.05)
Z × Age			0.02
			(0.05)
Employed			−0.04
			(0.07)
Z × Employed			0.003
			(0.07)
Unemployed			−0.002
			(0.06)
Z × Unemployed			−0.05
			(0.09)
Retired	−0.11	−0.08	0.06
	(0.35)	(0.35)	(0.36)
Z × Retired	0.22	0.24	0.17
	(0.24)	(0.24)	(0.26)
Z	−0.10	−0.08	−0.02
	(0.21)	(0.21)	(0.22)
Constant	1.42***	1.45***	1.35***
	(0.39)	(0.39)	(0.43)
Observations	1,798	1,798	1,691
Akaike Inf. Crit.	1,592.23	1,620.50	1,549.24
		Hungary	

*p<0.1; **p<0.05; ***p<0.01

Standard errors in parentheses.

Models are estimated using a multilevel model with intercepts varying by locality. Z indicates that the respondent was randomly assigned to receive the treatment version of the list experiment. Local Control is an additive index of indicators that take a value of 1 if the locality has a mayor who is an incumbent, a co-partisan with the national executive, or from the same party as the plurality in the city council. Retrenchment Coalition is the average of the standardized proportions of the anti-workfare constituency: the employed and retirees. Expansion Coalition is the average of the standardized proportions of the pro-workfare constituency: the unemployed and Roma. Retrenchment X Expansion is the interaction of the pro- and anti-workfare constituencies. Poverty Rate is the proportion of inhabitants who are below the poverty line. Debt Rate is the proportion of survey respondents by locality who reported being in debt. Mayor Margin is the margin of victory of the mayor. Population is the population. Roma, Female, Age, Employed, Unemployed, Retired, Debt and Poor are individual-level variables coded from our surveys. All but Age and Poor are binary. All continuous variables are standardized.

B6: Hungarian Locality Questionnaire

Name of locality... ... ...
Time interview starts:
2014... ..... Month... ... ... day... ... hour minute
SD1. Gender of Respondent

1. Male

2. Female

SD2. Can you tell me please what year you very born?
_____ Year

First, I am going to ask you some questions regarding politics.

I am going to read some statements about events that happened or could have happened at times of elections. Please recall the elections held on April 6, 2014, and tell me how many of these events happened in your locality. You do not need to tell which ones happened, only how many. With the help of this answer sheet, please follow the statements I am reading. For each question, I am going to tell you which answer sheet you will have to look at.

I am going to read some statements about events that happened or could have happened during elections.

Please recall the elections of 6 April, 2014, and tell me how many of these events happened in your locality. You do not need to tell which ones happened exactly, only how many.

- One of the candidates was attacking his/her opponent.
- None of the candidates engaged in negative campaigning.
- I met one of the candidates in person.

[Answer Sheet One]
0 – None
1 – One
2 – Two
3 – Three
4 – Four
88 – Don't know
99 – No answer

I am going to read some statements about events that happened or could have happened during elections. Please recall the elections held on April 6, 2014, and tell me how many of these events happened in your locality. You do not need to tell which ones happened exactly, only how many.

- Several candidates visited our locality.
- One of the candidates promised to protect animal rights.
- None of the candidates visited our locality.
- **I was worried that a family member would lose employment in the public works program if I voted for the wrong candidate (sensitive item).**

[Answer Sheet 2]
0 – None
1 – One

2 – Two
3 – Three
4 – Four
88 – Don't know
99 – No answer

I am going to read some statements about events that happened or could have happened during elections. Please recall the elections held on April 6, 2014, and tell me how many of these events happened in your locality. You do not need to tell which ones happened exactly, only how many.

- There were Fidesz posters in my neighborhood.
- None of the parties had posters in my neighborhood.
- **I expected a favor from the mayors' men if I voted well (sensitive** item)
- I got into a fight over politics

[Answer Sheet 3]
0 – None
1 – One
2 – Two
3 – Three
88 – Don't know
99 – No answer

I am going to read some statements about events that happened or could have happened during elections. Please recall the elections held on April 6, 2014, and tell me how many of these events happened in your locality. You do not need to tell which ones happened exactly, only how many.

- Most people rushed to vote at very early hours of the morning.
- People went to vote at different times of the day.
- **I worried that I would owe money to my creditor if I voted badly (Sensitive** item)
- The election commission did not have enough ballots for every person who wanted to vote

[Answer Sheet 4]
0 – None
1 – One
2 – Two
3 – Three
4 – Four
88 – Don't know
99 – No answer

I am going to read some statements about events that happened or could have happened during elections. Please recall the elections held on April 6, 2014, and tell me how many of these events happened in your locality. You do not need to tell which ones happened exactly, only how many.

- I saw some Jobbik posters in our locality.
- **During the last elections, I was offered a gift, drink or food in exchange for my vote (sensitive question)**

- I did not see any Jobbik posters.
- I met one of the candidates also in person.

[Answer Sheet 5]
0 – None
1 – One
2 – Two
3 – Three
88 – Don't know
99 – No answer

I am going to list some more statements in connection with the elections. Please recall the elections held on April 6, 2014. How many of these events happened to you, or in your locality?

- A candidate representing Jobbik visited our locality.
- **Somebody tried to convince me not to vote (sensitive question)**
- I did not see anybody campaigning for Jobbik.
- Some of the candidates were especially good-looking.

[Answer Sheet 6]
0 – None
1 – One
2 – Two
3 – Three
4 – Four
88 – Don't know
99 – No answer

Now I would like to ask some personal questions.

D1. Do you?
01 – work full time
02 – work part time
03 – work on short-term contracts
04 – work in the workfare program
05 – are unemployed
06 – are on maternity leave, child care fee, child care allowance, child raising support
07 – are a housewife/househusband, homemaker, stay-at-home mother
08 – are a student
09 – are retired
88 – Don't know
99 – No answer

D2. IF YOU WORK: QUESTION D1 CODE 1–4
How many days did you work in the past month?
.... days
88 – Don't know
99 – No answer

D3. The monthly income of your household is:
1 – Less than 50 thousand forints
2 – Between 50 thousand and 100 thousand forints or

3 – Over 100 thousand forints
88 – Don't know
99 – No answer

D4. As far as you know, how many people are there in your locality who offer credit to poorer people when they get into a difficult situation?
.... people
88 – Don't know
99 – No answer

D5. Do owe money to anybody?
1 – Yes
2 – No
88 – Don't know
99 – No answer

D6. Is there a workfare program in your locality?
1 – Yes
2 – No
88 – Don't know
99 – No answer

D7. Did a member of your immediate family receive benefits from the workfare program?
1– Yes
2 – No
88 – Don't know
99 – No answer

D8. Which party do you feel closest to?
1 – Fidesz
2 – MSZP
3 – Jobbik
4 – Other,.... ....
7 – I do not feel close to any party
88 – Don't know
9 – No answer

D9. IF ANSWER TO D8 IS CODE 1–4
How close do you feel to this party?
1 – Very close
2 – Somewhat close
3 – Not very close
88 – Don't know
99 – No answer

D10. Did you vote at the time of the last election?
1 – Yes
2 – No
88 – Don't know
99 – No answer

D11. Thinking of the ballot you just cast, which of the following statements is closest to your opinion?
1 – My ballot is secret and people cannot see how I voted
2 – My ballot is not secret and people can see how I voted

88 – Don't know

99 – No answer

D12. Would you describe yourself as somebody belonging to a minority group that is discriminated against in this country?

1 – Yes

2 – No

88 – Don't know

99 – No answer

D13. How likely are you to give someone in your locality 500 forints if he asks for it?

1 – Very likely

2 – Likely

3 – Unlikely

4 – Very unlikely

88 – Don't know

99 – No answer

D14. Now imagine that that this person in your locality had given you 500 forints last month when you were in need. How likely are you to give that same person 500 forints if he asks for it?

1 – Very likely

2 – Likely

3 – Unlikely

4 – Very unlikely

88 – Don't know

99 – No answer

There are many problems in Hungary and none of which are easy to solve or can be solved with few resources. In the following questions, which of these problems are dealt too much, too little, or just the right amount by the government.

K1. Thinking about the policies of the government to improve the welfare of Roma, do you believe that . . .

1 – The government does too much

2 – The government does exactly the necessary steps

3 – The government does not do enough

88 – Don't know

99 – No answer

K2. In order to reduce crime

1 – The government does too much

2 – The government takes the necessary steps that are exactly needed

3 – The government does not do enough

88 – No answer

99 – Don't know

K3. There are people who think that those who are poor, are poor because they do not work enough. Others think that someone is poor because of bad circumstances. What do you think?

1 – People are poor, because they do not work enough

2 – People are poor becomes because of poor circumstances

88 – Don't know

99 – No answer

K4. Do you agree that children should be taught together, regardless of their abilities?

1 – Agree

2 – Disagree

88 – Don't know

99 – No answer

K5. How safe do you feel if you have to go somewhere alone after dark?

1 – I feel completely safe

2 – I feel safe

3 – I do not feel safe

4 – I do not feel safe at all

88 – Don't know

99 – No answer

B7: Romania Locality Survey

Good morning/Hello. We are conducting a study to better understand how the presidential election of 2014 unfolded. To discuss these issues, you have been randomly selected to participate in the study. All the answers you will provide will be anonymous. We will not communicate your answers to any person. Once the survey is completed, nobody will be able to identify the individual answers of any person participating in this survey.

I will read a number of statements that refer to the recent presidential election, held in November 2014. For each of these statements, I would like you to tell me how many of these events occurred here, in this locality. <u>You do not have to tell us which, only how many</u>. [EXAMPLES] To understand the questionnaire better, please tell me how many of the following three statements are true?

- It is summer now.
- There is a church in our locality.
- There is a store in our locality.

How many statements are true?_____

0 – None   1 – One   2 – Two   3 – Three   4 – Four   99 DK

- Some people in our locality are employed in agriculture.
- Traian Băsescu was born in our locality.
- Our locality is situated in a mountainous area.

How many statements are true? _____

0 – None   1 – One   2 – Two   3 – Three   4 – Four   99 DK

L1. I would like you to think back to the recent presidential elections held in November 2014.

How many of these incidents happened to you?

- I knew where to go in order to vote.
- On the day of the vote, I had to go to the hospital, because I did not feel very well.
- **The priest in our locality told us to vote for a particular candidate.**
- Some of my relatives who live abroad visited me on the day of the vote.

How many statements are true? _____
0 – None   1 – One   2 – Two   3 – Three   4 – Four   99 DK

L2. I would like you to think back of the recent presidential elections held in November 2014. How many of these events happened to you?

- I waited in line in order to vote.
- When I went to vote, I saw some people who were drunk.
- **I was afraid to lose my social assistance benefits from the city hall** (*ajutoarele de la primărie*) **if I voted for the wrong candidate (sensitive question)**
- In our locality, the campaign unfolded without violence.

How many of these statements are true? _____
0 – None   1 – One   2 – Two   3 – Three   4 – Four   99 DK

L3. I would like you to think back of the recent presidential elections held in November 2014. How many of these events happened to you?

- At the polling place, I saw observers form Germany who had come to see how elections are administered.
- **A person employed at the city hall told me how to vote to serve me also in future (sensitive question)**
- The voting station was open when I arrived.
- Traian Băsescu visited our locality on the day of the elections.

How many statements are true? _____
0 – None   1 – One   2 – Two   3 – Three   4 – Four   99 DK

L4. I would like you to think back of the recent presidential elections held in November 2014. How many of these events happened to you?

- I could vote in our locality because there is a voting section.
- At the time of the last elections, I voted in England.
- I saw Victor Ponta in our locality on the day of the second round.
- **During the campaign, I was offered money or food to vote for a certain candidate (sensitive question)**

How many statements are true? _____
0 – None   1 – One   2 – Two   3 – Three   4 – Four   99 DK

L5. I would like you to think back of the recent presidential elections held in November 2014. How many of these events happened to you?

- During the campaign, I met both Victor Ponta and Klaus Iohannis personally.
- The people from the electoral commission asked me for my ID in order to vote.
- **A person I owe money tot old me that I will owe even more money if I don't vote for the right candidate (sensitive question)**
- I waited in line for a few hours in order to vote.

How many statements are true? _____
0 – None   1 – One   2 – Two   3 – Three   4 – Four   99 DK

L6. I would like you to think back of the recent presidential elections held in November 2014. How many of these events happened to you?

- I knew that Victor Ponta is one of the candidates for the office of presidency.
- During the last elections, I voted in France.
- **An influential leader of the Roma community told me how to vote (sensitive question)**
- On the day of the vote, I saw a large number of persons from the Republic of Moldova in our locality.

How many statements are true? _____
0 – None   1 – One   2 – Two   3 – Three   4 – Four   99 DK

L7. I would like you to think back of the recent presidential elections held in November 2014. How many of these events happened to you?

- I knew that Klaus Iohannis is of German origin.
- **Somebody told me to vote in a different locality (sensitive question)**
- I saw Klaus Iohannis here in our locality at the time of the runoff.
- There were violent conflicts among the people in our locality before the election.

How many statements are true? _____
0 – None   1 – One   2 – Two   3 – Three   4 – Four   99 DK

P1. Did you vote during the first round of the presidential elections?
1. Yes   2. No   98.DK   99. NA

P2. Did you vote during the second round of the presidential elections?
1. Yes   2. No   98. DK   99. NA

P3. At what time did you vote during the second round?_____ 98. DK   99. NA

P4. Do you agree with the following statement: Even though several persons told me whom to vote for, I voted for another candidate.
1. Yes   2. No   98. DK   99.NA

P5. Do you feel close to a particular party?
1. Yes   2. No   98. DK   99. NA
If **YES** → Go to **P6** and **P7**   If **NO** → Go to **P8**
[FILTER, If P5 is yes]

P6. Which party do you feel closest to?
1. PSD   2. PNL   3. Another party, (name)_____   99. DK/NA
[FILTRU, If P5 is yes] P7. How close do you feel to this party?
1. Very close   2. Close   3. Not very close   99. DK/NA

P8. When thinking about the elections that have taken place during the last years in Romania, did you vote during . . .

	YES	NO	DK/NA
1. The referendum to impeach president Băsescu held in July 2012?	1	2	99
2. The parliamentary elections held in December 2012?	1	2	99
3. The elections for the European parliament held in May 2014?	1	2	99

R1. Do you consider yourself a person who is . . .
1. Without religious beliefs
2. Not very religious
3. Somewhat religious
4. Very religious
98. DK
99. NA

R2. On average, how often do you attend church?
1. Daily or almost daily
2. Once a week
3. Several times a month
4. Never
98. DK
99. NA

R3. Do you believe in icons who make miracles?
1. Yes   2. No   98. DK   99. NA

R4. Do you believe in objects that have miraculous powers? ***********************
1. Yes   2. No   98. DK   99. NA

R5. Do you know persons who are not attending the Orthodox Church who live in this locality?
1. Yes   2. No   98. DK   99. NA

R6. A church in the locality has been renovated in the last two years?
1. Yes   2. No   98. DK   99. NA

D1. Before voting during the second round, were you aware of the difficulties in voting encountered by Romanians who live overseas?
1. Yes   2. No   98. DK   99. NA
If **YES** → Go to **D2**   If **NO** → Go to **D3**
[FILTER: Answer to D1 was *Yes*]

D2. How did you find out about the difficulties encountered by Romanians living abroad ?

1. By watching TV.	1. Yes	2. No	99. DK/NA
2. From relatives and friends who live in Romania.	1. Yes	2. No	99. DK/NA
3. From relatives and friends who live abroad.	1. Yes	2. No	99. DK/NA

D3. How do you communicate with your friends and relatives?

1. By phone	1. Yes	2. No	99. DK/NA
2. By email and SMS	1. Yes	2. No	99. DK/NA
3. Facebook	1. Yes	2. No	99. DK/NA
4. Twitter	1. Yes	2. No	99. DK/NA

D4. Among your relatives with whom you communicate at the moment, are there relatives who live abroad?
1. Yes   2. No   98. DK   99. NA

D5. How many persons do you know who live at present in France? _____ persons
D6. How many persons do you know who live at present in France? _____ persons
D7. How many persons do you know who live at present in France? _____ persons
D8. How many doctors do you know? _____ persons

SD1. Gender:

1. Male

2. Female

SD2. What is your age? _____ years old

SD3. What is your ethnicity?

1. Romanian   2. Roma   3. Hungarian   4. German   5. Another. Please name ethnicity

_____

SD4. What is the last school you have completed?

1. No school

2. Primary school

3. Gymnasium

4. Highschool

5. Vocational school

6. University and postgraduate studies

99. DK/NA

SD5. What is your occupation?

1. Independent (including home-maker or independent farmer)

2. Employed with formal employment contract

3. Employed without formal employment contract

4. I receive social assistance benefits

5. Retired

6. Student

7. DK/NA

SD6. The monthly income of your household is:

1. Under 900 RON

2. Between 900 and 1,500 RON

3. Between 1,500 and 3,000 RON

4. Above 3,000 RON

98. DK

99. NA

SD7. You or a member of your immediate family receives winter support from the city hall.
1. Yes   2. No   98. DK   99. NA

SD8. You or a member of your immediate family receives social assistance benefits from the city hall.
1. Yes   2. No   98. DK   99. NA

SD9. You or a member of your family owes a large amount of money to a person in this locality ?
1. Yes   2. No   98. DK   99. NA

SD10. How many persons in this locality do you know who offer loans to the people who find themselves in a difficult situation?
98. DK   99. NA

F1. Which candidate did you vote for during the first round of the presidential election?

1. Victor Ponta

2. Klaus Iohannis

3. Călin Popescu Tăriceanu

4. Elena Udrea

5. I did not vote during the first round

6. Monica Macovei

7. Kelemen Hunor

97. Another candidate _____

F2. What candidate did you vote for during the second round of the presidential election of November 2nd 2014?

1. Victor Ponta

2. Klaus Iohannis

98. DK/NA

F3. Thinking about your vote, which of the following statements is true?
1. My vote is not secret and people can see how I voted
2. My vote is secret is nobody knows how I voted
1. Statement 1 is true
2. Statement 2 is true
98. DK
99. NA

Do you agree with the following statements?	Yes	No	Don't know	This is not the case
F4. The mayor promised he will repair our roads if we vote for the right candidate.	1	2	99	97
F5. The priest from the locality told us to vote for one of the candidates.	1	2	99	97
F6. I was afraid I would lose support from the city hall if I did not vote for the correct candidate.	1	2	99	97
F7. A person from the city hall told me how to vote so that they can serve me in future.	1	2	99	97
F8. During the campaign, somebody offered me money or foodstuff to vote for a particular candidate.	1	2	99	97
F9. A person I owe money told me that I will owe more money if I don't vote for the correct candidate.	1	2	99	97
F10. An important person in the Roma community told me what candidate to vote for.	1	2	99	97
F11. Even though some people tell me whom to vote, nobody can find out what person I voted for.	1	2	99	97
F12. Somebody proposed to me to vote in another locality.	1	2	99	97

Survey vignettes

Time and Minute
Survey starts: | | |

Questionnaire Number:| | | |

Hello! My name is _____. I am a student in the department of Political Science at SNSPA. Together with the Foundation Innovation Research we are carrying out a study that seeks to understand better how the local elections of 2016 took place. To discuss these issues, we have selected you randomly, like in a lottery. All the answers you will provide will be completely anonymous. We will not communicate them to anyone. At the end, we will not be able to identify the individual responses of persons who participate in our survey.

R1. Do you consider yourself a person who is . . .
1. Without religious beliefs
2. Not very religious
3. Somewhat religious
4. Very religious
98. DK
99. NA

R2. On average, how often do you attend church?
1. Daily or almost daily
2. Once a week
3. Several times a month
4. Never
98. DK
99. 99. NA

R3. Do you believe in icons who make wonders?
1. Yes   2. No   98. DK   99. NA

R4. Do you believe in objects that have miraculous powers?
1. Yes   2. No   98. DK   99. NA

R5. Do you know persons who are not attending the Orthodox Church who live in this locality?
1. Yes   2. No   98. DK   99. NA

W1. Workfare vignette

Introduction (everyone)
I would now like to have a general discussion about the social assistance program. As you probably know, under the minimum guaranteed income law, people with low incomes can get social help. Instead, they have to provide working hours in the community's interest. Although they have low incomes, both elderly people and employees with workbooks cannot benefit from the guaranteed minimum income. Imagine now a place very similar to your locality. There are many low-income people living in this locality. Many of these people are Roma.

Control Scenario
Despite receiving a very large number of social aid applications, the mayor of this locality decided to provide the guaranteed minimum income only to persons who can prove that they meet the requirements of the law.

Favor Scenario
The mayor of this locality makes access to social assistance conditional on his political support. He encourages people who want to get these benefits to vote in local elections and vote for his party in parliamentary elections.

Coercion Scenario

The mayor of this locality conditions access to social policy benefits on political support. He has punished persons that did not vote for him during the local elections or who did not support his party during the parliamentary election, by cutting their access to social policy benefits and leaving them without any means of subsistence.

In your opinion . . .	Not at all	A little	Somewhat	Much	Very much	DK
W1.1. How acceptable is the behavior of this mayor?	0	1	2	3	4	99
W1.2. How correct was the behavior of the mayor?	0	1	2	3	4	99
W1.3. How democratic was the behavior of the mayor?	0	1	2	3	4	99
W1.4. How abusive was the behavior of the mayor?	0	1	2	3	4	99

W2_1. If this mayor was to compete in your locality, how likely would it be that some people voted for him?
1. Not at all likely
2. Unlikely
3. Somewhat likely
4. Quite probable
5. Very probable
99. DK

W2_2. If this mayor competed in your locality, how likely would he be winning the elections?
1. Not at all likely
2. Unlikely
3. Somewhat likely
4. Quite probable
5. Very probable
99. DK

W2_3. If the mayor of your locality would have acted this way, how likely would you vote for this mayor?
1. Not at all likely
2. Unlikely
3. Somewhat likely
4. Quite probable
5. Very probable
99. DK

W2_4. If the mayor in your locality would have acted this way, how likely would you vote for another candidate?
1. Not at all likely
2. Unlikely
3. Somewhat likely
4. Quite probable
5. Very probable
99. DK

VB1_5. If the mayor in your locality would have acted this way, how likely would you not vote at all?
1. Not at all likely
2. Unlikely
3. Somewhat likely
4. Quite probable
5. Very probable
99. DK

Do you think that this mayor . . . ?	Not at all	A little	Somewhat	Much	Very much	DK
W3_1. Tries to limit the number of persons who receive social assistance benefits in order not to reward laziness?	0	1	2	3	4	99
W3_2. Tries to reduce the number of recipients of social assistance benefits in order to help elderly persons?	0	1	2	3	4	99
W3_3. How good of a manager is this mayor?	0	1	2	3	4	99
W3_4. How honest is this candidate?	0	1	2	3	4	99
W3_5. Would this mayor be able to provide order in the locality?	0	1	2	3	4	99
W3_6. Would this candidate help poor people?	0	1	2	3	4	99
W3_7. How wealthy is this candidate?	0	1	2	3	4	99
W3_8. Do you think this candidate is a good family man?	0	1	2	3	4	99
W3_9. Would this candidate offer a job to someone like yourself?	0	1	2	3	4	99
W3_10. Would this candidate help people in your locality if they faced an emergency?	0	1	2	3	4	99
W3_11. Could the candidate solve problems in the locality?	0	1	2	3	4	99
W3_12. How much political experience does this candidate have?	0	1	2	3	4	99
W3_13. How good of a Christian do you think this candidate is?	0	1	2	3	4	99
W3_14. How much would this candidate fight against corruption?	0	1	2	3	4	99

How much do you agree with the following statements?	Totally disagree	Partially disagree	Neither agree, nor disagree	Partially agree	Totally agree	DK
If a person puts me in a difficult situation, I will also put her in a similar difficult situation	1	2	3	4	5	99
If someone makes a favor to me, I will return the favor	1	2	3	4	5	99
If somebody was kind to me, I will do everything to help that person	1	2	3	4	5	99
If a person insults me, I will insult her myself	1	2	3	4	5	99
The government should reduce the differences in incomes between rich and poor people by raising taxes on the rich	1	2	3	4	5	99
The government should reduce differences in income between rich and poor people, by increasing social assistance benefits for the poor	1	2	3	4	5	99
There are too many people who live off social assistance benefits and we should not reward the lazy from our own money	1	2	3	4	5	99
Social assistance benefits have to be reduced and it is better to use the money for public investments, such as roads	1	2	3	4	5	99

SD1. What is your gender?
1. Male
2. Female

SD2. What is your age? _____ years old

SD3. What is your ethnicity?
1. Romanian
2. Roma
3. Hungarian
4. German
5. Another. Please name ethnicity _____

SD4. What is the last school you have completed?
1. No school
2. Primary school
3. Gymnasium
4. Highschool
5. Vocational school
6. University and postgraduate studies
99. DK/NA

SD5. What is your occupation?
1. Independent (including home-maker or independent farmer)
2. Employed with formal employment contract
3. Employed without formal employment contract
4. I receive social assistance benefits
5. Retired
6. Student
7. DK/NA

SD6. The monthly income of your household is:
1. Under 900 RON
2. Between 900 and 1,500 RON
3. Between 1,500 and 3,000 RON
4. Above 3,000 RON
98. DK
99. NA

SD7. You or a member of your immediate family receives winter support from the city hall.
1. Yes   2. No   98. DK   99. NA

SD8. You or a member of your immediate family receives social assistance benefits from the city hall.
1. Yes   2. No   98. DK   99. NA

SD9. You or a member of your family owes a large amount of money to a person in this locality ?
1. Yes   2. No   98. DK   99. NA

SD10. How many persons in this locality do you know who offer loans to the people who find themselves in a difficult situation?
98. DK   99. NA

F3. Thinking about your vote, which of the following statements is true?
3. My vote is not secret and people can see how I voted
4. My vote is secret is nobody knows how I voted
1. Statement 1 is true
2. Statement 2 is true
98. DK
99. NA

Survey Experiments

C1: Balance Tests

The survey experiments were administered in Romania in July 2016 in 60 localities located in three counties: Olt, Giurgiu, and Teleorman. First we describe sample demographics and present the results of balance tests to assess whether the randomization was successfully implemented. We first present information on the welfare survey experiment and the vote buying survey experiment in Tables C1 and C2. In Table C3 we present information on the conjoint experiment on policy favors that we carried out in a separate sample.

Table C1 Welfare vignette sample demographics and balance tests

	Control Mean	Policy Favor Mean	Difference $T_{PF} - C$	p-value	Policy Coercion Mean	Difference $T_{PF} - C$	p-value
Female	0.59	0.58	−0.02	0.75	0.59	0.00	0.99
Age	54.66	55.58	0.92	0.61	53.61	−1.05	0.56
Poverty	2.08	2.14	0.06	0.57	2.13	0.05	0.65
Education	4.15	4.17	0.03	0.86	4.10	−0.04	0.78
Employed	0.56	0.45	−0.11	0.05	0.55	−0.01	0.88
Retired	0.40	0.45	0.05	0.33	0.37	−0.03	0.55
Unemployed	0.02	0.05	0.02	0.22	0.04	0.02	0.31
Social Assistance	0.01	0.02	0.01	0.39	0.02	0.01	0.60
Roma	0.05	0.04	−0.01	0.68	0.06	0.01	0.67

Table C2 Vote-buying vignette sample demographics and balance tests

	Control Mean	In-Kind Mean	Difference $T_{IK} - C$	p-value	Cash Mean	Difference, $T_{Ca} - C$	p-value
Female	0.56	0.54	−0.02	0.71	0.63	0.08	0.09
Age	54.49	55.43	0.94	0.55	54.69	0.20	0.90
Poverty	2.14	2.12	−0.03	0.78	2.06	−0.08	0.36
Education	4.14	4.22	0.08	0.56	4.07	−0.07	0.63
Employed	0.53	0.51	−0.03	0.57	0.50	−0.03	0.54
Retired	0.41	0.43	0.02	0.69	0.41	−0.01	0.91
Unemployed	0.03	0.04	0.02	0.32	0.03	0.00	0.80
Social Assistance	0.01	0.01	−0.00	0.99	0.04	0.03	0.02
Roma	0.06	0.03	−0.03	0.19	0.06	−0.01	0.81

Table C3 Favor conjoint sample demographics and balance tests

	Control Mean	Favor Mean	Difference	*p*-value
Female	0.45	0.47	0.02	0.44
Age	46.16	43.94	−2.21	0.01
Education	5.24	5.13	−0.11	0.12
Income	2.43	2.32	−0.11	0.03
PSD	0.33	0.32	−0.01	0.76

For the conjoint experiment, the randomization was fixed such that in every comparison there was one candidate who had offered policy favors to voters in exchange for their votes and another who had not. In Table C3, we present an analysis of the balance of covariates depending on whether the clientelistic candidate was presented as the first rather than second profile.

Table C3 suggests that there may be some imbalance in the sample: the differences in age and income across the groups who saw the clientelistic candidate as the first profile and those who saw it as the second profile are statistically significant. There is a small possibility (about 0.0025 percent) that both of these differences are just due to random chance. The other possibility is that the randomization procedure used was influenced in some way by demographic characteristics. To randomize the profiles we created 14 different questionnaires that had randomized combinations of five pairs of profiles. If these questionnaires we administered in groups (i.e., questionnaire 1 was given to respondents 1–25, questionnaire 2 to 26–50, etc.), and the order of respondents was influenced by demographic characteristics, this could introduce imbalance in the sample. We do not think that this imbalance is a major threat to our ability to draw conclusions in the study for two reasons. First, we note that the differences are quite small substantively. In the case of age there is a difference of about two years, and in the case of income a difference of 0.1 on a four-point scale. Second, we include the observable demographic characteristics as controls in our analyses.

C2: Measuring Policy Preferences

In order to test our prediction that policy preferences shape how citizens interpret clientelism, we also need to measure respondents' preferences for or against the workfare program. We do this with a battery of four questions that measure the strength of preferences for redistribution in general, and for the current distribution of welfare benefits. Using the average of these four questions, we form an index of anti-workfare preferences. Figure C1 presents the distribution of responses to the four questions on a five-point agreement scale. We use this measure in the survey experiments on welfare coercion and vote buying.

The average respondent in our sample has pro-redistribution preferences in general, as 50–60 percent of respondents strongly agree that the government should raise benefits for the poor and raise taxes on the rich. However, they are unhappy with the current distribution of benefits. More than 40 percent strongly agree that social assistance should be reduced in order to make investments in the village, and more than 50 percent strongly agree that there are too many lazy people living off state funds.

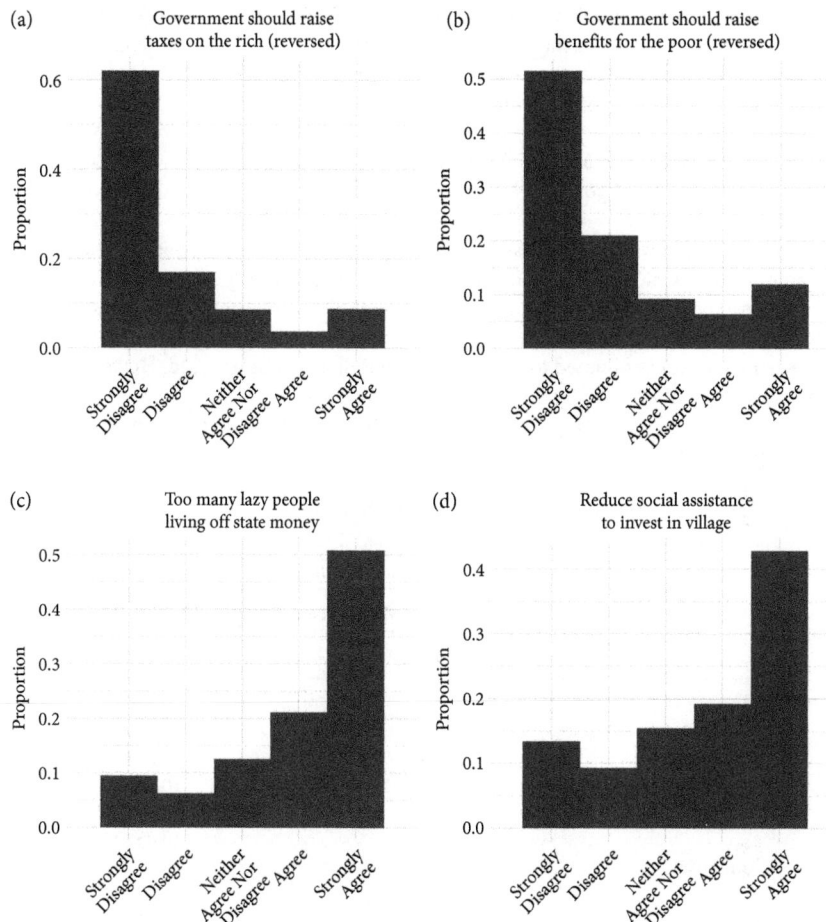

Figure C1 Distribution of anti-workfare attitudes by question

C3: Validation of Poverty as a Proxy for Preferences

In the policy favors conjoint experiment, we use poverty as a proxy for policy preferences. Our choice to use poverty is primarily driven by necessity, as this experiment was not conducted expressly for this project and didn't include measures of welfare policy preferences. However, we believe that poverty is a good proxy for welfare preferences and interesting in its own right for several reasons. First, poverty is the characteristic that is most commonly used in the literature on attitudes towards clientelism (Weitz-Shapiro 2012, 2014; Kramon 2016; González Ocantos et al. 2014). There are many explanations for why the poor might be more tolerant of or positive towards clientelism, but we argue that this heterogeneity is driven by their different policy preferences. Second, there are empirical reasons why poverty is a reasonable proxy for welfare preferences. In our sample for the welfare and vote buying survey experiments, poverty and pro-workfare policy preferences are very strongly correlated. Table C4 presents the results of an analysis of the correlates of anti-workfare preferences, the characteristic that we use to look at heterogeneous effects in the welfare and vote buying survey experiments. It shows that out of all the demographic characteristics that we measure, income has the strongest relationship with anti-workfare preferences.

Table C4 shows that out of all of the demographic characteristics that we measure, our income-based measure of poverty is the only characteristic that is consistently correlated with welfare preferences.

A one standard-deviation increase in poverty (equivalent to a 0.9-point increase on a four-point income scale) is associated with a 0.19 to 0.22 standard deviation increase on the anti-workfare index. This correlation is highly statistically significant. Other demographic characteristics also have logical relationships with anti-workfare preferences. Specifically, retirees tend to be more opposed to workfare, while Roma are less opposed. However, these relationships are not statistically distinguishable from zero.

These results suggest that poverty is a plausible though imperfect proxy for anti-workfare preferences.

Table C4 Correlates of anti-workfare preferences

	Dependent variable	
	Anti-Workfare Ideology	
	(1)	(2)
Female	−0.15*	−0.14*
	(0.08)	(0.08)
Age	−0.04	−0.05
	(0.06)	(0.06)
Poverty		−0.20***
		(0.05)
Employed	0.15	0.13
	(0.22)	(0.22)
Unemployed	−0.12	0.04
	(0.30)	(0.31)
Retired	0.16	0.21
	(0.24)	(0.24)
Education	0.13***	0.06
	(0.04)	(0.05)
Roma	−0.21	−0.19
	(0.19)	(0.18)
Constant	−0.05	0.34
	(0.23)	(0.24)
Observations	656	629
R^2	0.03	0.06

* $p<0.1$; ** $p<0.05$; *** $p<0.01$

Standard errors in parentheses.

Models are estimated using OLS. Poverty is a standardized four-category variable based on reported income. Female, Roma, Employed, Unemployed, and Retired are dummy variables. Age is a standardized version of the respondents age in years and Education is a standardized four-category variable.

C4: Welfare Scenario Supplementary Results

Disaggregated results

In this section we present results on the individual survey questions rather than aggregated outcome indices.

Table C5 and Figure C2 show that the negative effects of the policy favors and coercion treatments are consistent across the sub-indicators in the welfare policy index. The interaction term Clientelism: Policy Favors X Anti-Workfare Ideology is consistently negative and significant across both of the variables in the welfare policy index.

Table C6 and Figure C3 show that the negative effects of the policy favors and coercion treatments are consistent across the sub-indicators in the help deserving poor index. The

Table C5 Anti-workfare ideology and the social policy signals of policy favors and coercion—welfare index disaggregated

| | Dependent variable | | | |
| | Against Laziness | | Help the Elderly | |
	(1)	(2)	(3)	(4)
Clientelism: Policy favors	−0.44***	−0.43***	−0.50***	−0.49***
	(0.12)	(0.13)	(0.12)	(0.13)
Clientelism: Policy coercion	−0.61***	−0.57***	−0.55***	−0.53***
	(0.12)	(0.12)	(0.12)	(0.13)
Clientelism: Policy favors × Anti-Workfare Ideology	−0.23**	−0.25**	−0.24**	−0.23**
	(0.12)	(0.12)	(0.12)	(0.13)
Clientelism: Policy coercion × Anti-Workfare Ideology	−0.06	−0.04	−0.17	−0.12
	(0.13)	(0.13)	(0.13)	(0.14)
Anti-Workfare Ideology	0.04	0.04	0.12	0.10
	(0.08)	(0.09)	(0.09)	(0.09)
Constant	0.37***	−0.33	0.38***	−0.14
	(0.08)	(0.37)	(0.09)	(0.37)
Individual Controls		✓		✓
Observations	394	371	387	365
R^2	0.08	0.09	0.07	0.08

** p<0.1; ** p<0.05; *** p<0.01

Standard errors clustered by respondent in parentheses.

Models are estimated using OLS. All outcomes are standardized. Favor Treatment is a dummy indicating that the respondent was randomly assigned to the vignette in which the mayor offered a policy favor; Coercion Treatment is a dummy indicating that the respondent was randomly assigned to the vignette in which the mayor threatened to take away policy benefits; the residual category is the vignette in which the mayor refrains from clientelistic offers or threats. Anti-Workfare Ideology is a standardized continuous measure of the respondent's opposition to the existing state welfare programs. Individual controls include gender, age, income, ethnicity, education, and workfare eligibility.

(a)   (b)

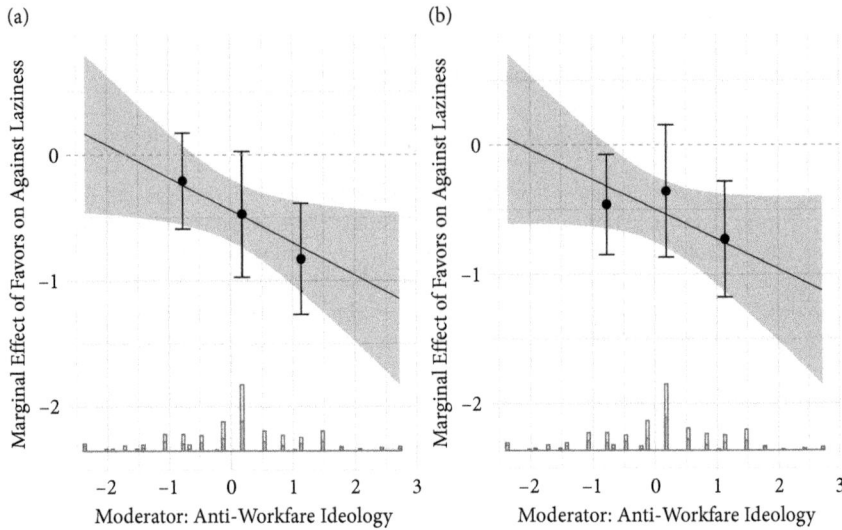

Figure C2 The marginal effect of favors on the sub-indicators in the Welfare Policy Index at varying levels of anti-workfare ideology

interaction term Clientelism: Policy Coercion X Anti-Workfare Ideology is consistently positive and significant across all three of the variables in the index.

Table C7 shows that the negative effects of the policy favors and coercion treatments are consistent across the sub-indicators in the management index. The interaction term Clientelism: Policy Coercion X Anti-Workfare Ideology is consistently positive and significant across the variables in the index.

Table C8 shows that the negative effects of the policy favors and coercion treatments are consistent across the sub-indicators in the corruption index. There are no significant interaction effects on any sub-indicators.

Table C9 shows that the negative effects of the policy favors and coercion treatments are driven by the variables Good Christian and Treats People Well. There are no negative effects on perceptions of whether the candidate is a good family man. It seems that voters interpret policy corruption as a signal of weak religiosity and a lack of ethics in most interpersonal relations, but do not believe that this behavior generalizes to conduct in the household. There are no significant interaction effects on any sub-indicators.

Table C10 shows that the negative effects of the policy favors and coercion treatments are consistent across the sub-indicators in the competitiveness index. There are no significant interaction effects on any sub-indicators.

Table C11 shows that respondents say that they would be less likely to vote for candidates who use policy favors or policy coercion, more likely to vote against them, and more likely to abstain from the election altogether. The negative effects of the policy favors and coercion treatments are consistent across the sub-indicators in the electoral punishment index. There are no significant interaction effects on any sub-indicators.

Table C6 Anti-workfare ideology and the social policy signals of policy favors and coercion—help deserving poor index disaggregated

	Dependent variable					
	Help the Poor		Help in Emergency		Job for You	
	(1)	(2)	(3)	(4)	(5)	(6)
Clientelism: Policy favors	−0.76***	−0.74***	−0.72***	−0.71***	−0.65***	−0.59***
	(0.11)	(0.12)	(0.11)	(0.12)	(0.12)	(0.12)
Clientelism: Policy coercion	−1.09***	−1.09***	−0.98***	−0.99***	−0.90***	0.94***
	(0.11)	(0.11)	(0.11)	(0.12)	(0.12)	(0.12)
Clientelism: Policy favors × Anti-Workfare Ideology	0.09	0.16	−0.03	−0.004	−0.04	−0.001
	(0.11)	(0.12)	(0.11)	(0.11)	(0.12)	(0.12)
Clientelism: Policy coercion × Anti-Workfare Ideology	0.24**	0.29**	0.17	0.22*	0.22*	0.29**
	(0.12)	(0.12)	(0.12)	(0.12)	(0.13)	(0.13)
Anti-Workfare Ideology	−0.09	−0.12	−0.06	−0.09	−0.16*	−0.19**
	(0.08)	(0.08)	(0.08)	(0.08)	(0.08)	(0.09)
Constant	0.67***	0.74**	0.59***	0.58*	0.57***	0.57
	(0.08)	(0.34)	(0.08)	(0.34)	(0.08)	(0.36)
Individual Controls		✓		✓		✓
Observations	392	370	392	371	368	346
R^2	0.21	0.25	0.18	0.20	0.16	0.21

* $p<0.1$; ** $p<0.05$; *** $p<0.01$

Standard errors in parentheses.

Models are estimated using OLS. All outcomes are standardized. Favor Treatment is a dummy indicating that the respondent was randomly assigned to the vignette in which the mayor offered a policy favor; Coercion Treatment is a dummy indicating that the respondent was randomly assigned to the vignette in which the mayor threatened to take away policy benefits; the residual category is the vignette in which the mayor refrains from clientelistic offers or threats. Anti-Workfare Ideology is a standardized continuous measure of the respondent's opposition to the existing state welfare programs. Individual controls include gender, age, income, ethnicity, education, and workfare eligibility.

Comparison of welfare preferences and income

In this section we present a comparison of poverty and welfare preferences in shaping how voters respond to public forms of clientelism. This analysis generally shows that welfare preferences explain more variation in how voters interpret the policy signals of public clientelism than poverty. Poverty on its own is a significant moderator of the relationship between favors and perceptions of a candidate's stance on workfare (but in the opposite direction of welfare preferences) and a significant moderator of the relationship between favors and perceptions of a candidate's personal qualities. By contrast, welfare preferences are significant moderators of perceptions of a candidate's position on the workfare program, perceptions of the candidate's likelihood of helping the poor, and management skills. All of the results on welfare preferences are robust to including the interaction of poverty and the treatments.

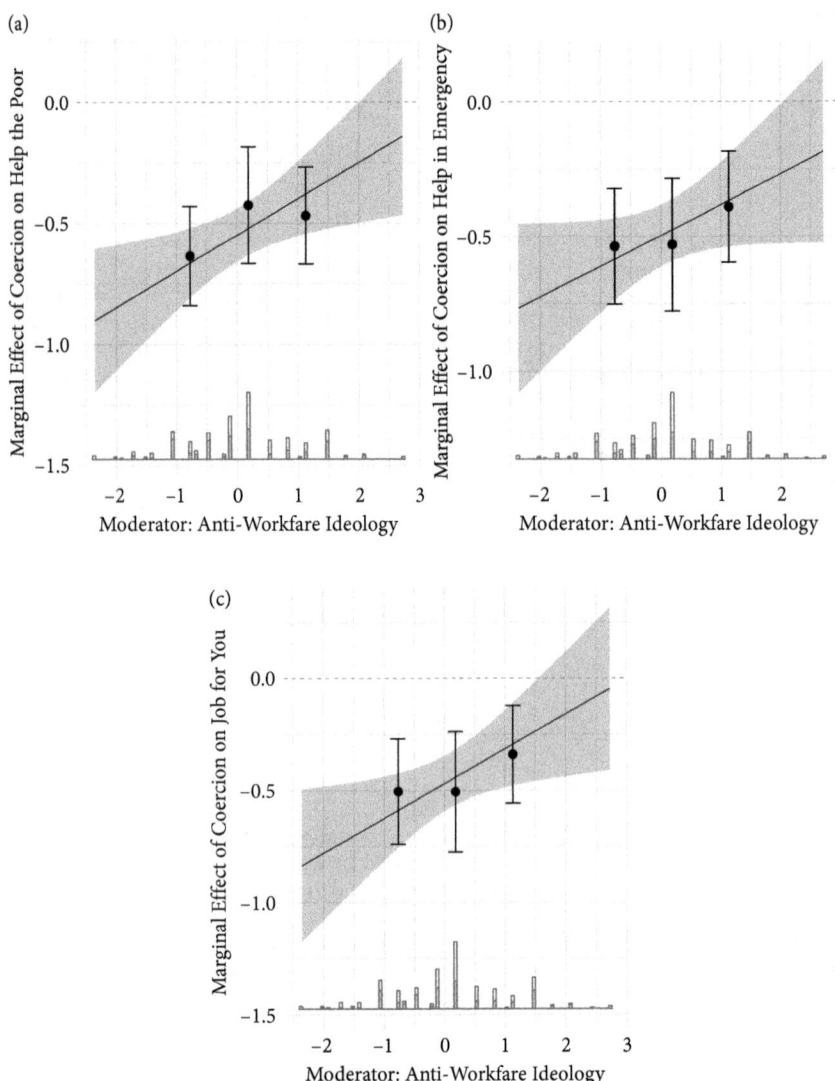

Figure C3 The marginal effect of coercion on the sub-indicators in the Help Deserving Poor Index at varying levels of anti-workfare ideology

Table C7 Anti-workfare ideology and the personal quality signals of policy favors and coercion—management index disaggregated

	Good Manager		Keep Order		Solve Problems	
	(1)	(2)	(3)	(4)	(5)	(6)
Clientelism: Policy favors	-0.80***	-0.79***	-0.88***	-0.91***	-0.74***	-0.73***
	(0.12)	(0.12)	(0.11)	(0.12)	(0.11)	(0.12)
Clientelism: Policy coercion	-1.05***	-1.05***	-1.09***	-1.09***	-1.01***	-1.01***
	(0.12)	(0.12)	(0.11)	(0.12)	(0.11)	(0.12)
Clientelism: Policy favors × Anti-Workfare Ideology	-0.01	0.02	0.03	0.06	0.01	0.05
	(0.12)	(0.12)	(0.11)	(0.11)	(0.11)	(0.11)
Clientelism: Policy coercion × Anti-Workfare Ideology	0.20	0.23***	0.23***	0.25***	0.21***	0.24***
	(0.13)	(0.13)	(0.12)	(0.12)	(0.12)	(0.12)
Anti-Workfare Ideology	-0.05	-0.08	-0.08	-0.08	-0.10	-0.11
	(0.09)	(0.09)	(0.08)	(0.08)	(0.08)	(0.08)
Constant	0.70***	0.61***	0.72***	0.47	0.65***	0.25
	(0.08)	(0.35)	(0.08)	(0.34)	(0.08)	(0.34)
Individual Controls		✓		✓		✓
Observations	368	349	394	375	401	380
R²	0.19	0.21	0.22	0.25	0.19	0.21

*** $p<0.1$; *** $p<0.05$; *** $p<0.01$

Standard errors in parentheses.

Models are estimated using OLS. All outcomes are standardized. Favor Treatment is a dummy indicating that the respondent was randomly assigned to the vignette in which the mayor offered a policy favor; Coercion Treatment is a dummy indicating that the respondent was randomly assigned to the vignette in which the mayor threatened to take away policy benefits; the residual category is the vignette in which the mayor refrains from clientelistic offers or threats. Anti-Workfare Ideology is a standardized continuous measure of the respondent's opposition to the existing state welfare programs. Individual controls include gender, age, income, ethnicity, education, and workfare eligibility.

C5: Vote-Buying Scenario Supplementary Results

Disaggregated results

Comparison of welfare preferences and other possible moderators

In this section we present a comparison of poverty, Roma ethnic status, workfare eligibility, and anti-workfare ideology in moderating how voters respond to a private form of clientelism, vote buying. This analysis shows that, as is the case with anti-workfare ideology, variation in poverty explains little to no variation in how voters view vote buying. Being a member of the Roma ethnic group, however, does seem to be associated with more positive reactions towards vote buying on several dimensions.

Table C8 Anti-workfare ideology and the personal quality signals of policy favors and coercion—corruption disaggregated

	Honest		Fight Corruption	
	(1)	(2)	(3)	(4)
Clientelism: Policy favors	−1.14***	−1.12***	−1.15***	−1.17***
	(0.11)	(0.11)	(0.11)	(0.11)
Clientelism: Policy coercion	−1.31***	−1.29***	−1.27***	−1.27***
	(0.11)	(0.11)	(0.11)	(0.11)
Clientelism: Policy favors × Anti-Workfare Ideology	0.10	0.13	0.11	0.18
	(0.10)	(0.11)	(0.11)	(0.11)
Clientelism: Policy coercion × Anti-Workfare Ideology	0.16	0.19	0.11	0.15
	(0.11)	(0.12)	(0.12)	(0.12)
Anti-Workfare Ideology	−0.11	−0.12	−0.16*	−0.18*
	(0.07)	(0.08)	(0.08)	(0.08)
Constant	0.90***	0.72*	0.91***	0.74*
	(0.07)	(0.32)	(0.08)	(0.32)
Individual Controls		✓		✓
Observations	397	375	384	363
R²	0.31	0.32	0.31	0.33

* $p<0.1$; ** $p<0.05$; *** $p<0.01$

Standard errors in parentheses.

Models are estimated using OLS. All outcomes are standardized. Favor Treatment is a dummy indicating that the respondent was randomly assigned to the vignette in which the mayor offered a policy favor; Coercion Treatment is a dummy indicating that the respondent was randomly assigned to the vignette in which the mayor threatened to take away policy benefits; the residual category is the vignette in which the mayor refrains from clientelistic offers or threats. Anti-Workfare Ideology is a standardized continuous measure of the respondent's opposition to the existing state welfare programs. Individual controls include gender, age, income, ethnicity, education, and workfare eligibility.

C6: Favor Conjoint Supplementary Results

Tables C24 through C26 present the results of the conjoint analyses with poverty interacted not only with the clientelism treatment but also with all the other categories. These tables are used to test whether (1) poverty is associated with a higher tolerance of all types of corruption, and (2) poverty is associated with lower sensitivity to any of the candidate characteristics.

Tables C24 through C26 show first that the poor are not more tolerant of all forms of corruption. By comparing the coefficients on the interactions of Business Experience: No corruption X Poor and Business Experience: Corruption X Poor, we can assess whether the poor are more likely to view all kinds of corruption more positively. In fact, while the poor do seem differentially likely to view business experience without corruption allegations as a positive signal of redistributive preferences and some personal characteristics, there is no such consistent differential effect when corruption allegations are involved.

Table C9 Anti-workfare ideology and the personal quality signals of policy favors and coercion—personal qualities index disaggregated

	Dependent variable					
	Good Christian		Family Man		Treats People Well	
	(1)	(2)	(3)	(4)	(5)	(6)
Clientelism: Policy favors	−0.68***	−0.65***	−0.02	−0.04	−0.40***	−0.43***
	(0.12)	(0.13)	(0.12)	(0.13)	(0.13)	(0.14)
Clientelism: Policy coercion	−0.95***	−0.96***	−0.07	−0.09	−0.58***	−0.59***
	(0.13)	(0.13)	(0.12)	(0.13)	(0.13)	(0.13)
Clientelism: Policy favors × Anti-Workfare Ideology	0.10	0.15	−0.18	−0.16	−0.13	−0.12
	(0.12)	(0.13)	(0.12)	(0.12)	(0.13)	(0.14)
Clientelism: Policy coercion × Anti-Workfare Ideology	0.04	0.08	−0.15	−0.16	−0.02	0.01
	(0.14)	(0.14)	(0.13)	(0.13)	(0.14)	(0.14)
Anti-Workfare Ideology	−0.11	−0.12	0.13	0.14	0.04	0.03
	(0.09)	(0.09)	(0.09)	(0.09)	(0.10)	(0.10)
Constant	0.60***	0.55	0.04	−0.33	0.33***	0.65*
	(0.09)	(0.36)	(0.09)	(0.37)	(0.09)	(0.39)
Individual Controls		✓		✓		✓
Observations	336	320	412	390	331	312
R²	0.16	0.18	0.01	0.04	0.06	0.09

* $p<0.1$; ** $p<0.05$; *** $p<0.01$

Standard errors in parentheses.

Models are estimated using OLS. All outcomes are standardized. Favor Treatment is a dummy indicating that the respondent was randomly assigned to the vignette in which the mayor offered a policy favor; Coercion Treatment is a dummy indicating that the respondent was randomly assigned to the vignette in which the mayor threatened to take away policy benefits; the residual category is the vignette in which the mayor refrains from clientelistic offers or threats. Anti-Workfare Ideology is a standardized continuous measure of the respondent's opposition to the existing state welfare programs. Individual controls include gender, age, income, ethnicity, education, and workfare eligibility.

Second, Tables C24 through C26 show that the poor do not generally interpret candidate characteristics differently than better-off citizens do. When it comes to candidate gender, party, or legislative experience, the evaluations of the poor and the better-off are not systematically different.

Finally, because our marginal effects plots showed some signs that respondent poverty does not have a linear relationship with the size of the treatment effect of policy favors, we conduct a robustness check in which we recode poverty as a binary variable. Tables C27 through C29 show the results for this analysis. The interaction of this binary version of poverty and the candidate characteristics remains significant in all of the regressions.

Table C10 Anti-workfare ideology and the personal quality signals of policy favors and coercion—competitiveness index disaggregated

	(2) (3) (4)			
	Dependent variable			
	Win Others' Votes		Win Election	
	(1)	(2)	(3)	(4)
Clientelism: Policy favors	–0.61***	–0.56***	–0.63***	–0.59***
	(0.11)	(0.11)	(0.11)	(0.11)
Clientelism: Policy coercion	–1.07***	–1.06***	–0.99***	–1.01***
	(0.11)	(0.11)	(0.11)	(0.11)
Clientelism: Policy favors × Anti-Workfare Ideology	0.13	0.16	0.12	0.13
	(0.10)	(0.10)	(0.10)	(0.11)
Clientelism: Policy coercion × Anti-Workfare Ideology	0.07	0.09	0.11	0.12
	(0.11)	(0.11)	(0.11)	(0.12)
Anti-Workfare Ideology	–0.06	–0.08	–0.05	–0.05
	(0.07)	(0.08)	(0.07)	(0.08)
Constant	0.60***	0.20	0.61***	0.43
	(0.07)	(0.32)	(0.08)	(0.32)
Individual Controls		✓		✓
Observations	457	432	454	429
R²	0.19	0.22	0.16	0.19

* $p<0.1$; ** $p<0.05$; *** $p<0.01$

Standard errors in parentheses.

Models are estimated using OLS. All outcomes are standardized. Favor Treatment is a dummy indicating that the respondent was randomly assigned to the vignette in which the mayor offered a policy favor; Coercion Treatment is a dummy indicating that the respondent was randomly assigned to the vignette in which the mayor threatened to take away policy benefits; the residual category is the vignette in which the mayor refrains from clientelistic offers or threats. Anti-Workfare Ideology is a standardized continuous measure of the respondent's opposition to the existing state welfare programs. Individual controls include gender, age, income, ethnicity, education, and workfare eligibility.

Table C11 Anti-workfare ideology and the personal quality signals of policy favors and coercion—electoral punishment index disaggregated

	Dependent variable					
	Win Your Vote		Lose Your Vote		Abstain	
	(1)	(2)	(3)	(4)	(5)	(6)
Clientelism: Policy favors	−1.21***	−1.19***	0.73***	0.67***	0.36***	0.37***
	(0.10)	(0.10)	(0.11)	(0.11)	(0.11)	(0.11)
Clientelism: Policy coercion	−1.40***	1.37***	0.79***	0.75***	0.27*	0.23*
	(0.10)	(0.10)	(0.11)	(0.11)	(0.11)	(0.12)
Clientelism: Policy favors × Anti-Workfare Ideology	−0.02	0.01	−0.02	−0.06	0.03	0.02
	(0.09)	(0.09)	(0.10)	(0.10)	(0.11)	(0.11)
Clientelism: Policy coercion × Anti-Workfare Ideology	0.03	0.07	0.03	0.01	0.04	0.02
	(0.10)	(0.10)	(0.11)	(0.12)	(0.12)	(0.12)
Anti-Workfare Ideology	0.01	−0.03	0.06	0.06	−0.08	−0.06
	(0.06)	(0.07)	(0.07)	(0.08)	(0.08)	(0.08)
Constant	0.97***	0.91***	−0.49***	−0.93***	−0.21***	−0.06
Individual Controls	(0.07)	(0.29)	(0.07)	(0.33)	(0.08)	(0.34)
		✓		✓		✓
Observations	454	430	449	425	451	427
R^2	0.36	0.35	0.14	0.14	0.03	0.06

* $p<0.1$; ** $p<0.05$; *** $p<0.01$

Standard errors in parentheses.

Models are estimated using OLS. All outcomes are standardized. Favor Treatment is a dummy indicating that the respondent was randomly assigned to the vignette in which the mayor offered a policy favor; Coercion Treatment is a dummy indicating that the respondent was randomly assigned to the vignette in which the mayor threatened to take away policy benefits; the residual category is the vignette in which the mayor refrains from clientelistic offers or threats. Anti-Workfare Ideology is a standardized continuous measure of the respondent's opposition to the existing state welfare programs. Individual controls include gender, age, income, ethnicity, education, and workfare eligibility.

Table C12 Anti-workfare ideology, poverty, and the social policy signals of policy favors and coercion

	Dependent variable			
	Workfare Retrenchment Index		Help Deserving Poor Index	
	(1)	(2)	(3)	(4)
Clientelism: Policy favors	−0.85***	−0.96***	−0.85***	−0.95***
	(0.28)	(0.28)	(0.25)	(0.25)
Clientelism: Policy coercion	−0.72*	−0.76***	−1.16***	−1.24***
	(0.28)	(0.28)	(0.25)	(0.25)
Clientelism: Policy favors × Anti-Workfare Ideology	−0.18	−0.20*	0.08	0.12
	(0.11)	(0.11)	(0.10)	(0.10)
Clientelism: Policy coercion × Anti-Workfare Ideology	−0.08	−0.06	0.25*	0.29***
	(0.12)	(0.12)	(0.11)	(0.10)
Clientelism: Policy favors × Poverty	0.20	0.24*	0.07	0.14
	(0.12)	(0.12)	(0.11)	(0.11)
Clientelism: Policy coercion × Poverty	0.10	0.11	0.09	0.12
	(0.12)	(0.12)	(0.11)	(0.11)
Anti-Workfare Ideology	0.08	0.07	−0.13*	−0.15*
	(0.08)	(0.08)	(0.07)	(0.07)
Poverty	−0.06	−0.07	−0.04	−0.06
	(0.08)	(0.08)	(0.07)	(0.08)
Constant	0.46*	0.04	0.66***	0.81***
	(0.19)	(0.35)	(0.17)	(0.31)
Individual Controls		✓		✓
Observations	396	390	407	401
R^2	0.08	0.11	0.21	0.26

* $p<0.1$; ** $p<0.05$; *** $p<0.01$

Standard errors in parentheses.

Models are estimated using OLS. All outcomes are standardized. Favor Treatment is a dummy indicating that the respondent was randomly assigned to the vignette in which the mayor offered a policy favor; Coercion Treatment is a dummy indicating that the respondent was randomly assigned to the vignette in which the mayor threatened to take away policy benefits; the residual category is the vignette in which the mayor refrains from clientelistic offers or threats. Anti-Workfare Ideology is a standardized continuous measure of the respondent's opposition to the existing state welfare programs. Poverty is a standardized measure of how poor the respondent is (the inverse of income) on a four-point scale. Individual controls include gender, age, ethnicity, education, and workfare eligibility.

Table C13 Anti-workfare ideology, poverty, and the personal quality signals of policy favors and coercion

| | | | | *Dependent variable* | | | | |
| | Management Index | | Anti-Corruption Index | | Personal Index | | Competitiveness Index | |
	(1)	(2)	(3)	(4)	(5)	(6)	(7)	(8)
Clientelism: Policy favors	-0.85***	-0.89***	-1.39***	-1.41***	-0.74***	-0.74***	-0.03	-0.08
	(0.25)	(0.25)	(0.26)	(0.26)	(0.24)	(0.24)	(0.26)	(0.26)
Clientelism: Policy coercion	-1.19***	-1.22***	-1.34***	-1.35***	-0.42*	-0.45*	-0.20	-0.25
	(0.26)	(0.26)	(0.26)	(0.26)	(0.23)	(0.24)	(0.26)	(0.26)
Clientelism: Policy favors × Anti-Workfare Ideology	0.04	0.06	0.14	0.15	0.04	0.05	0.05	0.04
	(0.10)	(0.10)	(0.10)	(0.10)	(0.09)	(0.09)	(0.10)	(0.10)
Clientelism: Policy coercion × Anti-Workfare Ideology	0.22*	0.24*	0.13	0.14	-0.01	0.001	0.11	0.11
	(0.11)	(0.11)	(0.11)	(0.11)	(0.10)	(0.10)	(0.11)	(0.11)
Clientelism: Policy favors × Poverty	0.03	0.05	0.11	0.12	0.19*	0.19*	-0.09	-0.06
	(0.11)	(0.11)	(0.11)	(0.11)	(0.10)	(0.11)	(0.11)	(0.12)
Clientelism: Policy coercion × Poverty	0.08	0.10	0.03	0.03	-0.02	-0.01	-0.05	-0.03
	(0.11)	(0.11)	(0.11)	(0.11)	(0.10)	(0.10)	(0.11)	(0.11)
Anti-Workfare Ideology	-0.10	-0.11	-0.14*	-0.14*	0.02	0.01	-0.08	-0.09
	(0.07)	(0.07)	(0.07)	(0.07)	(0.07)	(0.07)	(0.07)	(0.07)
Poverty	0.63***	0.52*	0.85***	0.75*	0.17	0.31	0.07	-0.004
	(0.17)	(0.32)	(0.17)	(0.32)	(0.16)	(0.30)	(0.17)	(0.32)
Individual Controls		✓		✓		✓		✓
Observations	410	404	399	393	418	413	380	374
R^2	0.23	0.25	0.35	0.35	0.09	0.09	0.03	0.05

* $p<0.1$; ** $p<0.05$; *** $p<0.01$

Standard errors in parentheses.

Models are estimated using OLS. All outcomes are standardized. Favor Treatment is a dummy indicating that the respondent was randomly assigned to the vignette in which the mayor offered a policy favor; Coercion Treatment is a dummy indicating that the respondent was randomly assigned to the vignette in which the mayor threatened to take away policy benefits; the residual category is the vignette in which the mayor refrains from clientelistic offers or threats. Anti-Workfare Ideology is a standardized continuous measure of the respondent's opposition to the existing state welfare programs. Poverty is a standardized measure of how poor the respondent is (the inverse of income) on a four-point scale. Individual controls include gender, age, ethnicity, education, and workfare eligibility.

Table C14 Anti-workfare ideology, poverty, and propensity to punish candidates who use policy favors and coercion

	Dependent variable	
	Electoral Punishment Index	
	(1)	(2)
Clientelism: Policy favors	0.78***	0.76***
	(0.18)	(0.18)
Clientelism: Policy coercion	1.00***	1.00***
	(0.18)	(0.18)
Clientelism: Policy favors × Anti-Workfare Ideology	−0.02	−0.03
	(0.07)	(0.07)
Clientelism: Policy coercion × Anti-Workfare Ideology	−0.02	−0.03
	(0.08)	(0.08)
Clientelism: Policy favors × Poverty	−0.03	−0.02
	(0.08)	(0.08)
Clientelism: Policy coercion × Poverty	−0.11	−0.11
	(0.08)	(0.08)
Anti-Workfare Ideology	0.02	0.02
	(0.05)	(0.05)
Poverty	−0.61***	−0.69***
	(0.12)	(0.23)
Individual Controls		✓
Observations	439	433
R^2	0.26	0.27

* $p<0.1$; ** $p<0.05$; *** $p<0.01$

Standard errors in parentheses.

Models are estimated using OLS. All outcomes are standardized. Favor Treatment is a dummy indicating that the respondent was randomly assigned to the vignette in which the mayor offered a policy favor; Coercion Treatment is a dummy indicating that the respondent was randomly assigned to the vignette in which the mayor threatened to take away policy benefits; the residual category is the vignette in which the mayor refrains from clientelistic offers or threats. Anti-Workfare Ideology is a standardized continuous measure of the respondent's opposition to the existing state welfare programs. Poverty is a standardized measure of how poor the respondent is (the inverse of income) on a four-point scale. Individual controls include gender, age, ethnicity, education, and workfare eligibility.

Table C15 Anti-workfare ideology and the social policy signals of vote buying—help deserving poor index disaggregated

	Dependent variable					
	Help the Poor		Help in Emergency		Job for You	
	(1)	(2)	(3)	(4)	(5)	(6)
Vote Buying: In-kind	−0.26*	−0.28***	−0.45***	−0.45***	0.40***	−0.43***
	(0.10)	(0.11)	(0.10)	(0.10)	(0.10)	(0.11)
Vote Buying: Cash	−0.81***	0.78***	−0.83***	−0.83***	−0.82***	−0.88***
	(0.10)	(0.10)	(0.10)	(0.10)	(0.10)	(0.11)
Vote Buying: In-kind × Anti-Workfare Ideology	−0.13	−0.11	−0.16	−0.14	−0.14	−0.09
	(0.10)	(0.10)	(0.10)	(0.10)	(0.10)	(0.11)
Vote Buying: Cash × Anti-Workfare Ideology	−0.07	−0.03	−0.09	−0.05	−0.06	0.04
	(0.10)	(0.11)	(0.10)	(0.10)	(0.11)	(0.11)
Anti-Workfare Ideology	0.03	0.04	−0.03	−0.04	0.002	−0.02
	(0.07)	(0.08)	(0.07)	(0.07)	(0.08)	(0.08)
Constant	0.37***	0.01	0.44***	−0.20	0.42***	0.10
	(0.07)	(0.30)	(0.07)	(0.30)	(0.07)	(0.31)
Individual Controls		✓		✓		✓
Observations	542	508	548	515	505	474
R^2	0.12	0.14	0.13	0.15	0.12	0.17

* $p<0.1$; ** $p<0.05$; *** $p<0.01$

Standard errors in parentheses.

Models are estimated using OLS. All outcomes are standardized. Vote Buying: In-kind is a dummy indicating that the respondent was randomly assigned to the vignette in which the candidate offered a meal; Vote Buying: Cash is a dummy indicating that the respondent was randomly assigned to the vignette in which the candidate offered cash; the residual category is the vignette in which the candidate offers nothing. Anti-Workfare Ideology is a standardized continuous measure of the respondent's opposition to the existing state welfare programs. Individual controls include gender, age, income, ethnicity, education, and workfare eligibility.

Table C16 Anti-workfare ideology and the personal quality signals of vote buying—management index disaggregated

	Dependent variable					
	Good Manager		Keep Order		Solve Problems	
	(1)	(2)	(3)	(4)	(5)	(6)
Vote Buying: In-kind	−0.43***	−0.49***	−0.51***	−0.53***	−0.46***	−0.50***
	(0.10)	(0.11)	(0.10)	(0.10)	(0.10)	(0.11)
Vote Buying: Cash	−0.86***	−0.88***	−0.93***	−0.91***	−0.84***	−0.83***
	(0.10)	(0.11)	(0.10)	(0.10)	(0.10)	(0.10)
Vote Buying: In-kind × Anti-Workfare Ideology	−0.13	−0.14	0.03	0.05	−0.05	−0.02
	(0.11)	(0.11)	(0.10)	(0.10)	(0.10)	(0.10)
Vote Buying: Cash × Anti-Workfare Ideology	−0.03	0.01	0.01	0.05	−0.03	0.01
	(0.11)	(0.11)	(0.10)	(0.10)	(0.10)	(0.11)
Anti-Workfare Ideology	0.04	0.03	−0.01	−0.02	−0.04	−0.05
	(0.08)	(0.08)	(0.07)	(0.08)	(0.07)	(0.08)
Constant	0.45***	0.11	0.48***	−0.03	0.44***	−0.21
	(0.07)	(0.31)	(0.07)	(0.29)	(0.07)	(0.30)
Individual Controls		✓				✓
Observations	519	487	550	516	537	504
R^2	0.13	0.15	0.14	0.16	0.12	0.16

* $p<0.1$; ** $p<0.05$; *** $p<0.01$

Standard errors in parentheses.

Models are estimated using OLS. All outcomes are standardized. Vote Buying: In-kind is a dummy indicating that the respondent was randomly assigned to the vignette in which the candidate offered a meal; Vote Buying: Cash is a dummy indicating that the respondent was randomly assigned to the vignette in which the candidate offered cash; the residual category is the vignette in which the candidate offers nothing. Anti-Workfare Ideology is a standardized continuous measure of the respondent's opposition to the existing state welfare programs. Individual controls include gender, age, income, ethnicity, education, and workfare eligibility.

Table C17 Anti-workfare ideology and the personal quality signals of vote buying—corruption index disaggregated

	Dependent variable			
	Honesty		Fight corruption	
	(1)	(2)	(3)	(4)
Vote Buying: In-kind	−0.57***	−0.60***	−0.67***	−0.70***
	(0.09)	(0.10)	(0.10)	(0.10)
Vote Buying: Cash	−1.27***	−1.28***	−1.18***	−1.19***
	(0.09)	(0.10)	(0.09)	(0.10)
Vote Buying: In-kind × Anti-Workfare Ideology	−0.08	−0.06	−0.004	−0.002
	(0.09)	(0.10)	(0.10)	(0.10)
Vote Buying: Cash × Anti-Workfare Ideology	−0.08	−0.05	−0.04	−0.04
	(0.09)	(0.10)	(0.10)	(0.10)
Anti-Workfare Ideology	0.05	0.04	−0.07	−0.05
	(0.07)	(0.07)	(0.07)	(0.08)
Constant	0.64***	0.07	0.64***	0.23
	(0.07)	(0.27)	(0.07)	(0.29)
Individual Controls		✓		✓
Observations	536	503	517	488
R^2	0.27	0.28	0.24	0.26

* $p<0.1$; ** $p<0.05$; *** $p<0.01$

Standard errors in parentheses.

Models are estimated using OLS. All outcomes are standardized. Vote Buying: In-kind is a dummy indicating that the respondent was randomly assigned to the vignette in which the candidate offered a meal; Vote Buying: Cash is a dummy indicating that the respondent was randomly assigned to the vignette in which the candidate offered cash; the residual category is the vignette in which the candidate offers nothing. Anti-Workfare Ideology is a standardized continuous measure of the respondent's opposition to the existing state welfare programs. Individual controls include gender, age, income, ethnicity, education, and workfare eligibility.

Table C18 Anti-workfare ideology and the personal quality signals of vote buying—personal qualities index disaggregated

	Dependent variable					
	Good Christian		Family Man		Treats People Well	
	(1)	(2)	(3)	(4)	(5)	(6)
Vote Buying: In-kind	−0.44***	−0.46***	−0.45***	−0.45***	−0.45***	−0.47***
	(0.11)	(0.11)	(0.11)	(0.12)	(0.10)	(0.10)
Vote Buying: Cash	−0.96***	−0.96***	−0.67***	−0.68***	−0.96***	−0.94***
	(0.10)	(0.11)	(0.11)	(0.11)	(0.10)	(0.10)
Vote Buying: In-kind × Anti-Workfare Ideology	−0.15	−0.14	−0.13	−0.13	−0.16*	−0.17*
	(0.11)	(0.11)	(0.11)	(0.11)	(0.10)	(0.10)
Vote Buying: Cash × Anti-Workfare Ideology	−0.08	−0.05	0.03	0.07	−0.09	−0.06
	(0.11)	(0.11)	(0.11)	(0.12)	(0.10)	(0.10)
Anti-Workfare Ideology	−0.01	0.01	0.01	0.01	0.05	0.07
	(0.08)	(0.08)	(0.08)	(0.08)	(0.07)	(0.07)
Constant	0.49***	−0.20	0.39***	−0.44	0.48***	−0.13
	(0.08)	(0.30)	(0.08)	(0.33)	(0.07)	(0.29)
Individual Controls		✓		✓		✓
Observations	471	447	464	438	555	523
R^2	0.17	0.20	0.08	0.11	0.16	0.17

* $p<0.1$; ** $p<0.05$; *** $p<0.01$

Standard errors in parentheses.

Models are estimated using OLS. All outcomes are standardized. Vote Buying: In-kind is a dummy indicating that the respondent was randomly assigned to the vignette in which the candidate offered a meal; Vote Buying: Cash is a dummy indicating that the respondent was randomly assigned to the vignette in which the candidate offered cash; the residual category is the vignette in which the candidate offers nothing. Anti-Workfare Ideology is a standardized continuous measure of the respondent's opposition to the existing state welfare programs. Individual controls include gender, age, income, ethnicity, education, and workfare eligibility.

Table C19 Anti-workfare ideology and the personal quality signals of vote buying—competitiveness index disaggregated

	Dependent variable			
	Win Others' Votes		Win Election	
	(1)	(2)	(3)	(4)
Vote Buying: In-kind	−0.18*	−0.22*	−0.32***	−0.36***
	(0.10)	(0.10)	(0.10)	(0.10)
Vote Buying: Cash	−0.45***	−0.49***	−0.49***	−0.50***
	(0.10)	(0.10)	(0.10)	(0.10)
Vote Buying: In-kind × Anti-Workfare Ideology	0.07	0.09	−0.07	−0.04
	(0.10)	(0.10)	(0.10)	(0.10)
Vote Buying: Cash × Anti-Workfare Ideology	0.09	0.13	0.15	0.19*
	(0.10)	(0.10)	(0.10)	(0.10)
Anti-Workfare Ideology	−0.09	−0.07	−0.11*	−0.09
	(0.07)	(0.07)	(0.07)	(0.07)
Constant	0.21***	−0.49*	0.27***	−0.13
	(0.07)	(0.29)	(0.07)	(0.29)
Individual Controls		✓		✓
Observations	616	579	612	574
R²	0.04	0.07	0.06	0.10

* p<0.1; ** p<0.05; *** p<0.01

Standard errors in parentheses.

Models are estimated using OLS. All outcomes are standardized. Vote Buying: In-kind is a dummy indicating that the respondent was randomly assigned to the vignette in which the candidate offered a meal; Vote Buying: Cash is a dummy indicating that the respondent was randomly assigned to the vignette in which the candidate offered cash; the residual category is the vignette in which the candidate offers nothing. Anti-Workfare Ideology is a standardized continuous measure of the respondent's opposition to the existing state welfare programs. Individual controls include gender, age, income, ethnicity, education, and workfare eligibility.

Table C20 Anti-workfare ideology and the personal quality signals of policy favors and coercion—electoral punishment index disaggregated

| | *Dependent variable* | | | | | |
| | Win Your Vote | | Lose Your Vote | | Abstain | |
	(1)	(2)	(3)	(4)	(5)	(6)
Vote Buying: In-kind	−0.54***	−0.58***	0.43***	0.45***	0.21*	0.22*
	(0.09)	(0.09)	(0.09)	(0.10)	(0.10)	(0.10)
Vote Buying: Cash	−1.13***	−1.14***	0.85***	0.88***	0.46***	0.44***
	(0.09)	(0.09)	(0.09)	(0.10)	(0.10)	(0.10)
Vote Buying: In-kind × Anti-Workfare Ideology	−0.07	−0.05	−0.04	−0.08	0.09	0.09
	(0.09)	(0.09)	(0.09)	(0.10)	(0.10)	(0.10)
Vote Buying: Cash × Anti-Workfare Ideology	−0.05	0.02	0.14	0.08	0.07	0.06
Anti-Workfare Ideology	(0.09)	(0.09)	(0.10)	(0.10)	(0.10)	(0.10)
	0.01	−0.005	0.02	0.03	−0.06	−0.04
	(0.06)	(0.06)	(0.07)	(0.07)	(0.07)	(0.07)
Constant	0.55***	0.03	0.42***	−0.45	−0.22***	−0.15
Individual Controls	(0.06)	(0.26)	(0.07)	(0.28)	(0.07)	(0.29)
		✓		✓		✓
Observations	611	573	609	573	618	580
R^2	0.22	0.25	0.13	0.15	0.04	0.05

* $p<0.1$; ** $p<0.05$; *** $p<0.01$

Standard errors in parentheses.

Models are estimated using OLS. All outcomes are standardized. Vote Buying: In-kind is a dummy indicating that the respondent was randomly assigned to the vignette in which the candidate offered a meal; Vote Buying: Cash is a dummy indicating that the respondent was randomly assigned to the vignette in which the candidate offered cash; the residual category is the vignette in which the candidate offers nothing. Anti-Workfare Ideology is a standardized continuous measure of the respondent's opposition to the existing state welfare programs. Individual controls include gender, age, income, ethnicity, education, and workfare eligibility.

Table C21 Alternative moderators and the policy signals of vote buying

	Dependent variable	
	Help Deserving Poor Index	
	(1)	(2)
Vote Buying: In-kind × Roma	0.15	
	(0.45)	
Vote Buying: Cash × Roma	0.80*	
	(0.39)	
Vote Buying: In-kind × Workfare Ineligible	–0.14	
	(0.17)	
Vote Buying: Cash × Workfare Ineligible	0.24	
	(0.17)	
Vote Buying: In-kind × Poverty		–0.01
		(0.09)
Vote Buying: Cash × Poverty		0.08
		(0.09)
Direct Effects	✓	✓
Observations	579	564
R^2	0.15	0.16

* $p<0.1$; ** $p<0.05$; *** $p<0.01$

Standard errors in parentheses.

Models are estimated using OLS. All outcomes are standardized. Vote Buying: In-kind is a dummy indicating that the respondent was randomly assigned to the vignette in which the candidate offered a meal; Vote Buying: Cash is a dummy indicating that the respondent was randomly assigned to the vignette in which the candidate offered cash; the residual category is the vignette in which the candidate offers nothing. Roma is a binary variable that takes a value of 1 if the enumerator identifies the respondent as a member of the Roma minority. Poverty is a standardized four-category variable that takes a higher value for respondent's who report a lower level of income. Welfare Ineligible is a binary variable that takes a value of 1 if the respondent is employed or retired.

Table C22 Alternative moderators and the personal quality signals of vote buying

	Management Index		Anti-Corruption Index		Personal Index		Competitiveness Index	
	(1)	(2)	(3)	(4)	(5)	(6)	(7)	(8)
Vote Buying: In-kind × Roma	−0.21		0.20		0.04		0.39	
	(0.45)		(0.47)		(0.44)		(0.46)	
Vote Buying: Cash × Roma	0.65*		0.76*		0.76*		0.45	
	(0.40)		(0.39)		(0.39)		(0.41)	
Vote Buying: In-kind × Workfare Ineligible	−0.001		−0.07		0.001		0.01	
	(0.17)		(0.17)		(0.16)		(0.19)	
Vote Buying: Cash × Workfare Ineligible	0.31*		0.25		0.19		−0.26	
	(0.17)		(0.17)		(0.16)		(0.19)	
Vote Buying: In-kind × Poverty		−0.06		0.0002		0.08		−0.23*
		(0.09)		(0.09)		(0.09)		(0.10)
Vote Buying: Cash × Poverty		0.05		0.06		0.08		−0.18*
		(0.09)		(0.09)		(0.09)		(0.10)
Direct Effects	✓	✓	✓	✓	✓	✓	✓	✓
Observations	592	574	569	553	576	560	618	600
R²	0.16	0.16	0.28	0.28	0.18	0.18	0.06	0.07

* $p<0.1$; ** $p<0.05$; *** $p<0.01$

Standard errors in parentheses.

Models are estimated using OLS. All outcomes are standardized. Vote Buying: In-kind is a dummy indicating that the respondent was randomly assigned to the vignette in which the candidate offered a meal; Vote Buying: Cash is a dummy indicating that the respondent was randomly assigned to the vignette in which the candidate offered cash; the residual category is the vignette in which the candidate offers nothing. Roma is a binary variable that takes a value of 1 if the enumerator identifies the respondent as a member of the Roma minority. Poverty is a standardized four-category variable that takes a higher value for respondent's who report a lower level of income. Welfare Ineligible is a binary variable that takes a value of 1 if the respondent is employed or retired.

Table C23 Alternative moderators and the electoral punishment of vote buying

	Dependent variable	
	Electoral Punishment Index	
	(1)	(2)
Vote Buying: In-kind × Roma	0.61*	
	(0.32)	
Vote Buying: Cash × Roma	–0.14	
	(0.28)	
Vote Buying: In-kind × Workfare Ineligible	0.05	
	(0.12)	
Vote Buying: Cash × Workfare Ineligible	–0.01	
	(0.13)	
Vote Buying: In-kind × Poverty		–0.09
		(0.07)
Vote Buying: Cash × Poverty		0.02
		(0.07)
Direct Effects	✓	✓
Observations	620	602
R^2	0.23	0.24

* $p<0.1$; ** $p<0.05$; *** $p<0.01$

Standard errors in parentheses.

Models are estimated using OLS. All outcomes are standardized. Vote Buying: In-kind is a dummy indicating that the respondent was randomly assigned to the vignette in which the candidate offered a meal; Vote Buying: Cash is a dummy indicating that the respondent was randomly assigned to the vignette in which the candidate offered cash; the residual category is the vignette in which the candidate offers nothing. Roma is a binary variable that takes a value of 1 if the enumerator identifies the respondent as a member of the Roma minority. Poverty is a standardized four-category variable that takes a higher value for respondent's who report a lower level of income. Welfare Ineligible is a binary variable that takes a value of 1 if the respondent is employed or retired.

Table C24 Poverty, candidate characteristics, and self-reported voting propensity

	Dependent variable
	Preferred Candidate
Clientelism: Policy Favors × Poor	0.09***
	(0.02)
Business Experience: No corruption × Poor	0.05*
	(0.02)
Business Experience: Corruption × Poor	0.02
	(0.02)
Political Experience: Legislative × Poor	−0.003
	(0.02)
Gender: Female × Poor	0.04*
	(0.02)
Party: PMP × Poor	0.003
	(0.03)
Party: PNL × Poor	−0.04
	(0.03)
Party: PSD × Poor	0.04
	(0.03)
Party: USR × Poor	−0.05*
	(0.03)
Poor	0.07***
	(0.03)
Direct Effects	✓
Individual Controls	✓
Observations	3,220
R^2	0.07

* $p<0.1$; ** $p<0.05$; *** $p<0.01$

Standard errors clustered by respondent in parentheses.

Models are estimated using OLS. The outcome is a dummy variable indicating that the respondent thought that the candidate profile was better on the dimension under question than the alternative profile with which it was presented. Data is analyzed at the level of the candidate profile such that the full data frame of 3,220 includes ten observations (two from each of five pairs) per respondent. The base case for Clientelism is no policy favors. The base case for Business Experience and Political Experience is no experience. The base case for Party is the ALD. Individual controls include gender, age, education, and a dummy indicating that the respondent supports the PSD.

Table C25 Poverty, candidate characteristics, and perceived personal characteristics

	Dependent variable	
	Good Manager	Honest
	(1)	(2)
Clientelism: Policy Favors × Poor	0.07***	0.08***
	(0.02)	(0.02)
Business Experience: No corruption × Poor	0.03	0.06***
	(0.02)	(0.02)
Business Experience: Corruption × Poor	0.02	0.03
	(0.02)	(0.02)
Political Experience: Legislative × Poor	0.01	0.02
	(0.02)	(0.02)
Gender: Female × Poor	0.01	0.03
	(0.02)	(0.02)
Party: PMP × Poor	−0.02	0.02
	(0.03)	(0.03)
Party: PNL × Poor	−0.03	0.01
	(0.03)	(0.03)
Party: PSD × Poor	−0.002	0.05*
	(0.03)	(0.03)
Party: USR × Poor	−0.004	−0.01
	(0.03)	(0.03)
Poor	−0.05*	−0.10***
	(0.03)	(0.03)
Direct Effects	✓	✓
Individual Controls	✓	✓
Observations	3,220	3,220
R^2	0.04	0.07

* $p<0.1$; ** $p<0.05$; *** $p<0.01$

Standard errors clustered by respondent in parentheses.

Models are estimated using OLS. The outcome is a dummy variable indicating that the respondent thought that the candidate profile was better on the dimension under question than the alternative profile with which it was presented. Data is analyzed at the level of the candidate profile such that the full data frame of 3,220 includes ten observations (two from each of five pairs) per respondent. The base case for Clientelism is no policy favors. The base case for Business Experience and Political Experience is no experience. The base case for Party is the ALD. Individual controls include gender, age, education, and a dummy indicating that the respondent supports the PSD.

Table C26 Poverty, candidate characteristics, and self-reported voting propensity

	Dependent variable
	Preferred Candidate
Clientelism: Policy Favors × Poor	0.09***
	(0.02)
Business Experience: No corruption × Poor	0.05*
	(0.02)
Business Experience: Corruption × Poor	0.02
	(0.02)
Political Experience: Legislative × Poor	−0.003
	(0.02)
Gender: Female × Poor	0.04*
	(0.02)
Party: PMP × Poor	0.003
	(0.03)
Party: PNL × Poor	−0.04
	(0.03)
Party: PSD × Poor	0.04
	(0.03)
Party: USR × Poor	−0.05*
	(0.03)
Poor	−0.07***
	(0.03)
Direct Effects	✓
Individual Controls	✓
Observations	3,220
R²	0.07

* p<0.1; ** p<0.05; *** p<0.01

Standard errors clustered by respondent in parentheses.

Models are estimated using OLS. The outcome is a dummy variable indicating that the respondent thought that the candidate profile was better on the dimension under question than the alternative profile with which it was presented. Data is analyzed at the level of the candidate profile such that the full data frame of 3,220 includes ten observations (two from each of five pairs) per respondent. The base case for Clientelism is no policy favors. The base case for Business Experience and Political Experience is no experience. The base case for Party is the ALD. Individual controls include gender, age, education, and a dummy indicating that the respondent supports the PSD.

Table C27 Poverty, candidate characteristics, and perceived policy positions – Binary poverty

	Dependent variable		
	Help Low Income	Help in Emergency	Create Jobs
	(1)	(2)	(3)
Clientelism: Policy Favors	−0.11***	−0.12***	−0.15***
	(0.03)	(0.03)	(0.03)
Clientelism: Policy Favors ×	0.19***	0.14***	0.18***
Poor (Binary)	(0.03)	(0.04)	(0.03)
Poor (Binary)	−0.10***	−0.08***	−0.09***
	(0.03)	(0.03)	(0.03)
Direct Effects	✓	✓	✓
Individual Controls	✓	✓	✓
Observations	3,220	3,220	3,220
R^2	0.05	0.03	0.04

*p<0.1; **p<0.05; ***p<0.01 Standard errors clustered by respondent in parentheses.

Models are estimated using OLS. The outcome is a dummy variable indicating that the respondent thought that the candidate profile was better on the dimension under question than the alternative profile with which it was presented. Data is analyzed at the level of the candidate profile such that the full data frame of 3,220 includes ten observations (two from each of five pairs) per respondent. The base case for Clientelism is no policy favors. The base case for Business Experience and Political Experience is no experience. The base case for Party is the ALD. Individual controls include gender, age, education, and a dummy indicating that the respondent supports the PSD. Poverty is a binary variable that takes a value of 1 if the respondent reports earning below 1500 RON.

Table C28 Poverty, candidate characteristics, and perceived personal characteristics—binary poverty

| | *Dependent variable* | |
| | Good Manager | Honest |
	(1)	(2)
Clientelism: Policy Favors	−0.15***	−0.21***
	(0.03)	(0.03)
Clientelism: Policy Favors × Poor (Binary)	0.15***	0.15***
	(0.03)	(0.03)
Poor (Binary)	−0.07***	−0.07***
	(0.03)	(0.03)
Direct Effects	✓	✓
Individual Controls	✓	✓
Observations	3,220	3,220
R²	0.04	0.07

* p<0.1; ** p<0.05; *** p<0.01

Standard errors clustered by respondent in parentheses.

Models are estimated using OLS. The outcome is a dummy variable indicating that the respondent thought that the candidate profile was better on the dimension under question than the alternative profile with which it was presented. Data is analyzed at the level of the candidate profile such that the full data frame of 3,220 includes ten observations (two from each of five pairs) per respondent. The base case for Clientelism is no policy favors. The base case for Business Experience and Political Experience is no experience. The base case for Party is the ALD. Individual controls include gender, age, education, and a dummy indicating that the respondent supports the PSD. Poverty is a binary variable that takes a value of 1 if the respondent reports earning below 1,500 RON.

Table C29 Poverty, candidate characteristics, and self-reported voting propensity—binary poverty

	Dependent variable
	Preferred Candidate
Clientelism: Policy Favors	−0.21***
	(0.03)
Clientelism: Policy Favors × Poor (Binary)	0.19***
	(0.03)
Poor (Binary)	−0.09***
	(0.03)
Direct Effects	✓
Individual Controls	✓
Observations	3,220
R^2	0.06

* p<0.1; ** p<0.05; *** p<0.01

Standard errors clustered by respondent in parentheses.

Models are estimated using OLS. The outcome is a dummy variable indicating that the respondent thought that the candidate profile was better on the dimension under question than the alternative profile with which it was presented. Data is analyzed at the level of the candidate profile such that the full data frame of 3,220 includes ten observations (two from each of five pairs) per respondent. The base case for Clientelism is no policy favors. The base case for Business Experience and Political Experience is no experience. The base case for Party is the ALD. Individual controls include gender, age, education, and a dummy indicating that the respondent supports the PSD. Poverty is a binary variable that takes a value of 1 if the respondent reports earning below 1,500 RON.

Bibliography

Ágh, A. (1998). *The politics of Central Europe*. London: Sage.

Ágh, A. (2000). Party formation process and the 1998 elections in Hungary: Defeat as promoter of change for the HSP. *East European Politics and Societies* 14(2): 288–315.

Ágh, A. (2016). The decline of democracy in East-Central Europe: Hungary as the worst-case scenario. *Problems of Post-Communism* 63(5–6): 277–87.

Ahlquist, J. S., K. R. Mayer, and S. Jackman (2014). Alien abduction and voter imperson-ation in the 2012 US General Election: Evidence from a survey list experiment. *Election Law Journal* 13(4): 460–75.

Allina-Pisano, J. (2008). *The Post-Soviet Potemkin village: Politics and property-rights in the Black Earth*. New York: Cambridge University Press.

Anderson, L. (2000). *Practicing democracy: Elections and political culture in imperial Germany*. Princeton, NJ: Princeton University Press.

Arlacchi, P. (1983). *The mafia business: The mafia ethic and the spirit of capitalism*. London: Verso.

Asociatia Pro Democratia (APD) (2009). Sondaj de opinii și percepții privind fraudarea alegerilor. Unpublished Manuscript, Bucharest.

Aspinall, E. (2014). When brokers betray: Clientelism, social networks, and electoral politics in Indonesia. *Critical Asian Studies* 46(4): 545–70.

Auyero, J. (1999). "From the client's point(s) of view": How poor people perceive and evaluate political clientelism. *Theory and Society* 28(2): 297–334.

Baland, J. and Robinson, L. (2008). The political value of land: Political reform and land prices in Chile. *American Journal of Political Science*. 56(3), 601–19.

Ban, C. (2014). *Dependență si dezvoltare: Economia politică a capitalismului românesc [Dependency and development: The political economy of Romanian capitalism]*. Cluj-Napoca: Editura Tact.

Banégas, R. (1998). Marchandisation du vote, citoyenneté et consolidation démocratique au Bénin. *Politique Africaine* 69: 75–88.

Banerjee, Abhijit, Donald P. Green, Jeffery McManus, and Rohini Pande (2014). Are poor voters indifferent to whether elected leaders are criminal or corrupt? A vignette experi-ment in rural India. *Political Communication* 31(3): 391–407.

Banfield, E. and J. Wilson (1965). *City Politics*. New York: Cambridge University Press.

Bauer, A. (1995). *Chilean rural society from the Spanish conquest to 1930*. New York: Cambridge University Press.

Beck, L. (2008). *Brokering democracy in Africa: The rise of clientelist democracy in Senegal*. New York: Palgrave Macmillan.

Bensel, R. F. (2004). *The American ballot box in the mid-nineteenth century*. New York: Cambridge University Press.

Biroul Electoral Central [Various years]. *Rezultate electorale din România*. Available at http://www.alegeri.roaep.ro.

Blair, G. and K. Imai (2012). Statistical analysis of list experiments. *Political Analysis* 20(1): 47–77.

Blaydes, L. (2006). Who votes in authoritarian elections and why? Determinants of voter turnout in contemporary Egypt. Presented at APSA 2006. Available at http://citeseerx.ist.psu.edu/viewdoc/download?doi=10.1.1.457.5619&rep=rep1&type=pdf.

Boone, C. and N. Kriger (2012). Land patronage and elections: Winners and losers in Zimbabwe and Côte d'Ivoire. In Dorina Bekoe, ed., Voting in fear: Electoral violence in sub-Saharan Africa, 75–116. Washington: United States Institute of Peace.

Bozóki, A. (1989). Mi a Fidesz és mi mi nem? [What is Fidesz and what is not?] Magyar Narancz.

Bozóki, A. (1992). A magyar pártok 1991-ben. In P. Sándor and L. Vass, eds, Magyarorsz'ag politikai évkönyve 1991-röl. Budapest: Demokrácia Kutátosok Magyar Központja Alapítvány.

Bozóki, A. (2002). The Hungarian Socialists. In J. T. Ishiyama and A. Bozóki, eds, The Communist successor parties of Central and Eastern Europe, 89–115. Armonk, NY: Sharpe.

Bratton, M. (2008). Vote buying and violence in Nigerian election campaigns. Electoral Studies 27(4): 621–32.

Bratton, M. (2013). Voting and democratic citizenship in Africa. Boulder, CO: Lynne Rienner.

Bratton, M. and N. Van de Walle (1997). Democratic experiments in Africa: Regime transitions in comparative perspective. New York: Cambridge University Press.

Brusco, V., M. Nazareno, and S. Stokes (2004). Vote buying in Argentina. Latin American Research Review 39(2): 66–88.

Carlson, E. (2015). Ethnic voting and accountability in Africa: A choice experiment in Uganda. World Politics 67(2): 353–85.

Chandra, K. (2014). Patronage, democracy and ethnic politics in India. In D. A. Brun and L. Diamond, eds, Clientelism, social policy, and the quality of democracy, 135–74. Baltimore, MD: Johns Hopkins University Press.

Charnay, J.-P. (1964). Les scrutins politiques en France de 1815 à 1962: Contestations et invalidations. Paris: Armand Colin.

Charntornvong, S. (2000). Local godfathers in Thai politics. In Ruth McVey, ed., Money and power in provincial Thailand, 53–73. Copenhagen: Nordic Institute of Asian Studies.

Chubb, J. (1981). The social basis of an urban political machine: The case of Palermo. Political Science Quarterly 96(1): 107–12.

Chubb, J. (1982). Patronage, power and poverty in southern Italy. New York: Cambridge University Press.

Collier, P. and P. C. Vicente (2012). Violence, bribery, and fraud: The political economy of elections in sub-Saharan Africa. Public Choice 153(1–2): 117–47.

Conroy-Krutz, J. (2013). Information and ethnic politics in Africa. British Journal of Political Science 43(2): 345–73.

Conroy-Krutz, J. and C. Logan (2012). Museveni and the 2011 Ugandan election: Did the money matter? Journal of Modern African Studies 50(4): 625–55.

Cornelius, W. (1977). Leaders, followers and official patrons in urban Mexico. In S. Schmidt, J. Scott, C. Lande, and L. Guasti, eds, Friends, followers and factions: A reader in political clientelism, 337–54. Berkeley: University of California Press.

Cramer, K. (2016). The politics of resentment: Rural consciousness in Wisconsin and the rise of Scott Walker. Chicago, IL: University of Chicago Press.

Crawford, K. (1996). East Central European politics today. Manchester: Manchester University Press.

Csizmadia, E. (1999). Pártok és agytrösztök [Parties and think tanks]. Politikatu-dományi Szemle 7(4): 1–31.

Csoba, Judit. (2010). A közfoglalkoztatás régi-új redsere. Útközben az "Ut a munkähoz programban." *Esély* 1: 1–124.

Davis, William. (1910). *The influence of wealth in Imperial Rome*. New York: Macmillan.

Diaz-Cayeros, A., F. Estévez, and B. Magaloni (2016). *The political logic of poverty relief: Electoral strategies and social policy in Mexico*. New York: Cambridge University Press.

Djankov, Simeon, Rafael La Porta, Florencio Lopez-de-Silanes, and Andrei Shleifer (2010). Disclosure by politicians. *American Economic Journal (Applied Economics)* 2(2): 179–209.

Eaton, K. and C. Chambers-Ju (2014). Teachers, mayors, and the transformation of clientelism in Colombia. In D. A. Brun and L. Diamond, eds, *Clientelism, social policy, and the quality of democracy*, 88–113. Baltimore, MD: Johns Hopkins University Press.

Economist Intelligence Unit (1997). *Country report: Hungary*. London: EUI.

Ekiert, G. and S. Hansom (2003). *Capitalism and democracy in Central and Eastern Europe: Assessing the legacy of communist rule*. New York: Cambridge University Press.

Elster, J., C. Offe, and K. U. Preuss (1998). *Institutional design in post-communist societies: Rebuilding the ship at sea*. Cambridge: Cambridge University Press.

Enyedi, Z. (2005). The role of agency in cleavage formation. *European Journal of Political Research* 44(5): 697–720.

Enyedi, Z. (2006). Accounting for organisation and financing: A comparison of four Hungarian Parties. *Europe-Asia Studies* 58(7): 1101–17.

Enyedi, Z. (2014). The discreet charm of political parties. *Party Politics* 20(2): 194–204.

Enyedi, Z. and L. Linek (2008). Searching for the right organization: Ideology and party structure in East-Central Europe. *Party Politics* 14(4): 455–77.

Enyedi, Z. and G. Tóka (2007). The only game in town: Party politics in Hungary. In P. Webb and W. White, eds, *Party politics in new democracies*, 147–78. Oxford: Oxford University Press.

Emerson, R., R. Fretz, and L. Shaw (2011). *Writing ethnographic fieldnotes*. Chicago, IL: University of Chicago Press.

Fehr, E., K. Hoff, and M. Kshetramade. (2008). Spite and development. *The American Economic Review* 98(2): 494–9.

Fehr E. and S. Gachter (2000). Cooperation and punishment in public goods experiments. *The American Economic Review* 90(4): 980–94.

Finan, F. and L. Schechter (2012). Vote-buying and reciprocity. *Econometrica* 80(2): 863–81.

Fish, M. S. (2001). The dynamics of democratic erosion. In Richard D. Anderson Jr., M. S. Fish, S. E. Hanson, and P. G. Roeder, eds, *Postcommunism and the theory of democracy*, 11–53. Princeton, NJ: Princeton University Press.

Foltz, W. J. (1977). Social structure and political behavior of Senegalese elites. In S. W. Schmidt, J. C. Scott, C. Landé, and L. Guasti, eds, *Friends, followers and factions: A Reader in Political Clientelism*, 422–38. Berkeley: University of California Press.

Fox, J. (1994). The difficult transition from clientelism to citizenship: Lessons from Mexico. *World Politics* 46(2): 151–84.

Friedrich, P. (1968). *The Legitimacy of a Cacique. Local-level politics: Social and cultural perspectives*, 243–70. Chicago, IL: Aldine Pub. Co.

Fujiwara, T. and L. Wantchekon (2013). Can informed public deliberation overcome clientelism? Experimental evidence from Benin. *American Economic Journal: Applied Economics* 5(4): 241–55.

Gabor, Daniela. (2010). *Central banking and financialization. A Romanian account of how Eastern Europe became subprime*. Basingstoke: Palgrave Macmillan.

Gambetta, D. (1993). *The Sicilian Mafia: The business of private protection*. Cambridge, MA: Harvard University Press.

Garrigou, A. (1992). *Le vote et la vertu: Comment les Français sont devenus électeurs*. Paris: Presse de la Fondation Nationale des Sciences Politiques.

Geddes, B. (1994). *Politician's dilemma: Building state capacity in Latin America*. Berkeley: University of California Press.

Gelman, A. and J. Hill (2007). *Data analysis using regression and multilevel hierarchical models*. New York: Cambridge University Press.

Gherghina, S. (2013). Going for a safe vote: Electoral bribes in post-communist Romania. *Debatte: Journal of Contemporary Central and Eastern Europe* 21(2–3): 143–64.

Gherghina, S. (2014). *Party organization and electoral volatility in Central and Eastern Europe: Enhancing voter loyalty*. New York: Routledge.

Giraudy, A. (2007). The distributive politics of emergency employment programs in Argentina (1993–2002). *Latin American Research Review* 42(2): 33–55.

Giugăl, A. (2015). The presidential election of 2014 in Romania: Electoral continuity and discontinuity. Available at https://papers.ssrn.com/sol3/papers.cfm?abstract_id=2691301.

Glynn, A. N. (2013). What can we learn with statistical truth serum? Design and analysis of the list experiment. *Public Opinion Quarterly* 77(S1): 159–72.

Golden, M. and B. Min (2013). Distributive politics around the world. *Annual Review of Political Science* 16: 73–99.

Gonzalez-Ocantos, E., C. K. De Jonge, C. Meléndez, J. Osorio, and D. W. Nickerson (2012). Vote buying and social desirability bias: Experimental evidence from Nicaragua. *American Journal of Political Science* 56(1): 202–17.

González-Ocantos, E., C. K. De Jonge, and D. W. Nickerson (2014). The conditionality of vote-buying norms: Experimental evidence from Latin America. *American Journal of Political Science* 58(1): 197–211.

Gosnell, H. F. (1968 [1937]). *Machine politics: Chicago model*. Chicago, IL: University of Chicago Press.

Gottlieb, J. (2017). Explaining variation in broker strategies: A lab-in-the-field experiment in Senegal. *Comparative Political Studies* 50(1): 1556–92.

Grzymała-Busse, A. (2002). *Redeeming the communist past: The regeneration of communist parties in East Central Europe*. New York: Cambridge University Press.

Grzymała-Busse, A. (2003). Redeeming the past: Communist successor parties after 1989. In G. Ekiert and S. Hansom, eds, *Capitalism and democracy in Central and Eastern Europe: Assessing the legacy of communist rule*, 157–81. Cambridge: Cambridge University Press.

Grzymała-Busse, A. (2006). *Rebuilding Leviathan: Party competition and state exploitation in post-communist democracies*. New York: Cambridge University Press.

Hainmueller, J., D. Hangartner, and T. Yamamoto (2015). Validating vignette and conjoint survey experiments against real-world behavior. *Proceedings of the National Academy of Sciences* 112(8): 2395–400.

Hainmueller, J., D. J. Hopkins, and T. Yamamoto (2014). Causal inference in conjoint analysis: Understanding multidimensional choices via stated preference experiments. *Political Analysis* 22(1): 1–30.

Hainmueller, J., J. Mummolo, and Y. Xu (2016). How much should we trust estimates from multiplicative interaction models? Simple tools to improve empirical practice. Working Paper, Princeton University.

Hale, H. E. (2014). *Patronal politics: Eurasian regime dynamics in comparative perspective*. New York: Cambridge University Press.

Hanham, H. J. (1959). *Elections and party management: Politics in the time of Disraeli and Gladstone*. London: Longmans.

Henrich, J., R. McElreath, A. Barr, J. Ensminger, C. Barrett, A. Bolyanatz, J. C.Cardenas, M. Gurven, E. Gwako, N. Henrich, and C. Lesorogol (2006). Costly punishment across human societies. *Science* 312(5781): 1767–70.

Hicken, A. (2011). Clientelism. *Annual Review of Political Science* 14: 289–310.

Holland, A. and B. Palmer-Rubin (2015). Beyond the machine: Clientelist brokers and interest organizations in Latin America. *Comparative Political Studies* 48(9): 1–38, 1186–223.

Holland, A. C. (2016). Forbearance. *American Political Science Review* 110(2): 232.

Humphreys, M. and A. M. Jacobs (2015). Mixing methods: A Bayesian approach. *American Political Science Review* 109(4): 653–73.

Ilonszki, G. and S. Kurtan (1995). Hungary. *European Journal of Political Research* 28(4), 359–68.

Institutul Naţional de Statistică (2011). *Recensămîntul populaţiei si al locuinţelor*. Bucureşti: Institutul Naţional de Statistică.

Ishiyama, J. T., ed. (1999). *Communist Successor Parties in Post-communist Politics*. Carmack, NY: Nova Science.

Kahneman, D., J. L. Knetsch, and Richard Thaler (1991). The Endowment Effect, Loss Aversion, and Status Quo Bias. *Journal of Economic Perspectives* 5: 193–206.

Kahneman, D. and A. Tversky (1979). Prospect theory: An analysis of decisions under risk. *Econometrica* 47(2): 263–91.

Karl, T. L. (1995). The hybrid regimes of Central America. *Journal of Democracy* 6(3): 72–86.

Key, V. O. (1934). The techniques of political graft in the United States. PhD diss., University of Chicago.

Kitschelt, H. (1992). The formation of party systems in East Central Europe. *Politics and Society* 20(1): 7–50.

Kitschelt, H. (1995). Formation of party cleavages in post-communist democracies: Theoretical propositions. *Party Politics* 1(4): 447–72.

Kitschelt, H. (2000). Linkages between citizens and politicians in democratic polities. *Comparative Political Studies* 33(6): 845–79.

Kitschelt, H. (2002). Constraints and opportunities in the strategic conduct of post-communist successor parties: Regime legacies as causal arguments. In A. Bozoki and J. Ishiyama, eds, *The Communist successor parties of Central and Eastern Europe*, 14–40. London: Sharpe.

Kitschelt, H. (2003). Accounting for post-communist regime diversity: What counts as good cause? In G. Ekiert and S. Hansom, eds, *Capitalism and democracy in Central and Eastern Europe: Assessing the legacy of communist rule*, 49–86. New York: Cambridge University Press.

Kitschelt, H. (2011). Clientelistic linkage strategies: A descriptive exploration. In *Workshop on Democratic Accountability Strategies*, Unpublished Manuscript, Duke University.

Kitschelt, H. and S. I. Wilkinson (2007). *Patrons, clients and policies: Patterns of democratic accountability and political competition*. New York: Cambridge University Press.

Klein, X. (2003). *Gültig—ungültig. Die Wahlprüfungsverfahren des Deutschen Reichstages 1867–1918*. Marburg: Elwert.

Kopecký, P. (2006). Political parties and the state in post-communist Europe: The nature of symbiosis. *Journal of Communist Studies and Transition Politics* 22(3): 251–73.

Kopecký, P., P. Mair, and M. Spirova (2012). *Party Patronage and party government in European democracies*. New York: Oxford University Press.

Kornai, J. et al. (1986). The soft budget constraint. *Kyklos* 39(1): 3–30.

Központi Statisztikai Hivatal (2013a). *Évi Népszámlálás. Területi adatok. Baranya megye*. Pecs: Központi Statisztikai Hivatal.

Központi Statisztikai Hivatal (2013b). *Évi Népszámlálás. Területi adatok. Borsod-Abaùj-Zemplén megye*. Miskolc: Központi Statisztikai Hivatal.

Központi Statisztikai Hivatal (2013c). *Évi Népszámlálás. Területi adatok. Baranya megye*. Miskolc: Központi Statisztikai Hivatal.

Kramon, E. (2016). Electoral handouts as information: Explaining unmonitored vote buying. *World Politics* 68(3): 454–98.

Krekó, P. and G. Mayer (2015). Transforming Hungary—together? An analysis of the Fidesz-Jobbik relationship. In M. Minkenberg, ed., *Transforming the transformation? The East European radical right in the political process*, 183–205. New York: Routledge.

Kühne, Thomas (2003). *Dreiklassenwahlrecht und Wahlkultur in Preussen 1867–1914: Landtagswahlen zwischen korporativer Tradition und politischem Massenmarkt*. Düsseldorf: Droste.

Kurer, O. (2001). Why do voters support corrupt politicians? In A. K. Jain, ed., *The political economy of corruption*, 63–86. New York: Routledge.

Kurtzman, D. H. (1935). Methods of controlling votes in Philadelphia. PhD diss., University of Pennsylvania.

Kuziemko, I., R. W. Buell, T. Reich, and M. I. Norton (2014). Last place aversion: Evidence and redistributive implications. *Quarterly Journal of Economics* 129(1): 105–49.

Landé, C. (1977). Introduction: The dyadic basis of clientelism. In S. W. Schmidt, J. C. Scott, C. H. Landé, and L. Guasti, eds, *Friends, followers and factions: A reader in political clientelism*, xiii–xxxvii. Berkeley: University of California Press.

Larreguy, H. A., C. Montiel Olea, and P. Querubin (2017). Political brokers: Partisans or agents? Evidence from the Mexican teacher's union. *American Journal of Political Science* 61(4): 877–91.

Lawson, C. and K. F. Greene (2014). Making clientelism work: How norms of reciprocity increase voter compliance. *Comparative Politics* 47(1): 61–85.

Lemarchand, R. (1972). Political clientelism and ethnicity in tropical Africa: Competing solidarities in nation-building. *American Political Science Review* 66(1): 68–90.

Lemarchand, R. (1981). Comparative political clientelism: Structure, process and optic. In S. Eisenstadt and R. Lemarchand, eds, *Political clientelism, patronage and development*, 7–32. Beverly Hills, CA: Sage.

Lieberman, E. S. (2005). Nested analysis as a mixed-method strategy for comparative research. *American Political Science Review* 99(3): 435–52.

Lindberg, S. I. (2003). "It's our time to chop": Do elections in Africa feed neo-patrimonialism rather than counter-act it? *Democratization* 10(2): 121–40.

Magaloni, Beatriz (2006). *Voting for autocracy: hegemonic party survival and its demise in Mexico*. New York: Cambridge University Press.

Magyar, B. (2016). *Post-Communist mafia state: The case of Hungary*. Budapest: Central European University Press.

Mares, I. (2015). *From open secrets to secret voting: Democratic electoral reforms and voter autonomy*. New York: Cambridge University Press.

Mares, I., A. Muntean, and T. Petrova (2018). Economic intimidation in contemporary elections: Evidence from Romania and Bulgaria. *Government and Opposition* 53(3): 486–517.

Mares, I. and G. Visconti (2019). Voting for the lesser evil: evidence from a conjoint experiment in Romania. Political Science Research Methods, 7(3), 1–14.

Mares, I. and L. E. Young (2016). Buying, expropriating, and stealing votes. *Annual Review of Political Science* 19: 267–88.

Mares, I. and L. E. Young (2019).Varieties of clientelism in Hungarian elections. *Comparative Politics* (51)3: 449–480.

Mares, I. and B. Zhu (2015). The production of electoral irregularities: Economic and political incentives. *Comparative Politics* 48(1): 23–41.

Marx, K. (1963 [1852]). *The Eighteenth Brumaire of Louis Bonaparte.* New York: International.

Meyer-Sahling, J.-H. (2008). The rise of the partisan state? Parties, patronage and the ministerial bureaucracy in Hungary. In P. Kopecký, ed., *Political Parties and the State in Postcommunist Europe*, 24–47. London: Routledge.

Meyer-Sahling, J.-H. and K. Jáger (2012). Party patronage in Hungary: Capturing the state. In P. Kopecký, P. Mair, and M. Spirova, eds, *Party patronage and party government in European democracies*, 163–85. Oxford: Oxford University Press.

Morlang, D. (2003). Hungary: Socialists building capitalism. In J. L. Curry and J. B. Urban, eds, *The Left transformed in post-communist societies*, 61–98. Lanham, MD: Rowman and Littlefield.

Murer, J. S. (2002). The Romanian PDSR and the Bulgarian Socialists in comparative perspective. In A. Bozoki and J. T. Ishiyama, eds, *The communist successor parties of Central and Eastern Europe*. Armonk, NY: Sharpe.

Nichter, S. (2014). Political clientelism and social policy in Brazil. In *Clientelism, social policy, and the quality of democracy*, 130–51. Baltimore, MD: Johns Hopkins University Press.

O'Dwyer, C. (2004). Runaway state building: How political parties shape states in post-communist Eastern Europe. *World Politics* 56(4): 520–53.

O'Dwyer, C. (2006). *Runaway state building: Patronage politics and democratic development.* Baltimore, MD: Johns Hopkins University Press.

Offe, C. (1994). *Der Tunnel am Ende des Lichts.* Frankfurt: Campus.

Oliveros, V. (2013). A working machine: Patronage jobs and political services in Argentina. PhD diss., Columbia University.

Oliveros, V. (2016). Making it personal: Clientelism, favors, and the personalization of public administration in Argentina. *Comparative Politics* 48(3): 373–91.

Oprea, M. (2006). *Chipul mortii: Dialog cu Vladimir Bukovski despre natura comunismului.* Bucuresti: Polirom.

Özbudun, E. (1981). Turkey: The politics of clientelism. In *Political Clientelism, Patronage and Development*, 249–70. London: Sage.

Pande, R. (2011). Can informed voters enforce better governance? Experiments in low-income democracies. *Annual Review of Economics* 3(1): 215–37.

Penfold-Becerra, Michael. 2007. Clientelism and social funds: evidence from Chavez's Misiones. *Latin American Politics and Society* 49(4): 63–84.

PDSR (2000). The political program of the PDSR. Technical report, Party of Democratic Socialism in Romania.

Pilenco, Alexandre (1928). *Les mœurs electorales en France.* Paris: Éditions du Monde Moderne.

Powell, J. D. (1970). Peasant society and clientelist politics. *American Political Science Review* 64(2): 411–25.

Przeworski, A. (1991). *Democracy and the market.* New York: Cambridge University Press.

Putnam, R. D. (1973). *The beliefs of politicians: Ideology, conflict, and democracy in Britain and Italy*. New Haven, CT: Yale University Press.

Racz, B. (1993). The socialist-left opposition in post-communist Hungary. *Europe-Asia Studies* 45(4): 647–70.

Racz, B. (2000). The Hungarian socialists in opposition: Stagnation or renaissance? *Europe-Asia Studies* 52(2): 319–47.

Remmer, K. L. (2007). The political economy of patronage: Expenditure patterns in the Argentine provinces, 1983–2003. *Journal of Politics* 69(2): 363–77.

Robinson, J. A. and R. Torvik (2009). The real swing voter's curse. *American Economic Review* 99(2): 310–15.

Rogers, Francis James (1906). *Parliamentary elections and petitions with appendices of statutes, rules and forms*. Vol. 2. London: Stevens and Sons.

Roper, S. D. (2008). The influence of party patronage and state finance on electoral outcomes: Evidence from Romania. In P. Kopecký, ed., *Political parties and the state in postcommunist Europe*, 112–32. London: Routledge.

Rouquié, Alan (1978). Clientelist Control and Authoritarian Contexts. In *Elections without choice*, 19–35, ed. Guy Hermet, Richard Rose, and Alain Rouquié. New York: Wiley.

Rueda, M. R. (2017). Small aggregates, big manipulation: Vote buying enforcement and collective monitoring. *American Journal of Political Science* 61(1): 163–77.

Rupnik, J. and J. Zielonka (2013). *Democracy in Central and Eastern Europe: The state of the art*. Thousand Oaks, CA: Sage.

Rupnik, J. and J. Zielonka (2016). Introduction: The state of democracy 20 years on: Domestic and external factors. *East European Politics and Societies* 27(1): 3–25.

Schatzberg, Michael (2001). *Political legitimacy in Middle Africa: Father, family, food*. Bloomington: Indiana University Press.

Scheiner, E. (2006). *Democracy without competition in Japan: opposition failure in a one-party dominant state*. New York: Cambridge University Press.

Scheppele, K. L. (2014). Legal, but not fair: Viktor Orban's new supermajority. *New York Times*, April 13. Available at https://krugman.blogs.nytimes.com/2014/04/13/legal-but-not-fair-hungary/.

Schmidt, S., J. Scott, C. Lande, and L. Guasti, eds. (1977). *Friends, followers and factions: A reader in political clientelism*. Berkeley: University of California Press.

Schneider, M. (2015). Whither the quid pro quo? Essays on party-voter linkages and distributive politics in rural India. PhD diss., Columbia University.

Scott, J. (1969). Corruption, machine politics, and political change. *American Political Science Review* 63(4): 1142–58.

Scott, J. (1972a). *Comparative political corruption*. Englewood Cliffs, NJ: Prentice Hall.

Scott, J. (1972b). Patron–client politics and political change in Southeast Asia. *American Political Science Review* 65(4): 1142–58.

Scott, J. (1990). *Domination and the arts of resistance: Hidden transcripts*. New Haven, CT and London: Yale University Press.

Scott, J. and B. Kerkvliet (1977). How traditional rural patrons lose legitimacy: A theory with special reference to Southeast Asia. In S. W. Schmidt, J. C. Scott, C. H. Landé, and L. Guasti, eds, *Friends, followers and factions: A reader in political clientelism*, 439–58. Berkeley: University of California Press.

Shefter, Martin (1994). *Political parties and the state: The American historical experience*. Princeton, NJ: Princeton University Press.

Sniderman, P. M. and D. B. Grob (1996). Innovations in experimental design in attitude surveys. *Annual Review of Sociology* 22(1): 377–99.

Soare, S. C. (2007). Romanian parties membership: A regional comparative analysis. Paper presented at the Conference on EU enlargement, University of Salford.

Stokes, S. (2005). Perverse accountability: A formal model of machine politics with evidence from Argentina. *American Political Science Review* 99(3): 315–25.

Stokes, S., T. Dunning, M. Nazareno, and V. Brusco (2013). *Brokers, voters, and clientelism: The puzzle of distributive politics*. New York: Cambridge University Press.

Szelényi, I. (2015). Capitalism after communism. In B. Magyar and J. Vasarhelyi, eds, *Twenty-five sides of a post-communist mafia state*, 637–49. Budapest: Central European University Press.

Szöke, Alexandra. (2014). (Un)employment and workfare schemes in rural Hungary—a longitudinal study of the regulative changes of the public work programme. Working paper, Erste Foundation.

Szombati, K. (2016). The revolt of the provinces: Anti-gypsyism and right-wing politics in rural Hungary. PhD diss., Central European University.

Tarrow, S. (1995). Review: "Bridging the quantitative–qualitative divide in political science: Designing social inquiry: Scientific inference in qualitative research," by Gary King, Robert O. Keohane, and Sidney Verba. *American Political Science Review* 89(2): 471–4.

Tavits, M. (2013). *Post-communist democracies and party organization*. New York: Cambridge University Press.

Tóka, G. (1996). Voting Behaviour in 1990. In G. Tóka, ed., *The 1990 election to the Hungarian National Assembly*. Berlin: Sigma.

Toole, J. (2003). Straddling the east–west divide: Party organisation and communist legacies in East Central Europe. *Europe-Asia Studies* 55(1): 101–18.

Van Biezen, I. (2003). *Political parties in new democracies: Party organization in Southern and East-Central Europe*. Basingstoke: Palgrave Macmillan.

van de Walle, N. (2007). Meet the new boss, same as the old boss? The evolution of political clientelism in Africa. In H. Kitschelt and S. Wilkinson, eds, *Patrons, clients and policies: Patterns of democratic accountability and political competition*, 50–67. New York: Cambridge University Press.

van de Walle, N. (2014). The democratization of clientelism in sub-Saharan Africa. In D. A. Brun and L. Diamond, eds, *Clientelism, social policy, and the quality of democracy*, 230–52. Baltimore, MD: Johns Hopkins University Press.

Wallander, L. (2009). 25 years of factorial surveys in sociology: A review. *Social Science Research* 38(3): 505–20.

Waller, M. (1995). Adaptation of the former communist parties of East-Central Europe: A case of social-democratization? *Party Politics* 1: 473–90.

Wang, Chin-Shou and Charles Kurzman (2007). Dilemmas of electoral clientelism: Taiwan. *International Political Science Review* 28(2): 225–45.

Weiner, M. (1967). *Party building in a new nation: The Indian National Congress*. Chicago, IL: University of Chicago Press.

Weitz-Shapiro, R. (2012). What wins votes: Why some politicians opt out of clientelism. *American Journal of Political Science* 56(3): 568–83.

Weitz-Shapiro, R. (2014). *Curbing clientelism in Argentina: Politics, poverty and social policy*. New York: Cambridge University Press.

Wertheimer, A. (1987). *Coercion*. Princeton, NJ: Princeton University Press.

Wilkinson, S. I. (2007). Explaining changing patterns of party-voter linkages in India. In H. Kitschelt and S. I. Wilkinson, eds, *Patrons, clients, and policies: Patterns of democratic accountability and political competition*, 110–40. New York: Cambridge University Press.

Wilson, J. Q. (1961). The economy of patronage. *Journal of Political Economy* 69(4): 369–80.

Winters, M. S. and R. Weitz-Shapiro (2013). Lacking information or condoning corruption: When do voters support corrupt politicians? *Comparative Politics* 45(4): 418–36.

Wolfinger, R. E. (1972). Why political machines have not withered away and other revisionist thoughts. *Journal of Politics* 34(2): 365–98.

Wurfel, D. (1963). The Philippines. *Journal of Politics* 25: 757–73.

Wurfel, D. (1991 [1988]). *Filipino politics: Development and decay.* Ithaca, NY: Cornell University Press.

Zamchiya, P. (2011). A synopsis of land and agrarian change in Chipinge district, Zimbabwe. *Journal of Peasant Studies* 38(5): 1093–122.

Zolberg, A. R. (1968). The structure of political conflict in the new states of tropical Africa. *American Political Science Review* 62(1): 70–87.

Zolnay, J. (2012). Abusive language and discriminatory measures in Hungarian local policy. In M. Stewart, ed., *The Gypsy "menace": Populism and the new anti-gypsy politics*, 25–42. London: Hurst.

Index